THE AMUSEMENTS OF
OLD LONDON

———

VOLUME THE FIRST

THE LONG ROOM AT BAGNIGGE WELLS, 1776

THE AMUSEMENTS OF OLD LONDON

BEING A SURVEY OF THE SPORTS AND PASTIMES
TEA GARDENS AND PARKS, PLAYHOUSES
AND OTHER DIVERSIONS OF THE PEOPLE
OF LONDON FROM THE 17TH TO
THE BEGINNING OF THE
19TH CENTURY

By WILLIAM B. BOULTON

Two Volumes in One

VOLUME THE FIRST

BENJAMIN BLOM  New York/London

THESE LITTLE ESSAYS

THE RESULT, IN PART, OF MANY HOURS OF

PLEASANT LABOUR IN HER COMPANY

I DEDICATE

WITH ALL AFFECTION TO

MY MOTHER

First Published 1901
Reissued 1969 by
Benjamin Blom, Inc., Bronx, New York 10452
and 56 Doughty Street, London, W.C. 1

Library of Congress Catalog Card Number 75-828.20

Printed in the United States of America

PREFACE

THIS work is an attempt to survey the amusements
of Londoners during a period which began, approximately, with the Restoration of King Charles the
Second and ended with the accession of Her Majesty
Queen Victoria. These somewhat arbitrary boundaries of the subject were adopted for what seem to be
sufficient reasons. In the almost complete absence of a
periodical literature there is little record of the lighter
moments of Londoners before the first of those great
events; the era which began with the last inaugurated
a revolution in social England which, among greater
matters, transformed the nature of its amusements,
and in so doing has suggested a natural limit to our
subject. Anyone seeking conviction as to the com-
pleteness of that transformation has only to be reminded that athletics of all kinds have assumed the
place they fill in modern life since the Queen came to
the throne, and that of the organised amusements of
Londoners during the period we have chosen for our

inquiry two only survive in a recognisable form to-day, the Play and the Social Club.

The amusements of Old London are only to be studied properly in the periodicals which record them, and in the lighter memoirs and letters of the times. The author has relied almost entirely upon these sources of information, but has made use of certain admirable collections of them dealing with particular subjects, all duly mentioned in the text.

WILLIAM B. BOULTON.

London, *September* 1900.

CONTENTS

VOLUME THE FIRST

CHAPTER I

*THE DIVERSIONS OF HOCKLEY IN THE HOLE,
AND AT FIGG'S*

CHAPTER II

LONDON AL FRESCO—THE TEA GARDENS

CHAPTER III

THE MASKED ASSEMBLY

CHAPTER IV

THE PLAY TABLES

CHAPTER V

THE COCKPIT

CONTENTS

CHAPTER VI

THE PLAY AND THE OPERA

LIST OF ILLUSTRATIONS

VOLUME THE FIRST

BULL-BAITING

DRAWN BY H. ALKEN

AMUSEMENTS OF OLD LONDON

CHAPTER I

THE DIVERSIONS OF HOCKLEY IN THE HOLE, AND AT FIGG'S

IT was very usual during the early years of the eighteenth century to encounter in the streets of the city of London a band of men marching in a kind of military order to the beat of kettle-drums, with colours flying and drawn swords, and followed by a numerous retinue distributing handbills to passers-by. The handbills contained particulars of surprising entertainments to be enjoyed at Hockley in the Hole, an establishment of great renown which stood in what was afterwards Ray Street, Clerkenwell, a street which disappeared in some great scheme of municipal improvement about forty years ago. Hockley in the Hole was a kind of theatre or arena of the old type which originated in Elizabethan times, and provided accommodation for bull and bear baiting, dog-fights, and contests for prizes between gladiators

armed with the sword or with cudgels or quarter-
staffs, and such like entertainments. It was, indeed,
the lineal successor of the Bear Garden at Bankside,
and its earlier years were perhaps contemporary with
the later of that famous institution. At the beginning
of the last century Hockley was the headquarters of
what, by later generations, was known as the "fancy,"
that is, the organisation of rather low caste sporting
characters who devoted themselves to forms of sport
not actually forbidden by the statute-book, but still
more or less frowned upon by the respectable and
law-abiding.

Hockley in the Hole was a tumble-down affair
even in its prime. It was surrounded by ruinous
houses inhabited by very shady characters; by low
taverns and raffish institutions for the training of
bull and fighting dogs, and the whole vicinage was
subject to periodical overflowings of the adjacent
Fleet ditch, upon whose banks indeed Hockley was
built. It derived its name from a word meaning "a
muddy field," and in no way belied the appellation.
There was an atmosphere of blackguardism about
the place and its entertainments from the first; there
were, for example, rumours of dark passages to the
banks of the Fleet for the convenience of gentry who
attended its diversions and had particular reasons for
avoiding constables and Bow Street officers. Years
after Hockley had vanished, they dug up a valise
marked " R. Turpin " in a house adjoining, together
with a choice collection of skeleton keys, which you may

see figured very convincingly in Mr. Pinks' excellent
"History of Clerkenwell." At the time we are considering, Hockley was the chosen home of the sports we
have mentioned, and of other miscellaneous entertainments of a character vastly pleasing to the popular taste
of that day, diversions which are happily to-day things
of the past. But Hockley, with similar institutions at
Tothill Fields, Westminster, at Saffron Hill, Clerkenwell, and later, at Marylebone, continued traditions of
sport which had had a very considerable vogue under
distinguished auspices in earlier times. In the days of
William the Third and Anne, sporting butchers and
low gamesters were the chief of their patrons, though
people of condition appeared at intervals in the half-
crown " pleasant cool gallery for gentlemen" hung
with tattered tapestry. From these humble and disreputable entertainments emerged later, as we shall
see, the great institution of the London Prize Ring,
an institution which provided the national amusement of a century. In the early days of Anne and
the first Georges, the diversions of Hockley filled a
large place among the pleasures of the lower orders
of Londoners, and it is very probable exercised a vast
influence on their character.

Hockley itself provided a not inconsiderable
amount of material for the annalists and social
historians of those times, and was decidedly the
chief of the group we have named. The exact
date of its establishment is uncertain; it probably
succeeded the Bear Garden in Bankside, which sur-

vived from the reign of Elizabeth to that of William the Third. There is mention of " a newe Beare Garden " at or near Islington so early as 1641, which may or may not be an allusion to Hockley itself. But the first of its advertisements which have come down to us dates only from the last year of the seventeenth century, and in the following June the Grand Jury of Middlesex began to complain of the impudence of its professors, who distributed their handbills to the sound of drums, and in defiance of the king's trumpeter, who had the monopoly of street music in those times.

" We having observed," said the Grand Jury, " the late boldness of a sort of men that stile themselves masters of the noble science of self-defence passing through this city with beat of drums, colours displayed, and swords drawn, with a numerous company of people following them dispersing their printed bills, thereby inviting persons to be spectators of those inhuman sights, which are directly contrary to the practice and profession of the Christian religion, whereby barbarous principles are instilled in the minds of men; we think ourselves obliged to represent this matter, that some method may be speedily taken to prevent their passage through the city on so unwarrantable a design."

The exhibition which incurred these animadversions of the Grand Jury was the prize fight with swords, which we shall examine later, and was in reality a much more harmless affair than it seemed ; but the sportsmen were clearly breaking the law in the matter of the musical procession, and for the next few years they evaded the penalties of the magistrates by withdrawing the music. Advertisements thenceforward appeared at regular intervals in the *Postboy*, announcing their displays as " trials of skill," to take place at such an hour at " His Majesty's Bear Garden at Hockley in the Hole, without beat of drum." This assumption of a royal title was not without humour, and with the use of the words " vivat Rex " at the end of such announcements was no doubt a claim of Hockley to represent the tradition of the old Bear Garden of Queen Elizabeth at Bankside, then lately extinct. In any case, at the time we are considering, the place received such patronage as enabled it to rank as one of the chief amusements of the town for the next half century, and its strange contests between the " masters of the science of self defence," with sword and with fist, and its bull and bear baitings were noticed by half the essayists and satirical poets of the first two Georges as typical of the brutal tastes of Englishmen.

Bear-baiting, one of the chief diversions of Hockley, was, it is said, introduced into England in the reign of King John by a band of Italians, and exhibited to that monarch at Ashby-de-la-Zouch "for his Highness's amusement, wherewith he and his court were highly delighted." Fosbrooke, the antiquarian, records that in feudal days the bears were maintained, and their instructors paid, by a tax levied upon the peasantry, who were allowed free admission to the spectacle of the baiting. Bull-baiting, no doubt, came a little later, and both were in great vogue under the Tudors. Bear-wards, in the days of Elizabeth, were the appanages of great nobles, and the bears themselves were public characters. It was Slender, was it not, who had " seen Sackerson loose twenty times," or so he told Anne Page. The Queen herself was a great connoisseur in the sport; so much so, that she deprecated the competition of the playhouses, and issued orders from the Privy Council forbidding the acting of plays on Thursdays, the chosen day for the bear-baitings at Bankside. The Lord Mayor supported her Majesty with an injunction to the same effect, and gave reasons " that in divers places the players do use to recite their plays to the great hurt and destruction of the game of bear-baiting and such like pastimes which are maintained for her Majesty's pleasure." These were the palmy days of the sport; under the Stuarts it suffered a distinct loss of caste, and by the time Anne came to the throne both bear and bull baiting had declined into low forms of entertainment, much beloved of butchers and draymen, but still patronised more or less furtively at Hockley by persons of high station.

The particulars of those unedifying sports of bull and bear baiting were taken much for granted by the scribes of the last century, but there is much richness of detail to be gathered from earlier writers, details which changed little until the suppression of both amusements in quite modern times. Both bulls and bears were chained to a staple in the arena or pit by a chain of about fifteen feet in length, so that the defending animal had relative freedom of movement over a circle of thirty feet. " They," said old Hentzner in 1598, "are fastened behind, and thus worried by great English bulldogs, not without great risque from the horns of the one and the teeth of the other." The dog, attended by his owner, was held in front of the chained animal by the ears until he was wild with fury, and then let go. The plucky dog went straight at the head of the bull or bear, the middling one took an occasional nip, and bayed just out of reach of the quarry and of the staff of his master, who accompanied him into the pit ; the coward at the first encounter sought refuge from both bull and man by running under the legs of the quarry, and was frequently trampled dead. Both bull and bear were often decorated with huge rosettes stuck between their eyes with pitch. This practice had the advantage of giving the dog something which would come away with his teeth, and as it was fixed on the most dangerous spot, so to speak, of the whole beast, a dog which seized the rosette and dropped back into the ring shaking the trophy as part of his enemy was hugely prized.

There is an excellent account of such a baiting by Misson, the French advocate, who was in England during the reign of William the Third, a period just before the prime of Hockley in the Hole. The experienced bull, it would seem, took things coolly at

first.   He kept his feet close together, so as to avoid
any attack from beneath, and presented a horn at the
advancing enemy.   The horn, as we learn, was either
blunted at the point or provided with a sheath, which
minimised the risk of a gore.   Great trouble was
often taken to equip the bull properly in the matter
of horns.   Writes Mr. John Houghton, F.R.S., in
1694: "Some keep him (the bull) on purpose for the
sport of baiting, cutting of the tips of his horns, and
with pitch, tow, and such like matters, fasten upon
them the great horns of oxen."   We learn also, from
that gentleman's same work on husbandry, that many
butchers were accustomed to bait their bulls before
killing, thereby making, as they held, "his flesh more
tender and proper meat fit to be eaten."

The old bull who knew his business relied chiefly
upon getting the dog in the hollow of these long
horns, either provided by nature or by the care of his
master, as Mr. Houghton describes, and upon dis-
abling it by a toss in the air and a drop of perhaps
thirty feet on the hard floor of the pit.   The experienced dog knew the danger, and avoided it as
much as possible by crouching on the ground in the
preliminary fencing for an opening, which usually
preceded the rush for the throat.   If the bull made
his coup, the dog went flying into the air, often into
the boxes twenty feet above the pit, as when Mr.
Evelyn saw one dropped into a lady's lap in the third
tier in 1670.   Pepys noticed a similar incident about
the same time.   When the dog was in the air there

was a rush of his friends to break his fall: "some with their backs, to give him a soft reception, and others with long poles, which they offer him slant-ways, to the intent that sliding down them it may break the force of his fall." The high-bred bulldog was little discouraged by the toss unless disabled by the shock; indeed, there are instances recorded of dogs with broken legs returning to the charge. If the dog got home "with his eye teeth he sticks to him like a leech, and would sooner die than leave his hold; you might cut him to pieces joint by joint before he would let him loose. What is to be done then? While some hold the bull, others thrust staves into the dog's mouth, and open it by main force." Thus M. Misson. We learn other details from a much later authority, the author who furnished out Mr. Henry Alken's well-known plates on British Sports with letterpress. The dogs usually were silent in attack, and aimed, as a rule, "at the eye, lips, under jaw, and throat of the bull." The bull's roar, we are told, was much appreciated by connoisseurs, and he was allowed a hole in the ground in which to rub his wounded muzzle at proper intervals. On the other hand, he was often infuriated by being tortured with hot irons, and that almost within living memory.

In bear-baiting, which was perhaps rarer than bull-baiting, on account of the greater scarcity of the quarry, there was even more risk for the dog. The bear was less vulnerable by reason of its coarse fur, and its powers of offence were greater, the hug being

often employed against the dog with great effect.   At
other times the dogs were frequently crushed by the
bear rolling when seized.

Such were the main features of the bull and bear
baitings at Hockley in the Hole on the Mondays and
Thursdays of each week throughout the year, the
entertainments being often preceded by a parade of
the animals in the streets.   Thus Gay, in "Trivia,"
alludes to such a procession :—

> " When through the streets, with slow and solemn air,
>   Led by the nostril walks the muzzled bear ;
>   Behind him moves, majestically dull,
>   The pride of Hockley Hole, the surly bull.
>   Learn hence the period of the week to name,
>   Mondays and Thursdays are the days of game."

But there were variations and *divertissements* from
the main scheme of the entertainment.   One of these
was the not very intelligible joy of whipping a blind-
folded bear.   " Here often follows that of whipping a
blinded bear, which is performed by five or six men
standing circularly with whips, which they exercise
upon him without any mercy.   As he cannot escape
from them because of his chain, he defends himself
with all his force and skill, throwing down all he can
within his reach and are not active enough to get out
of it, on which occasions he frequently tears the whips
out of their hands and breaks them."

An advertisement of 1710 gives such details of the
miscellaneous forms of sport to be enjoyed at Hockley

that our information on the subject would hardly be complete without a quotation in full.

"At the Bear Garden, Hockley in the Hole, this is to give notice to all gentlemen gamesters and others, that on this present Monday is a match to be fought by two dogs, one from Newgate Market against one from Honey Lane Market, at a bull, for a guinea, to be spent." That guinea to be spent speaks eloquently of the quality of the audiences of Hockley, and suggests a fine circulation of pewter mugs from the "Coach and Horses" next door. "Five let goes out of hand," proceeds the advertisement, "which goes fairest and farthest wins all. Likewise a green bull to be baited, which was never baited before;" the green bull was, no doubt, a fine opportunity of entering young dogs; "and a bull to be turned loose with fireworks all over him; also a mad ass to be baited. With a variety of bull and bear baiting, and a dog to be drawn up with fireworks. To begin exactly at three of the clock."

This entertainment of May 1710 was, we believe, a special occasion, inaugurating a new management. There had been a dreadful tragedy a year before, when Mr. Preston, the proprietor of the establishment, had been attacked by one of his bears, and "almost devoured before his friends were aware of his danger." A sermon, as we read, was preached upon the sad event in the neighbouring church of St. James' by the Rev. Dr. Pead, under whom the parishioners of Clerkenwell then sat. The general

doings at Hockley were calculated to furnish texts
for many sermons.   But this tragedy, we are afraid,
was not taken in any chastened spirit by the frequenters of the place; it quite likely provided the
best advertisement Hockley ever received, and drew
increased crowds of "gentlemen gamesters and others"
to the support of the Widow Preston, who continued
the management of her unlucky husband.

For the next ten years, indeed, there is ample
evidence of the prosperity of the place.   Old collections of handbills and the old files of the news-sheets
of those days teem with notices of the diversions of
Hockley.   There are various details to be gathered
from a consideration of these.   We read of "two bear-
dogs to jump three jumps apiece at the bear, which
jumps highest, for two shillings to be spent."   The
bear was evidently a valuable property, and not often
baited to the death, and the dogs were matched against
each other for a definite match of a certain duration
only—a short test of courage and agility, and not
necessarily a fight with the bear to a finish.   There is
frequent mention, too, of "the famous bull of fireworks, which pleased the gentlemen to admiration."
Then we read of "twenty dogs to fight for a collar,
and the dog that runs farthest and fairest wins the
collar, with other diversions of bull and bear baiting, it
being a day of general sport by all the old gamesters."

On other occasions there was more finality in the
arrangements.   Thus in 1716: "At the request of
several persons of quality, on Monday, the 11th of

this instant June, is one of the largest and most mischievous bears that ever was seen in England to be
baited to death, with other variety of bull and bear
baiting, as also a wild bull to be turned loose in the
game-place with fireworks all over him. To begin
exactly at three o'clock in the afternoon, because the
sport continues long."

Such sports as these were purveyed continuously to
Londoners at Hockley and at the other establishments
we have mentioned. There was a distinct variation
from the ordinary show in an attraction advertised to
take place at a bear garden " at the backside of Soho
Square" in 1716. "At the desire of several persons
of quality a leopard 12 feet in length to be baited to
death, and gentlemen who chuse to risk their dogs
are allowed to assist. The leopard on view at the
Boarded House, Marylebone Fields." A leopard of
12 feet long to be baited to death suggests long odds
against any number of dogs. We read also of "An
African Tyger on a stage four feet high to be worried
by six bull and bear dogs for £100" at Hockley in
the following year. Sometimes the proceedings would
be varied by a fight between dogs of different breeds,
as when Mr. Evelyn saw such a contest at the Bear
Garden at Bankside in 1670, and tells us of "the
cruel mastiff" being beaten by "the Irish wolfhound,
which was a tall grey hound and a stately creature
indeed,"—a reference of interest to that extinct breed
of Irish wolfhound, a specimen of which is painted by
Vandyke in one of his great portraits of Lord Strafford.

Hockley, it is clear, only continued the tradition of the Royal Bear Garden in Southwark, and hardly improved upon some of the brutalities practised there under distinguished auspices. Malcolm, for example, records a most surprising entertainment advertised by the Bankside management in 1682. "Notice was given in the papers that on the 12th of April a horse of uncommon strength, of eighteen or nineteen hands high, would be baited to death at His Majesty's Bear Garden at the Hope, on the Bankside, for the amusement of the Morocco Ambassador, and many of the nobility who knew the horse, and any others who would pay the price of admission. It seems this animal originally belonged to the Earl of Rochester, and being of a ferocious disposition, had killed several of his brethren, for which misdeeds he was sold to the Earl of Dorchester, in whose service committing several similar offences he was transferred to the worse than savages who kept the Bear Garden. On the day appointed several dogs were set upon the vindictive steed, which he destroyed or drove from the arena. At this instant, his owners determined to preserve him for a future day's sport, and directed a person to lead him away. But before the horse had reached London Bridge, the spectators demanded the fulfilment of the promise of baiting him to death, and began to destroy the building. To conclude, the poor beast was fetched back, and other dogs being set upon him without effect, he was stabbed with a sword."

The diversions of Bankside were over, or nearly so, before Hockley came into repute as the home of the same entertainments, but Hockley at one period seems to have had a dangerous competitor in Mr. Wells, of the Bear Garden, Marylebone. Thus a newspaper of 1721 speaks of the death of that gentleman as a distinct relief to Madam Preston at the old establishment in Clerkenwell. "By the decease of Mr. Wells," remarks the journal, "the original bear garden in Hockley in the Hole is now likely to be thronged, especially since all the gamesters are resolved to bait every Monday and Thursday; and the gladiators have promised frequently to test their skill there, the brutes to box, the furmity and hasty-pudding eaters to gobble down their guttage at Madam Preston's and no other place." A poet, too, broke into song on the same occasion.

> "Shed, ye inhabitants, a flood of tears,
> Howl, all ye dogs, roar, all ye bulls and bears,
> Ye butchers weep, for ye no doubt are grievers
> And sound his loss with marrow-bones and cleavers—
> Wells is no more, yet death has been so kind
> That he hath left the bulls and bears behind."

There is ample evidence that the journalistic prophet of the continued prosperity of Hockley was well inspired, and we will quote a very full advertisement of that establishment of the date of 1730, both as a proof of this and also as completing our knowledge of the varied amusements of the places which had the torture of animals as their chief attraction.

"At His Majesty's Bear Garden at Hockley in the Hole, this present Monday, three great matches will be fought.

"First, a brindled dog from Hampstead to fight against a fallow-coloured bitch from Chelsea; to fight ten let goes apiece at the famous Newington Bull for half a guinea each; the dog or bitch which goes farthest in or fairest, wins the money.

"Secondly, a fallow-coloured dog from Whitechapel to fight against a fallow-coloured from Spittlefields Market, both to fight let go for let go at the famous Cambridge Bull for one guinea each, the dog that is killed or runs away, loses the money.

"Likewise, a mad bull to be dressed up with fireworks and turned loose in the game-place.

"Likewise, a dog to be dressed up with fireworks over him and turned loose with the bull amongst the men in the ground, also a bear to be turned loose at the same time, and a cat to be ty'd to the bull's tail.

"*Note.*—The doors will be open at four and the sport begin between five and six o'clock, because the diversion will last long and the days grow short."

The month fixed for the saturnalia here described was August, and the eloquence of this handbill would not be improved by any comment of our own.

The exhibitions of bear and bull baiting, and the other variations of animal torture which we have been considering, were fixed, as we have said, for Mondays and Thursdays. There was no lack of diversion at Hockley and similar establishments on the other days of the week, when their hospitalities were dispensed to clients whose tastes were broad enough to include contests in which the human animal was alone engaged; and although from a modern point of view these are not edifying, we turn to them with some relief. The term prize-fight has come in our day to convey an idea which

differs greatly from its original meaning of the days
of Anne. The great institution of the Prize Ring,
which flourished well within living memory and found
employment for that strange army of heroes who
supported themselves by the strange industry of
punching each other's heads, was a later development
of the prize-fight of Anne and the early Georges.
The original prize-fight, though apparently a very
fearful encounter between armed men, was in reality
a much less dangerous affair than the serious encounter
with the fist which delighted our forefathers of later
years, and decided the ownership of so much of their
money in the form of stakes. The prize-fight of
Hockley in the Hole and of Figg's amphitheatre in
the Oxford Road, though usually performed with
lethal weapons, or with cudgel and quarter-staff at the
least, was much less of a reality, and was organised
solely for the purposes of exhibition and of the resulting gate-money.

Side by side in the same papers with the advertisement of bull and bear baitings we have quoted, or
printed on similar handbills, began to appear announcements of the strange and varied encounters
which went to make up the prize-fight of the same
times. These advertisements usually took the form
of a public challenge of one gladiator by another, or, as
they loved to term themselves, " Masters of the Noble
Art of Self-Defence," a phrase, by the way, which was
in great favour with the boxers of a later period.
Hockley in the Hole was the favourite place for these

encounters, as we have said; the eminence of one of
their professors, Mr. James Figg, gave much renown
to an establishment set up by that gentleman in the
Oxford Road, as a private speculation of his own, and
they flourished also at the other establishments devoted to bull and bear baiting, notably at the old
Bear Garden itself at Bankside. The meeting was
always arranged beforehand, and the challenges appeared in the same issue of the paper, or were printed
on the same handbill. They usually had a very
martial ring about them; there is, for example, more
ardour than modesty in the following, quoted from
a handbill preserved in the Harleian collection, and
dated July 3rd, 1709 :—

"At the Bear Garden at Hockley in the Hole, near Clerkenwell Green, a trial of skill shall be performed at the noble science
of self-defence, on Wednesday next, at two of the clock precisely.

"I, George Grey, born in the city of Norwich, who have fought
in most part of the West Indies—viz., Jamaica and Barbadoes, and
several other parts of the world—in all twenty-five times, and upon
the stage, and never yet was worsted, and being now lately come
to London, do invite James Harris to meet and exercise at these
following weapons, viz., backsword, sword and dagger, sword and
buckler, single falchion and case of falchions.

"I, James Harris, master of the noble science of self-defence,
and formerly rid in the Horse Guards, and have fought an hundred and ten prizes, and never left the stage to any man, will
not fail, God willing, to meet this brave and bold inviter at the
time and place appointed, desiring sharp swords and from him
no favour.

"No person to be upon the stage but the seconds. Vivat
Regina."

In the first year of the eighteenth century, we may learn from the *Postboy* that Mr. John Terrewest, of Oundle, in Northamptonshire, was desirous of meeting Mr. William King, who lately fought Mr. Joseph Thomas, at the usual weapons. Mr. King, we find, was in no way backward: "I, William King, will not fail to meet this bold inviter, desiring, &c. *Note.*—There is lately built a pleasant cool gallery for gentlemen." The pleasant cool gallery, we imagine, was not at all superfluous, for we gather from another advertisement that the doors "will be open at 3 and the masters mount at 6." It does not require great imagination to picture the incidents and temperature of a three-hours' vigil with a typical audience of Hockley in the Hole, on a summer afternoon in a close ill-ventilated booth, with the fashionable accompaniments of beer and tobacco.

We have the advantage, indeed, of the observations of a very notable eyewitness upon the proceedings which followed such challenges as we have quoted. Mr. Richard Steele was present at one of these encounters, and he wrote and told the *Spectator* all about it. Steele, as we know, had a very keen eye for the peculiarities of his contemporaries, and his *Spectator*, No. 436, describing the humours of Hockley, is not the least human of the many pictures of the life of Queen Anne which we owe to that delightful pen.

A gentleman at Hockley was apparently a rarity, for Miss Preston, the daughter of the ill-fated patron of the place, who was later to be slain by his own bear, noticed Dick, and brought him a cup of water to mitigate the heat and the tedium of the waiting. He noticed that the damsel was very fair, fair enough, indeed, "to be the proper Amaryllis on these occasions," and Dick, in his own inimitable way, fell a-musing on a proper regulation of the combat which should make Elizabeth Preston the lady of one of the combatants, "and her beauty in comparison with that of some other nymph the subject matter of the challengers."

The challenge had been handed about, as we have already described, "printed on a whitish brown paper, put into my hand in the street." James Millar, it appears, lately come from the frontiers of Portugal, had heard of the fame of Timothy Buck of London, and had invited him to a meeting at Hockley.

Steele shows us the humours of the crowd waiting for the appearance of the combatants, the scuffling for good places, the "discontent of several active persons in the pit, who thought they were placed rather according to their fortune than their merit"; and the rush of these active ones to the galleries. Here "dispute between merit and property brought many to the ground, and raised others in proportion to the highest seats by turns for the space of ten minutes."

There was a sudden hush and a cessation of all dispute when the combatants appeared. " Miller is a man of 6 ft. 8 in. in height, of a kind but bold aspect, well fashioned, and ready of his limbs." Buck had "a perfect composure which engaged the judgment." Millar came on "preceded by two disabled drummers, to show, I suppose, that the prospect of maimed bodies did not in the least deter him. There ascended with the daring Millar a gentleman with a dogged air, as unsatisfied that he was not a principal. This son of anger lowered at the whole assembly, and weighing himself as he marched round from side to side with a stiff knee and shoulder, gave intimations of the purpose he smothered until he saw the issue of this encounter." We learn that the combatants each wore a ribbon on his sword arm, a survival, as Dick opined, of "the custom of wearing a mistress's favour on such occasions of old."

The men, stripped to their shirts, advanced to the middle of the stage, shook hands, and set to. It is difficult to know what rules governed these encounters; the swords were certainly sharp and blood flowed freely, but there was never a serious attack with the point, and there is only record of a single death as a result of half a century of fighting, and that an accidental one from blood-poisoning. No padding was used, apparently, no masks or jackets, which are necessary even in foil practice to-day, and yet it is certain that great injury was as a rule avoided.

In this particular fight witnessed by Steele, "Millar's heat laid him open to the rebuke of the calm Buck by a large cut on the forehead. Much effusion of blood covered his eyes in a moment, and the huzzas of the crowd undoubtedly quickened his anguish." The human and sympathetic touch which is seldom absent from Steele's writing, especially when there is a woman concerned, does not fail him here. In the midst of the tumult he had eyes " for a poor nymph in the gallery who suffered for Millar, and burst into a flood of tears." Millar's head was bound up, and he came on again " with a little rage." " The next was a warm, eager onset, which ended in a decisive stroke on the left leg of Millar. The lady in the gallery during this second strife covered her face, and for my part," writes Dick, " I could not keep my thoughts from being mostly employed in the consideration of her unhappy circumstance in that moment, hearing the clash of swords and apprehending life or victory concerned her lover in every blow, but not daring to satisfy herself on whom they fell." Millar's wound was a deep one, and was " exposed to the view of all who could delight in it." The proceedings ended with a challenge from Millar's second to fight Buck that day fortnight at the same weapons, " he declaring himself the master of the renowned Gormon, but Buck denied him the honour of that courageous discipline, and asserting that he had himself taught that champion, accepted the challenge."

It is never safe to take such a master of the ironic method as Steele too literally, but another contribution of his to the *Spectator* may perhaps supply a clue to the mystery of the strange safety of the combatants in these struggles with deadly weapons. Dick, writing in the name of "Scabbard Rusty," describes a

conversation he had overheard while sitting in a box
of an alehouse, "near the renowned seat of honour,
Hockley in the Hole." To him entered "two masters
of the science," and he heard them agreeing to quarrel
on the first opportunity, which was fixed no later than
the same evening "at a meeting of the fraternity of
basket hilts." "Will you give cuts, or receive?" said
one of these warriors to the other. "Receive," was
the reply. "Are you a passionate man?" "No,
provided you cut no more and no deeper than we
agree." Steele thought his readers ought to be
acquainted with these facts, in order that the people
might not pay their money to see real fighting and
be cheated.

Before the development of boxing, which we trace
in another chapter, these contests with the sword had
a great vogue among the sporting lights of those early
times, and the cult of "the noble science of self-
defence," of which they were the expression, found
employment for a large body of gladiators. The
most eminent of these were fortunate in a contemporary biographer, who has rescued their names from
oblivion, and has preserved for us some interesting
details of the mysteries of their profession. Captain
John Godfrey is as helpful to us in the matter of the
early prize-fight of Hockley and Figg's amphitheatre
as in tracing the development of pugilism from the
primitive encounters of Taylor's booth in the Oxford
Road a few years later. His curious quarto of 1753
is as eloquent upon the proper strokes of the sword

as upon the virtues of the blow with the fist in the
stomach or under the ear, which had such sterling
value for the earnest pugilist.   Listen to his cold-
blooded exposition of the niceties of the science of
the sword, and the proper objects to be kept in view
by those who practised it.

"In battles fought upon the stage," says the captain,
"you will find all inside cuts to be much deeper and
severer than the outside . . . they are more likely to
hit the face, which being more tender than the head,
will sooner carry the battle. . . . An outside throw,
especially if it be made slanting with a kind of back
sweep, must hit him in the face, and this sweeping
turn carries a direct edge."   Then the wrist of your
opponent should be attacked as often as possible, for
an assault on that vulnerable spot, properly driven
home, obviously finished the contest in your favour.
"The most dangerous cut of the sword to your
opponent," says Godfrey, "is the inside blow at the
wrist; the instant you hit him in the inside of the
wrist your victory is secure."   You may learn the
virtues of the drawing-stroke in going down to the
leg, the very stroke apparently which decided the contest which Steele witnessed in favour of Mr. Buck, in
the captain's quarto.   The whole essay has a blood-
thirsty flavour, but the profession was certainly less
dangerous than it appeared, and the chief object of
the exhibition fight was, we believe, a slashing flesh-
wound, which might produce a good show of blood.

The characters of the masters of this strange pro-

fession are also displayed on a generous scale by the
captain. He begins with the very men whom Steele
watched at Hockley. "Timothy Buck was a most
solid master . . . he was the pillar of the art, and all
his followers who excelled built upon him. Millar
was the palpable gentleman through the prize-fighter;
he was a most beautiful picture on the stage, taking
in all his attitudes, and vastly engaging in his demeanour. There was such an easy action in him
and agreeable smile in the midst of fighting that one
could not help being prejudiced in his favour."

William Gill was "a swordsman formed by Gill's
own hand," the captain never beheld anybody
better for the leg than Gill; "his cuts were re-
markably more severe and deep" than the ordinary.
Why, when he fought Butler, the Irishman, Butler's
leg was laid quite open, "his calf falling down to his
ancle." Poor Butler got blood-poisoning from the
wound and died, the only recorded martyr of the
sport.

"John Parkes of Coventry was a thorough swordsman, heavy, slow, and inactive, but of stanch judgment." Sutton, on the other hand, had "a nimble
body and very agile joints under a heavy head."
"Mr. Johnson is a stanch swordsman and a thorough
master of the true principle of the backsword, but
I must take the liberty to say that his joints are stiff
and slow in action. Mr. Sherlock must be pronounced
an elegant swordsman with uncommon merit, but is not
faultless. I have seen Mr. Sherlock," continues the

captain, "engaged with a man of far less abilities than himself, when, upon a bare stamp of the other's foot and a movement of his sword, he has hurried back with precipitation." Finally, "John Delforce, the only rival to Figg's memory, is so well known for a cudgeller on the stage that I need not lose any time in reviving him to thought." Cudgel-playing, that is, single-stick, was the rehearsal for the fuller glory of the fight with the steel.

It was a queer way of getting a living, to be sure, this submission of the body to blood-letting and hacking, which, however, was usually under very good control, and always stopped at the right moment, without the loss of an eye or limb, much less of a life. The fact speaks volumes for the swordsman-ship of the performers and for their sobriety. We imagine that these heroes of Hockley were vastly more respectable members of society than the patrons who flocked to see them bleed. They often became the darlings of the public and notable personages in certain circles. Millar was given a commission in the army, and assisted the young Duke of Cumberland in the suppression of the rebellion of the "Forty-Five." A Mr. John Sparks whom Millar was reputed to have beaten, a fact which inspired Mr. Buck to challenge him, was thus described on his tombstone in Coventry churchyard : "To the memory of Mr. John Sparks, a native of this city. He was a man of a mild dis-position, a gladiator by profession, who, having fought three hundred and fifty battles in the principal parts of Europe, at length quitted the stage with honour and applause, sheathed his sword, and with Christian resignation submitted to the grand victor in the 62nd year of his age, anno salutatis humanae, 1735." The epitaph would not disgrace the tomb of a bishop.

We have mentioned Mr. Figg's separate establishment in the Oxford Road; this was really a place of greater respectability than Hockley and the rest; it was the first of the London schools-of-arms, a place of tuition in the "noble science of self-defence" for such patrons as Mr. Figg could attract from the better classes, and an exhibition from which the coarser attractions of Hockley were excluded. There were no bear-baitings or dog-fights at Figg's, and its shows were confined to the various displays of the prize-fighting profession, of which Mr. Figg himself was the acknowledged *doyen*.

"Figg," says Captain Godfrey, with a fine enthusiasm, "was the Atlas of the sword, and may he remain the gladiating statue. In him strength and resolution and unparalleled judgment conspired to form a matchless master. There was a majesty shone in his countenance and blazed in all his actions beyond all I ever saw." Such of this majesty as it was possible to preserve by the graphic arts still blazes from the portrait of Figg in mezzotint by Faber, and in several engravings by Mr. Hogarth, who much appreciated Figg as a model. This paragon amongst prize-fighters was a native of Thame, in Oxfordshire, and was indeed a notable figure in the sporting circles

of his day. His patrons were of a higher grade in
the social scale than the average audiences of Hockley;
the bloods from "White's" and the "Cocoa Tree"
were often at Figg's, and there is frequent mention
of the entertainments he provided at his amphitheatre
in the annals of the first half of the last century.
"We took coach to Figg's amphitheatre," says Byrom
in his Journal in 1725, "where Mr. Leicester paid
2/6 for me. Figg and Sutton fought. Figg had a
wound, and bled pretty much. Sutton had a blow
with a quarter-staff just above his knee, which made
him limp, so they gave over." Figg fought Sparkes
before the Duke of Lorraine and Count Kinski and
suite in 1731. "His Serene Highness was extremely
pleased," we are told, "and expressed his entire satisfaction, and ordered them a handsome gratuity."
You will see Figg's portrait in the right-hand corner
of Hogarth's fine plate of Southwark Fair, where he
rides a pony with a very martial air, and draws attention to his honourable scars by prodigious pieces
of sticking-plaster on his closely shaven head. He
appears, too, in the same artist's "Modern Midnight
Conversation," and also, it is said, in Plate II. of the
"Rake's Progress." Mr. Hogarth etched for Figg a
business card or ticket of admission to the amphitheatre, which may yet be found in collections of that
artist's engravings.

Figg, we learn, was the sworn foe of all Irishmen,
and fought his 271st battle with Mr. Holmes in
October of 1735, a statement which is not without

interest as a measure of the danger of the prize-fight with swords. His advertisements are curious and of a historical or poetical cast, introducing allusions to Cæsar and Marius, laurels, cedars of Lebanon and cypresses, and hinting at early graves and tombstones for his opponents. He was undoubtedly a very expert swordsman, a notable master of the quarter-staff, and perhaps the first professional pugilist of whom anything is recorded, in which latter capacity we examine his career elsewhere.

We have dealt, so far, with the chief attractions of these curious and almost forgotten places of amusement, but there was one feature common to nearly all of them which still claims mention. In 1722 appeared the following advertisement, which was no doubt typical of many others :—

" *Challenge.*—I, Elizabeth Wilkinson, of Clerkenwell, having had some words with Hannah Highfield, and requiring satisfaction, do invite her to meet me on the stage and box for three guineas, each woman holding half a crown in each hand, and the first woman that drops her money to lose the battle.

"*Answer.*—I, Hannah Highfield, of Newgate Market, hearing of the resoluteness of Elizabeth Wilkinson, will not fail, God willing, to give her more blows than words, desiring home blows, and of her no favour. She may expect a good thumping."

"They maintained the battle for a long time," says the *London Journal* for June of 1722, describing this strange battle, "to the no small satisfaction of the spectators."

These Amazons were much in evidence both at Figg's and elsewhere, and their encounters, no doubt, supplied a pleasant change from the ordinary attractions of the place. The challenges were certainly arranged beforehand, like those emanating from Mr. Steele's acquaintance in the inn box, and the "words" referred to by Elizabeth were no doubt exchanged over a friendly pot of porter at some favourite house of call near the Fleet Ditch. The pious appeal to Providence was common in that day, and survives still, in the form of "D.V.," in those curious announcements which one reads in the local papers, when school children and the congregations of suburban chapels are challenged to the contests of the tea urn and muffin. The artificial character of the quarrel and of its preliminaries, however, does not appear to have diminished the realities of the encounter. The ladies were dressed in "close jacket, short petticoats, and holland drawers, and with white stockings and pumps." There is much eloquence in that condition of holding a half-crown in each fist. The lady who forgot the rule in the vehemence of the onset and resorted to her natural weapons, lost the day. The punishment of the encounter was thus limited to the thumps referred to by Hannah, and that thoughtful condition of the half-crown excluded the scratchings and hair-pullings which might have been expected in the circumstances. There was evidently a recognised band of these hardy women, for we read of "Mrs. Stokes, the city championess," desiring to meet "the Hibernian Heroine" at Figg's for a nominal stake.

Nor were feminine encounters confined to the contests of the fist. Strange as it may seem to modern ideas, prize-fighters with the cold steel were at times assisted by their spouses, and matched against other greatly daring ladies who had the help of their husbands. Thus, as Malcolm relates in 1725, "Sutton, the champion of Kent, and a courageous female heroine of that county fought Stokes, at Figg's, and his much admired consort of London. £40 was to be given to the male and female who gave most cuts with the swords, and £20 for most blows at quarter-staff, besides the collection in the box."

The entertainments we have described, both at Hockley and similar places, and at Figg's, continued their course with little interruption until about the middle of the last century, by which time the disappearance of Hockley and such like places had banished bull and bear baiting to the suburbs and provinces, and pugilism had taken the place of the prize-fight with the sword. Like many of the amusements of the period, they were attacked from time to time by the puritanical body, but always with indifferent success. They resisted presentment by Grand Juries, memorials to quarter sessions, and sermons by the clergy, from bishops downward. The activity of certain sections of the public where public amusements were concerned was a remarkable feature of the social life of the eighteenth century, as indeed it is of that of our own times. It was particularly in evidence when any natural convulsion brought terror or suffering to the community. Nerves upset by a great storm or by the shock of an earthquake would find a cause for such visitations in a Providence outraged by the enormities of the masquerade, the license of the playhouses, or the ribaldry of Hockley in the Hole. The great storm of 1703 produced Mr. Addison's fine compliment to the Duke of Marlborough in the famous image of the angel riding the whirlwind, and it produced also an agitation against cakes and ale in many forms. Incidentally, too, it saved the lives of many devoted cocks who were accustomed to immolation by the practice of the "cockshy" on Shrove Tuesday, a function which was suppressed during the consternation which followed the dreadful visitation of 1703. But Hockley survived all agitation, and its final overthrow was the result of the growth of London and the municipal improvements which accompanied it. The whole district was drained and its level raised in 1756, when it is probable the bear garden disappeared. The cult of the London prize-ring had already supplanted the attractions of its contests with sword and quarter-staff, and its bull and bear baitings found patronage further afield.

Both those sports remained lawful amusements until the year 1835, and there are persons still living who can remember having seen bulls baited in public places, such as the Bull Ring in Birmingham, for example—a name which still echoes the sport. Well on in this present century famous bulls were taken progresses from county to county, and matched

BEAR-BAITING

DRAWN BY H. ALKEN

against local dogs. There was a benevolent gentleman of Wokingham who was so devoted to the
diversion of bull-baiting, that he left provision in his
will for two bulls to be baited yearly for the amusement of the people of his native town ; and it is said
that the bulls are still purveyed to the beneficiaries,
but in the form of beef. So late as 1802, an attempt
at parliamentary interference with bull and bear baiting, though backed by the efforts of such men as
Sheridan and Wilberforce, was defeated. Mr. Windham, who successfully resisted the measure, looked
upon it, we are told, " as the first result of a con-
spiracy of Jacobins and Methodists to render the
people grave and serious." Bull and bear baiting
thus had a legal status until 1835, when a career of
the sport during nearly seven centuries of English
life was closed by an Act of Parliament.

There have been many headshakings over the moral
enormities of those old amusements of Englishmen
which seem entirely justified. The present is certainly not the moment to defend them. At their
worst, they were less cruel than the bull-fight in Spain
of to-day, because they were encounters between
animals handicapped into something like equality,
and furious with rage. The casualties were generally confined to the dogs, who in an average afternoon lost two of their number. The sickening
cruelty of non-combatant animals done to death,
like the terror-stricken horses of the bull-fight, was
at least avoided. At their best, they were certainly

less cruel than the low meetings for closed coursing common a few years ago, and the iniquities practised upon helpless pigeons at some of the low modern shooting-matches, in order to add to the eccentricities of their flight.

The personal encounters between the professors of the sword we put upon a different footing altogether. They were certainly unedifying as popular spectacles ; but we rank the danger to their exponents as much less than that of the players of a North Country football match of to-day, or even of the referee.

In considering the whole subject, we have to remember that indifference to suffering was a national asset in the days when the British Empire was in the making, and that it is quite possible that modern sentiment might take a moderate swing back in the same direction were the new century now about to open to bring with it the hardening of men's hearts, which comes with years of war and the pressgang. At the present moment, however, hardly a single trace of these old amusements of the town survives. The descendants of Figg and Millar are nowhere recognisable ; Hockley in the Hole may be very faintly and innocently reflected in the unprepossessing features of the bow-legged, underhung bulldogs which grin at us from the stands of the kennel shows.

CHAPTER II

LONDON AL FRESCO—THE TEA GARDENS

LONDON has always shown a disposition to make the best of a short summer and a fickle climate. You may turn to the letters, or diaries, or news-sheets of any period since that of the Stuarts, and find continuous record of a public ever ready to support an entertainment which included among its attractions the consumption of victuals in the open air. The peg upon which this attraction was hung has never been a matter of great moment. Highly-born people flocked to Spring Gardens in the days of Charles the First without intending to play bowls. The Mulberry Garden of the same times was only an attractive title for an open-air restaurant. Music and the promenade were the excuses for eating suppers at Vauxhall. The waters of Bagnigge Wells were little drunk by the humbler people who flocked there, except in the form of tea. And coming to more recent times, the fireworks and the "twenty thousand additional lamps" of the Vauxhall and Cremorne of the first half of the present century had less to do with the success of those famous institutions than the bad food and worse liquor, which Londoners are ever ready to pay for at exorbitant rates if only served out of doors.

There is, in fact, an unbroken tradition of *al fresco* entertainment in London over a period of two centuries at least. From the days of Charles the First until well on in the present reign, there is continuous record of junketings in one part of the town or another. Let us turn to the accounts of these old merrymakings, scattered in newspapers and magazines; preserved in advertisements, often of an almost touching quaintness; in letters and memoirs, and chance phrases of the diaries of generations long since asleep; in the records also, it must be confessed, of police courts and hostile licensing authorities. The draughtsmen and the engravers of a century were often busy with the doings at these places, and will give us much help in repeopling their forgotten shades and arbours, and in recalling a phase of social life which provided one of the chief relaxations of numbers of our citizen ancestors.

We know little or nothing of the *al fresco* entertainment in London before the days of Charles the First, and its vogue may be said to have come to an end with the extinction of Cremorne within the memory of those not yet past middle age; just as the need of open air relaxation in London was growing sorest, as it would seem. That, as we say, gives a period of over two centuries during which the *al fresco* entertainment flourished, a space of time in which London and the needs of its inhabitants have been totally transformed. It is important to remember this fact, and to think of the London of all but the present century as a great centre of population indeed, but compared with its present huge bulk, as a relatively small town. Take any old map, for example, of the middle years of the period we have marked out as that of the London *al fresco*, 1750 to 1760, the palmy days of its vogue, and trace the boundaries of London upon it. When George the Third came to the throne, London, including Westminster, was bounded by Oxford Street and Holborn on the north, by the river on the south, by the outer boundary of the city on the east, and by Hyde Park, Arlington Street, and St. James' Street on the west. All the rest of modern London was suburban merely, or open and pleasant country interspersed with wild heaths, and dotted with ancient villages. That country stretched out fingers and touched the city wall itself at Finsbury and the Tower. The fashionable dwellers in the Savoy and the lawyers of the Temple looked across the river to the hills of Surrey and Kent; and there is room for reflection in the fact that the Zoological Gardens, which were not opened till 1828, had for years to be fenced against the hares and rabbits which nibbled the bark off their shrubs and dug up their bulbs.

It was in and about a town of such dimensions then, and with such surroundings, that the *al fresco* entertainment took origin and developed, a town thickly populated and stuffy, it is true, the bulk of whose inhabitants lived and died within the limits of their

own streets, but still a town whose innermost slum
was within easy walk of a delightful country, and
whose suburbs were without the distressing squalor
and vulgarity of architecture which make for some of
us the oldest part of London to-day its most cheerful
part. It was the citizens of such a town, sober
merchants and shopkeepers, apprentices, sempstresses,
and artisans who worked continuously, but leisurely
and without much stress, during the week and spread
themselves over an area of many square miles on
Sundays, who formed the chief patrons of the *al fresco*
entertainment. The lawyers and military men who
filled the chief of the few recognised professions of
the last century, supplied their quota of course, and
the aristocracy came to most of the *al fresco* entertainments at one time or another, but merely as incidental
visitors. The *al fresco* entertainments of the aristocracy
were the great gardens of Vauxhall and Ranelagh, and
these two famous places of resort had a character all
their own as such, which makes it desirable to treat of
them in a separate chapter. In this, we ask the reader
to follow us through the more humble of the tea
gardens and spas, most of which had some special
attraction of cake and ale, or bowling-green or fives
court of its own, which might recommend it to the
patronage of a special *clientèle* in a day when competition between such places was often severe.

The first *al fresco* entertainment in London of which
there is anything like a full account, although open to
the public, was not, it is true, of a very democratic

character, or supported by the patronage of any but
persons of a certain condition.   Spring Garden at
Charing Cross was of royal origin, and Charles the
First was there accustomed to rub shoulders with his
subjects in what was practically a part of his own royal
gardens at Whitehall.   The place took its name from
a spring or fountain, which, in the pleasant fashion of
those times, was contrived to sprinkle those who came
to consult the sun-dial.   It is difficult to understand
how the public first gained admission to Spring Garden.
Its earliest attraction seems to have been a bowling-
green, "and there was kept in it," says Gerrard, writing
to Strafford in 1634, "an ordinary of six shillings a
meal, continual bibbing and drinking of wine all day
under the trees; two or three quarrels every week.
It was grown scandalous and insufferable, besides,
my Lord Digby being reprehended for striking Will
Crofts in the King's Garden, he answered that he took
it for a common bowling-place where all paid money
for their coming in."   This irregularity of Lord Digby
and Will Crofts led to an interference by the royal
authorities.   We are told that Spring Garden was
"put down for one day," but Queen Henrietta inter-
ceding, "it was reprieved for this year, but hereafter it
shall be no more bowling-place."

This garden, therefore, which we take to be the
forerunner and the model of the later *al fresco* entertainments of London, was obviously in full swing in
1634, and the displeasure of King Charles and of
others in authority later notwithstanding, it survived,

with some temporary eclipses, for thirty years at least.
It is difficult to think of Charing Cross as a sylvan retreat at this moment, but there is surely fascination
for the Londoner in this description of the place by
Mr. Evelyn in 1658: "The enclosure not disagreeable for the solemness of the grove, the warblings of
the birds, and as it opens in the spacious walks of St.
James's," and it is recorded that ten years earlier, viz.
in 1648, James Duke of York and Colonel Bamfield
passed into and out of Spring Garden in making their
escape from the Palace of St. James's "in the guise of
gallants come to hear the nightingale." To think to-
day of nightingales at Charing Cross!

There were other aspects of these gardens which
commended themselves less to the sober lover of trees
and solitudes, although he appears to have made much
use of the place. A great deal of what is known of
Spring Garden, indeed, is owing to Mr. Evelyn's recorded observations. "The thickets of the garden,"
he said, "seem to be contrived to all advantages of
gallantry, for it is usual here to find some of the
young company till midnight after they have been
refreshed with the collation which is here seldom
omitted at a certain cabaret in the middle of this
paradise, where the forbidden fruits are certain
trifling tarts, neats' tongues, salacious meats and bad
Rhenish; for which the gallants pay sauce, as indeed
they do at all such houses throughout England."
We learn elsewhere that the collation was at the
rate of six shillings a head, which, allowing for the

increased value of money and the poorness of the Rhenish, is surely a not ungenerous figure for a meal of cold meat.

It is not surprising to learn that Spring Garden attracted the serious attention of the Puritans. The jocular doings under the trees, the wine-bibbings and the quarrels, were reasons enough for the benevolent interference of the Parliament. It is quite in the natural order of things therefore to read that "Cromwell and his partizans had shut up and seized upon Spring Garden, which till now (1654) had been ye usual rendezvous for the ladys and gallants at this season." We again quote Mr. Evelyn. In the year of the Lord Protector's death, however, the place was again in full blast, and Mr. Evelyn, after going to see a coach race in Hyde Park, "collationed in Spring Garden."

This collation, indeed, was the great attraction of the place. It was difficult in those days to get a meal anywhere away from home, the coffee-houses had not yet arisen, and most of the taverns lay far eastward of Charing Cross. Great people then lived either in the city or just out of it, and Spring Garden, with its luncheon, was a convenient halting-place for refreshment on the way to, or returning from Hyde Park, where the promenade of the ring, the foot and chariot races, were at this time great attractions. "The manner is," says Mr. Evelyn, "as the company returns (from Hyde Park) to alight at the Spring Garden . . . but the company walk in it at such a rate you would think that all the ladies were so many Atalantas contending with their wooers."

One of the last references to the place is from the invaluable Mr. Pepys, whose fuller report on the doings there would have been very welcome. He went there, it seems, in May of 1662, with his wife's maids, "and the wenches gathered pinks. Here we staid, and seeing that we could not have anything to eate, but very dear and with long stay, we went forth again." But the days of Spring Garden were already numbered. It occurred, no doubt, to the keeper of the Privy Purse of King Charles the Second's needy Court that the situation of the place was adapted to more profitable uses, and it was soon devoted to those of building. Here arose the groups of houses first known as Inner and Outer Spring Garden, where lived a succession of people of condition till the tide of fashion again flowed westward. The name of the Spring Garden was adopted by the New Spring Gardens at Lambeth, which we examine elsewhere under the title of Vauxhall, but it still lingers about the spot where the County Council deliberates to-day upon the licensing of other forms of entertainment for Londoners.

The *al fresco* tradition of those days was supported by another garden farther west, the Mulberry Garden, which covered the site of the present Buckingham Palace and gardens. We take little account of a bowling-green opened in 1635 by "a gentleman barber," during a temporary eclipse of Spring Garden,

"in the fields behind the mews in Piccadily," because
it was really a gaming establishment, "made to enter-
tain gamesters and bowlers at an excessive rate . . .
where they bowl great matches" (Gerrard to Strafford). It fulfilled the usual destiny of such places,
became known as Shaver's Hall, in pleasant allusion
to the "gentleman barber" who founded it, and its
remains could be traced in the tennis-court at the
corner of James Street until quite recent times. The
Mulberry Garden, however, was of the true class of
open-air entertainment, "ye only place of refreshment about ye town for persons of ye best quality
to be excessively cheated at," says Mr. Evelyn in
1654, Cromwell at that time having laid his heavy
hand on Spring Garden.

Although the records of the Mulberry Garden are
somewhat scanty, it had certainly a great vogue during
the reigns of both Charleses and the Commonwealth,
for half the dramatists of the Restoration make their
characters move in its walks and arbours, and eat its
tarts and cakes, and it was of sufficient importance as a
place of public resort to give a title to one of Sedley's
comedies. There is historical record of the place also.
It was quite like Charles the Second to violate his own
proclamation against the drinking of toasts during a
debauch at the Mulberry Garden. Mr. Pepys too
was there in 1668, and found it "a very silly place,
worse than Spring Garden, and but little company,
only a wilderness that is somewhat pretty." But years
later candid Samuel was much better pleased, the

circumstances perhaps being more propitious, for
entertainment at another's expense is ever a good
softener of criticism. "To the Mulberry Garden,"
says Samuel, "where Shere is to treat us with a
Spanish Olio . . . he did do it mighty nobly, and the
Olio was indeed a very noble dish such as I never saw
better or any more of. We left other good things
which would keep till night for a collation, and with
much content took coach again, meeting The. Turner,
Talbot, Batelier and his sister in a coach, and with
us to the Mulberry Garden, and thereafter a walk to
supper upon what was left at noon, and very good,
and we mighty merry." It is in such passages as this
that the memory of the place is preserved, or in the
gossip of contributors to *Sylvanus Urban*, who remembered "to have eat tarts with Mr. Dryden and
Madam Reeve at the Mulberry Garden, when our
author advanced to a sword and chedreux wig."
Wycherley, Etherege, Sedley, Shadwell, will tell us
of the "pleasant divertissement" of the place; of
cheesecakes and tarts and arbours and dinners "in the
dining-room of Mulberry Garden House"; of ladies
and gentlemen who made love together till twelve
o'clock at night. The place was closed about 1674,
when the *al fresco* tradition of London passed into the
keeping of Vauxhall. It is worthy of note that the
soil of Mulberry Garden is still open to wind and sun
in the gardens of Buckingham Palace, which gives
its memory a distinction rare among these old
pleasaunces, which for the most part, as we shall see,

lie buried to-day under acres of unlovely bricks and mortar.

It was in those two old pleasure gardens of the Stuart times then, as we believe, that the tradition of the London *al fresco* originated. But its real development waited upon the times when England, emerging from the troublous days of the civil wars and revolutions, at last found time and opportunities for enjoyment under the more settled rule of Anne and the first Georges. There was feverish enjoyment of a sort for Londoners, of course, during those restless days of the Restoration; but an enjoyment clouded with the shadow of an impending Nemesis which was palpable to the great body of Englishmen as long as there was a full-blooded Stuart on the throne. Mr. Pepys himself felt it at one of those very gardens when the doings of Harry Killigrew and of other "very rogues" made Samuel's "heart ake," as we shall see when we come to Vauxhall. But it was only when England settled down under the wise rule of the sagacious Walpole, who first discovered the capacity of the English for managing their own affairs, that London really began to enjoy itself, and one of the first evidences of that welcome change in the national fortune was the multiplication of those popular and innocent places of open-air entertainment in and round London.

It is quite natural to find the citizen of low-lying London lifting his eyes to the hills and turning for solace from his labours chiefly to the pleasant country

which then rolled towards the sun from the heights of
Hampstead and Highgate. It is difficult to-day to
think of the unpromising districts now covered by
Clerkenwell, Pentonville, and Islington, to say nothing
of the suburbs farther north, as open country, with
pastures, woods, and streams, yet such it was almost
within living memory. The New River, which to-day
flows into our waterpipes, and even the Fleet River,
which perhaps helps to flush our sewers, were in the
days of which we write streams with fat meadows, and
buttercups, and placid cattle, the delight of generations of true cockneys from Holborn and the city.
The springs of this upland country sloping to the
Thames bubbled up in various places charged with
" chalybeate " or " sulphur," as the doctors of that
day believed, and provided an excuse for a dozen or
more of " spas," and " waters " or " wells," each with
its gardens and long room and special body of patrons,
who perhaps accepted the efficacy of its waters, and
certainly enjoyed the diversions of the place.

A tea garden occupied the very site of the present
underground railway station at King's Cross ; others
jostled each other on the spot which is now a very
wilderness of railway bridges and shunting grounds
behind the great termini in the Euston Road. As
time went on such places spread over a tract of country
which included Bayswater on one hand and Stepney on
the other, stretched out to Kilburn and Hampstead,
Hornsey and Dalston, and studded generously the
whole district so included with these open-air enter-

tainments, the names of whose springs or proprietors
or attractions are yet preserved in the names of the
streets which to-day cover their ancient delights.

In the very centre of that grimy district of Clerkenwell, for example, on a spot which has recently been
again restored to light and air by the opening of
Rosebery Avenue from the Gray's Inn Road to King's
Cross Road, was situate a very typical tea garden of the
last century, Islington Spa, or the New Tunbridge Wells.
The place could boast a respectable antiquity before
its end came, for it offered its attractions to the subjects of King James the Second and of Queen Victoria
alike, and its doings provided copy for such widely
separated historians of their times as Ned Ward and
Pierce Egan. Like many other of the north London
pleasure gardens, it owed its origin to the discovery
of a spring of " chalybeate" water, and a year or so
after that event there is mention of one of its early
proprietors in the *London Gazette* (1685), "Mr. John
Langley of London, merchant, who bought the Rhino-
ceros and Islington Wells." For the ten years following it had quite a vogue as a watering-place, and
became the frequent theme of the poets of Grub
Street, who were employed to sing its praises. When
the eighteenth century opened Islington Spa was a fine
going concern; to the medicinal attractions of its
waters were added the amusements of a tea garden,
and the amenities of the place, like those of many
others, began to expand in sympathy with the more
generous views of life then becoming common among

Londoners.   Ned Ward will tell you of its lime trees, its coffee-house, its dancing saloon, its raffling shop, and its gaming tables.   A tame doctor was kept on the premises to administer the waters, which were supplementary now to the pleasures of music, dancing, and the promenade.   Islington Spa became a great place of popular resort, where city madams, sempstresses, and clerks could rub shoulders on occasion with people of a higher rank, and its arbours were much affected by city apprentices and their sweethearts with a weakness for plum cake.   Other less desirable visitors followed, as was usually the case in these public places—sharpers, frail women, and pickpockets, and even on occasion gentlemen of the road. They took my Lord Cobham's watch from him there about the middle of the century, and doings at the play-tables were not above suspicion.

Like many of its competitors Islington Spa had varying fortunes until, in 1733, in the month of May, it occurred to the Princesses Caroline and Amelia to attend regularly and take its waters.   These royal ladies were duly saluted with twenty-one guns, and all London flocked to the gardens to see a real princess.   Their visit brought sudden prosperity to the place ; the proprietor, it was said, took £30 of a morning in entrance money alone, and Mr. Pinchbeck, the toyseller, seizing the psychological moment, did a large trade in fans bearing a representation of the place, which may still be found in collections of those interesting objects.   It was in that very year that Mr.

George Bickham, jun., made a very pretty drawing of
Islington Spa, and engraved it at the head of a copy
of verses set to music, which celebrate some of the
charms of the society which gathered there. The
engraving shows the company taking the waters in
a very quaint and delightful courtyard and garden,
and assisted by a contemporary letter from a young
lady who was there soon after we can revive the
pleasures which such places afforded for our ancestors,
and measure the gulf between the Islington of that
day and this. "New Tunbridge Wells is a very
pretty and romantick place," says the letter, "and the
water much like Bath water, but makes one vastly
cold and hungary." It made Lady Mary Wortley
Montagu giddy and sleepy, it seems, but her ladyship left it on record that she derived much benefit
from its use. Even as late as 1803 we learn from
Malcolm, in that valuable work of his where are
preserved so many interesting particulars of the life
of the century which had just closed, that "the
gardens were very beautiful, particularly at the
entrance. Pedestals and vases are grouped under
some extremely picturesque trees, whose foliage is
seen to much advantage from the neighbouring fields."
We do not doubt it ; a garden of any sort of a century
old has a beauty of its own, but there is pathos for a
Londoner in the thought that such a picture existed
in Clerkenwell during the present century. The
beginning of the end, however, came soon after.
Charlotte Street, afterwards Thomas Street, arose on

part of the site in 1810, and Eliza Street was built over the original entrance, a new one being made from Lloyd's Row. The gardens, thus curtailed, struggled on till 1840, when the end came by the building of two rows of houses, known as Spa Cottages. The well itself was enclosed in an outhouse of the dwelling of a former proprietor, and its waters were offered at sixpence a quart by an enterprising surgeon. It seems almost incredible that they continued to run until the year 1860. But all interested in the past of this enormous County of London will be grateful to Mr. Philip Norman and Mr. Warwick Wroth, who visited the spot independently in 1894, and after a search in the outhouse discovered a cellar containing the old spring, dry, indeed, but still surrounded by the remains of its grotto, its steps, and its balustrade, the relics of its better days.

A similar institution, which proved a formidable rival to Islington Spa, was the famous gardens of Bagnigge, opened by a Mr. Hughes in 1759, in grounds which are now covered by the Phœnix Brewery, a little north of Clerkenwell Police Court, and by part of the great building yard of the Messrs. Cubitt in the Gray's Inn Road. There were traditions of merrymaking about this pleasant spot long before Mr. Hughes made his venture. Bagnigge House, which gave its name to the gardens and wells, was a country residence of Nell Gwynn, where King Charles the Second and his brother James delighted at times to take breakfast with that lady. Mr. Hughes appears to have

discovered the capabilities of the place quite by accident. As a great amateur of gardening he was much
troubled by the difficulty of growing his pansies and
carnations, and in seeking for the cause he discovered
that their roots were beset by the percolations of two
springs of water. Analyses of these waters disclosed
the fact that one was "a chalybeate of a ferruginous
character, with an agreeable subacid tartness, apt to
produce a kind of giddiness, and afterwards a pro-
pensity to sleep if exercise be not interposed." Thus
Dr. Bevis, the analyst and adviser to Mr. Hughes.
The other, we learn on the same authority, was a
"carthartic, which left a distinguishable brackish bit-
terness on the palate," and three half pints were sufficient for most people. The ingenious Mr. Hughes
sank wells to collect these health-giving streams,
ran pipes into an ornamental dome supported on
pillars in the classic taste, which he called the Temple,
and provided Londoners with a new spa or watering-
place—just as George the Third mounted the throne
of his grandfather.

Such was the origin of Bagnigge Wells, a place of
resort for the true-bred cockney for half a century.
Nell Gwynn's dining-room, the banqueting-hall of
Bagnigge House, a room of a generous spaciousness
nearly eighty feet by forty, provided a pump-room or
promenade. The old gardens were laid out with
clipped hedges of yew; formal walks ran between
alleys of box and holly; there were arbours covered
with sweetbrier and honeysuckle for tea-drinking;

ponds containing gold fish, then not often seen; a
fountain with Cupid bestriding a swan, and leaden
statues of Phyllis and Corydon—perhaps those very
figures which to-day give a quaint interest to one of
the galleries of South Kensington. The Fleet River,
crossed by three rustic bridges, divided the gardens
into two unequal parts, the eastern and smaller portion
being devoted to people whose tastes were less modish
than those of the patrons of the pump-room. Here
pleasant seats were provided on the banks of the
stream for such "as chuse to smoake or drink cyder,
ale, &c., which are not permitted in other parts of the
garden." The severity of the formal garden too, as
we read, declined upon the eastern bank of the Fleet
and melted away into the pleasing rusticity of willows,
elder bushes, burdock and water plants, which were
well known to artists seeking opportunity for the
study of natural foliage.

The programme of amusement at this cockney
paradise was very typical of the London *al fresco* in
its prime. In the morning the place was chiefly at
the disposal of the invalids who believed in the efficacy
of its waters, and who, at the height of its vogue, were
to be found at Bagnigge in hundreds. Many of these
partook of the early breakfast which was provided for
the austere ones, who drank the waters in an orthodox
manner on an empty stomach. A good organ, presided over by Mr. Charles Griffiths, provided music in
the pump-room for the gouty and the lame: the pump-
room with its panelled walls, low ceiling, its armorial

bearings, its bust of Nell Gwynn in a niche in the wall, "bordered with festoons of fruit and flowers, moulded in delf earth, and coloured after nature," and its general pleasant flavour of antiquity. As the day wore on the invalids withdrew and the place was prepared for another class of customers. The citizens, their wives and daughters, came for their afternoon outing ; the long room if the weather threatened, and the arbours if the sun shone, were filled with sober parties of shopkeepers or with boys and their sweethearts, drinking tea and eating the bread and butter and the buns baked on the ground for which the place was famous. Negus was another of the products of Bagnigge held in much favour, and there were cider and ale for the more jovial spirits who smoked under the shade of the Fleet willows and watched the games of skittles and Dutch pins which were played in the eastern part of the gardens during the long summer evenings.

It was on Sundays, however, that Bagnigge was seen at its best. Its nearness to the city, its undoubtedly pleasant surroundings, and the quasi-fashionable character imparted to the place by the patronage of the well-to-do invalids who drank its waters, made it the paradise of the city matron for a quarter of a century at least. From May till October, Holborn and Cheapside and Smithfield put on their Sunday best and emptied themselves into Bagnigge as the Sabbath afternoons came round. Half the bad poets of the last half of the century sang one aspect of the place or another. Listen to Mr. William Woby in the "Shrubs of Parnassus" on its springs—

> ". . . and stil'd the place
> Black Mary's hole, there stands a dome superb
> Hight Bagnigge, where from our forefathers hid,
> Long had two springs in dull stagnation slept;
> But taught at length by subtle art to flow
> They rise; forth from oblivion's bed they rise;
> And manifest their virtues to mankind."

That was one way of saying what the proprietor said much more directly in his daily advertisement. "Mr. Davis takes this method to inform the publick that both the chalybeate and the purging waters are in the greatest perfection ever known and may be drank at 3d. each person, or delivered in the pump-room at 8d. per gallon. They are recommended by the most eminent physicians for various disorders as specified in the hand-bills."

But there were not wanting versifiers of better equipment. Here is Mr. Churchill, for example, in 1779 with a metrical study quite as convincing as Mr. Davis's prose—

> "Thy arbour Bagnigge, and the gay alcove
> Where the frail nymphs in amorous dalliance rove,
> Where 'prentice youths enjoy the Sunday feast,
> And city madams boast their Sabbath best,
> Where unfledged Templars first as fops parade,
> And new made ensigns sport their first cockade."

The prentice's song, too, is not without some suggestion of local colour—

> " Come, prithee make it up, Miss, and be as lovers be,
>   We'll go to Bagnigge Wells, Miss, and there we'll have some tea ;
>   It's there you'll see the lady-birds perched on the stinging
>   nettles,
>   And chrystal water fountains, and shining copper kettles ;
>   It's there you'll see the fishes, more curious they than whales,
>   They're made of gold and silver, Miss, and wags their little
>   tails."

Finally, Mr. Colman in his prologue to Mr. Garrick's " Bon Ton " gives the city madam's view of what then constituted the mode—

> " Bon Ton's the space 'twixt Saturday and Monday,
>   'Tis riding in a one horse chair on Sunday,
>   'Tis drinking tea on summer afternoons
>   At Bagnigge Wells with china and gilt spoons."

With these varied attractions for various classes of customers, Bagnigge during nearly half a century had a not surprising vogue. There was some attempt at a promenade in fine dresses on Sundays, where aspiring young men about town, who were not quite the mode, graduated in deportment for the brighter glories of Ranelagh and Vauxhall. There came of course the usual hangers-on of respectability, the ladies of doubtful reputation, the " bloods of humour," copper captains, and even on occasion famous highwaymen, like the eminent John Rann, or Sixteen-stringed Jack, who was wont to display his hectoring graces in the gardens. Such incidents, however, gave a pleasant adventurous interest to a visit to Bagnigge ; a highwayman, so long as he escaped the justices, was a not unpopular character, and the ordinary citizen lost no caste in taking a glass with one of these heroes at a tea garden or a tavern. It is recorded, however, that this particular hero gave such offence at Bagnigge on a certain Sabbath afternoon in July of 1774, that he was incontinently pitched out of the windows of the Long Room by the outraged citizens, a fall which preceded his final overthrow by Jack Ketch at Tyburn by just four months.

It is not surprising to find the artists busy with a place which attracted so much of the life of the time. There was the excellent publisher, Carrington Bowles, who preserved so much for us of the social life of the century, who has left two or three excellent mezzotints among his series. One, the Bread and Butter Manufactory, shows the fashionable Sunday parade in the long room ; another, the typical citizen Mr. Deputy Dumpling and his family enjoying an afternoon in the gardens. The place is figured in the frontispieces and illustrations of many parish histories and London guide-books of a past day. Men like Sanders painted it, and engravers like I. R. Smith transferred its beauties to the copper. Finally its amenities provided subjects for many able amateurs whose sketches and drawings enrich great collections like those of Mr. Crace and the Guildhall Museum.

On the extensive piece of ground which is to-day enclosed more or less roughly by Marylebone Road, High Street, Marylebone, Weymouth Street, and Harley Street, was the other notable public garden of the northern district of London, famous for half a century as Marylebone Gardens. We make no apology for reminding the modern Londoner that Marylebone remained a rural village until well on in the reign of George the Third, a village separated by fields from the Oxford Road, and receiving much benefit from the attractions of these gardens, which came to be much appreciated by the well-to-do and respectable people who began to build and occupy the good houses of Portman and Cavendish Squares. As in the case of the great majority of the London *al fresco* establishments, the later prosperity of the garden was reared upon the small beginnings of a tavern or public-house. The Rose of Normandy was a small place of this sort on the eastern side of the High Street, famous since Stuart times for its bowling-greens. Those same bowling-greens were acquired from the gardens of the Marylebone Manor House, which stood till 1791 on the site of the present Devonshire Mews. People of condition played bowls at the Rose until well on in the eighteenth century, and left their substance at its gaming-tables. Mr. Pepys found the Rose "a pretty place" in 1668, and Sheffield, Duke of Buckingham, as Mr. Pope reminds us, spent much of his time on its pleasant lawns, dined there once a year with his friends, and was accustomed to wind up the annual proceedings with the genial toast, "May as many of us as remain unhanged meet here again next spring." There were occasional illuminations too at the Rose, and concerts of music on the king's birthday, acrobatic exhibitions, and flying men, all of which

foreshadowed features of the management of the later
gardens of which the Rose was the forerunner.

It was only, however, in the summer of 1738 that
the proprietor of the tavern, Mr. Daniel Gough, realis-
ing its capabilities, threw the place open to the public
as an *al fresco* entertainment, and first made a regular
charge of admission to what he called his " Marybone
Gardens," much increased then and later by additions
from the grounds of the Manor House.   The venture
seems to have been quite successful from the first.
The evening entertainment of good music, which continued the tradition of the place, was apparently much
appreciated, for in the three following years there is
record of the building of a substantial garden orchestra,
an organ by Bridge, and the " House or Great Room "
for balls and suppers.   The place attained almost
immediately the dignity of the silver token or season
ticket, admitting two people for the whole summer,
and there is evidence of the increasing prosperity of
the establishment in the progressive prices, from twelve
shillings to a couple of guineas, charged for these relics,
which are still to be seen at the British Museum and
in other collections.

There is a very pleasant flavour of sober reasonable
enjoyment by worthy and respectable people suggested
by the numerous records of these old gardens—of their
early years at least; of simple rational amusement in
pleasant surroundings widely different from the fiercer
joys of some other establishments we shall notice in
the course of our inquiry.   The peace-loving public

who gave the place its vogue disported themselves
among the ancient trees and parterres in the old garden
of the Manor House; shady elms and planes, some of
which still give dignity to the houses south of the
Marylebone Road, made a pleasant retreat where they
could eat their syllabubs and cake, and listen to the
music of Handel and Arne.   On the west they looked
right on to pretty Harrow-on-the-Hill; northward
their view was bounded by the wooded heights of
Hampstead and Highgate, and on the east there was
nothing but green fields and open country between the
gardens and the rising moon.   There were surely
worse conditions in which to hear " Where the Bee
Sucks," or "Blow, Blow thou Winter Wind," for the
first time, than surrounded by pretty faces in Marylebone Gardens in the early days of George the Third;
and London has gained little, one imagines, by the
exchange of these simple pleasures for some of its
amusements to-day.

Music, as we have said, was one of the great traditions of the place.   From the first we hear of musical
rarities at the gardens.   There was Mr. Stanesby, jun.,
for example, who in 1738 produced " two grand bas-
soons, the greatness of whose sound surpass that of any
other bass instrument whatever," and a little later Mr.
Ferron performed on "the Pariton, an instrument
never played in publick before."   For thirty years, too,
there was a succession of famous vocalists.   Mary
Anne Falkner, the pretty ballad singer, who fascinated
half the young men of the middle century; Tommy

Lowe, the tenor, whose warblings were for many seasons one of the attractions of Vauxhall, and Mrs. Vincent, who sang " Let the Merry Bells go Round," to the accompaniment of "a new instrument called the tintinnabula " ; Charles Bannister gave his popular imitations of other well-known singers, anticipating a favourite entertainment of our own variety theatre ; Nan Catley, the prima donna from Covent Garden ; Defesch, the famous violinist; Dibdin, of Drury Lane; the fresh full voices of "the young gentlemen from St. Paul's choir," and scores of others, made the groves of Marylebone melodious for two generations.   The great Handel himself was often in the gardens listening to the performances of his own cantatas, and Dr. Arne was to be seen conducting his own glees, with a visage "like two oysters in a plate of beet-root," as Mr. Sheridan unkindly recorded in describing the Doctor's eyes and complexion.   Harmony and decorum were the features of Marylebone Gardens at its prime, broken rarely by a quarrel under the trees, or the rudeness of a royal visitor like the burly Duke of Cumberland.

The pleasant amenities of the place appear even in the announcements of its simple pleasures.   The naïve and quaint advertisements of Miss Trusler, the daughter of one of the proprietors of the place at its best, could never have issued from the raffishness of Islington or the vulgarity of Bagnigge Wells. Said this lady in 1759, " Mr. Trusler's daughter begs leave to inform the nobility and gentry that

she intends to make fruit tarts during the fruit
season, and hopes to give equal satisfaction as with
the rich cakes and almond cheesecakes. The fruit
will always be fresh gathered, having good quantities
in the garden, and none but loaf sugar used and
the finest Epping butter. Tarts of a twelvepenny
size will be made every day from one to three o'clock.
New and rich seed and plum cakes are sent to any
part of the town." Marylebone, to be sure, was an
Arcadia under the presidency of such a genius as
this. It was, in fact, a place where the gentry who
had country houses in the village hard by could
send their children and their nursemaids in the
summer days and evenings without fear of untoward
molestation, and where they themselves could, and
indeed often did, take their breakfast under the planes
in the sun and the gentle breezes of the hayfields with
which the gardens were surrounded.

Not that Marylebone was without its mild excite-
ments on occasion. It is recorded that pretty Miss
Fountayne, a relation of " Dr. Fountayne's, a dean
of the Established Church," was one day taking the
air in the gardens when she was saluted by a young
man of a gallant bearing, who boldly kissed her before all the quality. The lady started back shocked
and surprised, as in duty bound. " Be not alarmed,
madam," said the gentleman, " you can now boast
that you have been kissed by Dick Turpin."

On an occasion of a much later date it is painful
to record that Dr. Johnson was concerned in a slight

disturbance at Marylebone. The place was then on the downward grade, and its good musical attractions had been diluted by more or less unsatisfactory displays of fireworks, displays which generally marked the beginning of the end of the better class of the London *al fresco*. The Doctor had been attracted by the fame of Mr. Torre's fireworks, and went to see them with his friend George Steevens. The afternoon had proved wet, there were few people present, and the management announced that the fireworks, "being water-soaked," could not be fired. "This," said the Doctor, "is a mere excuse to save their crackers for a more profitable company; let us both hold up our sticks and threaten to break those coloured lamps, and we shall soon have our wishes gratified. The core of the fireworks cannot be injured; let the different pieces be touched in their respective centres and they will do their offices as well as ever." Moved by this very Johnsonian eloquence, some young men broke the lamps; but the respective centres of the different pieces remained untouched, and the uninjured cores still refused to do their offices. Such troubles, however, were rare at Marylebone, and its decorous joys, its harmonious concerts, its simple banquets of syllabubs and negus, of coffee and plumcake, are the theme of a score of kindly allusions in the memoirs and diaries of the past. Its groves and its great room, its latticed arbours and its fine company are reflected in the fine engraving published by J. Tinney in 1755, and many knowing connoisseurs contend that its simple beauty inspired the lovely painting by George Morland called the "Tea Garden," the plate after which by Smith is now one of the prizes of the sale rooms.

We have described at some length these three old places of amusement, because they are, as we believe, typical specimens of the very numerous class of similar establishments, usually of smaller extent and fewer pretensions, but still having each its own special attraction for a special body of patrons, and each with a record of prosperity, fleeting often, but real at one stage or other of its career. There was often a prodigious competition between neighbouring establishments. Islington Spa, for example, had an enterprising competitor at its very gates in the London Spa, a name given to a spring discovered in a tavern garden on a spot marked now by the junction of Exmouth Street and Rosoman Street. This institution was advertised by its proprietor, Mr. Halhead, as as good, if not better, than the opposition affair over the way "so mightily cry'd up." He produced something in the shape of a garden, and London Spa became famous as a rendezvous of milkmaids on May day. His "chalybeate," when brewed, made ale of a surpassing richness, with which the pleasure-seekers of the Welch Fair in the adjoining Spa Fields were accustomed to wash down the orthodox dish of roast pork eaten at those merry-makings in pleasant derision of the Jews. Within a hundred yards of the London Spa were the New Wells, with a reputation from quite early times for a quasi theatrical and spectacular entertainment.

Here, by ordering a pint of wine, you could hear Mr. Blogg sing the "Early Horn" or "Mad Tom" to a kettledrum obligato; or gaze upon a "fine collection of large rattlesnakes, one having nineteen rattles; a young crocodile imported from Georgia, and a cat between the tyger and leopard, perfectly tame." As time went on history was reflected in the entertainments of the New Wells. Admiral Vernon captured Portobello again; the Duke of Cumberland as "Courage" suppressed the rebels of the "Forty-Five," and that surprising lady, Hannah Snell, who served as a marine, by the name of James Grey, at the siege of Pondicherry, and had been wounded more than once, went through "her military exercises in her regimentals."

At the Mulberry Gardens, again, in Clerkenwell, a place of generous size, with a clear pond of water and a great mulberry tree with seats to watch the skittle players, you could hear "honest Jo Baker beat a trevally on his side drum the very same that he beat before his Grace the Lord Duke of Marlborough after the battle of Malplaquet." The Mulberry Gardens had their John Bull proprietor with a genius for advertisement, who engaged British musicians only, as holding that "the manly vigour of our own native music is more suitable to the ear and heart of a Briton than the effeminate softness of the Italian." The honest joys of the Mulberry Gardens in due season were blotted out by the House of Detention, and now the present huge pile of the quadrangle of the existing

Clerkenwell School-board buildings occupies the site of its once pleasant shades.

At the Lord Cobham's Head, off the present Farringdon Street, anglers might find board and lodging on reasonable terms, a pleasant garden with shady groves of trees, and "a fine canal stocked with very good carp and tench fit to kill." Farther east, too, just off what is now Old Street, behind St. Luke's Hospital, was Perilous or Parlous Pool, a place so named because in Elizabethan times "divers youths by swimming therein have been drowned." For a century and a half Perilous Pool was a noted place for the joys of duck hunting, until in 1743 a man named Kemp changed its name to Peerless Pool and made of it a resort for perspiring citizens for another century. He embanked the pool, surrounded it with a grove of trees, provided it with marble steps and a marble vestibule for dressing, "with a small library of light literature," made of it in fact a fine open air swimming-bath of sixty yards by thirty, and had his reward in a flourishing subscription and a body of patrons who paid two shillings for a single bath. Besides the swimmers, he attracted the support of another class by constructing a grand artificial canal stocked with carp, tench, and other fish for cockney sportsmen. Baldwin Street occupies the site of that canal to-day, and the name of the bathing-place, which remained open until the middle of the present century, still lingers in that of "Peerless Row."

Roam, indeed, where you will about those vast acres of brick and mortar of the northern half of the great

County of London, if you have still heart for the enterprise, and you will find its most unlovely holes and
corners teeming with the memories of these well-nigh
forgotten places of pleasure.   The present inferno of
the Metropolitan station at King's Cross is excavated
from the once famous gardens of St. Chad's Well,
where a century and a half ago hundreds drank its
medicinal waters of a morning and its tea of an afternoon, without the fear of typhoid before their eyes.
The great surgeon Abernethy was often to be seen at St.
Chad's Well, and the local Dr. Blimber, "Mr. Measall,
the master of Gordon House Academy, Kentish Town,
was used to march his young gentlemen once a week
to take the waters" and so save doctor's bills.   Stand
amongst the railway arches and shunting grounds at
the back of St. Pancras Station and realise, if you can,
the pleasant gardens of Pancras Wells in the middle
of hayfields, with a view of the northern heights of
Primrose Hill and Hampstead, reckoned fine, the old
church of St. Pancras on its borders, and footpaths
from Gray's Inn in full view of the gardens, whence the
proprietor could count his customers approaching and
form his estimate of their wants.   Pancras Wells, too,
had a competitor at its gates in the Adam and Eve
Tea Garden, where they kept cows for the making of
syllabubs, and men played trapball of a summer evening and the children watched a little squadron of toy
frigates on the pond.

Eastward again, in Pentonville, stood White Conduit House, in a space bounded approximately to-day

by the present Penton Street, Cloudesley Road, Alton Street, and Denmark Road, another of the great tea gardens in the north which vied with Bagnigge and Marylebone. Here did generations of citizens partake of "hot loaves, tea, coffee, and liquors in the greatest perfection, and milk from cows which eat no grains," enjoy the views from the windows in the Long Room, "from whence is the most copious prospects and airy situation of any now in vogue," as the proprietor was careful to point out. White Conduit House had its "pleasing walks prettily disposed," its "genteel boxes," with paintings in the Flemish manner, its alcoves let into its clipped hedges, and its avenues of shady trees, and was the delight of numbers of Londoners for a century. It had also its own code of deportment. It was reckoned the mode at White Conduit House to tread on the skirt of the damsel whose acquaintance you wished to make, apologise for your clumsiness, and suggest an adjournment to an arbour for tea by way of amends. White Conduit House, too, has an interest of its own for most Englishmen, for did not Mr. Bartholomew the proprietor, in 1754, provide bats and balls for his customers, and encourage the game of cricket in the adjoining meadow, and so lay the foundations of the vast organisation of the modern game? There is no doubt about it at all. The place continued the headquarters of cricket in London for twenty years; men of condition played their matches there, and in 1784 the club which met in that meadow included the Duke

of Dorset, Lord Winchilsea, Lord Talbot, Colonel
Tarleton, and no less a light of the cricket world than
Thomas Lord, the founder of the Marylebone Club.

The history of these and a score of other entertainments in the open air is recorded in the fugitive
literature of their times, admirably collected and
arranged in works like that of Mr. Warwick Wroth
of the British Museum, with its orderly references and
authorities which make it a model of what such a
work should be.   In such records you may learn how
the "Three Hats" at Islington was perhaps the home
of the modern equestrian entertainment, afterwards
brought to perfection by Philip Astley, where "Johnson the Irish Tartar rode a single horse standing on
his head;" how citizens with a taste for the placid
old game of bowls went to Dobney's in the Pentonville Road, to the Belvidere Tea Gardens hard by, to
the Black Queen Coffee House and Tea Gardens,
Shacklewell Green, or to Cuper's Gardens over the
river.   Dobney, we find by the way, had another
curious attraction about 1772, when Mr. Daniel
Wildman, the Bee Master, gave a fearsome exhibition
on horseback, "standing upright, one foot on the
saddle and the other on the horse's neck, with a
curious mask of bees on his face; he also rides,
standing upright on the saddle, with the bridle in
his mouth, and by firing a pistol makes one part of
the bees march over a table and the other swarm in
the air and return to their places again."

Each one of all these humble places had some

special attraction of its own.   There was Copenhagen House, on the site of the Clock Tower of the Cattle Market at Islington, famous for its fives, where John Cavanagh, the prince of fives players, whose fine play is commemorated in an essay of Hazlitt's, was wont to astonish spectators with his skill at the game, eschewing the volley, "but seldom missing a return off the ground, though it rose no more than an inch." There is a human story of the origin of fives at Copenhagen House, telling how the maid of the tavern, hailing from Shropshire, meeting an acquaintance from the same county, and talking over the game, which was one of the diversions of their native place, improvised a fives ball, made an appointment for a day later, and played a game against the end of the house, which delighted the onlooking topers and so started the tradition of fives at Copenhagen House. The very gable where the maid and her friend played their historic game remained the theatre of the famous contests which followed, and the cooks in the kitchen were said to recognise the severe returns of Cavanagh on the wall, and, "as the meat trembled on the spits," to remark, "There's the Irishman again."

All the roads, indeed, that led out of London to the north and west, were avenues which led pleasure-seekers to open air entertainments of one sort or another.   Belsize House was a country mansion on the west side of Haverstock Hill, opened in 1720 by a Welshman "with an uncommon solemnity of music and dancing," with a park wilderness and garden a mile in circumference "filled with a variety of birds which compose a most melodious and touching harmony," as we are assured. Cakes and ale were much in evidence at Belsize House, and foot and galloway races "six times round the course." In 1726 they "hunted a fat doe to death with small beagles," when sportsmen were invited "to bring their own dogs if not too large."

Farther north still was Hampstead with its famous wells and gardens, and a local clergyman and chapel for those amorous couples who could not afford the journey to Gretna Green. Its later Assembly Room with its fugitive fashion is embalmed in much of the fiction of the last part of the century, and there Mr. Samuel Rogers "danced minuets in his youth and met a great deal of good company." Visits to Hampstead in those days were in the nature of an expedition which called for the services of the daily stage coach. Perhaps the most northerly point of attraction for pleasure-loving Londoners was the Spaniards Tavern, unless Kilburn Wells or New Gorgia in Turner's Wood, or Hornsey Wood House, could claim that distinction. The Spaniards had its pebble walks laid out by the ingenious Mr. Staples with curious devices of the Signs of the Zodiac, the Tower of London, Adam and Eve, and the Great Pyramids and its "prospect of Hanslope Steeple within eight miles of Northampton and Langdon Hill in Essex, full sixty miles east," unless the imagination of its advertisers betrayed them. Between these outposts and the

Thames, Bayswater Gardens in the Bayswater Road on the west, and Spring Garden in the Mile End Road on the east, there were a dozen or it may be a score of similar places which claim and receive attention in a history of the town, but must be passed over here with such mention.

We have been concerned so far with the places of entertainment which flourished on the *al fresco* tastes of the Londoner at various periods, but nearly all lying on the north side of a line continued east and west of what is now approximately Oxford Street. It was on this side of London that the *al fresco* tradition of the tea garden attained its greatest splendour, mainly, as we believe, from the natural love of a town dweller for rising ground and brisk air, partly from the variety which two little rivers gave to that country, and also by reason of the attractions of the semi-fashionable crowds who at times gathered round one or other of its numerous spas.

South London, however, was not without its open air attractions, which had a flavour of their own, differing widely from that of the places we have already considered. The attractions of the South London districts were less simple and less respectable. With an unconscious humour, many of them advertised their mineral waters in competition with the spas of the north; waters pumped from wells which would fill at a few feet below the surface of what was practically the huge marsh between Rotherhithe and Vauxhall; waters which Dr. Rendle opines could have been nothing more than the mere soakage of a swamp. But their main attractions were more or less feeble imitations of the glories of Vauxhall, and their patrons were, speaking generally, of a less innocent cast of mind and less easily amused than the citizens who flocked northward to Islington or Hampstead, or westward to Marylebone.

One of the chief of the South London group which shared with the peerless Vauxhall the distinction of an approach by water, was Cuper's Garden, on the south side of Waterloo Bridge, through the very centre of which modern progress drove the Waterloo Bridge Road. Cuper's Garden took its name from an old servant of the Howard family, who, just at the end of the seventeenth century, laid out a big patch of the marsh land with walks and bowling-greens, contrived to give it some flavour of dignity and distinction by dotting the place with mutilated statues presented to him by his patron upon the demolition of Arundel House, and opened the place as a public garden, which had a measure of success for some sixty or seventy years. At first music and dancing were the chief attractions, and 'prentices and sempstresses the chief of its patrons, and there is a not untuneful set of verses which reflect some of the simple joys of those early days, beginning—

> "'Twas down in Cupid's Gardens
>   For pleasure I did go,
> To see the fairest flowers
>   That in that garden grow."

But under subsequent proprietors, notably one Ephrain Evans and his widow, the place developed more upon the lines of Vauxhall, with orchestras, fireworks, and illuminations, and promenades under the trees, where "pretty young women were accustomed to parade dressed like young men, and wearing swords." Such diversions at times attracted a deal of fashionable company, Horace Walpole and the Prince of Wales among others, who gave distinction to the assembly and occupation to the pickpockets. It was upon that rock of careless management that Widow Evans, "a well-looking, comely person," finally split, when the Act of 1752 established authorities for the "better regulating of places of public entertainment," and licences became necessary for such as Widow Evans. Cuper's Garden was refused a licence amidst the lamentations of the widow, who was forced to retire upon the tavern and a mere tea garden. The widow was apparently a woman of some resource, for when her orchestra was thus silenced she advertised her tea and the subdued attractions of the place, with the remark that there still "remained some harmony from the sweet enchanting sounds of the rural warblers."

Finch's grotto was another South London garden in what is now the Southwark Bridge Road, where the proprietor, Finch, inheriting a house and garden, was not long in discovering the inevitable spring of medicinal water, and made "a grotto and a natural and beautiful cascade," aspired to the dignity of season tickets, and returned a modicum of refreshment, "half a pint of

wine, cake, jelly, or cyder," in exchange for the one
shilling admission. Stray royalties, like the wild York
and the silly Gloucester, would come to listen to the
music at Finch's, or perhaps to gaze at the singers
of such beauty and notoriety as Sophia Baddeley of
Drury Lane and Vauxhall, the heroine of many wicked
stories of those days.

The present Spa Road, Bermondsey, takes its name
from Bermondsey Spa Gardens, where Mr. Keyse,
the self-taught painter, enclosed some acres of waste
ground, discovered the usual spa, and with his pictures of green-grocers' stalls and butchers' shops, his
cheery personality, his cheery brandy, his lamps in
imitation of Vauxhall, his prima donnas and burlettas,
contrived to keep the place open for thirty years. At
the Helena Gardens, Rotherhithe, the tradition of the
al fresco lingered perhaps latest of all. There singers
warbled and dancers capered, infant prodigies of six
delighted or bored audiences, and orchestras scraped
until the year 1881. At the Belvidere Gardens, just
above Cuper's Garden, on the Thames, the proprietor
advertised "the choicest river fish which they (his
patrons) may have the delight to see taken." The
Flora Gardens, the Temple of Apollo, and the Temple
of Flora were classically named establishments near
what is now the Westminster Bridge Road, one with
an "Apollonian promenade and a pallid moon between
brilliant transparencies," and claiming credit for "the
superior excellencies of music and wines, and the chas-
tity and dignity of the place," all of which virtues and

advantages, however, did not avert the suppression of the place by the magistrates in 1793. The Dog and Duck, St. George's Spa, on the site of the present Bethlehem Hospital, was an *al fresco* entertainment which had its origin in the popular sport of duck hunting, ran through the whole gamut of mineral water, tea gardens, musical entertainments, and fireworks, and expired finally in an atmosphere of raffishness and blackguardism.

To conclude, and not to omit mention of any notable district which was a centre of *al fresco* entertainment, we may notice the little group of tea gardens for which Chelsea was famous: Strombolo House, the beauty of whose fireworks enabled the proprietor to charge the high price of half a crown for admission, and anticipate the glories of the Crystal Palace to-day; Jenny's Whim, with its bowling-green, cock-pit, and ducking-pond, its alcoves and prim flower-beds, its pond where mechanical mermaids and fishes rose at intervals to the surface, and its recesses where Harlequin and Mother Shipton started up when an unseen spring was trodden upon by the visitor. Finally Brompton had its Florida Gardens just west of Gloucester Road, on the south side of the present Cromwell road, a rural retreat with clipped hedges, terraces, and shady walks, "well adapted for gallantry and intrigue," where Mr. Hiem grew cherries, strawberries, and flowers, supplied "fresh fruit every hour in the day, ice creams, wine, cyder, tea and coffee," also " Berne Veckley, an elegant succedaneum for bread and butter, and eat by the noblesse of Switzerland."

It was among the delights of such places as these
which we have endeavoured to visit in the spirit that
former generations of Londoners took their modest
pleasures and the life of a couple of centuries of
London displayed itself. As a conclusion to our inquiry it may be of interest to speculate for a moment
on the causes of their decline. It would be easy to
account for the disappearance of the old London
pleasure gardens by pointing to the necessities in the
matter of building sites of a town which, since the first
vogue of the *al fresco* entertainment, has grown into a
province—a province of bricks and mortar. But such
a proposition would be merely plausible, because it is
certain that the London tea garden was moribund
before cheap corn created a vast population, and easy
communications distributed it in very unequal patches
over a country where most interests of beauty or enjoyment have been sacrificed to the exigencies of an industrial commercialism. The decline of the London *al
fresco*, we believe, followed a change in the taste of the
people themselves, that taste itself an inevitable consequence of an increasing population and an increasing
prosperity. The simple pleasures which satisfied the
London of Charles the Second left the London of
George the Third unmoved, and the pleasure-seeking
citizen of the London of William the Fourth had a
soul altogether above the placid joys of the London
of George the Third. If you seek conviction on the
point, read Pepys and Horace Walpole, Harry Angelo,
Pierce Egan and Captain Gronow, and compare the

different accounts of the pleasures of the town by each
of those recording angels.

It is quite easy to trace this change of taste in the
records of any of the old places of amusement we have
been considering. There was always the increasing
splendour of Vauxhall to be reckoned with by the
managers of them all, a sort of bull amongst tea gardens, against which every frog as time went on found
it necessary to distend itself, and usually burst in
the process. And so we find the harmless dissipations
of the teapot and muffin gradually supplanted by
fare of a headier character, and the simple pleasures
of the organ in the Long Room, the ballad-singer, and
the prim decorum of the promenade yielding to joys
of a fiercer kind and forgathering of a different character, a change which led often to presentations by
grand juries and contests with magistrates, and a
change invariably ominous of the end. At Bagnigge
Wells the Long Room became a concert-room, where
serio-comics gave "turns" much as they do at the
Pavilion to-day, and balloon ascents in the garden
became necessary to tickle the jaded palates of spectators surfeited by promenades among clipped hedges
and fountains. For years before White Conduit
House had closed its gates, forgotten and unregretted,
it had run through the whole changes of a variety
entertainment and the amusements of a country fair.
The fish-pond had been drained and filled in to make
room for a dancing saloon dedicated to Apollo, the
healthy joys of the early place, with its cricket and

white bread, had been exchanged for cheap fireworks, tight ropes, and conjurers like Mr. Chabert, who swallowed arsenic, oxalic acid, boiling oil and molten lead, and "entered a large heated oven supported on four pillars and there cooked a leg of lamb and a rump steak," which he obligingly divided among the spectators. Grand galas there and elsewhere rendered necessary the attendance of vigilant officers to prevent the entry of "persons in dishabille." At the delightful and decorous Marylebone, conjurers' entertainments and "Forges of Vulcan" in pasteboard and red-fire took the place of Acis and Galatea and "Where the bee sucks," and *fêtes champêtres*, "which consisted of nothing more than a few tawdry festoons and extra lamps," only moved more sophisticated audiences to resent the extra charge of five shillings by breaking the lamps and demolishing the scenery. The careers of the less famous gardens of the south and the west were almost invariably concluded in even less reputable circumstances, where the conduct of the raffish audiences attracted by their debased pleasures brought upon them the interference of the authorities.

There were others, of course, which were merely absorbed by the advancing wilderness of London, which planted gasometers in their pleasant parterres and dried up their springs for ever. Of these the elegists are topographers and antiquarians like Mr. Hone and Mr. J. T. Smith, who witnessed and regretted their departed glories. There is an almost touching description, for instance, by Mr. Smith of his visit to Bermondsey Spa

in the days of its decline: Smith himself the only
visitor, with his solemn banter of the artist proprietor's
pictures of savoy cabbages and knuckles of veal, and
the prima donna in silks and rouge singing her solo
according to contract and bowing her thanks for the
applause of the audience of one. Hone will tell you
of the forlorn aspect of St. Chad's Wells when its
waters remained undrunk and its patrons had sought
their pleasure elsewhere; of the "scene which the
unaccustomed eye might take for the pleasure-ground
of Giant Despair;" of "trees standing as if not meant
to vegetate, and nameless weeds straggling weakly upon
unweeded borders."

Such, however, were only the lamentations on the
short period of the decline of a phase of social life
which had fulfilled a purpose and had amused a large
proportion of the inhabitants of London for two hundred years. It is pleasant sometimes to think about
the London *al fresco* in its prime, and the delight and
enthusiasm of Londoners in the simple pleasures it
afforded, an enthusiasm which surely inspired the poet
who sang the beauties of the New River in those
haunting lines—

> "Farewell, sweet vale, how much thou dost excel
> Arno or Andalusia."

It is pleasant at times, as we say, to call their forgotten
pleasures to mind, to trace their forgotten boundaries,
and to hope perhaps for their resurrection in a translated form. We may remember, if we choose, that

London has received and is receiving, in exchange, parks and open spaces on a splendid scale, generously, and even royally administered in every respect except that of provision for its hunger and thirst. Mr. Pepys we feel convinced, could he revisit his beloved town, would not be enthusiastic about the buns and ginger-beer of, say, Regent's Park, or think that he had made in those viands a good exchange for Shere's Spanish olio at the Mulberry Garden. There are signs, however, that the taste for the *al fresco* amongst Londoners is not extinct; the success of such enterprises as the concerts at the Imperial Institute, at Earl's Court and elsewhere, the breakfasting in Battersea Park connected with the fashionable cycling of a few years ago, even the much abused Summer Club of Kensington Gardens, may be taken as signs of the times.

THE ROYAL MASQUERADE, SOMERSET HOUSE

DRAWN BY WILLIAM HOGARTH

CHAPTER III

THE MASKED ASSEMBLY

Curious antiquaries will tell you that human nature
has delighted in seizing every opportunity of disguising itself ever since the doings of mankind provided
material for their interesting researches. Whatever
your epoch or your nationality might have been, had
you encountered the misfortune of being born out
of the present incomparable age, your religion, your
pleasure, your prudery, or your wantonness, would have
prompted you at one time or other to throw off your
workaday dress, to hide your features in a mask or
domino, and conceal your identity for a time in the
habit and bearing of some one else. The erudite
Monsieur Pierre Larousse is of opinion that mankind
first took to changing its clothes as a relief from
misery. "*Il semble que l'homme ait voulu de tout temps
echapper ses misères en changeant d'habits.*" He began,
it would seem, by dressing himself up in the garments
which he attributed to his gods, and if his gods wore
none he was accustomed to divest himself of the
habiliments which his own daily life required. But
there were surely many other motives at work than
an attempt at an escape from misery in this per-

petual changing of garments. We doubt, for instance, whether it was misery which drove the ancients to disguise themselves for those surprising rites called Bacchanalia and Saturnalia, both of which functions we are assured were early instances of the masquerade or masked assembly. The carnivals, *fêtes des fous*, and *fêtes des innocents* of the Middle Ages were later examples of the masked assembly, as we are told, and all survivals of the Pagan rites, slyly adapted by the priests to the usages of the Christian Church, and inspired always by the eternal love of the human kind for disguise.

The fascination of the domino, indeed, is over all the ages, and has lent itself to every species of human interest or passion or design. An Inquisitor or an officer of the Vehmgericht put on a mask as he prepared some extra refinement of torture for his victim. A bravo who set out to earn a few pieces by sticking a knife into some superfluous lover serenading a girl in a Venetian balcony, slunk off in cloak and vizard. The same interesting article of dress was very useful to the sportive dame of the Restoration, who enjoyed the jokes of Wycherley or Sedley at the play, and wore the mask to conceal such blushes as those jokes produced, or to hide the fact that the wearer was already past blushing. The disguise of a fancy character was a convenient and favourite means of intercourse between the amorous swains and maidens of the carnivals, bals masqués, or masquerades, stories of which enliven the social records of every civilised nation since modern history began to be written. Claude Duval or

James Maclane found the black velvet of much assistance when they set out to lift purses on Hounslow Heath or Banstead Downs. The same protection gave the same feeling of security to the artists whose unpopular duty it was to relieve Mary Stuart, say, or Raleigh, or King Charles of their heads. The palmy days of disguises of all sorts and for all purposes were over before the present century began, but you may still trace certain aspects of the cult of the masquerade, shorn indeed of most of its ancient glory, but still of true pedigree, in the calico dances of the modern suburban villa and the rather dreary functions at Covent Garden Theatre. The practical use of the vizard, too, is revived occasionally in these prosaic days, when a Ribbonman waits for a landlord behind a fence with a blunderbuss, or Captain Moonlight places a land-grabber against a stone wall and shoots his legs from under him.

A consideration of all that has been recorded of the proceedings of people who have adopted disguises of one sort or another, for one of the hundred motives which have suggested their use, would convince the most innocent and amiable of critics that very little of good has ever been done in disguise. It was pleasantly held by an essayist of the last century that the first masquerade known and recorded was that change of personality which resulted in such disaster in the Garden of Eden. Developing the idea, this correspondent of the *Gentleman's Magazine* claimed the circumstances and environment of that entertainment to prove that the *Ridotto al fresco* with which Mr. Jonathan

Tyers delighted his patrons in the gardens of Vauxhall in the reign of George the Second was no new thing. It is an ingenious theory, like many others which appeared under the auspices of Sylvanus Urban, and, if true, would account for much that took place in masquerade in later times. There was much eating of forbidden fruit of various sorts, revelry and diversion of a distinctly worldly kind, by the people who made a practice of dressing themselves up in the habits of other times and personalities. The decorum which we may hope regulated their ordinary living was, as a rule, most certainly left behind with their ordinary dress when they assumed the domino and took their chair to the bal masqué, the masquerade, or the Ridotto.

It is worthy of note that the masked assembly was never an institution which had any great vogue among the common people, either in this country or elsewhere. The wearing of masks or of disguises in private life was from very early times the exclusive privilege of the great or of those who imitated them. It was in Italy, and at Venice especially, that the wearing of the vizard or domino first grew out of the practices of the Carnival into a habit with people of condition, that Carnival itself being, as we suggest, a development of the quasi heathenish fêtes of the mediæval church. Here as elsewhere it was the noble, or the man of fashion, or the professional adventurers of both sexes, who adopted the motley for the purposes of intrigue or pleasure, and seldom the merchant or shopkeeper. In France, too, as soon as there was any sign of the people availing themselves of the diversions which the public use of the mask provided for their betters, the great powers stepped in and made regulations confining its use to their own order.   In that happy country, it was ordained in 1535 that no citizen should be allowed to appear masked, save during the Carnival, under pain of death, and whole shopfuls of vizards and dominos were seized and confiscated.   The French nobles, headed by the king himself, might ruffle it about the streets of Paris, kiss honest Matthieu's daughter and lift Matthieu over the quay into the Seine if they saw fit, but if honest Matthieu availed himself of the same convenient disguise for his own purposes of pleasure or revenge, they took off his head, as when two unfortunate citizens suffered that fate for that particular crime at Toulouse, so late as 1626.   So too when the vizard was put to quite innocent uses in the England of Tudor times as a covering for a lady's face, both as protection from wind and from the free glances of the gallants, it was confined to women of social position; and the less innocent proceedings which flourished under its kindly shelter in later days were those of the highly placed and leisured classes. The virtues and vices of the mask were thus in all times and countries the virtues and vices of a small and particular section of the community.   Such as they were, they descended from above and did not ascend from below, and at their best or worst they never succeeded in penetrating more than a few of the upper strata of society.   It is our interesting task in this chapter to follow the records of the use of the mask or domino or fancy dress in England.

The vogue of the masked assembly was long in reaching this country, and the masquerade had been a favourite diversion of generations of continentals before its introduction here. It is quite in accordance with its modish reputation to find the masquerade introduced to Englishmen under the highest auspices. "On the daie of the Epiphany at night," says Hall's Chronicle of the year 1513, "the king, with eleven others, were disguised after the manner of Italie, called a maske, a thing not seen afore in England. They were apparelled in garments long and brod, wrote all with golde, and visers, and cappes of golde, and after the banket done, these maskers came in with the six gentlemen disguised in silk, bearing staffe torches, and desired the ladies to dance. Some were content, and some that knew the fashion of it refused, because it was not a thing commonly seen, and after thei danced and commoned together, as the fashion of the masks is, they took their leave and departed, and so did the queen and all the ladies."

We have here an early record of the true masked assembly in England, undeveloped as yet into the masquerade which, as we shall see, was an exotic and very striking feature of the fashionable amusement of London of the eighteenth century, but still exhibiting on a small scale the essential qualities of that entertainment. The true masquerade was a gathering of people every one of whom was in disguise, and its attraction consisted wholly of whatever diversion the ingenuity or the freedom of its members could extract from that condition.   The masque which Ben Jonson and Inigo Jones provided for the diversion of the court was a different affair altogether, theatrical and spectacular in its essential character, where the maskers were actors who provided amusement for a separate audience, as at any other theatrical entertainment.   In the masquerade proper the company were at once actors and audience together, and in the light of the subsequent experience of the English in its pleasantries, the fact that those ladies of Henry's court " who knew the fashion " refused to dance with the maskers is not without eloquence.

The masked assembly thus introduced into England under distinguished auspices was still many years in establishing its vogue.   It was, as we have said, an exotic, a plant of foreign origin, reared originally in a country devoted to the superstitions of Papistry, and finding little to agree with it in the robust air of England after the Reformation.   There is little recorded of masked assemblies during the later times of the Tudors, or, for that matter, during the more genial days of the Stuarts.   The rising Puritan feeling in the days of Charles the First was shocked by a masque encouraged by Queen Henrietta Maria at Whitehall on a Sunday in February of 1634.   This was not a true masquerade, but a masque presented by the members of the Inns of Court as a protest against Mr. Prynne's condemnation of the stage and of women

actors, when he alluded to the queen's rehearsal of Mr.
Montague's "Shepherd's Pastoral," an animadversion
which cost that patriot his ears. The queen, however, made the occasion a hybrid between a masque
and a masquerade by giving her royal hand to one of
the maskers in the dance. The crowd were incapable
of drawing fine distinctions, and objected to the appearance of the lawyers in disguise, especially on the
Sabbath. "The detestation of disguise natural to a
freeborn Briton, and the profanation of the Lord's
Day, so decently observed among us," as we read,
"roused the indignation of the publick so as to cause
an insurrection in Whitehall." The people opposed
her Majesty's guards, her Majesty's guards dragooned
the people, a scuffle ensued, "and about half-a-dozen
of the people were killed of one side and two or three
guards of the other," a very unhappy ending indeed
to that afternoon's pleasure of the queen and the Inns
of Court.

It is not at all singular that the masquerade should
have languished during the stormy days which followed; there was little place even for very modest
joys in the London of Puritan England, and still less
for such anathema as the mixture of the sexes in the
unholy diversions of a company all in disguise, where
the innocence of a young quaker might find itself in
very embarrassing circumstances with the best will in
the world, and the freedoms of youth and wantonness
had the best possible opportunities for displaying
themselves in their most luxurious form. But the

Restoration, with its laughter-loving court and its opportunities for the Catholic religion, with its bevy of beauties at Whitehall ready for any cantrips in the world, was an epoch which one would have thought favourable for the development of this attractive form of amusement.   And yet Pepys and Evelyn and De Grammont are strangely silent on the matter.   There was no vogue of the masquerade as yet, so much is clear from their pages.   But they all make mention of an entertainment at court which makes it plain that the diversion introduced to England by King Henry the Eighth was still alive within its shores.

It was in February of 1664 that Mrs. Pickering told Mr. Pepys "of the manner of a masquerade before the king and court the other day where six women, my Lady Castlemaine and the Duchess of Monmouth being two of them, and six men, the Duke of Monmouth and Lord Arran and Monsieur Blanfort being three of them, in vizards and in costly and antique dresses did dance admirably and most gloriously." Evelyn was there himself.   "I saw a masque performed at court by six gentlemen and six ladies surprising his Majesty, it being Candlemas Day."   From De Grammont we learn some particulars of the entertainment.   It was a device of the good-natured Queen Catherine of Braganza, it seems, to amuse the king, and no surprise to his Majesty, who knew all about it. Some of the lighter spirits of that reckless company seized the occasion for tricks which were quite prophetic of the later developments of the masquerade.

Miss Hamilton feigned the queen's handwriting in a letter to Lady Muskerry, who was fat and had one leg shorter than the other, and commanded her ladyship to dress in a habit of a lady of Babylon. De Grammont tells us of the poor lady's search among the Levant merchants of the city for particulars of such a dress, of her appearance outside the palace asking every courtier who entered if he was her partner, of De Grammont himself, a little late, making his joke about the " phantom masker " he had met outside to the king, " the masker with at least sixty ells of silver tissue about her, not to mention a sort of pyramid upon her head adorned with a hundred baubles." Miss Hamilton was rather frightened at her joke when the king commanded the strange masker to be introduced, and Lord Muskerry recognising his foolish lady in De Grammont's description rushed out of the room on that errand and conducted the poor creature out of harm's way. Such was the typical fun of the court of Charles the Second, and we shall see as we proceed that this flavour of cross purposes and confusion of personalities was very typical also of the final development of the masquerade in England a hundred years later.

It is upon such scanty material as is furnished by the gossip of these writers that we have to rely in tracing the origin and progress of the masked assembly in England. Sometimes in turning an old magazine or newspaper there is to be found some slight record which helps us. There is a bill set out in *Notes and*

Queries which carries on the tradition to 1673, a bill for "masquerading cloaths made by William Watts deceased, by his Majesty's order, and His Majie. also ordered the Duke of Monmouth to bespeake them." The bill included "a rich flowered venetian suite laced with silver lace and all furnitures, £59, 17s." —this for Mr. Sands. Mr. Hazzard, Mr. Isaac, Mr. Preist, and Mr. Caine had each "the like in all particulars," and "four bask habitts more at £11, 11s. per piece." Another gentleman paid for a "sheapherds habitt with all furnitures £30, 7s. 10d.," and a "Divell's shape" for Mr. Hazzard cost him £5, 15s. 6d. Mr. Hazzard thus had three suits for one occasion, a fact which teaches us that the masquerade had reached its development as early as 1673, for one of the chief delights of a wealthy man seeking his pleasure at the masquerade of the eighteenth century at the King's Theatre or at Mrs. Cornely's was to appear successively in two or three different dresses on the same evening.

It was only, however, when England began to settle down at the beginning of the last century that the masquerade established itself and became noticeable among the amusements of the town. Addison and Steele were on the spot to take note of its first public appearance in their *Tatlers* and *Spectators*, and their humorous moralisings on the subject leave us in no doubt whatever as to the nature of those early assemblies. It is quite easy to fill in our outline of the typical English masquerade from those pleasant pages where one or other of the authors projects himself into some fancied character whose personality should give point to the speculations he wishes to convey to his readers. Addison is " a Director of the Society for the Reformation of Manners," Steele is " the Undertaker of the Masquerade ; " Addison again will assume the character of a " future historian " living in our own times, only the better to look back and touch the events of his own with his gentle satire.

The *Spectator* had appeared no longer than a week when he laid his finger upon the " midnight mask which has of late been frequently held in one of the most conspicuous parts of the town, and which I hear will be continued with additions and improvements." The conspicuous part of the town here mentioned, as we learn from a contemporary advertisement, was a public room in Spring Gardens, where it was announced as an " evening entertainment, and no persons admitted unmasked or armed."

The fashionable character of the partakers in this modish dissipation is humorously suggested in Addison's pleasant banter. " As all the persons who compose this lawless assembly are masked we dare not attack any of them in our way, lest we should send a woman of quality to Bridewell or a peer of Great Britain to the Compter," wrote Addison as " Director of the Society for the Reformation of Manners." There happens to be corroboration of the truth of these remarks, which is an eloquent commentary upon the character of the people attending these early meetings, and also upon the reluctance of the authorities of

those days to bring highly placed people into disrepute.
A few years later there was a raid by the officers upon
a notorious meeting-place, the White Lion in Wych
Street, where, as a historian records, "the pernicious
and general custom of wearing masks enabled half
repentant sinners to mix with the most profligate of
the female sex and indulge in excesses which they
would not have dared to commit had their features
been exposed."   The constables appeared suddenly in
the midst of the revels and compelled the whole company to unmask, when they discovered "females of
some distinction, tradesmen's wives and their daughters,
and many women of another class, a collection which
really surprised each other, the vicious hardly credit-
ing that they were in such good company, and the
novitiates frightened at the features of unmasked
depravity."

We have been unable to follow the fortunes of
this particular assembly before the magistrates, but
a similar raid made later at Exeter Change supplies
further comment upon Mr. Addison's pleasantry.
The High Constable of Westminster descended upon
a masquerade at midnight and made a great haul,
which he duly displayed before Mr. Fielding. That
eminent magistrate sat up all night to hear the charge,
"but several of them being found to be persons of
distinction, the justice, not thinking proper to expose
them, after a severe reprimand dismissed them all."

"The women either come by themselves," says
Addison, describing the amenities of the masquerade

of 1711, "or are introduced by friends, who are
obliged to quit them upon their first entrance to the
conversation of anybody that addresses himself to
them." This by the way was one of the rules of the
true masquerade, which was its chief attraction for the
frisky maid or matron of those days. Introductions
were unknown, and absolute incognito was possible
for all who wished to preserve it. The mask and
domino were inviolable, except indeed to the police, and
any infringement of that rule by a masker led to the
inevitable chastisement of the offender by the other
men in the room, of which there are numerous fatal
results recorded. "But," continues Mr. Addison,
"there are several rooms where the parties may retire
and show their faces by consent. Whispers, squeezes,
nods and embraces, are the innocent freedoms of the
place, and the whole design of this libidinous assembly
seems to terminate in assignations and intrigues."
Go with Addison, too, as the Young Templar to the
Tuesday's masquerade, see him claimed as a brother
by a half-dozen female quakers, taken out to dance
the minuet by a "woman of the very first quality,"
who negligently displays a watch with a coronet upon
it, listen to his subsequent lamentations at having
"mistaken a cloud for Juno," and you will be under
no delusions as to certain aspects of the masquerade
of Queen Anne. Listen also to Dick Steele in his
humorous character of "Undertaker of the Masquerade." The incongruity of the talk and the dresses
amused Dick. "The misfortune of the thing is that

people dress themselves in what they have a mind to be and not what they are fit for.   There is not a girl in the town but let her have her will in going to a mask and she shall dress as a shepherdess. . . . The last day we presented everybody was so rashly habited that, when they came to speak to each other, a nymph with a crook had not a word to say but in the pert style of the pit, we had a judge who danced a minuet with a quaker for his partner, while a half-dozen harlequins stood by as spectators, a Turk drank me off two bottles of wine, and a Jew eat me up half a ham of bacon."

The humourists of the *Spectator* thus first drew attention to a subject which for the next half century occupied half the censors in the periodical press and produced an agitation against this particular form of entertainment which was more violent in expression and barren in result than any on record.   The masquerade absolutely throve on opposition.   As time went on it was presented by grand juries, denounced by pamphleteers, suppressed by a royal proclamation, but it survived them all.   The Bishop of London took its enormities as the text of a sermon in 1726, rivers of ink flowed down the pages of Craftsmen, Prompters, London and Gentleman's Magazines.   It was the subject of facetious and satirical efforts in prose and verse in would-be smart journals which are infinitely more depressing to read than the serious lucubrations of the dignified clergy.   They wrote dreadful plays upon it, where heiresses with fortunes were disposed of and married to needy adventurers by convenient parsons waiting round the corner; Edwin from the country taking Angelina to taste its delights has his bride abducted, takes to drink, and describes his ruin in very maudlin prose over whole pages of a monthly review. Mr. Henry Fielding wrote satires upon it of a very different calibre; and Mr. Hogarth, inspired no doubt by a love of morality, but drawing some inspiration also from the theatrical interest which the popularity of the masquerade was ruining, made it the subject of some of his most ferocious plates. There were strange financial proposals too from amateur chancellors of the exchequer, who proposed to levy taxes upon all tickets for these ungodly diversions and to devote the proceeds to the Foundling Hospital, an institution which they declared was populated by the amours which were kindled by the opportunities of the masquerade. Grave statisticians drew attention to what they contended was an appalling fact, that the vogue of the masquerade quadrupled the normal number of divorces, and pious God-fearing people, whose nerves were sorely shaken by the two smart shocks of earthquake which startled London towards the middle of the century, pointed to the judgment of heaven which these unholy revels were calling upon the town.

It was precisely during the period of this continued opposition, which stretched practically from the days of Queen Anne to those of George the Third, that the masquerade established itself as one of the chief amusements of the upper classes of society in London. Middle class England might still cherish its memories of the Puritans, but there were other views in high quarters, and a mere newspaper agitation was of little effect in a day when four-fifths of the population could not read.   The diversions of an aristocracy, too, were moderately safe from interference by legislation provided by a Parliament whose two houses were composed of the aristocracy and its nominees.   The well-born and well-placed classes of Anne and the Georges, in short, with King George the Second at their head, enjoyed the *fredaines* of the masquerade, and determined to keep them in spite of the bishops and the moralists of the press.   And they succeeded perfectly.

Fashionable London was very much aided in that natural desire by the appearance in England of one of those geniuses who is usually forthcoming to give practical shape to the wants of any body of people with an itching for amusement, for which they are able and willing to pay.   Beau Nash at Bath, Robert Arthur at White's Club, William Brooks at Brooks's, Almack at his Assembly Rooms in King Street, Crockford at the big gaming club in St. James's Street, were all men who came forward to give practical shape to some desire of a body of well-to-do patrons.   The man who came to the rescue of the masquerade in the early quarter of the last century was the Swiss adventurer, John James Heidegger.

Heidegger, though an adventurer, was an adventurer of a very favourable type, and was possessed of many amiable qualities. He had left his paternal home, the pastor's house at Zurich, in consequence of some youthful intrigue, and had wandered about Europe for a quarter of a century living by his wits and acquiring knowledge of men and cities. Some quasi diplomatic mission from his native country brought him to England in 1708, at the age of nearly fifty. Nothing came of the mission, however, and he remained in London, thinking, no doubt, that England was as good a place to pick up a living as another. Heidegger enlisted in the Guards, a regiment in which you might at that time find very well-born men among the rank and file. He is described as a man of great social qualities, and as possessing the ugliest face ever seen on living shoulders. We can quite believe both stories, for the place the Swiss Count, as he was called, took in a ridiculously exclusive society is a proof of the one, and the surviving portraits of him by Vanloo and others leave no doubt about the other. There are a score of facetious allusions to his lack of beauty in verse, prose, and the graphic arts, and the undoubted fact is embalmed in a score of amusing anecdotes. Lord Chesterfield told his importunate tailor, Mr. Jolly, who was dunning his lordship for his bill, that he would not pay him until he could produce an uglier man than himself. He induced Heidegger to wait with him at his lordship's levee the next morning, and got his money. Heidegger's social success may be measured by the fact that White's Club at the Chocolate House thought him worthy of membership, an honour that exclusive society was very apt to deny to acknowledged rank and conspicuous merit. Heidegger was the very man to organise the management of an amusement of which fashionable London was eager to partake, to rescue it from the attacks of its enemies, of the clergy, and of the press, and to lift it out of its rather dubious surroundings at Spring Gardens and elsewhere.

Heidegger's eventual assumption of the office of *Surintendant des plaisirs d'Angleterre*, a title given him by young Mr. Henry Fielding, unless that gentleman's line is only an echo of some popular epithet, was more or less accidental. A year after he came to England he was clever enough to collect a subscription which enabled him to produce an opera at the Queen's Theatre in the Haymarket. The opera was a nondescript affair, apparently, called "Thomyris," written in English, and furnished out with airs from other operas of the Italian composers, Bonocini, Scarlatti, and the rest. But it brought the Swiss Count much gold, and it established for him a connection with the theatre. He came to be consulted on operatic and theatrical matters, gave often good advice on the conduct of opera, which was at the time in a very poor way, and as time went on he acquired the very useful reputation of a sound critic in theatrical and operatic matters. He had the good fortune to recommend some decorations or arrangements at the Haymarket with which his Majesty King George the First expressed himself mightily pleased. The great world took him up and caressed him; princes gave him amethyst snuff-boxes set in gold; if my lady wanted a rout arranged at her town house in Lincoln's Inn Fields, or at the country mansion, or if there was a musical entertainment or a dancing assembly to be arranged at a public room, Mr. Heidegger was called in and did the thing to perfection. It was a sure sign of notoriety at least, if no great honour, to gain even distant allusion in Mr. Pope's pleasant writings. Mr. Heidegger's personal appearance is thus lightly touched upon in that poet's description in the "Dunciad" of the bird which accompanied the Goddess of Dulness—

> " A monster of a fowl,
> Something betwixt an Heidegger and owl."

Heidegger came to be spoken of as *arbiter elegantiarum*. King George, who loved both masquerade and opera, gave him much countenance; he was made Master of the Revels, and became manager of his Majesty's Theatre in the Haymarket, where he co-operated with Mr. Handel in the production of opera. "He then set about improving another species of diversion," says one of his biographers, "not less agreeable to the king, which was the masquerades."

Knowing what we do of the king's fondness for those entertainments, it is very comic to read some of the appeals of the opposition in the old magazines to the morality of his Majesty in the matter of the masquerade. Said some austere moralist, writing to the *Gentleman's Magazine* in 1747, "The king has showed a noble contempt of Italian Operas by discouraging them as much as he can, and I doubt not but that masquerades will meet with the same disapprobation with him." We know that George discouraged opera by protecting Heidegger and by accepting him as manager of the Haymarket; it is stated also that his Majesty was so pleased with one of his masquerades that he presented Heidegger with £1000. The fact is that although masquerades were bad enough from some points of view, they were not opposed upon their demerits alone. There was much interested malevolence in these attacks in the newspapers, generally inspired by the theatrical interests, which were suffering from the competition of the new amusement. The charge that masquerade was as bad as opera was no very grave reflection on the masquerade, but from the actor's point of view one was as pernicious as the other, and he lifted up his voice against both, with the periodical press as a mouthpiece.

Mr. Nichols, who wrote that valuable work on the art of Mr. Hogarth, tells a funny story which throws much light on Heidegger's relations with his patrons, and is not without its value as a picture of a fashionable masquerade. It also gives us some interesting glimpses of the personality of the man himself, of his good-nature and his appalling ugliness. The wild

Duke of Montagu, it seems, invited several hard-drinking friends to the Devil Tavern in Fleet Street, and included Mr. Heidegger in the company. The rest were in the plot, and were either hardened enough to drink fairly with Heidegger and prevail, or they shirked their liquor as he took his. In either event he was soon dead drunk and under the table, whence he was duly carried into a bedroom and laid on the bed in a profound sleep. The duke then sent for a waxwork maker, the daughter of Mrs. Salmon who lived nearly opposite the Devil Tavern in Fleet Street. This artist was instructed to make a plaster mould of the sleeping Master of the Revels, and from the mould thus obtained was made a facsimile in wax of the unconscious Heidegger's face, which was duly coloured after nature.

This frolic took place a few days before a masquerade at the Haymarket at which the king had announced his intention of being present. The duke then bribed Heidegger's valet to tell him what clothes his master was to wear on the occasion; provided a similar dress, and made up a man of Heidegger's stature with the clothes and the mask into a perfect double of that gentleman. The king, the Duke of Cumberland, and the Countess of Yarmouth and some others of the court were all in the plot. The arrival of the king, who was in mask, was only known to the general company by the band in the gallery playing "God Save the King" as his Majesty seated himself. The order to strike up the national anthem was given by Heidegger when informed of the royal arrival by the officers of the court. Heidegger went to the musicians as usual, who began the tune. As soon as his back was turned, however, the false Heidegger advanced, countermanded the order, and substituted for the loyal anthem the Jacobite and treasonable song " Over the Water to Charlie." The room was at once in an uproar, and Heidegger himself both frightened and furious. He rushed back to the gallery, stamped and swore, accused the musicians of being drunk and conspiring to ruin him. He then retired to one of the smaller rooms, when the sham Heidegger, imitating Heidegger's own voice, again stepped into the middle of the room in front of the gallery, damned the musicians for blockheads at the top of his voice, and requested to know why they were not playing " Over the Water to Charlie " as he had told them. The tune was again changed to " Charlie," which brought back Heidegger to the room. The company was again in an uproar. The Guards, who were not in the secret, were for going up into the gallery and pitching the musicians down into the floor, and were only restrained by the Duke of Cumberland. Shouts of "Shame, shame," arose from all parts of the room. Here the Duke of Montagu interposed and whispered into the ear of the Master of the Revels that the king was violently angry, and that he had best make his peace with his Majesty at once and then discharge the musicians, who were certainly mad. Heidegger was conducted to the presence for that purpose, and made his apology. He was turning away when he heard his own voice at his elbow exclaim, "Indeed, Sire, it was not my fault, but that devil's in my likeness." "Poor Heidegger," says Mr. Nichols, "turned round, stared, staggered, grew pale, but could not utter a word." The duke thinking, and with reason, that the joke had already gone far enough, here whispered the details of the plot in the ear of the poor Master of the Revels. He accepted the joke as well as he could, but declared that he would never conduct another masquerade until he had seen the mould made by "that witch the waxwork woman" broken up in his presence.

It is quite intelligible that with support and patronage in high quarters Heidegger could snap his fingers, as indeed he did, at bishops and pamphleteers. It is almost certain too that under Heidegger's management the character of the masquerade itself improved upon the irregularities which Steele and Addison noticed so humorously. It must be confessed also that Heidegger's opponents, liberal as they are in general abuse, are very sparing of specific charges. One of their few accusations which was supported by details of evidence, was that of the infringements of the gaming acts which went on at the masquerade. It was inevitable that in a mixed company, where no one was refused who could produce a fancy dress of some sort and the necessary twenty-seven shillings for the ticket, some irregularity should occur at intervals.

The magistrates occasionally made raids on the masquerade to discover highwaymen who were supposed to be present in the gaming and lottery rooms, but generally with ill success, though on one occasion they made a haul of an ingenious gamester who was passing rouleaux made up of halfpence for the orthodox rouleaux made up of twenty-five guineas. But the general charges of the Craftsmen and Connoisseurs are not convincing. "Infamous assemblies which tend more effectually to corrupt the morals of the people than all the plays and interludes which were ever acted"; "Venetian balls introduced to corrupt the few remaining sparks of virtue yet left among us," are rather clumsily expressed charges which may have been true, but are lacking in precision. It is quite easy to see interested motives in the complaint of a political paper of "a Harlequin preceding Punch and making way with his wooden sword and giving to all he met, even to Royal hands, a printed bill as follows." The printed bill was a lampoon on Sir Robert Walpole about the "Norfolk company of Artificial Comedians" and "Robin's Great Theatrical Booth in Palace Yard," and George the Second laughed as he read it, we may be sure. General accusations, too, "that the vitiated taste for foreign pleasures is only relished by the most shameless among both sexes in the upper gradations of life," and "I observe with pleasure that masquerades are not supported by persons of high rank and large fortunes, but have of late been chiefly composed

of gamesters, players, women of the town, and at-
torneys' clerks," may be fairly held to cancel each
other.

On the other hand, Heidegger's advertisements
were highly suspicious. He issued his tickets at the
aristocratic White's Chocolate House, it is true, but
"persons of quality" were begged to be careful of
the tickets applied for in their names, and to return
superfluous ones "to prevent them falling into bad
hands." It is also stimulating to the imagination to
read that "sufficient guards would be stationed within
and without to prevent all disorders and indecencies,"
and that "strict orders are given not to deliver any
glasses or bottles from the sideboards, and to shut
them up early." A contemporary critic, too, of Mr.
Heidegger's efforts for the amusement of the quality
has quite the old ring of Dick Steele's lucubrations
in the *Spectator*. "I had like to have been knocked
down by a shepherdess for having run my elbow a
little inadvertently into her side. She swore like a
trooper, and threatened me in a very masculine voice.
But I was timely taken off by a presbyterian parson,
who told me in a very soft tone that he believed I was
a very pretty fellow, and that he would meet me in
Spring Gardens to-morrow night."

These wits, and others of greater power, did their
worst for Heidegger and his masquerades, but he
defied them all, and boasted of making £5000 a year
by the business. He was certainly a man of resource;
the king himself signed a royal proclamation against

the Masquerade ; Mr. Heidegger changed the name
of the next one to a Ridotto, and had the honour of
bowing his Majesty to his seat.

> "Thou Heidegger the English taste hast found
> And rul'st the mob of quality with sound ;
> In Lent, if masquerades displease the town
> Call 'em ridottos, and they still go down.
> Go on, Prince Phiz, to please the British nation
> Call thy next masquerade a convocation."

Later a Middlesex Grand Jury presented Mr.
Heidegger by name as "the principal promoter of
vice and immorality," and the Master of the Revels
about the same time had the honour of receiving King
George at his country house of Barn Elms, a house
where entertainments of another sort still flourish
under the auspices of the Ranelagh Club. Heidegger
and his entertainments thus throve on opposition and
grew fat on obloquy ; there is scarcely a single remark
preserved in the records of that time which is not a
hostile criticism of his undertakings or his morals, or
a scoff at his ugliness. Even when he died his epitaph was "the late Ct. H—d—g—r, pandour to the
British nation." But his biographers have a kindly
word for the old man, who distributed his wealth with
both hands among the poor and needy. There was
never a successful entertainment at the Haymarket
but that his agents carried help to poverty and suffering wherever they could find it, and he died "im-
mensely lamented, aged near ninety," in 1749, as the

London Post informs us, leaving to the British public the legacy of the perfected masquerade.

The British public, or that portion of it which counted most, the few thousands of fashionable people who composed London society, accepted the legacy with all thankfulness and lost no time in entering into its enjoyment. In the year following Mr. Heidegger's death, a grand Venetian Ball at the Haymarket excited the ire of a good many eloquent scribes who were unable to be present. "All the shameless ones among both sexes in the upper gradations of life" it seems assisted. It was "ushered in," we are told, "with a pompous preparation to engage the general attention. Our fribbles must puff it, our women of quality echo it at their card tables till it becomes the general talk and fires every profligate imagination with impatience to see this raree show of Venice. Pity it is that the list of names who have honoured the rites of Venice and Bacchus with their devotion in the Venetian worship cannot be had in order to disperse through the nation and mark out to public notice the worshippers there." No one regrets the absence of that list more than the present writer, but we have a shrewd suspicion that Mr. Heidegger's successors had the honour of his Majesty's presence on this occasion. Frederick Prince of Wales was not there, which was an excellent reason for the appearance of his august father. "What a sensible pleasure must it give all honest Britons that he whose virtues have rendered him so amiable in their eyes by every good

office of humanity and goodness within the little extent
of the power he is entrusted with, to miss the darling
name in the guilty roll; excellent man, worthy of the
public love and the triple c-r-n which he is one day to
wear." A scribe who could discover such virtues as
these in "Fred" might have been a little tolerant even
of the enormities of the masquerade, and all who have
read much in the records of the distressing family
quarrels between Norfolk House and St. James's will
recognise the probability that this panegyric of the
prince was a gentle reproof of the presence of the king
at the Haymarket. There was a guard of military
there too, which gave much scandal to the correspondent of Sylvanus Urban, as also to the magistrates, who declared that "the Venetian Ball tended
to encourage gaming and the corruption of the morals
of both sexes, was unlawful, and a public nuisance."
Perhaps it was, but the masquerade continued to
flourish like a green bay-tree both at the Haymarket
and elsewhere.

There were several new buildings about town which
arose about the middle of the century and lent themselves admirably to its purposes. One of the finest of
these was the Rotunda at Ranelagh, a fine circular
room of 150 feet in diameter, built by Mr. Jones,
the architect of the East India Company, in 1742, and
the lovers of masquerade were not slow to recognise
the possibilities of that fine room for their favourite
diversion. It is at Ranelagh, as we believe, that we
get the first view of the masquerade in its develop-

ment, and can form a clear idea of its attractions. So far we have been almost entirely dependent upon hostile criticism of a very destructive character for our details of the masquerade. At Ranelagh we have the invaluable assistance of such writers as Horace Walpole, and it is not without significance as to the interested nature of much of the criticism we have quoted, to find that the entertainments at Ranelagh escaped the worst of its slings and arrows. At Ranelagh, be it remembered, there was no stage for actors, and the masquerade did not displace those deserving artists, or silence the warbling of the prima donnas or the quavering male sopranos of the opera. These people had a distinct grievance at the King's Theatre, it must be admitted, and it is more than probable that the notes which were hushed by the popularity of the revels in Haymarket became vocal again under the auspices of Sylvanus Urban in the groves of Clerkenwell.

Heidegger was yet alive when they took a leaf out of his book at Ranelagh, and produced in 1749 the "Jubilee Masquerade in the Venetian manner," to celebrate the conclusion of the peace in that year. It was on the 1st of May that all London flocked to the pleasant gardens at Chelsea to see "by far the best understood and prettiest spectacle" that Mr. Horace Walpole ever saw in his life. Horry was quite enthusiastic, went back to Strawberry Hill to recover from the fatigue, and wrote to his "dear child," Horace Mann, at Florence, to tell him all about it. One of the managers at Ranelagh, it seems, who was a German, got at the Walmoden and induced her to persuade King George "to order it." George was nothing loth, we may be sure, from what we know of his tastes. Let Walpole tell the tale in his own words. "When you entered you found the whole garden filled with masks and spread with tents, which remained all night *very commodely*," says Horace in italics. "In one quarter was a maypole dressed with garlands, and people dancing round it to a tabor and pipe and rustic music, all masked, as were all the various bands of music, which were disposed in different parts of the garden, some like huntsmen with French horns, some like peasants, and a troupe of harlequins and scaramouches in the little open temple on the mount. On the canal was a sort of gondola adorned with flags and streamers, and filled with music rowing about. All round the outside of the amphitheatre were shops filled with Dresden China, Japan, &c., and all the shopkeepers in mask. The amphitheatre was illuminated, and in the middle was a circular bower composed of all kinds of firs in tubs, from twenty to thirty feet high, under the orange trees, with small lamps in each orange, and below them all sorts of the finest auriculas in pots and festoons of natural flowers hanging from tree to tree. There were booths for tea and wine, gaming-tables, and dancing, and about two thousand persons. In short, it pleased me more than anything I ever saw."

Thus Horace, and if you place him in the foreground of the picture he has preserved for us with most of the notabilities in London society in 1749, you have the Jubilee Masquerade at Ranelagh on May the 1st of that year. Nothing surely was ever more innocent, which was no doubt a reason for the silence of the critics who so belaboured the festivities at the Opera House. The show was so successful that it was determined to repeat it in the form of a sub-scription masquerade, " and people will go in their rich habits," Mr. Walpole prophesied to his correspondent. He was there again and saw the king " well disguised in an old-fashioned English habit," and the old gentle-man was much pleased, as we learn, when one of his subjects unwittingly asked his Majesty to hold her cup as she was drinking tea. The Duke of Cumberland was so fat that no disguise was sufficient to hide his royal identity. The Duchess of Richmond was made up as a Lady Mayoress of the time of James the First, and Lord Delawarr after a picture of Queen Elizabeth's Porter, which we may still see at Hampton Court Palace. Most of the chief figures of that Georgian society were there, Mrs. Pitt the famous beauty in " a red veil, which made her look gloriously handsome," Lady Kildare and the rest. Walpole, with his anti-quarian memory, noticed Lady Betty Smithson with " such a pyramid of baubles on her head that she was exactly like the princess of Babylon in Grammont "— poor Lady Muskerry, whom we saw so shockingly hoaxed by Miss Hamilton at Queen Catherine's masquerade. Last of all came a figure which brought a touch of that *abandon* of the early masquerades so deplored by the bishops and the pamphleteers into the innocent decorum which Horace records so pleasantly. Here was Miss Chudleigh, whose whole life was a masquerade, masquerading as Iphigenia prepared for the sacrifice, dressed up in flesh-coloured silk tights, "and so naked," says Walpole, "that you would have taken her for Andromeda." We really hesitate to state further details of this costume, which may be read in the letters of Mrs. Elizabeth Montagu. As a fact, however, it was really one of the most innocent of the lady's disguises. She was masquerading at this moment as Miss Chudleigh and a maid-of-honour to the Princess of Wales, and all the time she was twenty-nine years of age and the Countess of Bristol and the mother of a son. One wonders if she put on that astonishing costume for the benefit of King George the Second, who pretended to be in love with her, and gave her a watch "which cost thirty-five guineas, out of his own pocket, and not charged on the civil list." Anyway the charming creature masqueraded on to the end of the chapter, when old Tiger Thurlow ordered her to be burnt on the hand for masquerading as the Duchess of Kingston, when she masqueraded over to the continent. A strange figure this at the first masquerade we are able to people with real characters, and the other maids-of-honour were so shocked that they would not speak to her; and much she cared, no doubt.

It is quite obvious that by this time, either for good

or for evil, the masquerade was established among the regular diversions of the metropolis. There was no longer any necessity for hole-and-corner meetings; it had asserted its vogue against the opposition of the good people who really believed in its iniquities and of those others who may have been inspired by the same pious motives, but were certainly biassed by others of a more worldly character. If the masquerade had left untouched other interests at the Haymarket, we should have heard less of its enormities, the columns of the *Gentleman's Magazine* and similar periodicals might even have become trumpets for its praises, as they did when the quality began to flock to Ranelagh. "We might have challenged all Europe," wrote a correspondent of that excellent journal in 1755, in language strangely different from the fulminations of a few years earlier, "to shew us the diversion of a masquerade in the perfection with which it was there exhibited, either for the spaciousness of the room, the beauty of the ladies, the splendour of their jewels, or the elegance of their habits."

During the next ten years the taste for the masquerade spread all over the country, and its pleasures were even toned down to suit the decorum of the private houses of the great. Thus a "grand masquerade ball with music" was given in 1763 by his Grace the Duke of Richmond, "the vocal parts of which were performed by the nobility in masquerade." We again quote the actual words of the strangely tolerant *Gentleman's Magazine*, which assures us that the Dukes of York and Cumberland were present, together with over eight hundred of the quality, and that the "entertainment was in every respect grand beyond description." Side by side with the account of his grace's we may place the story of another of a different character, which supports our proposition of the general acceptance of the masquerade. "Nearly fifty persons, ladies and gentlemen of the hair-dressing class, were assembled at a house in the Borough for the purpose of entertaining themselves in the taste with a masked ball, but unfortunately for them the floor gave way, and some had their legs broken, and some were killed on the spot." Then there was a great function of the sort given by "the club at Arthurs'," which we still know as White's in St. James's Street, to fifteen hundred people, where "the illuminations were in the same style with those given by the King of Denmark, but much improved," as we are assured. The fashion even spread to the chaste solitudes of North Britain. "At Duff House, the jointure apartments of the Countess Dowager of Fife, was exhibited the first masquerade ever seen in Scotland. In order that proper decorum might be preserved, several ladies of distinction were there unmasked. Among them were the Countess Dowager of Moray, Lady Elphinstone, and Mrs. Mure, the lady of Baron Mure." Is it not admirable, this acceptance of the forbidden thing with the precaution of the unmasked dowagers? The masquerade indeed survived the chastening influence of the new young

King George the Third, and grew and flourished exceedingly in the early years of his reign. You will find it pervading most of the popular engravings of the period to which students owe so much. The artists of the Bowles prints were busy with the masquerade, and drew much inspiration from its incidents, shepherdesses coming home fast asleep in Sedan chairs, fast asleep, or drunk if you like to think evil, and the like. The caricaturists and cartoon draughtsmen, too, used the masquerade to convey all kinds of droll ideas. There were masquerades of politicians, of nations, of kings and potentates, what you will. Mr. Hogarth even drew masquerades of the Court, and hinted in his blunt manner at certain whispers which had great interest for the scandalmongers of the day. He placed my Lord Bute by the side of the Princess of Wales, and matched the young Prince George with the elusive little quakeress Hannah Lightfoot.

One of the most famous of the masquerades of the great period was that which inaugurated the opening of the Pantheon in Oxford Street in 1772. The occasion was marked by an incident which provided the sensation which was seldom wanting at a masquerade. It had been rumoured that the managers of the Pantheon had set their faces against the admission of certain ladies whose position in society was very well understood, ladies whose features still smile at us from some of the most attractive canvases of Sir Joshua Reynolds. "Women of slight character," it was said, were to be excluded, and "all the players."

White's and Almack's at once began to ferment at the thought, for Mrs. Baddeley, who had several friends in both of those notable institutions, was held to be strongly pointed at in the regulation. Lord Melbourne, who was a pillar of both clubs, was at the time writing those touching love-letters to Sophia which may still be read in her life by Mrs. Steel; those letters in which his lordship protests that he loves her "every minnit of his life, Satterday, Sunday and every day." There were Mr. William Hanger, Sir Charles Bunbury, Lord March and Mr. Conway, and a score of others, who resented the imputation upon the tuneful lady of Ranelagh and Vauxhall. So they assembled at Almack's, the old club-house in Pall Mall which is now the Marlborough Club, to the number of twenty, and started off in a body to escort Sophia in her chair to the entertainment. It must have been a pretty sight, these fine gentlemen all dressed for the evening grouped round the chair of the fair Baddeley, and tramping through the streets, up St. James's Street, where they were joined by the contingent from White's, making their number up to fifty, across Piccadilly, up Bond Street and down the Oxford Road and so to the Pantheon. It was a long walk for their buckled shoes and silk stockings, and one hopes that the weather was fine.

At the door was a guard of porters in livery armed with long staves, who were on the lookout for the Baddeley and her sisters in art. They put their staves across the door and said with much civility, that their

orders were to refuse admittance to all the players.
The fine gentlemen whipped out their swords; the
porters, frightened out of their lives, made way for
Sophia, and that lady marched triumphantly into the
fine room under a long canopy made by the crossed
swords of her gallant escort. The gentlemen, still
unappeased, refused to sheath their steel or allow the
music to proceed until the managers came forward to
apologise to the injured lady, and her friend Mrs.
Steel asserts, though it is scarce credible, that two
duchesses, those of Ancaster and Argyll, came forward
to express to Mrs. Baddeley the pleasure it gave their
graces to welcome such an ornament to the assembly.
Anyway there was a messenger ready to run off to
the Abington to tell her of the result of the Baddeley's
adventure, and there was no more opposition to the
" players " at the Pantheon.

You may read in the *Town and Country Magazine*
of the company which continued to flock to the Pantheon in spite of the Baddeley and the rest, the
Duchess of Richmond and Mrs. Damer, Lady Melbourne herself, Mrs. Bouverie and Mrs. Crewe, all
ladies of high *ton*, and besides all the bloods of
White's, such men as Sir Joshua Reynolds and
Goldsmith and Dr. Johnson. It was at the Pantheon that the Doctor contradicting Mr. Boswell's thrifty animadversions on the charge of half
a guinea for the entrance, declared that there was
half a guinea's worth of superiority over other
people who had not seen it. To have seen Sophia's

entrance under the swords was surely cheap at that figure.

Popular as the masquerade had become with the classes for whom it was specially purveyed, we imagine that its final glory waited for the appearance in London of a second professional organiser, a lady named Teresa Cornelys, upon whom the mantle of Mr. Heidegger may be said finally to have descended. Teresa Cornelys, if that were her true name, was a German singer who had tramped the continent during her youth and sung in half the cities of France and Italy, as the Pompeati. She seems to have arrived in England in 1757—to have met with indifferent success as a singer, and to have turned to the prevailing taste of the public assembly as a means of making a living. No one knows anything of her resources; her subsequent career would suggest that she was in monetary difficulties from the first. In any case the first information we have of Madame Cornelys in England is the announcement of her taking Carlisle House, an old mansion of the Howards, which stood on the site of the present Italian Church at the corner of Sutton Street in Soho Square. She decorated and enlarged the place, and solicited the suffrages of the aristocracy for public entertainments, concerts, balls and the like.

It is difficult to understand how an adventuress, as Teresa undoubtedly was, should have succeeded in gaining the support of her great patrons, as she undoubtedly did. But her subscription-lists filled up, and very early in the first year of her career we see her making acknowledgment of the fact by a thank-offering of an entertainment to the "upper servants of the quality." "On Saturday last (February 18, 1763), Mrs. Cornelys gave a ball at Carlisle House to the upper servants of persons of fashion, as a token of the sense she has of her obligations to the nobility and gentry for their generous subscription to her assembly. The company consisted of 220 persons, who made up fourscore couple in country dances, and as scarce anybody was idle on this occasion the rest sat down to cards." It was a not unskilful move on the part of Teresa, and she had her reward later in seeing Soho crowded with the chairs and coaches of her patrons. If we are to believe her, never was such a difficulty as in getting to those delightful rooms in Soho. She had endless suggestions for the guidance of coachmen and chairmen; she hoped her patrons might be brought "as prudently" to her doors as possible; "that the hackney coachmen will make no disturbance;" that they would forbear from quarrelling, and not run their poles through each other's windows. She had even proposals for the substitution of shutters for windows in the ladies' chairs as a cure for breakages. We take Teresa to have been wise in her generation, and not unskilled in the uses of advertisement.

This energetic lady tried every attraction to enlist the support of her patrons—balls, concerts, assemblies, operas, which she disguised as "harmonic meetings," morning concerts of instrumental music. The papers following the year 1763 are full of her advertisements; of her concerts under Bach and Abel; her "society nights" on Mondays; her elaborate distinctions in the colour of her tickets, "blue wrote upon the back, purple wrote upon the back"; of her prayers to her patrons to see to it that none of these precious tickets fell into bad hands; of her deprecation of the wicked rumours that she was jealous of Mr. Almack, who was opening an opposition concern down at those fine rooms in King Street. Her gratitude flowed out to her patrons in those finely-worded announcements in the *Public Advertiser*, where she "humbly hopes that she has not been wanting in duty and gratitude to her protectors, and she cannot sufficiently be thankful for the comfort she enjoys in this happy country which she hopes never to leave." Her wish was fulfilled to the letter, for she died in the Fleet Prison; for the moment, however, she had a very considerable success. Fashionably placed people protected her and flocked to her assemblies, and we read of notabilities from abroad, like the King of Denmark and the Prince of Monaco, making a tour of her rooms as one of the sights of the town, and expressing themselves highly pleased with their elegance. It was not, however, until 1770 that she bethought herself of the masquerade.

If we felt the want of a definite description of the details of the masquerade under Heidegger, there is certainly no lack of rich detail of the same entertainment under Mrs. Cornelys. The memoirs and the magazines of the day are full of the doings at Carlisle House. Artists like the graceful John Raphael Smith engraved groups of its frequenters, industrious students of the time have even raked up and put on record the items of its dressmakers' bills. All London flocked to see the "Circe of Carlisle House," with royalty at its head; a very unattractive Circe she was, to be sure, unless the mezzotint portrait published by Mr. Carrington Bowles strangely belies her. The bloods from Almack's, White's, and Boodles' gave private masquerades of their own at Teresa's rooms and under her management, and she had practically the patronage of all who counted for anything in the society of 1770 and the few years following.

It was on the 26th of February of that year that the crowd of great people in chairs and coaches to Mrs. Cornelys' masquerade really did produce the crush which Teresa had prophesied in her advertisements. " The principal nobility and gentry of this kingdom, to the number of near 800," as we learn from the reporter, " were present at the masked ball in Soho Square, and the Square and adjacent streets were lined with thousands of people whose curiosity led them to get a sight of the persons going to the masquerade." It is shocking to learn that the crowd behaved very familiarly to all this fine company; they stopped the coaches and chairs, made the occupants lower the windows, and held up lights "in order to display the figures to better advantage. The house was illuminated in the most splendid and picturesque manner imaginable with between three and four thousand waxlights."

We can fill the rooms, if we like, on that occasion with figures which are familiar to the students of the period.   George the Third did not affect the masquerade like his grandfather, but his royal house was represented by the Duke of Cumberland as Henry the Eighth.   The *Gentleman's Magazine* was enthusiastic about the characters of this famous assembly.   "The Duke of Buccleuch as the figure of Nobody, who, after entertaining himself and his friends sometime in that character, withdrew and appeared in a most elegant dress as an Hungarian Hussar.   Sir Richard Phillips was a double man, half miller, half chimney-sweeper, his dress was so admirably contrived that it required some observation which was his real front, and that not only when standing but also when walking, Sir Richard walking sometimes with one foot forward and sometimes the other."   Captain Coxe went as a gamester "with cards sewn all over his clothes, and a pack of cards in his hands which he was continually shuffling and offering to the company."   Horry Walpole's niece, the widow Waldegrave, who afterwards married the Duke of Gloucester, went as Elizabeth Woodville, "almost sinking under the weight of pearls and beads."   There was Miss Monckton, who was remembered in quite modern times as the eccentric Countess of Cork, as "an Indian Sultana, lovely in spite of her colour, with £100,000 in diamonds on her head-dress."   Mr.

Garrick was there as Bellarius, and Mr. Foote as a Turk; "the Duchess of Bolton as Diana, Diana herself," says the enthusiastic reporter, and "a Running Footman, the prettiest imagined dress in the ball, and showed that the universal opinion of the wearer's superior taste of dress of any kind has its foundation in truth, the Earl of Carlisle." The Duchess of Buccleuch was the Witch of Endor, and Mrs. Crewe and Lady Almeria Carpenter in the character of Ballad Singers so entertained the whole company that they were encored several times, when those ladies obligingly sang again.

In another number of the *Gentleman's Magazine* of a month later, "Miss Vizard" writes of this diversion to Lady Bab Evergreen at Bath—

> "When we entered this paradise, judge, my dear madam,
> With what pleasure we met our first ancestor, Adam,
> Good God! 'twas so awful to see whence we sprung,
> For the dress to his body most prettily clung."

There was never a masquerade without its sensation, and Captain Watson of the Guards provided this one. His effort was received with much disapproval. "A figure of Adam, the unavoidable indelicacy of the dress, flesh-coloured silk with an apron of fig leaves worked in it, fitting the body to the utmost nicety, rendered it the contempt of the whole company. The masque was universally shunned, and the party bore it with the greatest composure," says one report. From another we learn that "Captain Watson per-

sonated the part with great propriety and drollery."
At another of Mrs. Cornelys' entertainments, Luttrell,
the man whom the Court put up to oppose Wilkes in
the Middlesex election, came in a shroud and carried
his coffin about with him.   At another still a gentleman appeared in a thatched house, and could only be
seen through the window.   The cottage bore the insur-
ance company's badge on its front, which suggested
to a humourist who was present an attempt to fire
the thatch.

Teresa Cornelys had the support of all such fine
company as this for a succession of masquerades week
after week and season after season ; there were special
paragraphs in the news-sheets devoted to " Masquerade
Intelligence," and it was a recognised function of the
great ladies of society to give receptions on the night
of her entertainments, where the maskers put in an
appearance on their way to Soho.   And yet Teresa
came to utter grief and failed miserably.   How was
it ?   Walpole clears up the mystery perfectly.   " Mr.
Hobart, my Lord Buckinghamshire's brother," was
manager of the Opera in the Haymarket, and in 1770
he affronted Signor Guadagni, the Italian tenor of his
company, by promoting above Guadagni's sister, who
was the prima donna, the Zamperini, whom readers of
the Selwyn letter will remember as a particular friend
of Lord March.   Two great ladies, the Duchess of
Northumberland and Lady Harrington, took the
part of the Guadagni, and induced Mrs. Cornelys to
establish an opera for him at Carlisle House, the

"harmonic meetings" which we have already mentioned. As Walpole says, "Mr. Hobart began to starve, and the managers of the theatres were alarmed." Mr. Hobart informs against Cornelys, hauls her up before the magistrates, and she is indicted, not for her harmonic meetings, but "that she does keep and maintain a common disorderly house, and did permit and suffer divers loose, idle, and disorderly persons to be and remain during the whole night rioting and otherwise misbehaving themselves."

Such was the official description of Teresa's grand masquerades, and the disorderly persons included such offenders as the Duke of Gloucester, Mr. Garrick, Sir Joshua Reynolds, the Duke of Buccleuch, and Lord Carlisle, we suppose. Her opera and her Guadagni were the real offence, of course, and her masquerade only the occasion. Wonder of all, Sylvanus Urban began to shake his head again at Carlisle House, and we protest that, all of a sudden, they found another bishop to deplore the evils of the masquerade in that very year, when, as Walpole tells us, Mr. Hobart put the constables in motion and threatened Teresa with Bridewell. Worst of all, Teresa's creditors began to move, and not long afterwards the *Westminster Magazine* contained a very facetious account of the sale of poor Teresa's effects in the very rooms of her triumphs, with dreadful jokes about "Cupid turned auctioneer," and speculative criticisms upon the history of each of her chairs and sofas.

Justice may have been done on this occasion. It

was no doubt wrong of Teresa to smuggle an illegal opera into her rooms to compete with the patentee, but does not her experience, compared with that of Heidegger, throw much light on the continued opposition to the masquerade? Mark the difference in the lots of the two great purveyors of that diversion. Heidegger made a great fortune and entertained the king at his private house; Teresa Cornelys lost every penny she ever possessed or could borrow, and her final years were spent as the king's guest in the Fleet Prison. There were those points of difference between the two, the experience they both shared was the support of a pleasure-loving aristocracy and the opposition and persecution of the theatrical and operatic interest. That opposition which Heidegger successfully overcame, and was never aroused by the masquerades of Ranelagh or the Pantheon, overwhelmed poor Cornelys the moment she began to compete with the opera at the Haymarket. We now know something of Teresa Cornelys' antecedents, not that any one cared about them until she interfered with " Mr. Hobart, my Lord Buckinghamshire's brother," at the opera. Those who care to do so can read much about her early history in the memoirs of that diverting rascal, M. Jacques Casanova de Seingalt. If he is to be believed, which indeed is a large assumption, Teresa, in her youth at least, to use the approved phrase, "was no better than she should be." But which of us is? Certainly not the greater number of her patrons, or the persecutors who ran her down at last.

The poor creature, with age overtaking her, made some later attempts to revive the glories of Carlisle House, but all in vain.   Later still she was to be seen at an old mansion which stood at the end of a fine avenue of trees a little west of what is now Wilton Place.   Here, under the name of Mrs. Smith, she tried to entice people of fashion to a suite of rooms where she proposed to supply breakfasts and draughts of asses' milk.   She failed in this scheme also, and the poor old creature found a refuge in the Fleet, where in 1797 her troubles came to an end at last.   The masquerade which Heidegger fanned into a flame blazed up and burned out with Teresa Cornelys, and its vogue has never revived.   Peace to her memory.

A KICK-UP AT A HAZARD-TABLE

CHAPTER IV

THE PLAY TABLES

IT was in quite modern times, in the year 1845 in fact, that a paternal government, after much painstaking inquiry, decided to interfere in the development of what was originally an amusement of the leisured classes of the town, and decreed that facilities for high play in this country should be extinguished. That same diversion of the play table had by that year assumed proportions which made of it a portent. When her present Majesty came to the throne high play was no longer the distraction of a few hundred men of fashion at half-a-dozen clubs, but a great social vice which was eating into the heart of all classes of Englishmen. The passion of mankind for risking its effects upon the accident of chance—the length of a set of straws, the fall of a pair of cubes, the combinations of a number of pieces of pasteboard—is, as we know, as old as history itself. But it was reserved for the England of the eighteenth and early nineteenth centuries to display that passion in its most elaborate and refined form, and the most superficial student of social matters in England during that period would point without hesitation to gambling as the one diversion of all others which was characteristic of London from the reign of Queen Anne to that of Queen Victoria. It happens, also, that little is recorded of organised gaming before the first of those reigns, and, consequently, that the social records of the hundred and fifty years which preceded the Gaming Act of 1845 include most of what is known of the pastime, or the fashion, or the vice, call it what you will, in this country.

Such a period would include the organised gaming at court during the festivities of Christmas; it would pass to the development of hazard at White's and the coffee-houses; it would include the notable doings of Mr. Charles Fox and his friends at Almack's and Brooks's; the fashionable craze for faro which prevailed in society at the end of the last century; the palmy days of the hells of the West-end at the beginning of this; the scandal at Graham's in St. James's Street, which was the beginning of the end; and the crown and glory of high play at Crockford's between 1827 and the accession of her present Majesty.

There is, we believe, a very sufficient explanation of the growth of high play in England during the period we have indicated. The passion for play amongst modern peoples has invariably begun at the top of the social scale and spread downwards. The gilded youth of this country have always been the most eminent exponents of games of chance, and the fact that these gentlemen were pretty well employed during the troubled days of the Stuarts had as a natural consequence the other fact that the establishment of play as the chief amusement of the town waited on their leisure. This only came with the more settled days of Anne and the first Georges, when the bloods about town had first an opportunity to devote themselves to the study of hazard. In dealing, therefore, with gaming as the chief amusement of Londoners, we think we may ignore any reference to the isolated *coups* of the gamesters which are recorded at intervals since very early times, and, after a glance at the gaming at court, pass on to the rage for hazard at the coffee-houses, which was in full blast when George the First came over, spread gradually all over London wherever people with ready money met together, and established the rage for play which was only suppressed by the Gaming Acts of 1845 still in force.

The public gaming at court seems to have been a curious survival of early enactments which limited gaming of all sorts to the period of national rejoicing which came round with each Christmas. Under the Tudors and Stuarts it became the custom for the court to join in the Christmas festivities, by throwing open a room provided with a play table at which any of the lieges might risk his money against that of the court from the king downwards, and successive monarchs from Henry the Seventh to George the Second thus gave their royal countenance to gaming. The arrangements were under an officer of the Lord Steward's department called the Groom Porter, and were nominally limited to the period between Christ-

mas and the Epiphany. It is difficult to determine
how far the public were admitted to the presence of
the king himself. There was certainly a public room
where the meanest of his Majesty's subjects might
make his cast or set the stake of an opponent, of
which we have a vivid account from Mr. Pepys.

"To see how persons of the best quality do here
sit down and play with people of any, though meaner,
and to see how people in ordinary clothes shall come
hither and play away 100 or 2, or 300 guinnys without any kind of difficulty, and lastly to see the formality of the groome porter who is judge of all their
disputes in play and all quarrels that may arise therein
. . . is a consideration I never could have thought
had been in the world, had I not seen it."

It is probable, however, that the king's appearance
in public was only nominal, and that the royal operations were confined to a private room, and to play
with his chosen courtiers. Thus Mr. Evelyn records
that King Charles opened the revels on the evening of
January 6, 1662, by throwing the dice himself as a
first cast in the Privy Chamber. Mr. Ashton in his
"History of Gambling" thus describes the etiquette
of the court gaming. "When the king felt disposed,
and it was his pleasure to play, it was the etiquette
and custom to announce to the company that 'his
Majesty was out,' on which information all court
ceremony and restraint were set aside, and when the
royal gamester had either lost or won to his heart's
content, notice of the royal pleasure to discontinue

the game was with like formality announced by inti-
mation that 'his Majesty was at home,' whereupon
play forthwith ceased, and the etiquette and ceremony
of the palace were resumed."

There are incidents of this royal diversion which
are not without interest.   The animadversions of Mr.
Pepys and Mr. Evelyn, on the occasions when they
visited Whitehall, describe with some eloquence one
of the aspects of the court of the Restoration.   There
is a story of Lord Chesterfield, too, which we shall
glance at when we come to the time of George the
Second, which has its humour, and the fact that
George the Third abolished the custom and dismissed the groom porter with a gratuity, were quite
in keeping with the traditions of the austere morality
of that virtuous monarch.   But our chief interest in
gaming at court is to take note of the encouragement
that such an example in high places could not fail to
give to the particular vanity of Londoners we are
examining.   And in this connection it is worthy of
mention that the numerous Acts of Parliament which
were passed to discourage gaming during the early
years of the last century thoughtfully excluded the
precincts of the royal palaces from their operation.
Court gaming, however, affected the morals and the
worldly possession of but a few, and we pass to the
consideration of the first reign of hazard in London,
of which so much cannot be said.

It was at the coffee-houses, headed by White's
Chocolate House and the Cocoa Tree, that hazard

was to be seen at its glory. Very early in the century, as we see elsewhere, the more fashionable of the frequenters of White's had formed themselves into a club which met in private rooms of their own. The company at White's included all the leading men of the day, and it was to avoid meeting the rabble which flocked to the play tables downstairs that these gentlemen formed a private society with its own private accommodation. Dissipated and broken captains, sharpers, and even highwaymen of the more presentable type were constantly to be met at the Chocolate House; judges there were liable to meet the man whom they might afterwards have to sentence in the dock; it was no uncommon thing in those days to recognise a body swinging in chains on a heath outside London as a man with whom you had called a main at hazard a few weeks before at White's or at the Cocoa Tree. So the Ministers and great lawyers and men of fashion of Queen Anne's reign very naturally retired to their own rooms at the Chocolate House, where they could lose fortunes to each other in all privacy and decorum.

Hazard was a game of pure chance, in which skill or knowledge were at an utter discount, and the merest novice might contend with the case-hardened gambler on terms of perfect equality. The game, as we believe, has quite disappeared in England, and it may be of interest to recall its simple features. Hazard, of course, was a game played with dice, and could be shared by as many players as could find room at the

circular table where it was always practised. All the
players took the box in turn, and played against any or
all of the rest of the company when he made his cast.
The caster took the box, named a sum as his stake,
and placed it on the table. The company, or such as
wished to join in the game, then matched the caster's
stake with a sum of equal amount. The caster then
called his "main," by naming any number from five
to nine, rattled the dice in the box, and threw them
on the table. If the number of his main appeared he
won his stake and gathered up the money on the table,
when the box passed on to his left-hand neighbour.
There was another number to each main called a
"nick," and if that number appeared the caster also
won. If, however, neither main nor nick resulted
from the throw, the original main the caster had called
became what was known as the "chance" of the company, and the number he had thrown that of the caster
himself. He was then allowed three further casts, and
if neither of the chances appeared in the combinations
of the dice to decide the ownership of the stakes he
was judged to have "thrown out," and the box passed
on without gain or loss to either party. When, however, the chances were set up by the failure of the
main or nick, the "odds" were called by the groom
porter, an official like a marker at a billiard table, who
took his name from the old functionary who kept
the table at court. The odds were well known, and it
was consequently quite easy to determine the respective
values of the chances of caster and "setters," as the

company were called. If the caster's chance was the better one, he had the option of increasing his original stake to any amount he chose, the setters being required to match it to the extent of two-thirds only. Such were the outlines of hazard, a game which had obvious fascinations for a true gambler, in which pure luck was the chief factor, and the chances of all the players were fairly divided by the continual passage of the box.

Play at White's became notorious almost from the first, and the club became the object of a great deal of criticism from people who were opposed to dice or cards. It was a "pit of destruction" to one, the "bane of the English aristocracy" to another. Lord Lyttleton dreaded that a descendant might become a member and shake down the oaks of Hagley in the dice-box. Mr. Pope notices the doings of two of the early plungers at the club, the Duke of Bedford and Sir Theodore Jansen, and there is hardly a volume of letters or memoirs of the first half of the eighteenth century which does not contain an account of some outrageous cast at White's in which a whole fortune changed hands in a moment. The ordinary incident of an evening at White's, the losing of an odd thousand or two, attracted no notice. Sometimes reference to such trifles appear in the letters of some man who happened to be present. Thus Richard Rigby takes occasion to mention that Bob Bertie won a thousand, and that my Lord Masham was "fool enough to lose three thousand to Lord Bolingbroke."

But at frequent intervals some portentous cast was made; a young man was ruined at a throw, and the whole town rang with the rumour and with execrations of the club. Young Mr. Harvey of Chigwell, for instance, lost £100,000 to Mr. O'Birne, an Irish gamester. "You can never pay me," said O'Birne. "Yes, my estate will sell for the money," was the spirited reply. "No," said O'Birne, "I will win but ten thousand, and you shall throw for the odd ninety." They did so and Harvey won, lived to become an admiral, and to fight under Nelson at Trafalgar.

Such were a few only of the incidents of the gaming at White's which attracted attention from their sensational nature, but the distractions of hazard were by no means confined to the clubs and coffee-houses. It was a necessary qualification of a courtier of George the Second to be prepared to sit down with that monarch and the Suffolks and Walmodens and the other picturesque appanages of the court and lose a comfortable sum. Twelfth Night was always a fixture for a sitting of more than ordinary importance at St. James's. On one of these occasions luck was in favour of Lord Chesterfield, who won so much money that he was afraid to carry it home with him through the streets, and was seen by Queen Caroline from a private window of the palace to trip up the staircase to the Countess of Suffolk's apartments. He was never in favour at court afterwards. There were great doings, too, at court on Twelfth Night of 1753, when the king and court sat down to play "for the benefit of the groom porter." We may suppose that so much a cast was given to that official, but some of the royal players benefited as well, for we read in the *Gentleman's Magazine* that the Duke of Cumberland rose a winner of £3000, and that the losers were the Duke of Grafton and Lords Huntingdon, Holderness, Ashburnham, and Hertford.

Under such distinguished patronage the fashion for gaming spread, and half the doings of the society of which Mr. Horace Walpole was the minute historian, appear through an atmosphere of hazard, or loo, or faro. The young Duke of Hamilton, for instance, who married the incomparable Miss Gunning in such haste with a curtain ring, ogled that lady down the length of Lord Chesterfield's saloon, and paid so little attention to his game that he lost a thousand pounds at a hand. Papers of the didactic type like the *Guardian* published portentous homilies on the dangers of feminine gambling, occasioned by reports which appeared at regular intervals in the news-sheets of Lady This or Miss That having lost three thousand guineas at loo. There are delightful touches on the feminine side of the craze scattered about the literature of the period. There was Goldsmith's lady, for instance, who played on her deathbed with the parson, won all his money, and expired in the act of dealing for a final game in which her funeral expenses were the stake. There was the other lady, too, who being admonished by a divine on the evils of gaming, including the great waste of time, agreed with the remark that there was indeed a prodigious deal of time wasted in dealing.

Hazard at the clubs and in fashionable society was conducted with all decorum. It was unfashionable and unpardonable to show any display of feeling at losses or gains. The absence of anything like a scene at these sittings in high circles, where the circumstances were calculated to produce very varied emotions in the players, is remarkable. Neither was there ever an imputation of unfair dealing in such society. But as the taste for the dice-box spread into lower circles, organised cheating at low taverns and gaming-houses became a regular profession, and very demonstrative proceedings on the part of players were of daily occurrence. Dice loaded on one side with small quantities of metal so as to insure certain numbers turning up were used by cheats; more frequently a pair of dice were made so numbered that certain combinations could not be thrown with them. One of these numbers was chosen by the caster, who substituted the false dice for the fair ones in the preliminary rattle, and this number after the cast had been made became the chance of the setters. The caster, thus secure from loss, went on throwing until either his own chance turned up or he "threw out" under the rules, when the box passed on. Even with fair dice there were ways of cheating. It was said that dice could be brought out of the box in certain combinations in which they were placed in the box; the "stamp" was a recognised cast by which the cubes were merely uncovered without throwing; a "dribble" was a slow pouring out which allowed of the clever manipulation of a cube on the table by an expert, and at times the dice were thrown clean off the table in order that a confederate might change them either for fair or false ones as circumstances demanded.

It is no matter of surprise that the incidents which occurred at the disreputable establishments where such practices were common were often of a most exhilarating character. The papers of the middle of the century are full of reports of such occurrences, which often engaged the attention of the magistrates, and not seldom led to judicial proceedings at the Old Bailey, and to those dismal processions to Tyburn which were the most popular of spectacular exhibitions in those days. Every man of the company at a low hazard house, though himself quite prepared to cheat, was virtue itself in resisting cheating in others. The practice of tampering with dice was so well recognised that they made a rule to meet the difficulty, which allowed of a setter to call for a fresh set of cubes up to the very moment of the fall of the cast on the table. It is easy to understand the chagrin of a caster who had successfully smuggled loaded dice into the box, and saw his successful main anticipated and extinguished by a call for fresh dice while his cast was actually in the air. Such an incident was often followed by a free fight of a dangerous nature, in which the chairs and other movables were not the only weapons employed, like the general mêlée which is presented with much vigour in the "Kick up at a Hazard Table," one of Mr. Rowlandson's most spirited plates.

There is a famous anecdote of Lord Stair and his brother at a house of this sort, which is very illuminative of the amenities of such places. They had both set the caster and won his stake. He threw down the box and cursed the brothers to all eternity. They made no reply, but took up the box and coolly made a cast each as to which should have the pleasure of running the caster through the body. Lord Stair won. "O Stair, Stair," said his brother, "you have always been more fortunate in life than I."

The frenzy of losers at the tables sometimes took astonishing forms. There is record of a ruined man seizing the edge of the table in his teeth and dying in the act. The company fled horrified, and he was found by the watch, dead, with his eyes open, his face distorted, and his teeth driven far into the wood of the table. A Frenchman was seen to ram a billiard ball down his throat, whence it was removed by a surgeon; an Irishman put the lighted candle into his mouth. A gamester, whose nonchalance at repeated losses was remarked upon, opened his shirt and showed his breast all lacerated by his own fingernails. But connoisseurs declared that the most awful form of emotion was that when men wept like statues without moving a muscle of their face, and with nothing to show they were alive except the tears running down their cheeks. On the other hand, there is a delightful story of a winner who, when he realised a large sum, straightway made arrangements for food, clothing, washing, and lodging for ten years, in order to be able to look forward to that period of gaming undisturbed by any anxiety.

There seems to have been a lull in the rage for hazard following the vogue of whist, which was marked by the publication of Hoyle's Treatise in 1742. Whist, it would seem, was first played in England by people of humble station. Long before it mounted to the drawing-room it was a favourite game in the servants' hall under the strange title of "swobbers." Then some tradesmen who met at the Crown Coffee-house discovered the merits of the game, studied its rules, and brought it into notice, and Hoyle's Treatise established the game as a permanent favourite and created a new profession, that of teacher of whist to the quality.

Although whist never appealed to the real votary of the dice-box, it was a most important factor in spreading the love of gaming amongst the middle and lower classes. Hazard required a large company, a special table, and a considerable amount of ready money. Whist was played in holes and corners, at taverns and coffee-houses, by small tradesmen, clerks and apprentices. The game also lent itself as a ready instrument of cheating to the sharpers, and these gentry soon evolved a complete system of signs and symbols for use with confederates either playing or looking on. Blowing the nose meant a good hand, taking snuff a bad one; a cough conveyed information of an honour;

a confederate looking over the hands of opponents declared their strength or weakness by the manipulation of a tobacco pipe, called "piping." Exclamations in conversation, such as "Indeed," "Truly," "Upon my word," "I assure you," suggested leads of hearts, diamonds, spades, or clubs. Cards bent into "Kingston Bridge," or pared at the edges for certainty of cutting, fingers held up at looking-glasses, and scores of other devices were put into practice for the beguilement of the prosperous tradesman or young city merchant, who were usually the victims of the profession. There are curious treatises on the subject of cheating written with such a mastery of detail as could only have emanated from the sharper himself, and it became a practice in the more presentable houses to run curtains on rods meeting at the centre of the table, so as to separate each player in a cubicle of his own.

One of the most famous of the incidents of the public whist tables is enshrined in a venerable anecdote, which is well known but still worthy of quotation. A very prominent figure of the public play tables of the middle of the century was one Roche, a tavern bully nicknamed the Tyger, from his ferocious aspect and manners. The Tyger's reputation was much enhanced when, after a dispute with Lord March, he took that nobleman by the ears and lifted him out of the room. But his fame chiefly rests on his treatment of a foreign count, whom he noticed cheating at a game of whist. He took up the pointed candle snuffers and pinned the count's hand to the table, with the remark, "I ask your pardon if the ace of spades is not under your hand," which indeed proved to be the case.

There was another slight lull in high play in fashionable circles when the young king came to the throne in 1760, and gaming at court was banished with other picturesque customs which prevailed at St. James's under George II. George III. would have none of it, and withdrew his countenance from all connected with the great doings of the dice-box. Even White's took its cue from the courtiers who flocked at the club and intrigued against Mr. Pitt and the Whigs, and the gaming at the club sank to quite innocent proportions. It was probably the altered aspect of affairs at White's which induced some score of young men of fashion, many of them members of the old club, to form a new one more to their liking. It is certain that Almack's club in Pall Mall, afterwards so famous as Brooks's, was opened in 1764 for no other purpose than as a rendezvous for thorough-paced gamesters.

Private gaming undoubtedly reached its height at Almack's during the twenty-five years which followed the opening of the club. Early in the present century Mr. William Crockford presided over transactions which possibly surpassed in amount the sums which changed hands at Almack's, but, as we shall see, play at Crockford's was not of a private character, but partook of the nature of the proceedings at Monte Carlo to-day.

All the glories of hazard revived at the new club

in Pall Mall. There was no trace of the traditional Whig politics of Brooks's in the early list of Almack's; the members were young men of fashion without exception, and they displayed a juvenile ardour in their doings at the club which attracted every eligible gambler in London within a very short space of time. The town soon began to ring with the effects of the mains cast at Almack's, and the encounters between noted plungers at the hazard table in the great room divided the attention of the town with the last news from the revolted States, or the latest blunder of Lord North and the King.

Owing to the identification of the name of Mr. Charles James Fox with the very choicest of the exploits at Almack's, the gaming of that celebrated period has become almost a part of English history. Public attention at the time was fascinated by the contrast between the inspired orator of the House of Commons, and the ruined spendthrift at Almack's cleaned out of his last shilling and asleep with his head on the table after a continuous sitting of twelve hours. To-day it is a standing wonder that Fox's reputation should have survived the doings of those first twenty years at Almack's, and that the real merits of his great nature should have drowned all censorious recollection of the vices which he only assumed.

Fox, of course, was only one of many; to make up a typical company at Almack's between 1770 and 1780, we should gather with him round the green-table in the great room his brother Stephen and his

cousin Lord Ilchester, his bosom friends Fitzpatrick
and Hare, Lord March, George Selwyn and the young
Earl of Carlisle, Burgoyne and Rodney, when not on
duty abroad, and Lord Derby, Lord Bessborough, and
the Duke of Devonshire. A little later we should
include Lord Robert Spencer, Lord Cholmondeley,
Lord Thanet, and Mr. Dick Thompson. Gibbon
would be at the fire-place with his snuff-box, Garrick
would look in after the theatre, and Horace Walpole
limp in from the saleroom, but not to play. Horry
loved nothing better than to win fifty guineas from a
dowager at loo, but he never risked the proceeds of
his fat pensions and sinecures with the plungers at
White's and Almack's.

The doings of those gentlemen, however, had great
interest for Horace, and fill a not inconsiderable space
in his entertaining letters and memoirs, where he has
left us a description of such a gathering as we have
supposed. "They began," says Horace, speaking of
the youthful punters at Almack's, "by pulling off
their embroidered clothes, and put on frieze great-coats,
or turned their coats inside outwards for luck. They
put on pieces of leather such as are worn by footmen
when they clean knives, to save their lace ruffles; and
to guard their eyes from the light and to prevent
tumbling their hair they wore high-crowned hats with
broad brims and adorned with flowers and ribbons,
masks to conceal their emotions, and each gamester
had a small neat stand by him to hold a wooden bowl
with an edge of ormolu to hold his rouleaux."

Of all that careless company Mr. Charles James Fox
was the most conspicuous, partly because he played for
the excitement of play alone, and was, as it would seem,
absolutely indifferent to the consequences of his losses
to himself or his friends, and also because he gained a
great reputation in the House of Commons almost
from the moment of his election as a member, and the
public was naturally interested in the contrast between
the heaven-sent orator of Westminster and the im-
provident spendthrift at the club. Walpole recorded
with some humorous strictures that Mr. Fox lost
£11,000 at a sitting which began on the 4th of
February of 1771, and ended at five o'clock of the
afternoon of the following day. On the morrow he
delivered a speech on a religious question at Westminster, having prepared himself for the effort, as
Mr. Gibbon pointed out, " by passing twenty-two
hours in the pious exercise of hazard." " After the
debate," continues Walpole, " he went to White's,
where he drank till seven in the morning, thence to
Almack's, where he won £6000, and between three
and four in the afternoon he set out for Newmarket."
Within the week he was back again in London and
lost another £10,000. His brother Stephen in the
meantime lost £11,000 at Almack's, so that the
brothers in three sittings within seven days lost a
sum of £32,000. Gaming ran in the Fox blood of
that generation, and the passion may perhaps be regarded as a dispensation of Providence which incited
these young men, both under twenty-five, to choose

a speedy method of returning to the British public the vast wealth which had been accumulated in a short time by very questionable means by their father, Lord Holland. Their cousin, Lord Stavordale, the son of Lord Ilchester, who was a true Fox though he bore the name of Strangways, was another of the generous youths of the hazard-table. There is a pleasing glimpse of this young gentleman also preserved by Walpole. " Lord Stavordale lost £11,000 last Tuesday, but recovered it at one great hand at hazard. He swore a great oath. 'Now, if I had been playing deep, I might have won millions.' "

It would fill a volume to mention the recorded incidents of the great period of hazard which may be read in the many histories of gaming which have appeared during the last few years. Hazard was practised in almost every rank of society where men met together, and in all parts of the town. There were notable houses for the accommodation of the butchers and drovers of Smithfield, for Jews in Houndsditch, and for the apprentices and tradesmen of the city. The lawyers of the Inns of Court must have been among the most devoted supporters of the game, if we may believe an anecdote of the Middle Temple. The floor of the hall of that great society was taken up for repairs towards the end of the century, when it was found that no less than a hundred pair of dice had accumulated through a few holes in the boarding. The game has even left its mark on our language. To "crab" in the slang vocabulary is to speak disparagingly of a thing or a person, and is derived from a term of the game given to a combination of the dice which meant inevitable loss. There can be little doubt, also, that the slang expression to "nick," in the sense of taking possession, is a survival of the old term at hazard, the "nick," which allowed of the gathering in of the stake by the man who was lucky enough to throw it.

Somewhere between the years 1775 and 1780 the rage for the old game of hazard, which had been the favourite with gamblers since the beginning of the century, yielded its place quite suddenly to a round game at cards called faro. Faro, which is still popular in the United States, and is not unknown in illegal clubs kept by foreigners in Soho to-day, was an adaptation from the much older game of basset, which was the favourite game at court in Stuart times. Faro was played between the dealer or keeper of the "bank" and the rest of the company, and, like hazard, it gave excitement to as many people as could find room round the table. The idea of the game was quite simple, and recalls the "Self and Company," played by children. Each of the company placed his stake upon any card of the thirteen he chose, and when the stakes were all set the dealer took a full pack and dealt it into two heaps, one on his right hand the other on his left, two cards at a time. He paid the stakes placed on such cards as fell on the right-hand pack, and received those of such as fell on his left hand. The dealing of each pair of cards was called a "coup," and the dealer paid or received such stakes as were decided after each coup.

Such was the crude idea of the game of faro which engaged the attention of all London at the end of the last century, but there were numerous variations which gave the game a great interest to all sorts of gamesters. The bold and reckless spirit having won on the first coup might leave his winnings to accumulate until he reached a point in the game which was known as *soixante et le va*, when he could claim sixty-three times his original stake. Other rules allowed a timid player to withdraw his winnings each time and leave only the sum he first ventured, and between such extremes of boldness and caution there were endless facilities which gave all sorts of interesting options to the player, and provided the game with its undoubted fascination. Faro, indeed, was full of incident, and without a dull moment; there were no long intervals for dealing or shuffling, and it had a plausible air of fairness as between the dealer and the company. As a fact, however, the odds were enormously in favour of the dealer. He claimed all ties, that is, when the same card appeared on both packs, the last card but one of the pack delivered its stake to him upon whichever hand it fell, and there was the impalpable but very real advantage of what was known as the " pull of the table " in his favour. The deal never passed on, a faro table being known as a "bank" which was kept by an individual, or a partnership of two or more persons, and enormous sums were realised by such concerns.

Brooks's led the fashion in faro, as it had done in
hazard a few years earlier.   The game at the club was
conducted by one or two partnerships, which were
astonishingly successful at the expense of the general
body of players.   Charles Fox and Fitzpatrick were
early in the field, for in 1781 we learn from the invaluable Walpole that his " nephew, Lord Cholmondeley,
the banker *a la mode*," was demolished.   He and Sir
Willoughby Aston went early one night to the club
and set up a bank of their own.   When Fox and Fitzpatrick arrived, they resented the competition, attacked
the bank, and won above £4000.   "There," said Fox,
" so should all usurpers be served."   Lord Cholmondeley, however, recovered, and he and his partner,
" Mr. Dick Thompson of Grosvenor Square," had a
very successful career at the club.   Nephew Cholmondeley, it seems, confided to Lord Foley that he had
won £44,000 in 1787 alone.   " Gaming was never
higher," said Mr. Daniel Pulteney to his patron the
Duke of Rutland, " and the pharaoh bankers have had
some good pidgeons.   A Mr. Barton was at one time
out with a sitting at Dick Thompson's bank £92,000,
and cut, losing £24,000."   Another celebrated bank
at Brooks's, running at the same time, was a partnership between Lord Robert Spencer and Mr. Hare.
The profits of this business, for it was nothing else,
enabled Lord Robert to retire on a landed estate.
The success of the faro banks at Brooks's was such
that it led to the game being forbidden at White's by
a special rule of the managers.

The passion for faro, however, was by no means confined to the clubs; its advantages to the dealer were soon recognised, and the facilities it offered to all who could provide a room and a company gave an opportunity to a score of women of fashion to combine business with pleasure. Faro banks were kept at half the great houses in town. Some of the younger men at Brooks's chattered about the enormous sums that the keepers of the table were making; Lord Cholmondeley, it was said, had whispered to Lord Foley that he and his partner had cleared £44,000 in a season; Lord Foley passed the news on to Lady Duncannon, Lady Duncannon mentioned it to her sister the Duchess of Devonshire, and the sisters, invoking the aid of Lady Harrington and a friend of hers who knew where he could borrow £1000, got together a fund and opened a private faro bank under the most fashionable auspices, which we may take as typical of a score of others in the west end of the town. All the drawing-rooms in London, indeed, were ankle deep in cards, for it was the custom for the dealer to fling the pack across the room at the end of each deal of faro, and the players each consumed a duplicate card with every stake they laid. Playing-cards were so common at that time in private houses that it was usual to write notes upon the backs of them, and those notes may often be found among the correspondence of those days.

As time went on there was hardly a house of note in the West End which did not run its faro table.

The Prince of Wales and the Duke of York gave their royal countenance to the fashion by appearing daily at one or other of them, and it became the custom for a lady to hire a dealer at five guineas a night to conduct operations, and to suggest that the profits of the table went to him and not to the hostess. This, of course, was a very transparent device to disguise the commercial nature of the transaction; it gave a thin varnish of propriety to the proceedings, but deceived nobody. People who were sulky at losing their money talked dreadful scandal, and the whole society of the day was permeated with the sordid suspicions which until that day had been confined to the low hazard rooms at the taverns and dingy houses of the city.

The vogue for faro was finally killed by an open scandal which came into the courts in the year 1797. Three ladies of position—Lady Buckinghamshire, Lady E. Luttrell, and Mrs. Sturt—were each fined £50 for playing at a public gaming-table. The "public gaming-table" was kept at Lady Buckinghamshire's own house by a man named Martindale, one of a family who lived by organising the pleasures of the aristocracy. Martindale, as a fact, was only the convenient dealer hired at so much a night, but he suffered as a principal of the concern, and was fined £250. Lady Buckinghamshire's bank had been a prodigious success, and it might have gone on for years if her ladyship had been well advised. The bank, however, had been robbed of £500 by some unknown person, and instead of hushing the matter up, she was silly enough to accuse a servant of the robbery and to dismiss him. This individual, feeling himself ill-used, gave information to the police as to the real nature of her ladyship's assemblies, and the details of those gatherings were investigated by the bench, with the result we have mentioned. Mr. Gillray, the caricaturist, seized upon the occasion to produce some of his most ferocious designs, in which these ladies and others were represented as "Pharaoh's daughters in the pillory and at the cart tail," being flogged by Lord Kenyon, who had delivered some very excellent remarks upon the prevalence of gaming in high quarters from the bench in another gambling case which had come before him. "If any prosecution of this nature is fairly brought before me," said his Lordship, "and the parties are justly convicted, whatever may be their rank or station in the country, though they should be the first ladies in the land, they shall certainly exhibit themselves in the pillory." Mr. Gillray gave very adequate pictorial expression to that threat of the judge, with recognisable portraits of Lord and Lady Buckinghamshire, Mrs. Concannon, Lady Archer, Lady Mount Edgecumbe, and others who had the reputation of knowing more than they ought about faro. The public exposure in the courts, and the popularity of Mr. Gillray's prints, which were circulated in sets from Humphrey's in St. James's Street, like books from Mudie's to-day, extinguished the popularity of the game, and its vogue expired as suddenly as it had arisen in the year 1798.

We have been chiefly concerned, so far, with play in distinguished circles, but the rage had gradually and surely spread downwards, and by the beginning of the present century had infected all classes in the country. About the time that whist was becoming popular as a medium for gambling, a game of pure chance was introduced from the Continent. Some speculators set up a table at Tunbridge Wells for playing E.O., a species of roulette played with a ball on a special table, and did well at it. It was a game which lent itself admirably to cheating; the cubs which surrounded the table into which the ball rolled were manipulated so as to insure a win to the table-keeper; inclines were made on the surface of the table imperceptible to the eye, but sufficient to conduct the ball into winning cubs; the cloth was waxed and ironed smooth at particular places with the same object and result. Roly poly, as the game was popularly called, had a great vogue, and became a standing attraction at race meetings, country fairs, and even in the streets of London. The game provided a fat living for gangs of sharpers, who went on circuit like his Majesty's judges, hung together in a confederacy, and extended their organised operations on popular lines to London and the larger cities.

Turf transactions were often auxiliary to the gaming operations of these gentlemen; on the other hand, the profits of roly poly gave a start to more than one shining light of the turf. As instances of both we may mention Colonel O'Kelly, the owner of

Eclipse, who was placed on his legs by successful dealings with the E.O. table at race meetings; and Mr.
William Crockford, the prince of gaming-house proprietors, was a product of the combination of racing
and roly poly.

The immediate result of the organisation's operations in London was the establishment of cheap
gaming-houses all over the town. Hazard revived,
or rather descended from Brooks's and the Cocoa Tree
to shady houses in Soho, Covent Garden, and the
City, and people of humble condition were taught the
joys and the dangers of roulette, *rouge et noir*, and
macao for small stakes. Morley's was a noted cheap
hazard-house in the City, Miller's a famous hell of
the low type in Leicester Street, where loaded dice
were habitually used, and drunken clerks relieved of
their employers' money a hundred pounds at the time.
John Taylor, of the Bedford Arms, Covent Garden,
stood a siege of some hours against the sheriff's
officers, having thoughtfully provided his passages
with doors of wrought-iron. No. 19 Great Suffolk
Street had a subterranean passage into an empty house
in Whitcombe Street, through which proprietors and
customers escaped when the place was raided. At
No. 3 Leicester Square there was an exit over the
roofs, but one gentleman mistaking it was smoked
out of the chimney by the officers. Every other house
in the piazza of Covent Garden seems to have been
raided, but the profits were so great that the fines
were easily paid, and if a man here or there was im-

prisoned, his partners carried on the business at another place during his absence, and he came out to share the profits which had accumulated while he was doing his term. "I can easily pay £500," said Mr. Miller of Leicester Square after a second raid; he paid that sum, did his two years, and opened again round the corner.

The mischief these places did is almost incalculable; bankruptcies, embezzlements, duels, and suicides resulting from gaming were of weekly occurrence, and it would seem that half the tradesmen and clerks of London were before the magistrates or the coroners of the last years of the last century and the first quarter of this. Men sat at these houses for a week at a time, and ended by losing the clothes from their back and being turned out in their stockings and shirt, and perhaps the climax was reached when two men were interrupted in preparations for an execution on a lamp-post in the north of London, the one having lost his life to the other for the sake of the clothes to be gathered from the corpse.

There was a constant interchange of personnel both of proprietors and players between houses of different grades. A man who had started some low house in Covent Garden or the City, swelled out on the plunder of clerks and tradesmen until he was substantial enough to open a house of more pretensions farther west. On the other hand, a gamester who began in St. James's more often than not sank through different stages of raffishness until his final efforts were transactions in half crowns at the dirty resorts of butchers and apprentices in Houndsditch or the Barbican.

The success of the profession of table keeping was very evident by the opening years of the present century, when a whole shoal of pretentious establishments, where public gaming could be enjoyed in luxurious surroundings, sprang up in the very heart of the West End. St. James's and the very precincts of the court itself produced a swarm of these places in irreproachable circumstances, every one founded and conducted by men who had humbler experience elsewhere. Hazard and faro had gone out at the older clubs, and club gaming of the period was represented by extremely deep play at whist at White's and Brooks's. Macao flourished for a while at Wattiers, where the members lived on each other for some eight or ten years until their estates disappeared, and the club expired by the flight of its supporters to Boulogne. Beau Brummell, who asked the waiter for a flat candlestick and a pistol, and was immediately obliged with a pair of loaded weapons by a madman with whom he was playing, was a typical member of Wattiers. *Rouge et noir* and French hazard were played at some of the second-rate clubs like the Union and Graham's, but these games were the chief support of the hells of St. James's, and were played little elsewhere.

No. 77 St. James's Street was a well-known house devoted to *rouge et noir*, where the stake was limited to £50, which prevented any pigeon from recouping himself with a great plunge. There does not seem to be any record of cheating at houses of this class, but there was a steady turn in favour of the table which rendered it quite unnecessary, and usury at high rates added very much to the profits. Opposite No. 77 was a small house devoted to hazard exclusively, much frequented by Guardsmen, whom it steadily relieved of arrears of pay accumulated during the Peninsular War. Fielder Morley and Carlos kept the corner house of Bennet Street, known as the " House with the Red Baize Door." They had a service of plate at this establishment which was made from silver coin won from their clients. Abbot, Watson, and other partners kept a house at No. 10 St. James's Square, the " Pigeon Hole," where the stake was limited to what was considered moderate dimensions, which, however, was high enough to allow of an annual profit of £30,000. There were two houses in King Street, Mrs. Leache's at No. 6, and Mr. Davis's at No. 10. No. 27 Bury Street was one of the temporary resting-places of Mr. William Crockford in his wonderful career from the fish shop in Fleet Street to the palace in St. James's Street opposite White's. Smith, Pope, & Co., at 77 Jermyn Street, and Taylor, Phillips, & Co., at 71 Pall Mall, were famous and prosperous men in their day, and gave their sons and daughters a good start in life. Roubel's, at No. 40 Pall Mall, was a house run in the French mode, where the cookery was good, and losses always paid without grumbling, which was not invariably the case elsewhere. Roubel and his partners did exceedingly well

on the whole, but they suffered a serious reverse when
a party of pigeons dressed themselves up as officers
of the law, raided the place, and cleared away some
thousands in gold which were on the table at the
time.

Such were the houses at which round games flourished after their decline at the great clubs. They
steadily drained the pockets of the aristocracy of
England for nearly half a century, and there is scarcely
a great family to-day which does not still feel the
effects of the play that went on within their doors
sixty years ago. All the efforts of the law as it stood
were unable to suppress them; they suborned witnesses, bribed police officers, and, if the worst came to
the worst, paid fabulous sums to keep articles out of
newspapers and cases out of court. The history of
these places is contained in such productions as the
" Greeks," the " Pigeons," and the " Academicians,"
written by men who had been ruined at the tables, and
published at great risk by Stockdale of Pall Mall.
They are dreary reading at the best, with their tag
quotations from Virgil and Horace, their names in
asterisks, and their slang in italics, all in the style of
Tom and Jerry, surely the most atrocious prose into
which the English language has ever been twisted.
But they contain the facts and doings of a phase of
life which had profound results, and they prepared
the ground for the final conflagration when play burnt
itself out at Crockford's.

William Crockford was originally a fishmonger of

sporting tastes who kept a small shop in the Strand near Temple Bar. He began his career as a gamester by punting for half-crowns at a low gaming-house kept by a man named Smith in King's Place, and he was accustomed to return to the fish-shop with his winnings late at night, and drop them wrapped in brown paper into the basement without entering the house. He probably learnt the capabilities of gaming as a profession at King's Place, but his first real start in life was a successful turf transaction. Crockford began his career as a table keeper by the purchase for £100 of a fourth share in a little hell at No. 5 King Street; his partners were men named Abbot, Houldsworth, and Austin, and their doings were not above suspicion. He appeared next at a French hazard bank at No. 81 Piccadilly, where he and his partners were believed to have cleared £200,000 in a very short time. This is not surprising, when one reads of five men losing £100,000 at a sitting to the fishmonger and his partner Gye. This was the sum that Lord Thanet, Lord Granville, Mr. Ball Hughes, and two others contributed to the concern by a single night's " play." It was persistently said that cheating was practised at No. 81, and false dice, declared to have been found on the place, were exhibited in Bond Street for some time. It is quite certain that Crockford was sued by dozens of his victims, and that he kept every one of these actions out of court by compromise before the hearing. After the disclosures in Piccadilly, Crockford lay low for a time, during which his name was not much in evidence, though he kept himself in touch with the progress of gaming as a sleeping partner in one of the more fashionable of the hells of St. James's. It was shortly before 1827 that he conceived the idea of gathering the cream of the playing public under one roof, and Crockford's Club, built at a cost of £94,000, was the result.

There is one thing, and one only, to be said in favour of Mr. Crockford's enterprise, which is, that this establishment did away with the practice of gentlemen playing against each other for large sums. At Crockford's the game was one of Gentlemen *versus* Players, the players being always Mr. Crockford's officials at the French hazard table, and the sole object of his business was to win the money of his patrons. He had no other sources of profit; his establishment was an exclusive club with a very low subscription, and was open to such gentlemen only as could convince the committee of their eligibility. For their subscription, which was so small that members who did not gamble were accustomed to make a sort of offering of conscience money, by flinging a ten pound note on the play table at the end of the season, the best cookery and the finest wines in London were supplied to them gratis, and they had the companionship of the most fashionable male society of the day. Crockford was wise enough to leave all the social arrangements to a committee of gentlemen who conducted the ballots, elected and rejected whom they chose, and made entry to Crockford's as difficult as to

White's or Brooks's. The new club, in fact, at once took a tone similar to that of those aristocratic bodies, whose members were made eligible for election to Crockford's by one of its first rules. In exchange for the princely accommodation of his house, and such fare as was unobtainable at any other club in London for love or money, Crockford asked for nothing in return but that gentlemen should condescend to take a cast at his table at French hazard.

French hazard was a variety of the old game in which a good many of the fairly equal chances between caster and setter were rearranged in favour of the setter, the setter at Crockford's being Mr. Crockford himself as represented by his croupiers. The nicks of the old English hazard, for example, were restricted in favour of the setter, there was a fee called " box money " paid by every caster as he took the box, and there were other advantages in favour of the bank known, as at faro, as the " pull of the table." The working of the " pull of the table " was very well explained by one of Crockford's victims before the Royal Commission of 1844, whose report resulted in the present Gaming Acts. That gentleman declared that the " pull of the table " absorbed a hundred pounds in a little over two hours from any player who took the box regularly as it came to him, and that quite independently of any win or loss on the cast itself.

The men who walked into Crockford's with their eyes open to encounter these odds were the pick of the society of the day, the men who had fought the battles of the country under Wellington, and men who were making great reputations at Westminster, as well as mere butterflies like the Dandies who loafed through life at White's. They were most of them men of exceptional parts, and distinguished for shrewdness and ability in one walk of life or another, and yet in the short space of ten years, between the opening of the club in 1827 and the accession of her Majesty, their losses converted Mr. Crockford into a millionaire at least. There is absolutely no record of any considerable sum of money ever won at the place by a player. Mr. Thomas Duncombe, the eminent Radical reformer, once took away £1600 from the club, but the main result of his dealings with Crockford was a deficit of £132,000 in his affairs. Mr. Auriol, who was called "Crockford's Ugly Duckling," on account of the voracity with which he ate his suppers, had some fleeting luck in small sums, but there is no other mention of a single penny being taken away from his doors.

On the other hand, there is ample evidence that the gentlemen of England marched in a compact band through the fishmonger's establishment in St. James's Street, and left the greater part of their substance behind, and it is no exaggeration to say, as was remarked indeed at the time by men who partook of its pleasures, that Crockford's absorbed the entire ready money of a generation, and much of its landed estate.

Some of these losses are recorded in the memoirs of

the time, but only a very small proportion of the
whole, and they may be taken merely as an index of
what went on at the club.   The second Earl of Sefton
left £200,000 in Crockford's rooms during his life-
time, and his son the third Earl, who was also a noted
victim, honoured an acceptance of his father's after his
death in 1838 for another £40,000.   Sir Godfrey
Webster met Mr. George Payne on the steps of the
club and confessed to having just received a "facer."
The "facer" was the loss of £50,000 at a sitting.
Another Baronet lost £7000 at a cast, and £20,000
in the evening, of which the cast was but an incident.
Lord Rivers, Lord Chesterfield, Lord Anglesey, Lord
Combermere, Mr. Ball Hughes, Lord Granville, Count
D'Orsay, and a score of other well-known men of the
day, were all losers of enormous sums, and the smaller
victims were to be counted by hundreds.   All the
memoir writers of those times, from Croker to
Gronow, recorded the losses at Crockford's on almost
every page of their diaries, and yet wrote of the decay
of the famous club almost with tears.   "*O noctes
cœnæque deûm*," wrote Captain Gronow, moved by
the sight of the old club transformed into a restaurant
before the present Devonshire Club occupied the building.   "Alas poor Crockey's, shorn of its former
glory, has become a sort of refuge for the destitute,
a cheap dining-house.   How are the mighty fallen;
those who remember Crockford's in all its glory cast,
as they pass, a look of unavailing regret at its dingy
walls, with many a sigh to the memory of the pleasant

days they passed there, and the gay companions and noble gentlemen who have long since gone to their last home."

Nominally Crockford's was extinguished by the Gaming Act of 1845, but its glory had departed at least five years earlier. Mr. Crockford having won all the money about the town, began to make preparations for a retirement with his winnings; he began to exercise great care in cashing cheques, refused all credit for the counters with which play was conducted, and generally realised his securities. There is no doubt he anticipated the parliamentary interference with his profession which came later, and, with an astuteness which was quite typical of his whole career, withdrew from the concern before the crash came. Whatever his real position may have been with relation to the premises when the parliamentary commission began its labours, he managed to conceal them. He was dragged from his retirement to give evidence, but his examination was quite fruitless. He declared that he had made over his club to the committee of gentlemen who had always managed the social side of the undertaking, five years before, because his age prevented him from looking after the business as he ought. When asked as to the former transactions with his clients, he refused all information. It was not for a humble individual like himself, he said, to know anything about the private affairs of gentlemen of position. He continued dealings in turf matters at a smaller house in St. James's Street until he died, and there is a gruesome legend that his body was put into the chair he usually occupied in the window on the day of his death, which was also the day of a great race, so that there might be no repudiation of the vast liabilities which were depending upon the meeting.

High play in England, as we believe, burnt itself out in those orgies at Crockford's; there has certainly never since been a revival of anything like the doings at the fishmonger's. There were good reasons for the abandonment of the cult of the dice-box in high circles apart altogether from the legislative interference of 1845. The absorption of the ready money of an entire generation of the best families in England by an adventurer and by the Jews, who helped his victims to fulfil their obligations to him, was a very good excuse for a change in their taste in the matter of amusement. It happened also that one of the few great scandals connected with gaming in England occurred almost at the moment when Crockford was preparing to retire with the plunder. It is probable, indeed, that the great scandal at Graham's might of itself have killed the fashion; it is certain that it had as much to do with its decline as the disasters suffered by the pigeons at the hands of Mr. Crockford. Mr. Thackeray, who remembered those times, and who wrote of the incident at Graham's, was of that opinion.

At Graham's Club in St. James's Street a man of an old and honoured name was detected cheating at whist, and was denounced as a dishonest trickster in a newspaper, the *Satirist*.   He brought an action against his accusers, failed in it, went abroad, and died.   Such were the bare outlines of the tragedy, but the details of the trial disclosed ugly features in the circumstances which had much interest for thoughtful people, and undoubtedly tended to bring the whole institution of play for high stakes between gentlemen into great disrepute.

There were witnesses at that trial, some of them men of assured and even great position, who admitted that they had detected the accused in his cheating a hundred times before the exposure and yet had held their peace.   As the game was whist, and the same parties met and played regularly together, it is obvious that others must have shared in the proceeds of the accused man's infamy.   But his clubmates, who swore to having seen him repeatedly perform the trick known as *sauter la coupe*, that is, insure the turn up of a king or ace on his own deal, had apparently no scruples about sitting down with him in the same game, and presumably some of them were his partners on occasion.   At any rate, he had no difficulty in finding partners in a private club, and such partners were either partners of his guilt, or were themselves the victims of a guiltily suppressed knowledge which was common property among numbers of their clubmates.

The sordid details of the play at Graham's, as recorded in the account of that trial, are astonishing. One witness swore that he had seen the culprit *sauter la coupe* "fifty or a hundred times."   When asked why he did not at once denounce him, this gentleman replied that had he done so before the accused "had been blown upon," he, the witness, would have had no alternative between the window and the door. The circumstances were undoubtedly embarrassing, but this witness surely took no very exalted view of his duties as a gentleman when he refrained from speaking and continued to meet the accused at cards.

Other clubmates of that unhappy man, it appears, had long detected him in the act of marking cards with his thumbnail or by bending, in order to recognise aces or honours, and manipulate them to his own advantage. They had even collected many packs of cards so marked after he had left the table, caused them to be sealed up and attested, and several of such packs were duly produced in court. Another witness swore to having seen the culprit cheat by reversing the cut, so as to insure as a trump the card his own final shuffling had placed at the bottom of the pack. Another still described the hacking cough with which the accused was always seized as he took the cards cut by his adversary on the right, a cough which, he declared, so invariably produced a king as the trump that it was known in the club as ——'s king cough. And yet, as we say, all these men continued to play with this black sheep on terms of amity, and some of them, at least, must have shared in the profits of his backsliding, until a fourth-rate newspaper took up the charge which these bold spirits whispered about the town. The libel action failed, the man was ruined, and died broken-hearted, and Lord Alvanley made his epitaph : " Here lies —— waiting for the last trump." It was surely time that high play amongst gentlemen at clubs should cease.

Since those days of Crockford's and Graham's and the Gaming Act, high play has ceased to be any considerable part of the social life of London at clubs or elsewhere, and its occasional manifestations which will occur to the memory have been incidental only. The passion for the excitement of chance has found other channels for its gratification. We have our organised dealings in " differences " on the Stock Exchange, our starting-price merchants, and the columns of our sporting press. The wants of the " votaries of chance " of all classes are certainly amply provided for by one or the other of these institutions.

CHAPTER V

THE COCKPIT

NOT the least among the pleasures which a delighted London owed to the happy restoration of his Majesty King Charles the Second, was a revival of the very ancient and popular sport of cock-fighting. The sound of the word has already an antique ring for modern ears. It is only a faint echo to-day of another of those ancient diversions with which Englishmen amused themselves during centuries, the details of which are almost as strange to the average young man of these times as the manœuvres of *retiarius* and *secutor* in the arena, or the steps of the Pyrrhic dance. And yet cock-fighting, like bull and bear baiting, expired unregretted almost in our own times. The Statute-book will tell you that it was 5 & 6 William IV. cap. 59 that did the business and put an end to the joys of the cockpit both in town and country. The sport which had amused English monarchs since the days of the Plantagenets, and had enlisted their particular patronage and support, failed to commend itself to an age of Railways and Reform Bills. So, as we say, the Battle Royal, Long Main, Short Main, and Welch Main, were alike forbidden by the law, the profession of trainer or walker of fighting-cocks languished in the secluded villages of a score of English counties, and the whole cult of the cockpit was submerged in a moment, amidst the headshakings of a few reactionaries in knee breeches and blue coats, who saw great danger to the British spirit and the British nation in its decline. We seek here to revive its amenities for a short season, to peep into its headquarters at Westminster or Gray's Inn Lane, and to discover if possible its real place among the amusements of our cockney ancestors.

Antiquarians give the sport of the gamecock an imposing ancestry. There were a dozen or more essayists of the last century who, while expressing the opinion of a minority against its barbarities, were very curious about its origin, and illustrated their arguments with all manner of quaint researches. Chief among these was "the ingenious Mr. Pegge," who wrote a very imposing essay in *Archæologia* in the year 1776, in which he refutes many of the theories of his brother sages, and dates the first European cockfight in the days of Themistocles. That general, it seems, was leading the Athenian army against the Persians when he observed two cocks fighting. He stopped the march, called a halt and pointed out to his troops that the birds fought "not for the gods of their country, nor for the monuments of their ancestors, nor glory, nor freedom, nor for their children; but for the sake of victory, and that one may not yield to the other." There was probably a lady in the case, which, however, the general failed to mention. " From this topic," we are told, " he inspirited the Athenians, who beat the Persians, and a cock-fight to celebrate the event was an annual and even a religious fixture later in Athens." The young Athenians, however, began to see more fun than religion in the opposition of the two cocks, and converted the annual religious festival into a diversion of daily occurrence. Thus, according to the ingenious Mr. Pegge, began the tradition of the sport in Europe, which survived in this country until the other day, as it were.

We have little concern, however, with Mr. Pegge and his theories, or with the views of his opponents, who traced cock-fighting in England to a more direct contact with the East, which is admittedly its home. It is certain that the sport had taken root in England in very early days. Some contend that references by Cæsar to the fighting-cock point to its presence here in pre-Roman times; but the point is not of great interest to us one way or the other. It is more to our purpose that cock-fighting is recorded as the diversion of ingenuous schoolboys by Fitz-Stephen in the reign of Henry the Second; that it was prohibited by Edward the Third; that it was encouraged by Henry the Eighth, who built the first royal cockpit at Whitehall; that it was so much the vogue in high circles in the reign of Charles the First that Vandyck painted a picture of the court watching a match in the royal pit; that Oliver Cromwell quite naturally suppressed the diversion by an Act of 1654, and that, as we have said, all its ancient glories were revived by the joyful restoration of King Charles the Second. Modern England, as we contend, began with the days of that monarch, or soon after; we propose therefore to confine our survey of the sport to the days of his Majesty, and since.

"Being directed by sight of bills upon the walls," wrote Mr. Pepys, under date of December the 21st, 1663, "I did go to Shoe Lane to see a cock-fight at a new pit there, a sport I never was at in my life." We make no apology for giving a long quotation from that astonishing diary, because, as we shall see later, it is the best description of a cock-fight on record. "But, Lord," continues Mr. Pepys, "to see the strange variety of people—from Parliament man, by name Wildes, that was Deputy-Governor of the Tower when Robinson was Lord Mayor, to the poorest 'prentices, bakers, brewers, butchers, draymen, and what not—and all these fellows one with another in swearing, cursing and betting, and yet I would not but have seen it once. I soon had enough of it, it being strange to observe the nature of these poor creatures; how they will fight till they drop down dead upon the table and strike after they are ready to give up the ghost, not offering to run away when they are weary or wounded past doing further, whereas when a dunghill brood comes, he will, after a sharp stroke that pricks him, run off the stage, and then they wring off his neck without much more ado. Whereas the other they preserve, though their eyes be both out, for breed only of a true cock of the game. Sometimes a cock that has had ten to one against him will by chance give an unlucky blow, and will strike the other stark dead in a moment, that he never stirs more; but the common rule is that though a cock neither runs nor dies, yet if any man will bet £10 to a crown, and nobody take the bet, the game is given over, and not sooner.   One thing more, it is strange to see how people of this poor rank, that look as if they had not bread to put in their mouths, shall bet three or four pounds at one bet and lose it, and yet bet as much the next battle (so they call every match of two cocks), so that one of them will lose £10 or £20 at a meeting; thence having had enough of it."

Mr. Pepys' powers of observation were never better displayed than in this account, which gives, as the result of a first visit, all the essentials of a public cock match—essentials which changed hardly at all until the law stepped in and extinguished the whole institution of cock-fighting in 1835. The squalor of the company, the unyielding bravery of the birds, the chance which might give the victory to either side in a moment, the fascination of the conditions of the sport for gamesters who wanted to risk and win money, the intricacies of the rules for " pounding a cock," the general brutality and love of blood which distinguished the votaries of the sport—all these aspects of cock-fighting, which appear with such astonishing clearness in Mr. Pepys' account of his

single visit to the cockpit—remained as features of
the diversion for the next century and a half, and are
corroborated by a score of treatises and criticisms
ranging over the whole of that period.

There has been a great deal of learned speculation
among London topographers as to the exact spots in
the town which were devoted at different times to the
practice of cock-fighting. They are all agreed that the
first known cockpit in London was the Royal Cockpit,
built, as Stowe records, by Henry the Eighth, " out
of certain old tenements " in Whitehall. The Royal
Cockpit continued as the battle-ground of the royal
cocks until Cromwell laid his hands upon the court
of Charles the First and its diversions ; its site became
a royal theatre in the days of the Restoration, and is
believed to be occupied by a part of the offices of the
Board of Trade to-day. Until quite well on in the
present century the cockpit gave a name to a room of
the Privy Council, where ministers discussed the Royal
Speech with their parliamentary followers on the eve
of the opening of each session. There was another
famous cockpit, vaguely located as " at the back of
Gray's Inn Walk," which an apparently well-informed
contributor to *Notes and Queries* describes as the cockpit of London during the Restoration. Mains were
fought here so late as 1752 ; and there is a very
intelligent account of the building by Von Uffenbach,
the German traveller, in 1709–10 : " There is a house
specially built for it (cock-fighting) near Gray's Inn.
The house is round like a tower, and inside just like a

COCK-FIGHTING

DRAWN BY H. ALKEN

theatrum anatomicum, with the benches rising above each other all round, on which the spectators sit." Then his Majesty, feeling the want of a pit nearer the palace, built the famous Royal Cockpit in Birdcage Walk, at the junction of Queen Square with Park Street at the top of Dartmouth Street, where all the chief matches were fought until the year 1816, when Christ's Hospital, the owners of the ground on which it stood, piously refused to renew the lease. The savour of the cockpit still lingers in the name Cockpit Steps in that neighbourhood. Driven thus from their classic haunt in Birdcage Walk, the disconsolate cockers subscribed among themselves, and built another theatre in Tufton Street, where their entertainments flourished until 1828. This building may still, or could a year or so ago, be inspected in the St. John's Institute of Tufton Street. The last resting-place of the cock-fighters in London was the " New Cockpit Royal," in Little Grosvenor Street, Westminster, and there it remained until destiny in the shape of 5 & 6 William IV. cap. 59 levelled the blow which knocked cock-fighting out of the sporting life of this country.

Such were the official quarters of the sport of cock-fighting in London for nearly two centuries, but there were many other public cockpits. The short list we have enumerated leaves out the establishment in Shoe Lane visited by Mr. Pepys. It omits also another place in Aldersgate Street devoted to the sport, which Samuel heard mentioned in a criminal case at the Sessions House. Another cockpit of the Restoration was that " by the King's Gate in Holborn," where, in 1668, Pepys and Creed "went to the new cocke pit, and there saw the manner of it and the mixed rabble of the people." The present Drury Lane Theatre stands on the site of another house which, doubtless, derived its name of the Cockpit from an establishment for the accommodation of the cock-fighting gentry which occupied the site in yet earlier times. There were public cockpits in Jewin Lane, Bainbridge Street, Pickle Egg Walk, at New Vauxhall Gardens, at Old Gravel Lane near Blackfriars, and at St. George's in the East. These we know of from contemporary allusions; there were probably a score of others whose names have not survived. In any case, Londoners were reasonably provided with opportunities for the sport, of which, as we shall show, they availed themselves to the full.

Cock-fighting in England, in Tudor and Stuart times at least, was an affair mainly for country gentlemen; and the breeding and rearing of the different strains of cocks of the game, and their training and preparation for the pit, were among the solaces of the manor-house of those times. Roger Ascham wrote an essay on the sport; and Gervase Markham gave very particular directions about the " choyce, ordering, and dyeting of fighting-cocks for the battel," to use his own delightful words and spelling. But the public cock-fight of later times, such as Mr. Pepys describes, was usually a composite affair in which owners, or associations of owners, matched their cocks in public with an eye to the gate-money paid by spectators, which formed a very useful addition to the stakes. The old news-sheets are full of the advertisements of these entertainments. Here is one, dated 11th of February 1700, and relating to a match at the Royal Cockpit, built some thirty years earlier by Charles the Second :—

"At the Royal Cockpit, on the South side of St. James's Park, on Tuesday, the 11th of this instant February, will begin a very great cock match, and will continue all the week, wherein most of the considerablest cockers of England are concerned. There will be a battle down upon the pit every day precisely at 3 o'clock, in order to have done by daylight. Monday the 9th instant March will begin a great match of cock-fighting between the gentlemen of the city of Westminster and the gentlemen of the city of London, for six guineas a battle and one hundred guineas the odd battle, and the match continues all the week in Red Lion Fields."

In the following April, too, there was an announcement of another match for a week, "at four guineas a battle and forty guineas the odd battle," between the gentlemen of London and those of Warwickshire, at the "new cockpit behind Gray's Inn Walks." By the time Queen Anne was on the throne, indeed, the sport was one of the recognised public amusements of the town, much noticed by foreigners, and rather proudly regarded by the natives as a peculiarly British institution. Herr Von Uffenbach, already quoted, speaks of cock-fighting in 1710 as the "particular delight of the English, however barbarous it may appear to strangers;" while Mr. Thomas Sherlock, an English gentleman, writing to a friend in Paris about the same time, implored him to come over to England, if only to see a cock-fight and a parliamentary election, "there is such a celestial spirit of anarchy in those two scenes," he says, "that words cannot paint."

Although the sport in England is now as dead as Queen Anne herself, there is very little difficulty in reviving its details and in forming a very definite idea of the attractions which drew crowds of its patrons to one or other of the cockpits we have mentioned. Besides old writers like Ascham and Markham, there were a whole set of professors and lovers of the "Royal Recreation and Art of Cocking," as they termed it, whose works initiate us into its deepest mysteries. We may learn from such treatises as that of Mr. William Machrie with that very title, which issued from Edinburgh in 1705, or the "Compleat Gamester" of Mr. Richard Seymour of thirty years later, enough to enable us to train cocks and arrange a main to-day, if haply the breed of cocks of the game still survive, and the police would leave us unmolested.

You chose a cock, for instance, as we learn from Mr. Seymour, "for shape, colour, courage, and sharp heel. First, for his shape, you must not choose him neither too large nor too small; wherefore the middle-sized cock is the proper choice for your purpose. His colour ought to be either grey, yellow, or red with a black breast. . . . You may tell his courage by his proud, upright standing and stately tread in walking; and if he croweth very frequently in the pen, it is a courageous demonstration." Lastly, you may know the sharpness of his heel "when, upon every rising, he so hits that he extracts blood from his opponent, gilding his spurs continually, and every blow threatening immediate death to his adversary."

You may learn, as we say, from such books as these the infinite pains and care taken by the cockmasters to prepare their birds for the contest. There was never a moment, from the egg to the final gasp in the cockpit, that these brave birds were without the watchful care of their breeders and trainers. The sires and dams were selected with the greatest care— a care which sometimes included the robbery of a clutch of eggs from the roost of some famous strain of birds; for there was no false modesty in matters of this sort among amateurs in those days. "Fair water," a quiet neighbourhood, and a restricted harem were all conditions of the ideal *menage* which went to produce the best specimens of the cock of the game. "Walks at windmills, watermills, grange houses, lodges in parks and coney warrens," are consequently "very good walks," as we learn, "but that the latter is somewhat dangerous, being frequently haunted by polecats and other vermin."

As soon as the chickens were hatched, all signs were carefully watched which might determine the future character of the bird. Even if the young hen chickens showed any symptoms of a lack of spirit, they were destined for the pot almost from the shell. For the cockerel, there were grave portents in such apparent trifles as the manner of his crowing, as it would seem. If he crowed before he was six months old, or his crowing was "loud, clear, or unseasonable," he exhibited "infallible signs of cowardice and falsehood," and he was thenceforth dedicated to the spit. "On the contrary, the true and perfect cock is long before he obtains his voice; and when he hath got it, observes his hours with the best judgment." They fed him with strange foods as he increased in stature, provided him with cooling medicines, and watched him through his first year or "staghood," until his second August came round, and he was fit at any time between that month and the following May to be prepared for the arena.

Before appearing in the pit, the cock of the game was put through a course of training which would be the making of a modern athlete. It took six weeks to bring him to his prime. For the first four days of that period he was fed "with the crumb of old manchet cut into square bits, at sun-rising, when the sun is in his meridian, and at sun-setting; and let his water be from the coldest spring you can get it." After four days' feeding on this fare he was set to spar with another cock. For a sparring match they covered "the cocks' heels with a pair of hots made of bombasted leather," that is, they improvised a sort of boxing-gloves for these interesting birds. In these they sparred until you saw them "pant and grow weary." You then took your cocks up, and gave them "a diaphoretic or sweating," in which process, apparently, you buried them in a deep basket of straw, after a dose of sugar-candy, chopped rosemary, and fresh butter. Towards the evening you took them out of their "stoves," and "licked their eyes and head with your tongue;" for what reason does not appear from Mr. Seymour's treatise; but we may hope that both trainer and trained enjoyed the process.

Such were the opening days of the period of training of a cock of the game. His main diet afterwards consisted of a sort of biscuit, compounded of wheat and oat flour, ale, the white of egg, and butter. Upon this generous diet the cock was encouraged to take reasonable exercise by a device which, with his sparring, foreshadowed the later glories of the cockpit. His trainer took a dunghill cock into his arms, and showed it to the cock of the game, ran away, and by "permitting him to have now and then a blow," enticed him to follow. If he continued this exercise "in a fair, green close" for about half-an-hour, the cock of the game would begin to pant, which was a sign for you to pick him up, carry him to his pen, and give him "herb of the grace, hyssop, rosemary, and butter." Such a course of training—the run round the green close after the dunghill cock, alternating with sparring matches with his own kind at intervals of a day—consumed the first month; the last fortnight was a time of less strenuous exercise for the cock. He was not allowed to spar for fear of leaving his head sore; but moderate chasings in the field were still recommended until the last four days of all before the battle, which were passed in dignified ease and seclusion. He was, at the end of those four days of rest, trimmed for the fight. All feathers on the crown of the head were snipped off close with scissors, his hackles or neck feathers were moderately shortened, his rump trimmed close, and his tail cut into the shape of a short fan by the shortening of the typical curved tail feathers of the cock. Lastly, his pinions were trimmed feather by feather, each quill being cut at a slant in order that in rising a lucky stroke might take out the eye of his adversary. Finally, his legs were furnished with the deadly " gaffles " or spurs. These, some two inches in length, and curved like a surgeon's needle, were either of steel or of a silver alloy, as the nature of the battle determined. For a contest for any small stake below five pounds, the steel spur was used. For battles for stakes of five pounds and upwards, the silver spurs were prescribed by the rules, that metal being reckoned less deadly, and the fight for the larger stake being thereby fittingly prolonged.

It will be gathered from these particulars of the breeding, rearing, and training of the gamecock that cock-fighting was no poor man's amusement, and that the only chance the poor man got of assisting was in the capacity of spectator. The rearing and training of the cocks necessary to supply a main lasting a week at the Royal Cockpit, such as that which attracted "the most considerablest cockers in England" in 1700, was an expensive affair, when it is remembered that each bird was two years old and had been through all the details of rearing and training by a professional trainer or feeder such as we have described. The expert knowledge of the feeder was also very necessary for the proper handling of the birds in the pit itself, where the accidental infringement of one of the rules of the sport might give away the match from the best bird in England.

It was after such care and preparations as these in the case of the scores of individual cocks on each side which went to make up a grand match or "main," that the lovers of the sport forgathered for such a week's contest at Whitehall or Westminster or Gray's Inn Lane, according to the period in which the gathering took place. The company was headed either by the two wealthy patrons, each of whom provided a small regiment of devoted roosters, or by what we may term a small syndicate on each side, who united the produce of their several cock-walks for the grand encounter. The proceedings of a grand main of cocks were always preceded by a very important function, that of weighing and matching the combatants in pairs. A meeting for this purpose was arranged between the parties on a day which might precede that of the battle by a few days or weeks, as might be agreed, and its date was determined by such consideration as the distances at which the parties lived from each other or from the place of battle in London. The date of the meeting for weighing was solemnly fixed in the articles of the match, a document drawn up in proper legal form, which regulated the stakes and other conditions of the encounter, and was properly executed under the hands of each of the parties. It was, however, an understood thing that the birds once matched could be dealt with in any way afterwards, and where a reasonable period was allowed to intervene between the day of weighing and that of the battle, there was much manœuvring between the parties, who strove to get the better of each other in point of weight and condition. If, as we say, the dates fixed by the articles allowed of such devices, a cock was trained very fine and light for the weighing, and was afterwards fed on a more generous scale with the hope of adding weight which might assist him against his adversary without diminishing his activity. The training of cocks, indeed, and their preparation for the pit was every bit as scientific and as carefully studied as the elaborate attentions bestowed upon the heroes of the prize-ring, like Mendoza, or Humphrys, or Jackson.

The favourite cocks for a match at the Royal Cockpit or other important meeting were those of a middle weight. The exact range of these weights was fixed by the articles, which always provided a maximum and minimum. These weights were usually between 3 lb. 8 oz. and 4 lb. 10 oz., as we learn from a curious copy of such articles given at length in an old encyclopædia published when the "fancy" was at its zenith.[1] The competitors were allowed a single ounce of give and take, but it was quite usual, as we are told, for cocks to be matched at the weighing within a drachm of each other. If there were birds in either collection which exceeded the maximum weight, they were rejected from participation in the main, but might be matched privately against each other by their owners as each saw fit, and without reference to

[1] "Articles of Agreement made the . . . day of . . . Between . . . and . . . First, the said parties have agreed that each of them shall produce, show, and weigh at the . . . on the day of . . . beginning at the hour of . . . in the morning . . . cocks, none to be less than 3 lb. 8 oz. nor more than 4 lb. 10 oz., and as many of each party's cocks that come within one ounce of each other shall fight for £ . . . a battle, that is, £ . . . each cock in as equal divisions as the battles can be divided into six pits or days' play at the cockpit before mentioned. And the party's cocks that win the greatest number of battles matched out of the number before specified shall be entitled to the sum of £ . . . odd battle-money, and the sum to be staked in the hands of Mr. . . . before any cocks are pitted by the parties. And we further agree to produce, show, and weigh on the said weighing days . . . cocks for bye-battles subject to the same weights as the cocks that fight in the main, and these to be added to the number of cocks unmatched, and as many of them as come within an ounce of each other shall fight for £ . . . a battle, the number of cocks so matched to be as equally divided as will permit of, and added to each day's play with the main cocks. And it is also agreed that the balance of the battle-money shall be paid at the end of each day's play. It is also further agreed for the cocks to fight in silver spurs and with fair hackles, and to be subject to all the usual rules of cock-fighting as practised at the Cockpit Royal, Westminster, and the profits arising from the spectators to be equally divided between both parties after all charges are paid that usually happen on these occasions. Witness our hands this . . . day of . . . &c."—From *Ree's Encyclopædia*, 1819, Art. "Cock."

exact weights. Such cocks were called "shake-bags," a term of which it is difficult to guess the origin, unless it may have conveyed a suggestion of a remainder cock left in the bag after all the others had been matched. The term "main," too, suggests an engagement of less importance. This was the "bye-battle." The bye-battle was a sort of *divertissement* apart from the main, which was useful in filling up the hours of the meeting, and in providing opportunities for gaming for small operators, distinct from the great issues of the main. Bye-battles were arranged between favourite cocks under the rules and weights of the articles of agreement, and also between "shake-bags," upon such terms as commended themselves to their owners. Stakes laid upon bye-battles were not confused with those depending upon the battles of the main, and their results were, of course, not reckoned among the points of the great encounter.

The mains were of three orders or dimensions. The ordinary great meeting between cities or counties —the Gentlemen of London and the Gentlemen of Warwickshire, for example—was the Long Main. This, with its satellite bye-battles, aimed, as we have said, at providing continuous entertainment for a whole week, and we can understand that it was scarcely worth the while of the gentlemen of the provinces to make the long and expensive journey by coach or post of those days for an entertainment of less duration. The Long Main lasting a week, therefore, is what we must understand by a "main of cocks" fought at any considerable theatre in the London of Anne and the first two Georges at least.

Wherever the elements of the great contest of the Long Main were wanting, the wealth of the great owners or syndicates, or their royal leisure, the Short Main had a great vogue. The Short Main was subject to the same laws and regulations as the Long Main, but it was confined to a couple of days at the outside, and was often arranged for a few hours of a single afternoon. The Short Main was consequently much affected by amateurs of a sane ambition only; it was upon the Short Main, too, that the whole cult of the cockpit declined in the degenerate days following the Act of 1835, when its votaries were hunted from county to county by the police.

The third dimension of mains was that astonishing arrangement known as the "Welch" variety. We are told that a Welch Main was "generally fought for a purse, a gold cup, a fat hog, or some other prize." But any of those treasures seems but a poor reward for the conqueror in the Welch Main. To arrange a Welch Main in orthodox form, you and your brother amateurs collected thirty-two fighting-cocks. These were arranged in sixteen pairs, and each couple fought to the death. The winners, or such as survived, were again matched in pairs, and the battle renewed. The eight winners of this second contest provided four pairs for the third; the survivors of the third contest made a couple of pairs for the penultimate combat; and the final issue of the Welch Main lay between this pair of devoted fowl, from which the much-enduring winner of the whole contest emerged. From these particulars it will be seen that the brutalities of the sport were displayed in their most repulsive form in the Welch Main. Its opportunities for betting were no greater certainly than in the Long Main and its bye-battles; but it had great attractions for the choice spirits of the cockpit; and it was a matter of pride to the true connoisseurs of the sport that the Welch Main was practised nowhere outside of these fortunate islands.

There remains also to mention the Battle Royal, which was another variation of the sport of true British pedigree. "The Battle Royal consists in any number of fowls being put down together in the pit, and the last surviving fowl gains the prize." The Battle Royal must have been a mere saturnalia of bloodshed without any of the technical qualities which the connoisseur found in the Long and Short Mains. There could have been no betting, except perhaps in the mild form of a sweepstake, in such a pandemonium; but the spectacle of a score of cocks, fighting promiscuously together, was no doubt a very grateful spectacle for the true lovers of the fancy.

For all purpose of our inquiry, however, we may reject the Welch Main and the Battle Royal, and think only of the Long and Short Mains. The two owners of the competing cocks, or the representatives of the many individuals whose contributions of cocks went to make up the numbers required to keep a Long Main going, sat on opposite sides of the pit, and were called "masters of the match." Inside the pit itself were two other officials, known as "feeders or setters-to." The duties of these last were very important, and a failure in them was likely to lead to the loss by their principals of the particular battle in which it occurred. They first of all put the two birds beak to beak, and subsequently each rendered to his own bird such aid as was permitted by the rules of the cockpit. This was limited strictly to releasing the birds from any entanglement of their spurs, either with each other, or in the matting which always covered the pit, to pushing a wounded bird upon its legs again, but by no means lifting him, and to replacing both combatants in the centre of the pit when the heat of the fray had driven them to its edges. There was another official known as the "Teller of the Law," whose duties will presently appear.

It was a rule of the main that the lightest cocks should be fought first in the match, the next heavy in turn, and so on in order of their several weights until the last pair of the main was reached. The official stakes were so much on each battle between each pair of cocks, and a further large sum on the "odd battle" or issue of the whole series. The first sum ranged from two to ten pounds in ordinary cases, the latter was often of very large amount. An ordinary main at the cockpit at Westminster would be for £10 the battle and £500 the main, but famous meetings, both in London and the provinces, produced much larger stakes than these. There was a main fought at Lincoln, for instance, about the year 1820, in which £1000 was laid on each battle and £5000 on the main. The main in this case was a short one of seven battles only, but as one set of cocks carried off five events out of the seven, £8000 went to the fortunate owners in stakes alone, besides the bets, which were always a great feature of a cock-match. Mains of £100 the battle and £1000 the main were not uncommon, and it is beyond question that the "Royal Pastime" was in its time responsible for the shifting of a vast deal of personal property.

The main, as we say, began by the first pair of cocks being confronted by the setters-to, the birds being allowed to take a preliminary peck at each other while still in the feeder's hands. They immediately took the attitude of beak to beak which one sees in every poultry yard, and fenced for an opening. Enthusiasts have declared that there were all the intricacies of boxing in the real feinting and parrying which took place between two well-trained and experienced cocks. Then followed the real joining of battle, the "buckle to," as it was called. With two well-bred and well-matched cocks, as we learn from eye-witnesses of the latest of these encounters, there was little to be seen but a whirring mass of wings and feathers. There were sounds of blows with the gaffles, mere flipping apparently, which sometimes made the feathers fly, but which meant wounds and death to the brave cocks of the game.

The determination shown by the finest cocks was astonishing. It is no exaggeration to say that the best cocks of the game would show fight as long as a spark of life remained in their devoted bodies. They might be maimed and even blinded, but when confronted by their enemy they would concentrate what little vitality was left to them in the menacing ruffling of their hackles and an expiring peck. This was so well understood that a blinded cock was never declared beaten until his beak was rubbed against that of his adversary. The old writers are eloquent about the valour of the gamecock. Listen to the Reverend Mr. George Wilson, who published a pamphlet in black letter entitled "Commendation of Cockes and Cocke-fighting" in 1607 :—

"There was a cocke about Shrovetide last which in the cockepit in the citie of Norwich fought with a stronge and stout adversarie until such time as both his eyes were beaten out, his head sore wounded and shrewdly battered, and all his bodie most pitifully bruised, and then with a sudden astonishment of a sound blow which from his cruell adversarie he received, being beaten downe and lying for dead, not stirring any whit nor seeming otherwise (to the beholders) than to be starke dead, he suddenly started up contrary to all their expectations (when there was offered twenty shillings, yea twenty pounds, to be layd to one that there was no breath remayning in his bodye), and closed with his adversarie, at whom he stroke most violent blowes, and never gave over untill (to the amazement of the spectators) he had most valiantly slaine him."

" Oh strange action, oh stout heart, and undaunted

minde," continues the Reverend George, rising with his subject, and looking down with a fine scorn upon those who preferred hawking to cocking, "you that make so much account of a squeaking Castrell or a scurvie Hobbie as you do of a good hawk, you who think every dunghill craven to be as good as a cocke of the game, tell me (I say), did you ever see any of your base-bred cockes shewe such courage, or doe such an admirable action ?   Surely never ! "

We return from this flight with Mr. Wilson to the sober prose of the pit, where it was not always that such phœnixes as he commemorates in the lofty diction we have quoted were to be found. The fowls, though seldom wanting in courage, were at times not wanting in discretion, and were accustomed to withdraw after a round or two to recover breath and look for an opening which should take the enemy at a disadvantage. This was an incident of the game, natural and even pretty in itself, which, however, was only allowed within limits. Too long an indulgence in this ogling process by the many roosters engaged in a six days' main had obvious inconveniences for a party of squires who had come up to Westminster from York, say, or Cheshire. So the aid of the Teller of the Law was called in upon such occasions. As soon as one or both of the cocks refused to confront each other, that functionary "told the law," that is, he counted twenty twice over in a clear and deliberate tone. At the end of this recital the birds were seized by the feeders and again placed beak to beak. If they then fought it out and one was killed, everything went well and without further hitch.   If, on the other hand, they again took to ogling each other, the Teller of the Law counted ten only, and they were again placed beak to beak.   Sooner or later one of the poor brutes would show himself inferior in stamina or courage to the other, and fail to stand up against his adversary, when the law was again invoked.   Twice twenty were told by the teller, then ten, ten times over, if the bird still refused to fight.   At the end of each ten the words " once refused, twice refused," &c., were solemnly repeated, and if there was no response by the defaulter before the counting of the last ten the battle was delivered to his adversary.   Such were the mysteries of the Long Law, as the process was called.

When a cock was obviously beaten the telling of the Long Law was apt to bore patrons of the sport who were anxious to set their stakes on a fresh battle. It was then open to any of these gentry to invoke the aid of the "Short Law" by a process which was known as " pounding the cock," that is, of laying the odds of forty to one in crowns against him.   This was always done by throwing a hat or glove into the pit as a sign of offering the £10 to five shillings and the claiming of the Short Law.   The Short Law was the counting of twice twenty only, and then repeating in a loud and distinct voice three times, " Will any one take it."   If no one took the offer, the cock against which the odds were laid was declared beaten.   There was, however,

always some risk in the process of pounding, because
the most valiant of birds might be all the time dying
of a wound, and by toppling over before the finish of
the telling of the law, leave the victory to the apparently
beaten bird.   Then again, the odds being so tempting,
the mere possessor of a crown might take your bet and
trust to the chapter of accidents.   This was often done ;
good judges of cock flesh could distinguish between
want of breath and want of courage, and make a good
investment by accepting the pounding.   On such occasions the apparently moribund rooster, like the one
in the leading case cited by the Reverend George
Wilson, would often rise from his bier and present
the ten pounds to the discerning sportsman who had
shown confidence in him.

There was surely no lack of interest in a main of
cocks, and as all bets were paid upon the conclusion of
each battle, it is not surprising to learn, as Mr. Sherlock
declared in writing to his friend in Paris, that there
was a celestial spirit of anarchy about a cock match
which was lacking in most other forms of entertainment
except a general election.   Defoe writing in his " Journey through England," in 1724, says : " Cock-fighting
is the very model of the amphitheatre of the ancients.
I was at several of these matches, and I never saw a
cock run away.   There is a continued noise among the
spectators in laying wagers upon every blow each cock
gives.   I believe abundance of people get money by
taking and laying the odds on each stroke, and find
their account at the end of the battle, but these are

people that most nicely understand it. If an Italian or German saw the arrangement, and by any chance came into one of these cockpits, he would certainly conclude the assembly to be all mad by their continued outcries of ' six to four.' "

The excellent Mr. William Machrie, "Fencing Master in Edinburgh," was good enough to recite a code of rules for the cockpit, which he thought might be found " reasonable and just with respect both to wagerers and the cocks," and he began his code with the admirable sentiment, " All swearing and opprobrious language is to be punished." We are afraid that admirable rule was often broken by the patrons of the Royal Pastime. Mr. Pepys and Mr. Defoe, as we have seen, were both eloquent upon certain aspects of the company at a cock-fight, which suggest the possibility of much strong language ; and they are strongly confirmed by most of the pictorial material which deals with cock-fighting from the days of Hogarth to those of Henry Alken. A consideration of some of the remaining rules of the code suggest a reasonable occasion for some difference of opinion, which may well have led to strong language, if nothing worse. Rule VIII. says : " All losses are to be paid presently after each battle, in good and current money." Nothing seems fairer, but the next rule provides much food for reflection, and hints at some possible confusion in the exciting surroundings of a cock-fight, which may well have led to profane swearing. " If any hath made a wager and cannot call to mind with whom he hath laid the same, and desire publicly that if the party with whom he laid the wager would give him the one half of the same, and the losing party do not confess the lay and give the one half upon his demand, it shall be lawful for any man to tell him with whom he hath laid, and the party to pay the whole because he did not confess it."

Was ever a rule better calculated to cause assault and battery than this? Then too, " He that takes up his cock or yields the battle when the cock is fighting, without consent of the bye wagerers, pays their loss." When one considers the effect of the execution of such edicts as these upon the class of audiences who flocked to the cockpits, he can well understand the shock Mr. Pepys' respectable feelings encountered in Shoe Lane.

We take Hogarth's famous plate of a cock match to be a representation of a very typical meeting of the patrons of the sport during the reign of George the Second. All classes of the community are represented ; the blind man in the centre of the plate is a portrait of a notable gamester of those days, Lord Albemarle Bertie, a son of the Duke of Ancaster ; there is another man of blood, evidently a portrait, on the right of the picture, with the star of a great order on his breast. At the other end of the social scale are the sweep taking snuff, and the mean blackguard who is filching the note from the blind Bertie, and several other of the figures round the table. The middle classes are represented by the man on the left sneezing at the snuff dropped by the superfine Frenchman, by the Quaker who is offering up a prayer near the sweep, and by the deaf gentleman on the left with the ear-trumpet. The figure in the right-hand corner of the print, with the gallows chalked on his shoulder, may present a back view of Jack Ketch himself, or the emblem may be taken as humorously prophetic of the wearer's latter end. There are six separate individuals who are attempting dealings with his lordship at one and the same time, a state of things we imagine to be quite typical of the process of getting a stake laid at a cock match; and the two jockeys in the foreground, who touch the handles of their whips, display the orthodox method of saying " Done" to a bargain among the gentlemen of the pigskin of those days. You may see, too, a foot of each of the setters-to on either side of the table. There is a shadow across the arena which speaks with much eloquence to the initiated. Part of it may be construed into a figure of a man holding out what may be recognised as the shadow of a watch and seals. It was the pleasant custom of the cockpit of the reign of George the Second to make an example of those who incurred liabilities which they could not discharge "in good and current money," by hoisting them up to the roof of the amphitheatre in a basket, which was kept handy for the purpose, and properly furnished with a rope and pulley. The victim of the shadow in Hogarth's print is offering his watch and seals to escape from his position of ignominy. We think this wonderful plate may be placed by the side of

Mr. Pepys' vivid description of his visit to Shoe Lane as one of the best presentments of the humours of the cockpit existing.

The same "celestial spirit of anarchy" animates the other classic representation of a cock match— that of the Royal Cockpit at Westminster, by Thomas Rowlandson, which appeared in the *Microcosm* of London some sixty years later. The excellent plates of that collection throw an amazing light upon the London of that day and its manners, with very little help, indeed, from the appallingly bald and padded prose which accompanies them. There is here the same mixture of dresses, the same clamorous betting, and the same rowdyism—"a collection of peers, pick-pockets, grooms, gentlemen, *bon vivants*, and bullies," as the scribe of the *Microcosm* puts it alliteratively but unconvincingly, are mixed up and cursing at each other, threatening each other with horsewhips, and punching each other on the head. There can be no doubt, we believe, about the general character of the companies which met to take their pleasure at the cockpit all over the town and country, if this state of things prevailed at the headquarters of the sport. Dramatic stories of the savagery of cockers as a class may still be read in the columns of the periodical literature of the days in which the institution flourished. A man who was losing called down im-precations from heaven upon himself and his bird. If the bird was killed, might he die also, he shouted, and the awe-struck contributor to the *Gentleman's*

Magazine records how the bird was killed, and how they carried out the impious gamester stark dead a moment later.

It may be that the roughness of the company at the ordinary cock match induced some of the more reputable votaries of the sport to take greater pains for the concealment of their identity than was usual in some others. It is quite certain that generous as the amount of information as to the details of cock-fighting which has come down to us from earlier generations, there has survived very little record of the *personnel* of the sport. The famous cock-masters of the Annes and Georges are unknown; such celebrities as King Henry the Eighth, King James the First, and Mr. Alexander Pope, are all vaguely mentioned as patrons of the cockpit; but who the men were who supported its traditions during the greater part of the last century it is now hard to say. We do not think it was ever in great favour among the fashionable men of St. James's; one reads nothing of it in Walpole or the Selwyn letters; there is only a single reference to cock-fighting in a whole century of wagers recorded in the betting-book at White's. In the latter half of the century a main of cocks was a regular attraction at all the well-known race meetings, and the results are all solemnly entered in the *Sporting Calendar* for each year: how the gentlemen of Northumberland met those of Durham in 1775, and fought a main, which ended in a draw; or how Cambridge beat Lincoln at Newmarket in the following year. The sport was accepted so seriously, that Mr. Hoyle, who wrote his famous treatise on Whist about the middle of the century, took the trouble to calculate the odds with the utmost nicety, as when he gravely quoted the betting as $1 \frac{3843421}{7821875}$ to 1 against a certain contingency.

But we imagine, as we have said, that very notable people kept out of the cockpit in London, except on rare occasions, until well on in the present century; and that the gentlemen of London or Westminster, who advertised their matches in the papers, were not very representative of their order. An account which Mr. Grantley Berkeley gives of a visit to the Royal Cockpit at Westminster, where he saw the Duke of Norfolk, very early in the present century, suggests that his Grace, who was not at all particular in his company as a rule, was not a regular frequenter of that institution. It suggests also some reason for the absence of gentlemen from such entertainments. Berkeley remembered the duke "in a blue silk coat and lace ruffles, with which he was accustomed to wipe out the pan of his gun when out shooting." Said the duke to a friend, "Well, I don't understand why they should offer those odds; if I betted, I should say two to one on the yellow." "Done with you," said a coster, who had overheard his Grace's remark, "I'll take it;" and he gave the duke a slap on the shoulder by way of concluding the bargain. The real vogue of the sport as an amusement of gentlemen came a little later, when the men of fashion became less superfine in bearing, and took a larger interest in sports of the field.

To return to such names as are recorded as the patrons of the sport, the first of the famous cockers seems to have been Colonel Mordaunt, who took his cocks to the East to match them against those of the potentates of Hindostan. The plate by Earlom, after the painting by Zoffany, depicting the battle between the colonel's birds and those of the King of Oude, in Lucknow, in 1786, is much admired by collectors of sporting prints, and sometimes changes hands at Sotheby's at comfortable prices. The colonel found the strains of cocks in India superior to his own, and on the whole met with very indifferent success. Another great light of the cockpit was Dr. Bellyse, of Anslem, who died in 1829. He bred from seven to eight hundred chickens yearly, mostly of the " White Pile " or " Cheshire Pile " varieties, and was one of the great supporters of the annual meetings at Chester, which were very famous. The sport had the distinguished support of the Earl of Derby of the first quarter of the present century, who protected and fostered the famous breed of the " Knowsleys, the cocks black-breasted, with red hackles, the hens partridge-coloured, and the legs of both white." Black-breasted Birchins, Duns, Piles, Cuckoos, Blotch-breasted Reds were other strains much prized by the knowing ones. The Earl of Sefton, the coaching earl of the Dighton Prints, and of the Reform Bill, was another great patron of the cock-fighting cult, and the families of Warburton, Wilbrahams, Egertons, and Cholmondeleys were all well known as eminent members of the fraternity, as were also Lord Mexborough, the Cottons and the Meynells, Admiral Rous, Lord Chesterfield, and General Peel.

There were also breeders and trainers of great renown in extensive business during the first thirty years of the present century, who were often looked up to by their clients much as are the great magnates of the training establishments for racehorses of to-day. Gilliver, a Staffordshire man, and Potter, who looked after Lord Derby's cocks, were famous names; Porter and Gunn were renowned in the art of setting-to and conducting the manipulations of the pit, and the appropriately-named Charles Faultless was unequalled in the nice operation of heeling the birds, that is, of attaching with waxed thread to the best advantage the murderous gaffles or spurs.

We have drawn almost all our information on the sport of cock-fighting from the writings of those who were its enthusiastic supporters, and have not concerned ourselves so far with the arguments or speculations of those who were opposed to its barbarities. There was, however, a continuous outcry against the sport, on the score of its cruelty, from very early times. The periodicals of the last century were not long together without some contribution which bewailed this aspect of the diversion, and its opponents often took strange ways of expressing their hostility in the public papers. Thus, in the *Gloucester Journal*

for 1756, some enemy thus addressed the local
"fancy" by advertisement :—

"This is to give notice to all lovers of cruelty and promoters
of misery, that at the George Inn, on Wednesday, in the Whitsun
week, will be provided for their diversion the savage sport of
cock-fighting, which cannot but give delight to every breast
divested of humanity, and for music, oaths and curses will not
fail to resound round the pit, so that this pastime must be greatly
approved by such as have no reverence for the Deity nor
benevolence for His creatures."

Mr. Pegge, too, of a quarter of a century later,
whom we quoted at the beginning of our inquiry, was
as convinced of the brutality of the sport as he was of
its antiquity, and was only one of a body of moralists
who inveighed against its practice for nearly a century,
an expression of public opinion which at last resulted
in the Act of 1835. This Act repealed another of three
years earlier, which had suppressed the sport within five
miles of Temple Bar, and in a set of merciful clauses
dealing with the sufferings of animals generally, extinguished cock-fighting throughout the country.

But in spite of this legislation cock-fighting did not
expire without a struggle. There was a great battle
at Elmore Farm, near London, presided over by the
Earl of Sefton, so late as 1850, and to evade the
police and bring a short main in a barn, or even
in a drawing-room, to a successful conclusion was a
favourite diversion with the sporting youth of this
country until quite recent times. There is an account
of such a meeting, which is naïvely humorous, in those

interesting but rambling memoirs of the Honourable Grantley Berkeley, showing how the Count de Salis, a magistrate, lent his premises near Cranford to Berkeley and his friends for the purpose, gave him the keys of the whole place, and then called in the police and hauled Berkeley before the Bench at Uxbridge. There was much fun excited by the non-appearance of the count, "the cock who would not fight," and Berkeley was fined five pounds. It is whispered that in even quite modern days a short main was a favourite diversion at two great English country houses at least, and later still a party of country gentlemen, including several magistrates, were within an ace of being caught by the police in the very act of cocking. That was about twenty-five years ago, but we hear little of such rumours to-day, and cock-fighting as a sport may be said to be extinct. We have fallen on evil days, and our sportsmen now watch foot-ball and cricket matches instead of sitting to see as many as a thousand cocks of the game slaughtered in a single week, as happened at a famous meeting at Newcastle one hundred and twenty years ago.

CHAPTER VI

THE PLAY AND THE OPERA

OLD Fynes Moryson, sketching in his sententious manner the characters of the nationalities he encountered in his famous itinerary, opined that "to pass over griefe the Italians sleepe, the Germans drinke, the Spaniards lament, the Irish howl, and the English go to playes." Moryson wrote of an age when the greatest of all playwrights was alive, and the English displayed a taste for the drama which took crowds of citizens to the Globe, to the primitive houses of Blackfriars, to the Fortune in Cripplegate, the Curtain in Shoreditch, and to half the inn yards in London. It is with that habit of haunting the playhouse, noticed so quaintly by the old writer, which the English have never since discarded, that we are concerned here. We wish to follow the audiences of former days into the playhouses which were from time to time opened for their patronage, and to take note of the humours of the different classes of playgoers in the different seats provided for their accommodation; from the King and Court in the Royal box to the humblest of his Majesty's subjects dropping orange peel or nutshells from the gallery into the pit. It is, as we

say, with that aspect of the theatre, of the good
people of all conditions taking their diversion at
the play, rather than with the actors and the lines
they recited at the footlights, that we are concerned
in this chapter, the last, indeed, a subject which has
already provided material for the able writers of many
volumes.

For all purposes of our inquiry, we date the modern
theatre from the days of the Restoration of his Majesty
King Charles the Second. It was only in that happy
reign that the persecution of the stage and of the
players at length became ineffective. The puritanical
opposition to everything connected with the drama,
which began perhaps with Archbishop Grindal, and
Gosson, the redoubtable parson of St. Botolph's, in the
reign of Elizabeth, and developed into the suppressions
of the Commonwealth, was now exchanged for the
patronage and protection of those in high places.
There has perhaps never been so good a friend to the
actor and to the theatrical interest generally as his
Majesty King Charles. The king, by granting a patent
to Mr. Tom Killigrew at the Cockpit in Drury Lane,
established that principle of monopoly in things dramatic which lasted till well on in the present reign. The
actors of Drury Lane were the king's servants and a
part of the royal household under the administration
of the Lord Chamberlain; a certain number of them
indeed wore his Majesty's uniform of red cloth and
silver lace, and ranked as Gentlemen of the Chamber.
The king's brother, the Duke of York, had his own

INTERIOR OF SADLER'S WELLS THEATRE

company at the Lincoln's Inn Theatre in Portugal Street, or at Sir Christopher Wren's house in Dorset Gardens under Davenant, with privileges scarcely less valuable, including a patent to which theatrical historians will trace back all the subsequent glories of the great house in Covent Garden. It was under his Majesty's auspices that women's parts were first played by women, and he was good enough, as we know, to honour the profession by forming very intimate alliances with some of those ladies. Lastly, there has never been a more assiduous playgoer than his Majesty King Charles himself.

We date our inquiries into the aspect of the theatres from the reign of King Charles, for another very sufficient reason. It was only when the invaluable diarists of that reign began to record their observations of the life of their times, that we get anything like a complete account of the interiors of the playhouses. It was Pepys and Evelyn who first enabled us to people the boxes and the pit with real figures, and performed for the seventeenth century what a host of contemporary writers have done for the theatrical matters of subsequent times. It is with the help of these diarists and the comments of the critical papers which came a little later, of the letter writers and memoir writers and essayists of a century and a half, that we seek to revive the aspect of the playhouse of former times, to consider the audiences which flocked to them, and to determine, it may be, from the attitude of those audiences, the place which the theatre has held among the amusements of succeeding generations of Londoners.

In turning our thoughts to the playhouses of the Restoration, it is important to forget a great part of the vast modern organisation of the stage, and, at first, to think only of a couple of small theatres occupied by the patent companies we have mentioned. These two companies, the King's and the Duke's, fortified by the patents accorded to Killigrew and Davenant, enjoyed what was practically a monopoly of purveying theatrical amusements to the town. The King's company occupied a building which arose on the site of the old cockpit in Drury Lane in the year 1663, and is the parent of the present building on the same site. The Duke's company filled a theatre extemporised by Davenant, in 1660, from a tennis-court in Portugal Street, on a site since absorbed by the museum of the Royal College of Surgeons. There were subsequent changes; the Duke's company, when Davenant died in 1671, and his lady with Betterton and Harris took over the management, went to a theatre built by Wren in Dorset Gardens, now Dorset Street and Salisbury Square, off Fleet Street. Dorset Gardens Theatre was a house of some architectural pretensions, with frontage on the Thames and an entrance for the convenience of audiences who came by water. So also, when the inevitable fire burnt out the King's company at Drury Lane in 1673, they occupied the vacated house in Portugal Street during the rebuilding of their own. Finally, the

King's and Duke's companies finding competition unprofitable, united their forces at Drury Lane in 1684, issued adventurers' shares and so established the venerable tradition of the renters at the patent theatre of old Drury. There were subsequent changes in which the relations between the two companies, or of certain of their members, were restored to their old conditions of competition at the two theatres. We shall find, therefore, that the interest of the play and its audiences whose amusement we seek to recall, are confined for a long period to a relatively small area.

It is quite easy, in thinking of theatrical entertainment in the light of our modern experience, to ignore many of the attractions which took people to the playhouse in those earlier days. The theatre of the Restoration was in reality much more of a social resort than the play or the opera as we know them. The pit of the playhouse of the Restoration was a social exchange, where the young man of condition displayed his graces and exchanged pleasantries with his fellows; where the man of wit discharged his carefully-prepared impromptus; and where the actors and actresses, not actually engaged on the stage, were accustomed to keep themselves in evidence by mixing freely and ostentatiously with the audience. The stage-door and the green-room, too, were attractions for a large class of men whose attentions to the actresses became a source of embarrassment to the management, but which was a remarkable feature of the theatrical life of the period upon which we have

very definite opinions of the managers themselves—
Colley Cibber and the rest. Finally, the patronage
which Charles the Second gave to both the theatres of
his time, and the nature of his relations with some of
his subjects who appeared with him in the royal box,
gave an interest to a visit to the play of those days
which is lacking in later and more sedate times.

There is scarcely any phase of the social life of
modern England which has received more minute
attention than that dealing with things theatrical;
and it is not difficult to revive the features of the
two London playhouses of the Restoration from the
labours of the historians of the stage. As a fact,
the theatre of those days differed little in essentials
from the theatre of to-day. The stalls of the fashionable houses of the West End have usurped the greater
part of the old pit; in other respects, those houses remain much as were their prototypes at Drury Lane, or
Lincoln's Inn, or Dorset Gardens, when King Charles,
in the box, nodded to Mr. Pepys by the side of a
pretty woman in the pit. The first tier, instead of
being partly open as to-day, was composed of boxes
continuously; the second tier contained many open
seats and a few boxes; the upper tier was the shilling
gallery as now, but without the refinement of the first
rows, railed off to make an "amphitheatre" at an
increased charge.

The stage ran out a distance of several feet beyond
the proscenium into the body of the theatre, and was
thus exposed on three of its sides to the spectators

who occupied the pit. The curtain, instead of rolling down as at present, worked in two halves on a rod thrown across the stage, behind the proscenium; and a great deal of the action of the play took place on this front portion of the stage which projected well into the house itself, to the great advantage both of actor and audience, as Mr. Colley Cibber, who lived to see this feature of the house altered, declared. It was at the front of this space, too, that those very epigrammatic prologues and epilogues of the period were spoken. Nelly Gwynn, say, as the distressful Valeria, would die to slow music; two walking gentlemen would advance to take away the corpse, Nell would break out with that surprising couplet—

"Hold, are you mad, you damned confounded dog,
    I am to rise, and speak the epilogue,"

trip to the front, and deliver Mr. Dryden's broad verses with a roguishness which in no way diminished their pronounced flavour. The other feature of the stage of the Restoration which distinguished it from that of to-day, was the mode of entrance for the actors. It was rarely, indeed, that the chief characters of a play came upon the stage from the wings. It was the curious custom of those days for Betterton or Kynaston, Mrs. Barry or Mrs. Bracegirdle, to enter and leave the stage through one of four doors, which were pierced through the proscenium, two on each side of the curtain, just where the stage-boxes came later, and gave access to the stage for the chief actors of the piece. We have to think, then, of the great part of the acting proceeding more amongst the audience than at present; the scenery and supers being more distinctly in the background, and the position in which the chief characters performed enabling them to make the most of the finest shades of play, both of voice and feature. Remove the modern footlights, and replace them by the light of moulded candles, hung from the flies and the proscenium, and you have the main outlines of the theatre of the Restoration.

The prices of the different parts of the house divided the audiences of those days into different social strata much as now, the main difference being between the pit of that day and this. The pit of the Restoration, though open at the same charge of half-a-crown, approximated more closely to the stalls of our own time in the rank of some of its patrons. A shilling took the apprentice to the gallery; a seat in a box on the second tier could be had for eighteen-pence; and in one of the lower boxes, in the best position on the first tier, for no more than four shillings. You could sit in the king's own box itself for that figure, if his Majesty were not present. Boxes were not let as units, as at present; and unless you took all the seats for yourselves and friends, you were always liable to have strangers sitting next to you; that, however, was an attraction in itself for the average playgoers of Charles the Second, when it went hard but his neighbour was some sprightly young woman in a vizard.

The actors and managers of those days, as of later, had different degrees of consideration for the different classes of their customers. Dryden's prologues and epilogues are full of complaisance for the "propitious angels" of the boxes, of derision and defiance for the occupants of the pit, the "nest of devils" with its free list of all the dramatic authors who had ever tempted fate and the managers with a manuscript of a play or a prologue ; its citizens who looked to have their money's worth ; and its smaller but dangerous band of beaux and men of quality, whose report of a play made or damned its success. "The Gods" were little considered by Killigrew and his successors ; the gallery, indeed, came to be the perquisite of the footmen of the people of quality who came early to keep their masters' places in the better portions of the house, a privilege which led to much trouble at a later period. Another curious feature of the management of the patent theatres of the early years of the reign of Charles the Second which points to its importance as a place of public meeting, was that regulation which allowed any one to walk into a playhouse without payment so long as he retired before the end of the act which was being played when he entered. It was thus common to see strangers walk into the pit, look round the house for a friend, and not finding him, go out without payment. The custom, however, led to such abuse, that the Lord Chamberlain abolished it after it had been in force some ten years or less.

There has probably never appeared in any age or language so minute account of the aspect of the theatre of a particular period as that contained in those entries of Mr. Samuel Pepys in that astonishing diary of the events of London between the years 1660 and 1670. We have little to do with Mr. Pepys' opinion of the acting or the plays. It may be that the " Midsummer Night's Dream," as he saw it presented, was " the most insipid, ridiculous play" that ever he saw in his life ; that " Othello" was "a mean thing," and that the " Tempest" had " no great wit"; that " Sir Martin Marall" was the greatest of all comedies, and that Thomas Betterton (as is quite likely) the greatest of all actors. Upon some or, indeed, all of these points Mr. Pepys' judgment may have been lacking, but no one has ever impeached his powers of observation, and it is certain that those who trouble to follow that quaint sinner in his pleasures may with little call on their imagination fancy themselves in the King's Playhouse at Drury Lane, the Duke's at Dorset Garden or Lincoln's Inn, or the Cockpit within the precincts of the court at Whitehall. There was little that escaped Samuel in any part of the house—he had an eye for the king sitting in the midst of a galaxy of beauty in the boxes ; for the citizens in the pit as well as for the actors on the stage ; and he knew as much about the toilette of Nell Gwynn as King Charles himself.

Among all the pleasures of the theatre of those days, one of the choicest for Samuel and for the ordinary citizen was certainly that of sharing the diversions of the place with his Majesty; there were all sorts of interesting details of life at court to be gathered by the plain man for the modest expenditure of half-a-crown for his seat in the pit. The waxing and waning of the beauty and influence of one lady of singed reputation; the appearance of another; the insolence of the newcomer at the height of her fortune; the boredom of the easy-going king at the familiarity of Palmer or Moll Davis; the indignation of the poor queen from Portugal at her surroundings, and many other particulars of the same sort were visible from time to time at Drury Lane or Dorset Gardens or the Cockpit at Whitehall, and insured a good return for his money for the ordinary playgoer.

Pepys could "never enough admire" the beauty of Madam Palmer, he "filled his eyes with her," "gazed upon her with much pleasure," felt troubled "to see her look dejectedly and slighted by people," protested that her beauty was in no way injured "by her late sicknesse." He saw Palmer almost on her first appearance ("with whom the king do discover a great deal of familiarity"); he noted her melancholy lack of smiles when Moll Davis was supposed to be in the ascendant, and he had a very shrewd foreboding of the effect of that ascendency when it was a patent fact. Was there ever a more suggestive commentary on that curious royal menage at Whitehall than that account of Mr.

Pepys of the aspect of the Duke's Playhouse in the afternoon of December the 21st, 1668? The Castlemaine had kept her footing for six years at least, but felt it slipping at last. "It vexed me to see Moll Davis in the box over the king's, and my Lady Castlemayne's head look down upon the king, and he up to her," says Mr. Pepys, "and so did my Lady Castlemayne once, to see who it was, but when she saw her she looked like fire, which troubled me." To use one of Samuel's own expressions, her ladyship's "nose was out of joynt" at Moll's exulting demeanour, so like her own, four years earlier, when she frisked into the king's box, seated herself at his Majesty's right hand, between his Majesty and the Duke of York, and "put the king himself as well as everybody else out of countenance." The Duke of York was more decorous in public, as a rule, than his Majesty, but the playgoer of 1663 could gaze upon his royal highness and his duchess at Whitehall "kissing and leaning upon one another," which Mr. Pepys considered "impertinent and unnatural dalliance," and the humours of the royal boxes at the play are surely very plain in his pages.

We can learn quite as much from him about other parts of the house. Samuel began his theatrical pleasures in the shilling gallery, as he was careful to record when he saw from the box of his more prosperous years, rather censoriously, the "abundance of 'prentices and mean people in the pit." ("So much the vanity of the age is to be observed in this parti-

cular," says Samuel on the occasion of his sixth visit
to Sir Martin Marall.) His experience in every tier
of the playhouses of his time makes him an authority
on the amenities of all. In the pit he sat by the
wits, was very careful to listen to Sedley's criticism of
another author's piece, to note Etheredge's curses of
the actors who were spoiling his own play, to listen to
Buckingham and Buckhurst and the beaux, whose report on the morrow was to make or mar the fortunes
of the comedy just presented for the first time. There
were no newspapers in those days, with columns open
to the professional critic, to advertise the success or
the ruin of the hopes of the dramatic author. The
production of the play was only communicated to the
public by a few broad sheets stuck on a post in the
town, and by its announcement from the stage at the
end of the previous performance. The pit then paid
its double price for a new piece, the wits flocked to
their corner near the stage, and their report after the
informal discussion at the end of the play, either in
the pit or in the actresses' dressing-rooms, decided
the fate of the piece.

It was a red-letter day for the playgoers of all ages
when women first came on the stage, and took the
place of those wonderful men actors, Kynaston and
the rest, whose presentment of female characters must
have been wonderfully efficient, if we may judge from
the enthusiastic reports which their performances inspired. Pepys first saw women on the stage in 1661 ;
it is said by historians of the drama that Mrs. Coleman,

who appeared at Rutland House five years earlier, was the first professional female actress. Many stories are told to account for this momentous change in the economy of the theatre. King Charles was kept waiting, it is said, and inquired the cause. "The queen is not yet shaved, your Majesty," was the reply, and its humour struck King Charles, we may be sure. No doubt the addition of a bevy of roguish actresses to the companies at the playhouses was as great an attraction to the king as it was to Mr. Pepys. Anyway, Killigrew and Davenant were both empowered to recruit their forces among the ladies, and we date one of the chief attractions of the stage from that happy reign.

There was much amusing incident among the audiences of those days, and we imagine that what the modern theatre had gained in decorum it has lost in interest. In place of the ice brought in during the intervals of the modern piece, oranges at sixpence each were purveyed by women of decided manners. Pepys is constantly recording money spent upon these delicacies for his womenkind at the play, " it costing me 8s. upon them in oranges," was a rueful entry in the diary. He had an unfortunate transaction, too, with one of these fruit merchants, when he had been round to see Mr. Harris behind the scenes, and " on returning the orange woman did come in the pit and challenge me for 12 oranges which she delivered to my order at a late play at night to give to some ladies in a box, which was wholly untrue." Samuel, however, paid up like a sensible man.

We gather that the pit seats consisted of mere rows of benches without backs, as in some theatres of to-day. "I was sitting behind in a dark place," says Mr. Pepys in a passage which gives vivid detail of the life of that time, "and a lady spit backward upon me by mistake, not seeing me, but after seeing her to be a very pretty lady I was not troubled at it at all." Pepys had ever a soft heart for a pretty face. He revelled in hearing a woman drown the voices of the actors by her laughter so long as she was comely, but was less tolerant of less fashionable neighbours. "Not so well pleased with the company at the house to-day," he records, "which was full of citizens;" "the house full of citizens, and so the less pleasant," is another entry. "Here a mighty crowd of citizens, 'prentices, and others, and it makes me observe that when first I began to bestow a play on myself, I do not remember that I saw so many by half of the ordinary 'prentices and mean people in the pit at 2s. 6d. apiece as now." It is quite easy to trace the growing popularity of the playhouse and Samuel's own growing importance in his pleasant pages.

But more often than not he was surrounded by the company he loved. He was delighted to sacrifice all his interest in the piece for the pleasure of the conversation of well-known people of fashion, even if only overheard. He was often by the side of Sedley, and drank in with delight the dramatic criticisms of that roystering spirit; "and he did at every line take notice of the dulness of the poet and badness of the action, and that most pertinently, which I was mightily taken with." We may hear, if we choose, Sir Charles's opinions on morals, as well as the dramatic unities, in his remarks recorded by Mr. Pepys, and wonder at the complaisance of the pit which preferred the witty reprobate's dissertations to the play they presumably went to hear. Pepys, assisted at another of Sir Charles's afternoons at the playhouse, and his account recalls the interesting custom, then prevalent among ladies of fashion, of appearing at the theatre in the vizard. The mask, which had been the usual wear of ladies out of doors in the reign of Elizabeth, was revived, after the Restoration, at the play. It was said that there was an excellent reason for the custom. The plays of Dryden or Mrs. Behn, or Sedley himself, were of a flavour, both in incident and language, that made it inadvisable for a modest woman to listen to them for the first time with a bare face. Whenever, therefore, a new piece was announced, which was at frequent intervals in those days, half the ladies in the house appeared in the black vizard, in order to take a taste of its quality without exposing their blushes. Pepys himself records the appearance of Lord Falconbridge " and his lady, my Lady Mary Crowwell, in the Duke's house in 1663;" "and when the house began to fill, she put on her vizard, and so kept it on all the play, which is of late become a great fashion among the ladies, which hides their whole face." The fashion spread downwards, and, it is to be feared, was used to cover frolics which were certainly not inspired by modesty; the mask, indeed, soon became the ensign of a lady of a defined position in society.

But here was Sedley to give Mr. Pepys an opportunity of preserving for our benefit a perfect reflection of one phase of life in the pit. "And one of the ladies," says Mr. Pepys, "would and did sit with her mask on all the play, and, being exceeding witty as ever I heard woman, did talk most pleasantly with him (Sedley), but was, I believe, a virtuous woman and of quality. He would fain know who she was, but she would not tell, yet she did give him many pleasant hints of her knowledge of him, and did give him leave to use all means to find out who she was; but pulling off her mask. . . . A more pleasant rencontre I never heard, and by that means lost the pleasure of the play wholly, to which, now and then, Sir Charles Sedley's exceptions against both words and pronouncings were very pretty."

There are other pictures of the playhouse within those pages which have surely never been surpassed. There is the house full of "parliament men, it being their holiday." A "gentleman of good habit" bought oranges from one of the women in the pit, was careless in his eating, "and did drop down as dead, being choked." Up runs "Orange Moll, and, with much ado, did thrust her fingers down his throat, and brought him to life again." We see the pit scattered by the summer "storm of hayle," which

drove through the cupola of the auditorium. Hart
is on the boards with a child in his arms, whose
mother is in the pit; the child cries, the mother
" by force " jumps upon the stage, and takes her
child away from the actor, and it pleases Mr. Pepys
" mightily to see the natural affection of the poor
woman." Lady Carnegie appears in a box " most
devilishly painted " ; Nell Gwynn in another has come
over from the Duke's theatre to see the play at
Drury Lane, " the jade Nell," as Mr. Pepys calls her
affectionately, the " bold merry slut who lay laughing there upon people." Mr. Beeston comes forward
to announce that a poor play, just acted to a half
empty house, will be repeated on the morrow; the
actor himself cannot keep his countenance, and the
pit breaks into a roar of derision. We see Mr.
Beeston on another day reading Mr. Kynaston's
part, that gentleman having been " exceedingly beaten
with sticks by two or three that assaulted him ; "
and we get an idea of how Sir Charles Sedley repaid
a jeer of the actor, or, as some say, a mere personal
resemblance heightened by a similarity of dress.
Sometimes, indeed, you might see a fracas on the
stage itself. In 1682, Mr. Charles Dering and Mr.
Vaughan had some little difference in the pit, drew,
and finding little room for their sword arms, rushed
up over the astonished fiddlers of the orchestra, and
fought at the front of the stage, " to the greater
comfort of the audience," as Dr. Doran quaintly
observes. It was a real fight, surely worth the half-

crown admission, for Mr. Dering got a thrust in the short ribs, and was carried out, bleeding, by the players; and Mr. Vaughan was marched off to Bridewell to await the issue of the encounter.

There are a score of these glimpses of the playhouse and its actors, and audiences and their humours, to be gathered from Mr. Pepys' masterpiece, now for the first time made accessible by Mr. Wheatley's splendid edition with its wondrous index. And the most interesting of them all is the portrait of that typical playgoer, Samuel himself, with his very soul laid bare for our inspection. He knows his weakness for the play, he enters solemn vows of abstinence with forfeits of a crown for the breach, and he records his falls more often than his resistance. " Hence much against my nature and will, yet such is the power of the devil over me, that I could not refuse it, to the theatre and saw ' The Merry Wives of Windsor' ill done." Quite early in 1661 he is "troubled to be seen by four of our office clerks which sat in the half-crown box, and I in the one and sixpence." He has a most engaging tone of superiority in reporting a remark of " an ordinary lady " in the pit who saw Lady Castlemaine for the first time " that she was well enough." He is in continual ecstasy about the beauty of one or the other of those ladies of the Court, most constant, however, to the Castlemaine, but appreciative of the Stewart, "with her little Roman nose," or "pretty witty Nell," or Mrs. Middleton "with a very excellent face, and body I think." If neither Hart nor

Nell nor Knipp were there the play, however good, would not please him. With Knipp present he would enjoy the worst of pieces even by the side of Mrs. Pepys. "But it is pretty to observe," he says, "how I did look up and down and did spy Knipp, but durst not own it to my wife, who do not like my kindness to her." Little wonder, indeed, for Mrs. Pepys surely had much to put up with. Samuel was decorum itself by her side, but when she was away he would find himself sitting in front of Knipp and Pierce, "who pulled me by the hair, so I addressed myself to them." Knipp sang a song up in the flies at the King's House which pleased Samuel mightily, "where Knipp, after her song in the clouds, came to me in the pit." Finally, the shameless rogue had the conscience to put on record his feelings at the performance of the "Virgin Martyr," where "the wind musique when the angel comes down is so sweet that it ravished me, so that it made me really sick, as I have formerly been when in love with my wife."

Mr. Colley Cibber mentions a real difficulty of those early managers when he remarks that access to the stage "was given as a bait to the unlicked cubs of the nobility." One of the greatest of the attractions of the playhouse for the audiences of the Restoration was the power of access to the mysteries behind the curtain. But the lounging men of fashion of that day were at the best a sad hindrance to the progress of the piece, ogling the actresses and elbowing the actors at the wings. As Cibber said in his alliterative style, "the

decencies of a drawing-room were exchanged for the
license of a lobby." It was his claim that, at the risk of
their lives, he and his colleagues had reversed the order
of things by refusing all entrance money at the stage
door, and "preserving to ourselves the right of chus-
ing our own company." It is interesting to learn that
the decorum of the drawing-room was eventually the
characteristic of Drury Lane under that distinguished
management ; of its deficiencies in the Restoration
there can be no doubt. There was always the chance
of one of those hectoring spirits falling foul of your
leading gentleman, as we have seen in the case of Sir
Charles Sedley and Mr. Kynaston. Mr. Pepys, too,
mentions a rumour "that my Lord Duke of Buckingham had soundly beaten Henry Killigrew at the King's
House, and taken away his sword, till the fellow
prayed him to spare his life." The pleasantries of
the young men in the tiring-room of the actresses, it
appears, were so pronounced that it was the custom of
the leading ladies to send away their young dressers
when the exquisites appeared. You may read of the
amenities of the green-room in a score of Mr. Pepys'
entries—how Nell Gwynn and Beck Marshall fell out,
and told each other a piece of their minds, which nothing
shall induce us to set down here. You may see another
aspect of the house behind the curtain in that visit
of Mr. Pepys to Mr. Harris in 1668 at the Duke's
House, "and there I observed much company come
to him, and the witts to talk after the play is done,
and to assign meetings." Then there was the famous

afternoon when he went with Knipp to the tiring-room or " woman's shift," where Nell was dressing herself, " all unready and is very pretty, prettier than I thought." He prompted Knipp in her part in " Flora's Fagaries," as he spells it, and giving the cues, listened to that vivacious minx as she ran through her speeches. He saw Nell look through the hole in the curtain, and swear terribly at the scanty numbers in the pit. " But to see how Nell cursed for being so few people in the pit was pretty ! " and the paint on their faces which wanted none made him " loathe them." " But Lord, their confidence, and how many men do hover about them as soon as they come off the stage, and how confident they are in their talk." We all know that famous passage, but we may search in vain for phrases better to present the green-room of the Restoration theatre, or the attraction that it had for half the audiences of those days, and the consequent troubles which Mr. Colley Cibber deplored.

As time went on, the audience, we believe, grew a little less primitive and more sedate ; the humours of the crush for the pit became more distasteful, and means were devised for making a visit to the play easier and more comfortable than it had been. You may find solemn edicts regulating the theatre and its audiences in great collections like the Calendar of State Papers ; how King Charles, being " advised that diverse people doe rudely presse, and with evil language and blowes, force their waye into the two theatres without paying the prices published," his Majesty declared such proceedings unlawful, "notwithstanding their pretended privilege by custom of forcing their entrance at the fourth or fifth act without payment." That "rudely pressing with evil language" seems strangely reminiscent of the days not very long gone by, before the days of the queue at the pit doors. But the audiences of the Restoration, or some members of them, had a way of avoiding the crush. We notice Pepys, on two occasions at least, records the employment of a substitute to hold his seat, a poor man or a boy sent on until the prosperous citizen might enter at his leisure when the house had filled. It soon became a custom, among the people of condition who affected the boxes, to send forward their servants to keep their places, and to display their liveries in the front seats, as one of the prologue writers hints. Shortly before the amalgamation of the two patent companies in 1682, it was weakly conceded to these servants that they might occupy the upper gallery at Drury Lane without charge. From that moment they became a very noisy, and, consequently, a very important part of the audience. "How often," says Mr. Cibber, 'have the most polite audiences, in the most affecting scenes of the best plays, been disturbed and insulted by the noise and clamour of these savage spectators." Dryden was very severe in one of his epilogues upon the same subject—

"They've grown a nuisance beyond all disasters,
     We've none so great, but their unpaying masters;'

and facetious advertisements on the subject of the servants at the play appeared in the papers. "Dropped near the playhouse in the Haymarket," says one of these in the *Female Tatler* for December 1709, "a bundle of horsewhips, designed to be used about the footmen in the upper gallery, who, almost every night this winter, have made such an intolerable disturbance that the players could not be heard, and their masters were forced to hiss them into silence. Whosoever has taken up the said whips is desired to leave them at my Lord Rake's porter, several noblemen resolving to exercise them on their backs the next frosty morning."

In the *Tatlers* and *Spectators* and *Guardians* of Steele and Addison you will find pictures of the audiences of the playhouses of their day, which are scarcely less vivid than the minute delineations of Mr. Pepys himself, for the speculations of those kindly authors often found a subject in the demeanour of the classes at the play. Steele and Addison were never more happy than in their badinage at the playhouse; we can follow the humours of all parts of the house in their pleasant pages, the whisper running along the row of boxes, the follies of the beaux, the fans and patches of the ladies; we can hear the claque and the cat-call in the gallery, and see the brow-beating and nose-pulling of the ruffians of the pit. We must be careful not to take those delightful authors too literally, for both were masters of the ironic method;

but with that reservation in mind, we can surely have no better companions than they in our search for the true aspect of the theatre of the early part of the last century.

From their speculations we conceive the playhouse to have toned down considerably since the days of Mr. Pepys. There is an air or refinement in the audiences of the times of the *Spectator* which we seem to miss in the pages of the Diary—a refinement with a charm all its own, notwithstanding its trivialities at which our authors laugh. What could be prettier than Addison's banter of the Whig and Tory ladies at the play, who wore patches on their faces, "disposed upon party lines," in his account of the Opera at the Haymarket in 1711. It has been quoted by serious historians as literally true; but we do not believe a word of it should be taken literally. Translated in the proper way, it provides us with an excellent picture of the opera of the days of Queen Anne, a picture of handsome women in the boxes, conspicuous by the exhibition of a new and rather silly fashion of spotting their faces with sticking-plaster.

"I noticed," says Mr. Addison, "two parties of very fine women that had placed themselves in the opposite side boxes, and seemed drawn up in a kind of array, one against the other. I found that they were patched differently, the faces on one hand being spotted on the right side of the forehead, and those upon the other on the left. In the middle boxes

were several ladies, who patched indifferently on both
sides of their faces. . . . The censorious say that
the patches turn to the right or to the left, according
to the principles of the man whose heart is aimed at.
Some, however, patch for the public good, as much
as for their private advantage; and several women of
honour do so with an eye to the interest of their
country." So it pleases Mr. Addison to banter on:
he tells us of Rosalinda, a famous Whig partisan,
who had unfortunately a very beautiful mole on the
Tory part of her forehead, which misled several
coxcombs "to converse in the wrong strain, when
on a sudden she has given them an unexpected
fire which sunk them all at once." We have
Nigranilla, too, "unhappy in a pimple, which forces
her against her inclinations to patch on the Whig
side."

So too, in that other paper of the same year, the
chattering vain woman of Mr. Addison's acquaintance
in the box is still a living image, the lady who broke
into a loud soliloquy at " Macbeth " before the rising of
the curtain, and wondered " when will the dear witches
enter," the lady who called to the young baronet in
the pit " to ask him whether Macbeth's wife was still
alive, and before he could give an answer fell a talking
of the ghost of Banquo." We seem to know that
lady and those others, the " whisperers who lay their
heads together in order to sacrifice everybody within
their observation, the laughers who keep up an insipid
mirth in their own corner, and it is to be observed

that their impertinence is ever loudest when the set happens to be made up of three or four females who have got what you call a woman's man among them." These are surely types which survive at theatres and elsewhere.

Steele, with his fine eye for women of all ages and conditions, is no less helpful to us in peopling the playhouse of Queen Anne; the honest fellow was never so happy as when gazing at a houseful of ladies placed in gradual rows in all the ornaments of jewels, silks and colours, "which gave so lovely and gay an impression to the heart that methought the season of the year had vanished, and I did not think it an ill expression of a young fellow who stood near to me that called the boxes 'those beds of tulips.'" Dick's impressionable eye catches a fine lady standing up and "did honour to herself and friend at a distance by curtseying, and gave opportunity to that friend to show her charms to the same advantage in returning the salutation," and we seem to see the crowded playhouse waiting for Mr. Cibber and Mrs. Barry to come on in the "Scornful Lady." Dick was often there to report the demeanour of those audiences. "There is a front row of virgins, the young married women in the second, while the rear is generally made up of mothers of long standing, undesigning maids and contented widows. A double entendre strikes the first row with an affected gravity, the second will venture at a smile, but the third take the conceit entirely and express their mirth in a downright laugh." We see thus the risky joke running round the circle of boxes.

Such are the impressions of the more fashionable parts of the audiences which we gather from a perusal of those inimitable papers, papers which seem to us more eloquent upon our subject than half the dry facts stored in the pages of more formal histories of the stage. But their pleasantry is by no means confined to those modish circles. " Mr. Spectator, I apply myself to you in the following case," wrote James Easy in January of 1712. " I do not wear a sword, but I often divert myself at the theatre where I frequently see a set of fellows pull plain people by way of frolic by the nose upon frivolous or no occasions. A friend of mine the other night applauding what a graceful exit Mr. Wilks made, one of these nose wringers overhearing him pinched him by the nose. I was in the pit the other night when it was very much crowded, a gentleman leaning upon me and very heavily, I requested him to remove his hand, for which he pulled me by the nose." James Easy was a very sober and prosperous linen-draper, by the name of James Heywood, of Fish Street Hill, and Addison very shrewdly allowed his letter to appear in his own language. It is certainly as eloquent of some aspects of the pit as in his own banter of that of the boxes.

Again, what language of the greatest severity could better chastise the dishonest absurdities of the claque than Addison's immortal paper on " The Trunkmaker in the upper gallery "? The text for that most humorous of all sermons begins the paper. "It has been observed that of late years there has been a certain person in the upper gallery of the playhouse, who, when he is pleased with anything on the stage, expresses his approbation by a loud knock upon the benches or the wainscot which may be heard over the whole house. The person is commonly known by the name of the Trunkmaker in the upper gallery."

It seems to us that since we were shown how Prince Hal and Falstaff both played the King, there have been few more humorous passages written than the variations Mr. Addison develops from this theme. The Trunkmaker was a large black man whom nobody knew, who was never seen to smile, "but upon hearing anything to please him takes up his huge oaken plank and laid it upon the next piece of timber that stood in his way with exceeding vehemence. If the audience does not concur with him, he smites a second time, and if the audience is not yet awakened, looks round him with great wrath, and repeats the blow a third time, which never fails to produce the clap. He is observed to be louder than ordinary every time the ghost in Hamlet appears ; he had broken half-a-dozen of oaken planks upon Dogget. When Nicolini first appeared at the opera he had demolished three benches in the fury of his applause; he seldom went away from any tragedy by Shakespeare without leaving the wainscot extremely shattered. The players cheerfully repair at their own cost whatever damages he makes ;

they had once a thought of erecting a kind of wooden anvil to make his strokes deep and mellow, but as this might not have been distinguished from the music of the kettle-drums, the project was laid aside." It was a great libel that he was bribed, but he had certainly saved many a good play and brought many a graceful actor into reputation, and the actors valued no applause which had not the sound of the oak plank in it. " His zeal for a good author is indeed outrageous, but his strokes are always just, and his admonitions reasonable." Such is Addison's method of preserving for us the humours of the gallery of his time, and the pleasantries of the practice common in those days, and perhaps since, of employing a paid fugleman to lead the laughter and applause of the house.

The crowding of actors upon the stage by fashionable loungers, which we noticed as a feature of the playhouse of the Restoration, was still known in the days of Anne. The custom increased, indeed, until the good queen issued an edict against it. "I saw," wrote a correspondent of Steele, or perhaps Steele himself, "a very lusty fellow, but withal a sort of beau, who getting into one of the side boxes on the stage before the curtain drew, was disposed to show the audience his activity by leaping over the spikes. He passed from thence to one of the entering doors, where he took snuff with a tolerable good grace, displayed his fine clothes, made two or three feint passes at the curtain with his cane, then faced about and appeared at t'other door. Here he affected to survey the whole house, bowed and smiled at random, and then showed his teeth, which were indeed, some of them, very white. During the time of acting he appeared frequently in the prince's apartment, made one at the hunting match, and was very forward in the rebellion." (These are all scenes from the play of "Philaster.")

It is almost incredible that audiences should have tolerated the state of things described in this letter, but there is no reason to believe they are exaggerated. By Queen Anne's day the abuse of the public trespassing on the stage had reached such a height that, as we have said, a royal proclamation was issued against it. "Whereas we are informed," said the *Gazette* of November 15, 1711, "that the orders we have already given for the reformation of the stage by not permitting anything to be acted contrary to religion or good manners, have in great measure had their good effect we proposed, and being further desirous of reforming all other indecencies and disorders of the stage, our will and pleasure therefore is, and we do hereby command, that no person of what quality soever shall presume to stand behind the scenes or go upon the stage either before or during the acting of any opera or play, and that no person go into either of our houses for opera or comedy without first paying the established prices for their respective places."

This edict of the queen was very well meant, no

doubt, but it was certainly not seriously enforced, or we should not have seen the stage crowded with spectators in Mr. Hogarth's painting of the scene in Newgate, in act third of "The Beggars' Opera." Here are Walker and Lavinia Fenton and Mrs. Egleton and Mr. Walker all playing in the midst of a crowd of distinguished spectators. There in the right-hand box is the great Duke of Bolton ogling Vinnie Fenton, whom he will presently remove from the stage and marry, and leave Mr. Rich and the British public without the most charming actress that ever played "Polly." Observe the satyr holding up the curtain above his grace's head and pointing the finger of scorn at his grace, which was Mr. Hogarth's way of suggesting the relations between his grace and Vinnie. In the box with the duke are Major Paunceford and Sir Robert Fagg, and Mr. Rich, the manager, talking to Mr. Cook, the auctioneer, and Mr. Gay, the author. The opposite box is full of other distinguished persons, all portraits, but who interest us less except to show how the spectators crowded the stage in 1727. The picture illustrates the theatre at Lincoln's Inn Fields perfectly, and is, indeed, the only representation of that departed playhouse known to be in existence.

That same play, too, of "The Beggars' Opera," and the hubbub it created, is as good an illustration as need be of the place things theatrical held in the society of those days. The legend of that wonderful opera is the best of all means of recalling the interests and the

fears, the jealousies and the defiances, which revolved
about the playhouse of 1728.

When Mr. Gay first showed the manuscript of his
"lyric drama," that is, a play with songs in it, with
Newgate and its occupants as background and characters, the idea of which he had taken from Dr. Swift,
Mr. Pope and the doctor both thought it hopeless.
Mr. Congreve was of a doubtful mind, and Mr. Rich,
who produced it at Lincoln's Inn, alone had faith in
the piece. It proved the greatest success ever known
on the stage at that time. The house was crowded
with an audience for sixty-three consecutive nights,
and Mr. Rich confessed to making £4000 out of it.
It made Rich gay and Gay rich, as was said by a
humourist of the period, the author drawing a not
uncomfortable sum from the proceeds.

There has grown up a vast amount of gossip and
chatter about this wonderful production, a play which
is not at all exciting to read in these days—apt, indeed,
to leave one unmoved. There are pretty simple songs,
where the charming Lavinia Fenton declared,

> " For on the rope that hangs my dear
> Depends poor Polly's life,"

and brought down the house with her pretty face
more than with the wit of the song. Mackheath,
too, has some humour; and one of the rogue's
sayings is alive to-day—

> " How happy could I be with either
> Were t'other dear charmer away."

But the great attraction of all was the rumour that the scene where Peachum and Lockitt fly at each other's throats was drawn from the life, from a similar encounter, in fact, between the two Secretaries of State, Sir Robert Walpole and Lord Townshend, which was believed to have taken place at his lordship's house in Cleveland Row. Whether there was truth in the rumour is beside the point; the people believed it, and enjoyed the scene very much; and Sir Robert Walpole was sensitive enough to get the Duke of Grafton to forbid the second edition of the play, which Mr. Gay set about preparing, and the whole society of the day, from the court downwards, was convulsed.

There is a very full account of it all in those diverting memoirs by Lord Hervey, the cynical Hervey who sneered at most of what he saw in his day. The Duchess of Queensberry, who was Mr. Gay's kind friend throughout his life, resented the interference of the Government, and put herself at the head of a movement to publish the improved play by subscription. Her grace was at court one day, when King George the Second came into the drawing-room, where her grace had buttonholed three men in a corner to solicit their subscriptions for her favourite. His Majesty condescended to ask her what she did. "What must be agreeable to any one so humane as his Majesty," said the spirited lady, "for it was an act of charity, to which she did not despair of bringing his Majesty to contribute."

And upon this her grace pushes her list for Mr. Gay under the royal nose, and solicits the help of his Majesty for the author of a work which had been suppressed a few days before for lampooning his Majesty's Minister. There is a great fuss, and Mr. Stanhope is sent to say that her grace's presence at court is not thought desirable for the future. Her grace says that for fear of mistakes she will send her answer in writing, and a pretty answer it is when it comes. Its grammar is shaky, but its meaning is unmistakable :—

"The Duchess of Queensberry is surprised and well pleased that the king has given her so agreeable a command as forbidding her to court, where she never came for diversion, but to bestow a great civility on the king and queen. She hopes that by so unprecedented an order as this, the king will see as few as he wishes at court, particularly such as dare to think or speak the truth. I dare not do otherwise, and ought not nor could I have imagined but that it would have been the highest compliment I could possibly pay the king and queen to support truth and innocence in their house.   C. QUEENSBERRY.

"P.S.—Particularly when the king and queen told me they had not read Mr. Gay's play. I have certainly done them right to justify my own behaviour rather than act like his grace of ——, who has neither made use of truth, honour, nor judgment in this whole affair, either for himself or his friends."

Such were the results which could grow out of an incident at the play in 1728, and we do not doubt in the least that the possibility of such developments made the theatre a much more amusing place than it is to-day.

The audiences of those days, indeed, were never long

without a sensation. There was the facetious Duke of Montague for instance, who provided the town with a nine days' wonder at the Haymarket Theatre in January of 1749. He advertised in an assumed name that he would "this evening at the Haymarket play on a common walking cane the musick of several instruments now used, to surprising perfection, and that he would on the stage get into a tavern quart bottle without equivocation, and there sing several songs, and suffer any spectator to handle the bottle, and that if any spectator would come masked, he would, if requested, declare who they were, and that in a private room he would produce the representation of any person dead, with which the person requesting it should converse some minutes as if alive. Gallery, 2s.; Pit, 3s.; Boxes, 5s.; Stage, 7s. 6d."

It seems strange that the theatre could have been let for such preposterous fooling, or that there were enough people to fill the theatre, with the Duke of Cumberland at their head, on that January afternoon of 1749. The meeting thus inaugurated took place, however, and has been famous ever since as the "Bottle Hoax."

The audience sat till long after the hour announced for the performance, without music and without the appearance of any actor or manager. It is easy to imagine the behaviour of the house, of whom, certainly, not one believed in the miracle they professed to be waiting to see; they were there, of course, merely for the fun and excitement of the inevitable riot. Reports of the banging of canes, stamping of

feet, and cat-calls still survive in various accounts of
the proceedings; but we take these manifestations to
be a very small part of the demonstrations, which at
length produced a man in front of the curtain. This
devoted servant of the duke announced that if, as he
feared, there might be no performance, the money
would be returned. On the other hand, a wag in the
pit announced: "If ladies and gentlemen will pay
double, the conjuror will get into a pint bottle," at
which pleasantry the house laughed derisively. Then
a young man of fashion arose, calmly lighted a candle,
and threw it on the stage, which was a very plain hint
for an attack upon the structure of the house. A
Scotch lady, who may have been present, but was
certainly inspired by the orthodox Jacobite hatred of
Butcher Cumberland, who was not long back from his
dragooning of the Highlanders, declares that the
prince was "the first that flew in a rage, and called
to pull down the house; he pulled his sword, and
was in such a rage that somebody slipped in behind
him, and pulled the sword out of his hand." However that may have been, there was a glorious and not
unnatural riot. The greater part of the audience
escaped from the theatre to wait events outside,
"some losing a cloak, others a hat, others hat, wig,
and sword also." A smaller and more active minority
remained inside, and devoted their attention to the
furniture and the decorations of the house. They
tore up the benches, broke to pieces the scenes—in
short, demolished the theatre entirely, "carrying away

the pieces into the street, where they made a mighty bonfire, the curtain being hoisted in the middle by way of flag," before the guards could arrive to prevent them, and no very great blame to them we think.

It was these endless possibilities of diversion of the early playhouses, apart altogether from the regular performances, which made, as we believe, a visit to the theatre a more exciting undertaking then than in later and more decorous times. You never knew what might happen. There might be a quaint surprise for his Majesty in the royal box, as when a cupid descended from the roof and presented King George the First with a programme of the play, with which conceit his Majesty was much pleased. Then you might watch King George the Second looking with greedy eyes at the pretty actress playing the intriguing chambermaid, until she turned upon the old man in the piece with the words, "You are villainously old ; you are sixty-six, and cannot have the impudence to think of living above two years." At this you would see his Majesty in the box, who was getting old himself, turn his back to the stage, and say in a voice heard all over the house, "This is damned stuff." Playgoers of those times could speculate upon the family quarrels at St. James's which kept his Majesty at Drury Lane and his royal highness, Prince Frederick of Wales, at the Lincoln's Inn establishment, and note that if a courtier of either court appeared at the opposition house, he lost his place forthwith.

There were these and many other diversions to be met with in the playhouses of the past which seem sadly lacking in those of to-day, though we hope that we receive due compensation in the ability of our players over Quin and Macklin, Wilkes, Nance Old-field, and Peg Woffington. If we are to believe Colley Cibber, it was no uncommon thing to see a disappointed swain of some pretty actress rise in the pit when she came on, interrupt her "by loud and various notes of mockery," and pelt her with rubbish which he had brought in his pocket for the purpose. Then there were endless possibilities of excitement when the pit was supreme, and, lacking its favourite actor or actress, or sore at some edict of the Lord Chamberlain, with any grievance indeed, real or fancied, in its mind, requested the ladies of the audience to withdraw, an omen significant of much; "overthrew the candles, called a council of war, and debated whether they should attack the harpsichord or not." The pit when roused, it seems, always attacked that instrument. They were also accustomed to send for drink, and deliberate over other methods of ventilating their grievances. Madame Chateauneuf failed to appear at Drury Lane in 1740. The ladies were sent home, and a nobleman of the rank of marquess, as we read, suggested that the proper course for the outraged audience to adopt, as it appeared to his lordship, was to fire the house. The proposal was gravely considered, but rejected as too severe a punishment for the non-appearance of the danseuse. They felt the

justice of the case would be met by smashing the
instruments of the orchestra, from the fife to the big
drum, eviscerating the boxes, and demolishing the
Royal Arms, and these disciplinary measures they
accordingly proceeded to carry out.

Then there were other great possibilities in the
continued presence of the audience on the stage.
Queen Anne's edict either failed altogether, or was
successfully evaded for years after its issue. There
was often a double row of spectators seated round
the stage ; nearly always a group of young men at
the wings among the players. In 1721 there was a
gang of a dozen or more, including a man of title.
Macbeth and his wife were about to begin the
murder scene, when his lordship strolled over the
stage to speak to a companion at the opposite wing.
Mr. Rich, the manager, was standing there too, and
told the peer he should never be admitted again. His
lordship slapped Mr. Rich's face, Mr. Rich smacked
his lordship's in return. There were half-a-dozen
swords out in a moment, and the audience were about
to witness a stage fight with an uncommon dash of
reality in it. Up rushed Mr. Quin, Mr. Ryan, and
Mr. Walker with their swords out, and drove the
beaux off the stage and into the pit. The beaux
clambered up into the boxes, cleared out the partitions
and sconces, and slashed the curtains, until Mr. Quin
and his watchmen and constables cleared them out,
and haled half-a-dozen before the magistrate. They
had to close the theatre for a week, and the king was

so angry that he ordered a guard of soldiers at the patent theatres, and there they remained until quite recent times as a memorial of the battle of the beaux with Mr. Quin and Mr. Rich in 1721.

Those guards were objects of interest for a century. At one time it was fashionable with the gallery to pelt them, until a few of the pelters were immured in the gatehouse prison. Later, one of the poor fellows was so amused at the impersonation of Sir Andrew Ague-cheek that he laughed himself into convulsions. Mr. Garrick, in tragedy, so touched the heart of another of these warriors, that he fainted, whereupon Mr. Garrick sent for him behind the scenes after the play and obligingly presented him with a guinea. It is reported that on the following evening his comrade in arms on the opposite side of the stage dropped as in a swoon, but that on this occasion there was no guinea forth-coming from Mr. Garrick, and thereafter the guard contrived to smother the feelings inspired by the acting of that great man.

We wrote in a former page of the weak concession which gave a sort of prescriptive right to the foot-men of the quality to the seats in the gallery at Drury Lane. It is astonishing that none of the able managers of those early years should have thought of the simple expedient of selling tickets for reserved places, instead of encouraging the footmen to take their seats by the side of early arrivals in the boxes, and play put and all-fours until their masters ap-peared, and they went upstairs to claim their places

in the gallery. The managers of later times paid
dearly for that concession, and the behaviour of these
people was a standing grievance with the management
and the audiences for years. Colley Cibber declares
that the original privilege was a jealous move of
Christopher Rich, who, deploring the popularity
of the actors and the pieces they played at the
Duke's House, admitted the footmen of the quality to
Drury Lane, as a bribe which might incite them " to
come all hands aloft in the crack of our applauses."
Mr. Rich's aspiration conveyed in this cryptic sentence
seems to have been fulfilled to the letter. " But, Sir,"
said the typical footman in the *Spectator*, " I am a
leader of the servants. I am he that keeps time with
beating my cudgel against the boards of the gallery
at an opera ; I am he that am touched so properly at
a tragedy when the people of quality are staring at
one another during the most important incidents ;
when you hear in the crowd a cry at the right place,
a hum where the point is touched in a speech, or a
huzza set up where it is the voice of the people, you
may conclude it is begun or joined, Sir, by your more
than humble servant, Thomas Trusty."

There were other aspects than these of the double row
of plush breeches in the gallery, and Drury Lane at last
screwed up its courage to get rid of what Mr. Cibber
described as " the most disgraceful nuisance that ever
depreciated the theatre." In 1737 the footmen were
incontinently turned away from the gallery doors.
There is a quite humorous account of what followed

in *Mist's Weekly Journal* for March the 12th of the
same year. " The footmen and other lively servants
attending the nobility and gentry in Drury Lane,
having on account of their vociferations during the
acts as well as the intervals been expelled the upper
gallery of the house in which they and their ancestors
had sat and voted in all affairs that came upon the
stage time immemorial . . . to the end that posterity
might see that they were not wanting to vindicate
the honour of their cloth, and maintain the whole
body of the livery in the full and free enjoyment of
their ancient rights and privileges, on Saturday night
a great number of them provided with staves and
truncheons assembled at the door of the said theatre."

The outraged footmen attended on the Saturday
night performance, which by 1737 had become the
most fashionable evening at the play, and in a great
body overpowered the attendants and overran the
stage, while a second party of them forced their
way and took possession of the gallery. Twenty-
five persons, it is stated, were injured in the affray
that followed. A magistrate in the house, Mr.
Justice de Viel, recognising the serious nature of
the disturbance, got up and read the Riot Act.
Frederick Prince of Wales and his princess were
there, and a vast number of the persons of rank
and fashion of the town as well, but withdrew with
the rest of the audience and left Colonel de Viel,
supported by foot-guards and the management of the
theatre, to deal with the rebellious footmen. Eighteen

were lodged in Newgate as a result. "The Welch footmen are said to have been the most contumacious in the affair," says Mr. Mist's scribe, "after mature consideration at the Goat and Harp alehouse." The incident, however, put an end to the tyranny of the footmen in the gallery, though the trouble only died away entirely after the men of plush had tried intimidation by dropping threatening circulars down the areas of the houses of all those whom they held to be opposed to the restoration of their privileges.

As the eighteenth century ran on into its middle years the number of theatres in London was slightly increased, and the opportunities of playgoers proportionately widened. There was a theatre at Goodman's Fields in Whitechapel which opened at intervals after 1729, and here in October of 1741, West End audiences had the wit to discover Mr. Garrick playing "Richard the Third" and to recognise his genius on the instant. The present Haymarket Theatre stands on a site immediately adjoining that of "the little theatre in the Haymarket," built in 1720. Early managers of the "little theatre," notably Mr. Henry Fielding, were much oppressed by the patentees of the old houses, though the house might be reckoned as one of the regular theatres of the town long before Mr. Foote obtained a licence for a "summer season" from May to September, as a solace for the accident of a broken leg which he had suffered in the company of a group of influential fashionables. Under Foote's management the Haymarket had great attractions for modish London, the attraction of seeing its own neighbours gibbeted in one or other of the performances of that actor.   Then there was a distinct gain to theatrical London in the substitution of Covent Garden Theatre for the old house in Lincoln's Inn Fields, a change which resulted in the migration westward of the company which represented the old patent which the Duke of York had granted to Davenant.   There was a droll story told concerning the closing of the Lincoln's Inn Theatre in 1732 which was no doubt religiously accepted by those good people who saw warnings in earthquakes against the iniquities of stage plays.   The last piece performed was, it was said, "Harlequin and Dr. Faustus," and the company included a whole troupe of stage fiends.   When the final performance was over, and the time came for the payment and dispersal of the company, there remained over "a supernumerary demon," the real article presumably, for he asked no wages but "flew up to the ceiling, made his way through the tiling and tore away one-fourth of the house."   This was surely a good reason for closing the rest of the edifice.

But the greatest addition to the amusement of fashionable London of the eighteenth century was the development of opera at the King's Theatre in the Haymarket, the house which was removed but a few years ago, and the site of which is now occupied by the Carlton Hotel and Mr. Tree's new theatre. Like some other of the theatres of London, it had its origin in the competition of the two patent companies.

In the early years of the century Vanbrugh and Congreve projected the theatre with the idea of providing a house where Betterton might act the plays which they proposed to write, in order to compete with the more prosperous King's Company at Drury Lane. The theatre was built by subscription, and was opened in 1705. It was then found that the size and architectural deficiencies of the house rendered it totally unfit for theatrical performances. A little later, opera suggested itself as a means of filling the new house, and the addition of opera to the other diversions of Londoners may, perhaps, be traced to the miscalculations of Mr. Congreve and Sir John Vanbrugh.

The new opera, as was only natural, encountered much opposition from the purely theatrical interest, and its early deficiencies were the subject of some merriment, and were perhaps fair game for the wits like Mr. Addison and Sir Richard Steele. The stage illusion, which is necessary in some measure to all performances of the kind, must surely have been wanting in a company where a leading singer from Italy warbled his part in his own mellifluous tongue, and his colleagues supported him in their own native English. Steele and Addison delighted in contrasting the productions at the Haymarket with those of the enterprising Mr. Powell, the puppet showman in the Piazza at Covent Garden, and always to that gentleman's advantage. "Those are the leading diversions of the town," said Steele in 1709, "and Powell has

set up 'Whittington and his Cat' against 'Rinaldo
and Armida.' At the opera the King of Jerusalem
is obliged to come from the city on foot, instead of
being drawn in a triumphant chariot with white
horses, as my opera-book had promised me, and he
had a very short allowance of thunder and lightning,
though I cannot in this place omit doing justice to
the boy who had the direction of the painted dragons,
and made them spit fire and smoke. He flashed in
his rosin in such just proportions and in such due
time that I could not forbear conceiving hopes of his
being one day a most excellent player, if, indeed, he
would only keep his head a little lower and hide his
candle." Then when live animals were introduced at
the Haymarket and at Mr. Powell's "motions," the
advantage still rested with the latter. "The sparrows
and chaffinches at the Haymarket as yet fly very
irregularly over the stage, and instead of perching on
the trees and performing their parts, these young
actors either get into the galleries or put out the
candles, whereas Mr. Powell has so well disciplined
his pig that he and Punch dance a minuet together."
At the puppet show " the scenes were managed very
dextrously," whereas at the opera " we were presented
with a prospect of the ocean in the midst of a delightful grove, and though the gentlemen on the stage
had very much contributed to the beauty of the grove
by walking up and down between the trees, I must
own I was not a little astonished to see a well-dressed
young fellow in a full-bottomed wig appear in the

midst of the sea, and without any visible concern taking snuff."

All this is excellent fooling, but it is fair to remember that some of Mr. Addison's reflections on the subject of opera may have been tinged with a pessimism born of his own failure in the same walk of art.

Opera was not long in emerging from its uneasy circumstances. King George the First patronised it, and gave a subscription of £1000, as well as his own name, to the Opera House, and from those early days opera and its attendant interests, the personalities of its singers and their rivalries, became, and long remained, the plaything of aristocratic London. Even in those times of social exclusiveness it was not reckoned undignified for a man of great family to identify himself with the management of opera as a means of increasing his income—there is mention of at least two such during the last century. Horace Walpole touched lightly upon Lord Middlesex's connection with the business in 1747 in one of those pleasant paragraphs of his. "Lord Middlesex," he says, "from his excellent economy in never paying the performers is likely to continue in the treasury." We see, too, in our chapter on the masked assembly, how fatal Mrs. Cornelys' interference with Mr. Hobart, Lord Buckinghamshire's brother, was to that hapless lady.

Fashionable London was so fond of opera in 1735 that it paid £5000 a year to Farinelli, and when that incomparable singer was at the Haymarket an enthu-

siastic lady in the boxes was heard to exclaim in her
ecstasy, " One God, one Farinelli." Then singers
and their competing merits were a continual joy to
generations of noble patrons, and their preferences
for one singer or another often inspired ladies of
high fashion with very unfashionable feelings. Thus
when the rival warblers Cuzzoni and Faustina were
appearing at the opera in 1726, they each had a party
of thick and thin supporters in distinguished circles.
There was the Countess of Pembroke at the head of
her party in a box, who was prepared to go all lengths
for Cuzzoni; the Countess of Burlington and Lady
Delawarr, with their train of young men in another,
were fierce and determined on behalf of the Faustina.
So when Cuzzoni came on the noble faction which
supported Faustina hissed her into silence, when
Faustina appeared she was shrieked off the stage by
the devoted band at the back of my Lady Pembroke.
It was a pretty incident and eloquent of the varieties
of diversion to be found at the opera of George the
First, an incident too which developed into a faction
fight and ended in the closing of the house for a
fortnight.

Such incidents as these are significant of the place
opera assumed among the amusements of the town,
and from the times of George the First until our
own, we may think of the Opera House as one of
the chief places of social resort in London. That
was a typical social afternoon at the opera, for instance,
in May of 1744, when the news came out that Mr.

Henry Fox had married Lady Caroline Lennox, the daughter of the Duke of Richmond, secretly and in defiance of her parents. Mr. Fox had prevailed on the young lady to go with him to the house of his friend Sir Charles Hanbury Williams, who had provided a parson in readiness, and there the knot was tied. The spirit of the young lady may be realised when we read that she had shaved off her eyebrows in order to make herself unpresentable to the other young gentleman whom her father and mother had provided in place of Mr. Fox. The news first reached fashionable London at the opera, and Williams was there himself to report it all to the young couple. The ducal family was of such very high standing that the marriage was reckoned a sad *mésalliance*, and it convulsed society for a season. "I saw the news of your marriage," wrote Williams, "run round the boxes like fire in a train of gunpowder." The performance of the Frasi was forgotten, the ladies leant across the partitions and whispered the news behind their fans, and the whole house in a few minutes was divided into two factions—of those who sympathised with the spirit of the young people, and those who deplored the troubles of the duke and duchess. It was whispered "that the rage of the duke and duchess was very high," that their great ball which had been arranged, and for which the town was waiting, had been countermanded, and that their graces had set out in dudgeon for Goodwood, and had issued a ducal ban upon all visitors to the offending daughter. Young Mr. Horace Walpole, hearing of this, walked round to Williams's box to know the earliest moment he might be allowed to call to pay his respects to the lady, a proceeding as characteristic of Mr. Walpole as is the whole incident characteristic of a typical audience at the opera of the time of George the Second.

Turning again to the theatre, no one looking through the annals of the stage since the middle of the last century can fail to be struck with the importance of the position which was gradually assumed by the audiences in their relations with the management. With the continual increase of the town and of the interest which the people began to take in public affairs, came the feeling that the exercise of a monopoly in theatrical matters imposed corresponding duties upon managers, and implied rights of audiences which had been too long ignored. From the times of the Restoration until the end of the reign of Queen Anne the humbler portions of the house had been made the butt for the facetious shafts of the epilogue writers, Mr. Dryden and the rest, who were wont to make merry over the dulness of their wits, the poverty of their domestic establishments, even of their personal appearance. But by the middle of the reign of George the Second the pit and gallery and the management were on a different footing altogether. The people, perhaps, first effectually asserted themselves in theatrical matters after the Licensing Act of 1737, when they determined to damn the first play which appeared under the auspices of the Lord Chamberlain, and they did so accordingly, much to the punishment of the author, Mr. Hildebrand Jacob, the quality of whose work was in no way taken into account. Even earlier than that year you may find in advertisements and announcements evidence that audiences as a whole began to receive greater consideration than formerly. There is quite a strange ring about the announcement from the Haymarket in 1735, for example, that " the company will continue to act as long as they shall deserve the favour of the town." Later the audiences began to assert their right to a voice in the very choosing of the piece. In 1755 Mr. Garrick found that unless he himself appeared every night he had great difficulty in filling Drury Lane, and as he felt himself unequal to the continued strain of nightly appearances, he produced, at great expense, the Chinese Festival, a ballet pantomime of a type then new but familiar since, which included a troupe of French dancers. War having in the meantime broken out between England and France, the Drury Lane audience would have none of the French dancers. At the first performance they intimated their objections with great candour from the pit, much to the amusement of His Majesty King George, who laughed at the tumult from the royal box. This produced some hissing against his Majesty and his dynasty, and his Majesty's approval of the piece had the effect of further increasing the trouble by ranging the fashion of the boxes on the side of his Majesty and Mr. Garrick.

That gentleman, anxious about the great expenses already incurred, was ill advised enough to repeat the performance, and by so doing managed to produce a riot of the first dimensions. After an exchange of defiance between the pit and the boxes, the gentlemen left their ladies, leaped gallantly into the pit, and drew their swords upon the citizens, the gallery meanwhile bombarding both parties with any missiles they found to hand, with great impartiality. The beaux, however, were soon overpowered, and the citizens having first smashed the harpsichord, proceeded to break up all the furniture of the house. They invaded the stage and reduced the elaborate scenery of the Chinese Festival to the merest ribbons. Still unappeased, they went on to Mr. Garrick's house in Southampton Street, and further asserted their right of interference by smashing his windows from basement to garret.

It was seldom, indeed, that actor or manager found any opposition to the clearly expressed wish of the house of the slightest use. There were greatly daring individuals who occasionally tried falls with angry houses, but always with indifferent success. Mrs. Siddons was once heard to say to a howling gallery, "Adieu, you brutes;" but we believe the noise going on at the moment prevented more than her companions on the stage from catching the remark. Another lady was momentarily successful in the face of a hostile audience, but her show of high spirit prevented her from ever appearing on the same stage again. Mrs. Montague was cast for Queen Eleanor in Hull's play of "Henry II.," but wishing for the more attractive part of Rosomond, given to Mrs. Hudson, turned sulky, pleaded illness as an excuse for not studying the part, and when the first night came, she sent an actor to explain to the audience that she intended to read her part. It was then suggested that she had better explain matters herself. With the book in her hand, and the saucy expression, "Who's afraid?" on her lips, she rushed on the stage. There she defiantly informed the pit that she *would* read the part, as she had had no time to study it. There was a roar of menace from the house, and some one shouted that they would rather have the cook-maid from the alehouse to read than Mrs. Montague. "Then," said that lady, "curse you all," flung the book of the play into the middle of the pit, and swept off the stage.

The eccentric George Frederic Cooke, too, was once called upon to apologise to a Liverpool audience for some slip or other. "What," he cried in derision, " an apology from George Frederic Cooke!" and continued, in pleasant allusion to Liverpool's connection with the slave trade, "There's not a brick in your infernal dirty town which is not cemented with the blood of a slave."

Nearly all the managers of the last century were fortunate in the patronage extended to them by royalty, and could usually reckon, during the reigns of the first three Georges at least, upon the great

attraction for the ordinary playgoer of the presence of
some member of the reigning house in the royal box.
Acting was the only art which George the First even
pretended to admire; he was very fond of ordering
the King's company down to Hampton Court, and
understood and enjoyed the political allusions of such
plays as " Henry the Eighth," which he was careful to
explain to the Prince of Wales. George the Second
enjoyed the play hugely, and was never so happy as
when watching a piece of the Restoration, with all its
indelicacies restored to the acting version by his own
royal command. The audiences of George the Third
had the satisfaction of his Majesty's presence on very
frequent occasions, but always to witness plays of the
greatest innocence. It must have been very cheerful
to hear his Majesty's hilarity ring round the house at
the smallest joke; we know he would laugh himself
almost into apoplexy when the clown in the pantomime
stole the goose or sat on the baby. He was so easily
pleased, that the actors sometimes made "gag" for
his especial benefit. They would make sly jokes at
his Majesty's agricultural pursuits, and his Majesty
would take the point with delight, and chuckle from
the royal box, "Hee, hee; good, they mean my sheep."
Then when they played the "Siege of Calais," where
there is a scene between two carpenters who have
made the scaffold for the execution, and a line,
" So the king is coming, and the king like not my
scaffold, I am no true man," Mr. Parsons, who was
playing the chief carpenter, went close up to the

royal box, and delivered an altered version in the words, " An the king were here, and did not admire my scaffold, I would say, damn him, he has no taste ; " and the king laughed louder than the house at the poor and impudent jest. The audiences of George the Third, too, were accustomed to find some amusement in the pieces commanded by the royal family on different occasions. Thus when the Duke of Gloucester appeared at the play with his duchess, Horry Walpole's niece, the widow Waldegrave, whom he had married in defiance of the Court, he commanded the piece " Jane Shore," as who should hint at the dangers of any but regular connections between royalty and its ladies. Then, too, only a week or so after the death of the Duke of Cumberland, with whom he was not on the best of terms, King George commanded " Much Ado About Nothing," to the great amusement of the waggish among his subjects.

But the occasion of all others in which the king appeared to the best advantage in the playhouse, was on that 5th of May 1800, when Hatfield fired at him from the pit ; and the brave king, after seeing that the queen and princesses were unhurt, quieted the fears of the Court Chamberlain who urged him to withdraw. " Sir, you discompose me as well as yourself," said his Majesty ; " I shall not stir a step," and he continued to look round the house with his single opera-glass, and all his subjects were delighted, for bravery never goes out of fashion.

It is conjectured by enthusiasts of the drama, that

when Mr. Garrick flashed on the stage in 1741, and
swept away in a breath all the antiquated and pompous
conventions which had almost strangled the art of the
stage since the days of Betterton,—the mouthings and
attitudes and sing-song recitatives in vogue with the
masters of the professions,—he had not only to exhibit a new art, but to create new audiences. There
must have been many playgoers who were unable in
a moment to part with the old traditions without a
struggle, or were prepared to accept all at once the
genius of the acting of the little man from the East
End Theatre at Goodman's Fields. But how complete that education must have become before Mr.
Garrick said farewell at Drury Lane in 1776, is
obvious from the accounts of that farewell which
have survived. The agreeable gossip, Mr. Harry
Angelo, was there himself with his mother and Mrs.
Garrick in the same box, and tells us all about it.
"I remember," he says, "that more tears were shed
when he had finished this touching part, and the
curtain dropped, than he had ever excited, perhaps,
mighty as his command might be over the passions
of his audience, when acting a character in the most
affecting tragedy." There is nothing at all suggestive
of a theatrical performance in the accounts of that
mournful occasion. People were heard sobbing after
they had quitted the theatre, and the solemnity of the
whole function was hardly exceeded when, ten years
later, the male fashion of the day turned out from
White's and Brooks's to follow the great player to

Westminster Abbey. That farewell at Drury Lane of Mr. Garrick's was a notable day in the annals of the theatre; a great artist's life-work accomplished, the most popular of the arts transformed by his genius, which had created new standards and new ideals, and a vast London audience acknowledging the fact with tears and lamentations.

And yet, the elevation which Garrick gave to the stage and its audiences notwithstanding, a spectacle or a sensation with a personal interest, like David's own farewell, for example, were ever the occasions which drew the crowded houses. From very early days it was the custom of managers of the patent theatres in lack of an attraction to admit all sorts of strange exhibitions to the stage, either as separate shows before the piece, or between the acts—acrobats and contortionists, cudgel players, hornpipe dancers, and the like. In 1736 the managers of Lincoln's Inn Theatre advertised that Mrs. Mapp, the famous bone-setter and quack doctress, would be present at the performance of "The Husband's Relief," and all London flocked to see that lady sitting serenely in a box, while the comic man of the piece came on and sang a song in her honour to the tune of "Derry Down," in which he derided the faculty, and declared that "the doctress of Epsom has outdone you all." Later, too, the management of the same house secured the attendance of "four Indian kings," these potentates being, as a fact, four Red Indian chiefs then on a visit to England. Their attendance was advertised, and the house was crammed to meet them. They sat in the centre box, and were thus invisible to the gallery. The gallery, not being able to see the kings, became riotous, and refused to allow "Macbeth" to proceed. Then Mr. Wilks came forward to assure the gallery that the kings were really in the house though they might not be visible to all parts of it. The gallery replied that it paid its money to see the kings, and meant to see them. After much negotiation the Indians were persuaded to go down to the stage, where, being provided with chairs, they sat out the performance.

That same perennial love of sensation has inspired half the audiences who have flocked to make the great occasions of the theatre. It was no mere love of fine acting which took all fashionable London to Covent Garden at ten in the morning on the 1st of December 1804, in order to be in time for the evening performance of Master Betty, the Infant Roscius. It is amazing to read the account of the sufferings of the audience who assembled to greet that prodigy. "Gentlemen who knew that there were no places untaken in the boxes and could not get up the pit avenues, paid for admission into the lower boxes, and poured from them into the pit in twenties and thirties at a time. . . . The ladies in one or two boxes were occupied almost the whole night in fanning the gentlemen who were beneath them in the pit. . . . Upwards of twenty gentlemen who had fainted were dragged up into the boxes ; several more raised their hands as if in supplication for mercy and pity." Is it not touching, and all this tribulation only to hear a young gentleman of fourteen play Selim in " Barbarossa "? The ingenuous British public never gave Garrick or Mrs. Siddons or John Kemble such a reception. One reads with wonder that the House of Commons adjourned on the motion of the austere Mr. Pitt, so that the legislators, having nothing better to think about in those times of Wellington and Napoleon, might have an opportunity of seeing the infant phenomenon. It is with satisfaction that one learns that Mrs. Siddons was too careful of the dignity of her art to play with the young gentleman, as was obligingly suggested to that lady.

It is not uninteresting in these days of a London of multitudinous playhouses to reflect that, until the Act of 1843 established free trade in theatres, the theatrical amusements of the town were still purveyed, nominally at any rate, under the old patents of Charles the Second, with the addition of the quasi accidental patent of the Haymarket and the aristocratic management of the opera at Her Majesty's. Such other theatres as opened their doors did so either on sufferance, by disguising their productions as burlettas or musical entertainments, or at the very imminent risk of being pounced upon by one of the patent managements. Licences of a temporary character were granted to some of these as time went on—to the Lyceum, for example, the Sanspareil, now the Adelphi, the

Olympic, and others. But in the main the mono-
polies of Drury Lane, Covent Garden, and the Haymarket were still acknowledged, though only with the
increasing reluctance of an increasing body of playgoers. But the last quarter of the last century and
the first of this had seen a change and development
in matters theatrical. Mr. Sheridan's imaginative
finance, which had succeeded the thrifty management
of Mr. Garrick at Drury Lane, had introduced many
other interests than his own in the fortunes of that
famous house, and eventually resulted in a management where the public were to some extent represented by a body of distinguished amateurs, of which
Lord Byron was one. Then, whenever a theatre was
altered or rebuilt, there was a constant effort on the
part of the managers to enlarge their houses, to increase the numbers of private boxes, and banish more
humble members of the audience to bad accommodation, where hearing and seeing were both difficult,
changes followed always by great popular discontent.

We imagine that the claims of aggrieved members
of the theatre-going public to a voice in the management, which we have already noticed in its early
development, found loudest expression in the Old
Price Riots at Covent Garden in 1809. These riots
were the direct result of the feelings of grievance and
resentment among the occupants of pit and gallery
at the treatment we have mentioned as usual whenever a theatre was rebuilt or remodelled. Mr.
Kemble, in rebuilding Covent Garden after the

great fire, proposed, among other changes, to add many new private boxes at the expense of the cheaper places of the house, and to raise the prices of seats in the pit by sixpence. He succeeded only in raising an agitation which filled his house with tumult night after night for exactly three months.

It was computed that for seventy-one nights, between the 18th September and the 16th December, no performance was possible on account of the uproar. The invention of new noises for Covent Garden became a fine art. One gentleman took a watchman's rattle, which he sprung from a private box at propitious moments; another occupied the centre of the pit with a large dustman's bell. Drums, horns, cat-calls, and bugles were the arms, so to speak, of the rank and file, while some of the more inventive geniuses of the opposition contrived to introduce live porkers into the theatre, their ears being pinched at proper intervals when a variation in the harmony was required. There was a regular performance called the O. P. Dance, which consisted, apparently, of a simultaneous and measured trampings of the feet all over the house. It was impossible to hear a word a few feet from the stage, and as soon as the curtain rose the audience turned their backs to the performers and devoted themselves to the diversions of the house. Any attempt at the arrest of individuals always led to a free fight, and the magistrates had little to do for three months but to settle disputes arising from the O. P. diversions at Covent Garden. The noise became so constant that it was a recognised thing, and communications passed between the two parties by means of large placards displayed by either side. Grave commercial potentates like the Governor of the Bank of England were called in as arbitrators, and declared that the enterprise would only show a profit of three per cent. on the capital outlay on the new theatre at the new prices, and that at the old rates there would be a loss of three-quarters per cent. per annum. The audience replied that it was not their fault if fancy salaries were paid to foreign actresses, or that the managers had neglected to insure the late theatre at more than a third of its value. Recognising, too, at that early period, the essential principles of free trade, they remarked, that if the monopoly of the patent theatres were ended, the managers might charge what they liked for their seats, and filch as many boxes from the pit as they chose, because the public could then go elsewhere for their diversion. After three months of this strife Mr. Kemble had to surrender, to withdraw all charges in the police courts, and to make an apology, and thus the right of the public to interfere in matters of administration was at last acknowledged and confirmed.

It is not uninteresting to note that almost at the moment when the popular element was asserting itself in the theatre all the fashion of London was engaged in concentrating itself at the opera. Just after the present century opened, there was a cult of deportment which developed in social London, and constituted a tyranny under which society groaned for a couple of generations. Beau Brummell and his set at the clubs in St. James's Street represented the male element of this autocracy of fashion, the lady patronesses at Almack's in King Street the feminine; and at the opera they both united their forces. The writers of the lighter memoirs of the period, Gronow, Grantley, Berkeley, and Lord Lamington, who, however, describes the antics of a later decade, are eloquent about the glories of the quality at the opera in those earlier years. There was the peerless Mr. Brummell, with his satellite exquisites in Fop's Alley, the interest of the whole mankind of the house, we are asked to believe, centred in the question of his raiment for the evening, echoed in the general remark, " How well got up is Brummell." The ladies of the grand tier, we are told, including the chaperons, were more anxious for his notice than for that of the Prince Regent. The opera, in fact, like Almack's, was a social function which entirely outclassed anything of the sort at Court after the retirement of the poor blind King George the Third. There was no question of getting in by the mere payment of money, a committee of ladies supervised the issue of every ticket, and a man or a lady went to the opera or did not, according as their social position was or was not considered worthy of that honour by the Lady Patronesses. Once there they had the pleasure of gazing upon those women whose beauty has inspired so many social writers to ecstasy—Lady Harrowby and her daughter,

Lady Mary Ryder, the Duchess of Argyll and the Ladies Campbell, Lady Stafford and Lady Elizabeth Gower, Mme. de Lieven, Princess Esterhazy, Lady Cardigan, and the rest. The performance did not matter in the least, as it would seem, for it is seldom mentioned in those panegyrics. The chief of the dandies displayed their graces with as much thought as the ladies—Mr. George Damer, Lord Foley, Mr. Henry Pierrepoint, Mr. Wellesley Pole, Mr. Charles Standish, Mr. Drummond, the old Sleeping Beauty Lumley Skeffington, and the others. It is very curious in these irreverent days to read the awe-struck frame of mind with which all this fine company was regarded, even by people who profess to have been in it. The Lady Patronesses who controlled London society from the time of the Regency until her Majesty came to the throne were accustomed to sit in conclave upon all the young men about to enter life, and decide as to whether or not they were eligible for admission to such stately functions as Almack's and the opera. "Only sixteen officers of the Guards were found worthy of that honour," as we are assured, and the whole circle of the elect of London society, even so late as 1840, did not exceed six hundred, according to Lord Willoughby d'Eresby, whose lady was one of its leaders. It was in the hands of this small coterie of people that the opera, as a fashionable institution, attained its natural development; on its first introduction into England, as we have seen, it soon became the plaything of an aristocracy, and it has remained so since. The support of the general public in the cheaper portions of the house is, no doubt, of greater importance now than formerly, but, after nearly two centuries, opera in England is still as dependent upon the support of a small and rich class as it was when Lady Delawarr and Lady Pembroke quarrelled about the respective merits of the Cuzzoni and the Faustina, or when the Lady Patronesses of George the Fourth were so careful in filtering its audiences.

It is at that point that we propose to take leave of our subject, the play and the opera as amusements of the people of London. Audiences since those times have displayed no very distinctive features, and the playhouse of the Regency differs little from that of Queen Victoria. The great event in theatrical matters of the present century was the abolishment of the exclusive rights of the patent theatres by the Act of 1843, a change which had been long foreshadowed, and resulted in the generous provision in the matter of theatres which we know and appreciate in these days.

END OF VOL. I

THE AMUSEMENTS OF
OLD LONDON

———

VOLUME THE SECOND

VAUXHALL GARDENS

THE AMUSEMENTS
OF OLD LONDON

BEING A SURVEY OF THE SPORTS AND PASTIMES
TEA GARDENS AND PARKS, PLAYHOUSES
AND OTHER DIVERSIONS OF THE PEOPLE
OF LONDON FROM THE 17TH TO
THE BEGINNING OF THE
19TH CENTURY

By WILLIAM B. BOULTON

VOLUME THE SECOND

CONTENTS

VOLUME THE SECOND

CHAPTER VII

LONDON AL FRESCO: VAUXHALL

CHAPTER VIII

THE FAIRS

CONTENTS

CHAPTER IX

THE PRIZE-RING

CHAPTER X

THE PARKS

CHAPTER XI

THE CLUBS AND COFFEE-HOUSES

CHAPTER XII

OF SUNDRY DIVERSIONS

LIST OF ILLUSTRATIONS

VOLUME THE SECOND

AMUSEMENTS OF OLD LONDON

CHAPTER VII

LONDON AL FRESCO : VAUXHALL

WE wrote in another chapter of the fondness of the Londoner of former times for taking his solace in the open air, of his habit of junketing under trees and in arbours, and of taking his modest refreshment in the scores of pleasant places which the enterprise of individuals placed at his disposal in almost every quarter of the town. We saw the tradition of the London *al fresco* in its origin at the Spring Garden at Whitehall, and followed it through most of the pleasant shades which made Islington and Clerkenwell, Marylebone, Brompton, Chelsea and Lambeth places of modest delight for successive generations of cockneys. In so doing, we suggested that the tradition of the open air entertainment in London, at one moment in great danger of losing its continuity, was supported by an institution on the banks of the river near Lambeth, where eventually it pros-

pered and developed until it made of its new resting-
place the crown and glory of the whole cult.   It
was at the New Spring Garden at Vauxhall, as
we hinted, that the tea garden of London attained
its zenith and offered to the man and woman of
fashion and breeding an entertainment more suited
to their tastes than the diversions provided for their
humbler fellow-citizens on a generous scale elsewhere.
The story of the famous gardens of Vauxhall we held
to be a theme worthy of a separate consideration, and
we now propose to complete our inquiry into the
history of the departed joys of the London *al fresco*,
by seeking to revive for a moment its final glories
at a spot which is to-day, perhaps, as little redolent
of groves and nightingales and whispering lovers as
any in London.   For it was in that unpromising
district just north and east of the grimy railway
station which still perpetuates the name, that Vauxhall Gardens spread their delights to an appreciative
town, delights of which you may read in terms almost
of ecstasy in the pages of a score of reputable authors
of the times and of a hundred less notable scribes.

It was, as we have said, in the year when the needy
Court of Charles the Second began to cover up the
pleasant lawns of the Spring Garden at Charing Cross
with the buildings which have kept the name alive
into our own times, that the London *al fresco* entertainment was in some danger of extinction.   The
numerous smaller tea gardens which we have examined elsewhere had not yet arisen, and the Mul-

berry Garden at Buckingham House, never destined
to a long career, was the single open air entertainment
available to Londoners near the town. There had,
however, long been traditions of merry-makings of
a modest nature at a spot which was then open
country, standing back from the river just behind
the southern end of the present Albert Embankment, where it joins Upper Kennington Lane. As
early as 1663 foreign travellers in England had
noticed a modest pleasure garden at Lambeth as a
feature of English life worth recording. Balthazar
Monconys speaks of the place as "lawns and gravel
walks dividing squares of twenty to thirty yards
enclosed with hedges of gooseberry trees within
which were planted roses." It is interesting to see
that he calls this pleasaunce the "Jardin Prin-
temps," a curious echo of the name of King
Charles's Spring Garden at Charing Cross.

Later, when the days of the Restoration came, there
is frequent mention of the place by Evelyn and Pepys.
Careful antiquaries indeed like Mr. Warwick Wroth
will detect record of two gardens side by side at
Lambeth, the new and the old Spring Gardens. But
we need not here assume the functions of those invaluable historians of a London which would be
forgotten in many of its most interesting aspects
but for their labours of love. It is enough for our
purpose that we can find record of a pleasant garden
up the river in those early times, where, as we have
said, we can watch the tradition of the London

al fresco taking shelter and reaching its highest development.

Here was Mr. Evelyn, for example, going up to inquire in 1661, when he found the "New Spring Garden at Lambeth a pretty contrived plantation," and we may follow the fortunes of the place in a score of pleasant allusions from his day until those of Addison and Dick Steele.   The founders of the place have left no trace of their personalities, and it is not until nearly a century after the first mention of Spring Garden at Lambeth that the true genius of the place, Mr. Jonathan Tyers, by his enterprise and ability established the Spring Garden at Vauxhall as the model of all places of the sort in Europe. But some of the notable men of the early days who enjoyed the pleasures upon which the later glories of the place were reared, have left us much comment on the doings within its boundaries, and with their help there is slight difficulty in repeopling its shades and arbours.

The accident of the identity of its name with that of the famous and modish royal garden at Whitehall was doubtless of some advantage to the New Spring Garden at Vauxhall.   Vauxhall, we may remark, took its name from a manor of South Lambeth named after Fulke de Breauté, the henchman of King John, who built a house there, called successively Fulke's Hall, Faukeshall, Foxhall, Vauxhall.   The name of Spring Garden was likely to attract much of the company of the place at Charing

Cross which had been displaced by the building schemes of his Majesty and the closing of the garden. The gardens had also another indubitable advantage in their situation near the banks of the river. When we consider the state of the roads in and near London until quite modern times, and recall the fact that until 1750 there was no bridge over the Thames between London Bridge and Kingston, we can appreciate the value of the river as a highway, and the help it brought to any place of entertainment near its banks. The fares on the Thames were extraordinarily moderate. There are regulations of the Corporation extant which tell us that the citizen wishing to go to Vauxhall by water could take a pair-oared wherry at Whitehall for sixpence, or if he was content with sculls for half that moderate fee. Then the journey by water was itself an attraction which brought advantages to the gardens. The place was in the country, and a visit in the heat of summer was something in the nature of an expedition to the substantial merchant from the city and his family. They were apt to stay longer and eat more after the little voyage, in which their appetites were sharpened by the fresh air of the river. The modest charges of the journey were as nothing to the class of patrons which made Vauxhall their own; they may, indeed, have been an advantage in acting as a kind of filter which excluded some of the rougher elements from the place. It is certain, in any case, that the Spring Gardens at Vauxhall from the first took a tone which distinguished them from the rest of such places in London; and this air of fashion Vauxhall retained until quite the closing days of its career of two centuries. Its glories were sadly dimmed before the end came, it is true, but at its lowest it always stood a little above the level of the competitors and imitators of its decline.

There is copious allusion to the early times of these famous gardens, as we say—allusion historical and literary, and over much of it is the right flavour of the Restoration. The humours of Spring Gardens at Charing Cross were removed to Spring Gardens at Vauxhall, with little maiming of their rites; there are the same rumours of syllabubs and cheesecakes, the same wandering of damsels through the close walks of the wilderness, the same whispering of gallants in love-locks to ladies in masks and flame-coloured gowns. Spring Gardens appear in the pages of Wycherley and Congreve, and Vanbrugh and Sedley, as a spot upon which much of the glitter and revelry of that reckless society, lately released from the bondage of the Puritans, displayed itself to the best advantage. The historical evidence of Mr. Samuel Pepys, too, is to the same effect. Samuel was there often, and in many moods; with the maids, with his wife, and without his wife but with other people's at times. The vice of the age, as exhibited by the company in the gardens, would shock him one day, and on another he would kiss Knipp in the arbour, "it being darkish." But that

quaint sinner can speak best for himself. "Thence
to the new one," he says in May of 1662, speaking of the Old and New Spring Gardens, "where I
never was before, which much exceeds the other;
and here we also walked, and the boy crept through
the hedge, and gathered abundance of roses, and,
after a long walk, passed out of the doors, as we
did at the other place." Those were quite early
days, both of the Restoration and of Samuel's prosperity and importance. He affected the place later
very frequently, and favours us with more particulars,
both of the gardens and the company.

In 1665, for example, there is local colour in the
record of another visit "By water to Foxhall, and
there walked an hour alone, observing the several
humours of the citizens . . . pulling off cherries and
God knows what." Two years later there was "A
great deal of company, and the weather and garden
pleasant, and it is very pleasant and cheap going
thither, for a man may go to spend what he will
or nothing—all is one; but to hear the nightingale
and other birds, and here fiddles, and there a harp,
and here a Jew's trump, and here laughing, and
there fine people walking, is mighty divertising."
We think Samuel's delight in the innocent pleasures
of Vauxhall, after the dark days of the Puritans and
the Plague and the Fire, with his new prosperity
growing upon him, is very human. And if inscription were wanted for the cenotaph of the departed
joys of the London *al fresco*, what better words

could be found than Pepys' elegy of the nightingale
and the Jew's trump?

But for the true aspect of the Vauxhall of the
Restoration, we must wait another year. Pepys left
record of three visits to Vauxhall in the summer of
1668, all within a few weeks, by which time he was
a man of mark, noticed by the king and the Duke of
York, and with a comfortable sum of money, still
growing, in his chest at Axe Yard. He had little
scruple about the company he kept, but much as
to that in which he was seen. His growing riches,
too, often gave him qualms when he thought of the
chances of the continuance of the circumstances in
which he was piling them up; every excess of that
reckless society gave him a shiver. Many of the
thoughts which constantly tormented the active brain
of the busy Samuel in those uneasy days find expression in the records of his visits to the Spring Garden
at Vauxhall in 1668, and certainly the humours of
the Restoration are there very perfectly reflected.
Listen to him.

"Walked and saw young Newport, and two more
rogues of the town, seize on two ladies, who walked
with them an hour with their masks on (perhaps
civil ladies)." Again: "Over the water with my wife
and Deb and Mercer to Spring Garden, and there
eat and walked; and observed how rude some of
the young gallants of the town are become, to go
into people's arbours where there are not men, and
almost force the women, which troubled me to see

the confidence of the vice of the age." Once more: "Over to Foxhall, and there fell into the company of Harry Killigrew, a rogue newly come back out of France, but still in disgrace at our Court, and young Newport and others, as very rogues as any in the town, who were ready to take hold of every woman that come by them. And so to supper in an arbour; but, Lord, their mad talk did make my heart ake."

The rogues must have been rude indeed to have shocked such a connoisseur in the art of dalliance as Mr. Pepys. Samuel little thought that the entries of that wondrous diary would ever be thrown open to the prying curiosity of later generations, that diary which surely of all books in the world has the merit of absolute veracity. Samuel never even deceived himself in those artless pages as to the real nature of his doings at Vauxhall or elsewhere. With his frolics with that long line of beauty from Betty Lane to Deb Willett entered against his account in his own hand he could have had few real qualms about "the confidence and vice of the age." His only trouble was as to how long it might last, with young Harry Killigrew and young Newport and the other "very rogues about town" going the pace as they were. Surely Samuel is the only man who ever made a clean breast of it, and the only human sinner whose reputation was ever established by the ordinarily disastrous process of being found out.

You may trace, as we say, the accuracy of Mr. Pepys' observations of the pleasantries of the early

Spring Gardens through the pages of the dramatists
of the Restoration, how the Hippolytas and Prues,
Thisbes and Mrs. Fancifuls, the flame-coloured petticoats, and the other figures of those joyous times
regarded the conveniences of its pleasant arbours.
Its pleasures and its vices were no better and no
worse than the other places of public resort of the
times, and at Vauxhall as elsewhere the flame of riot
and revelry of those reckless days blazed up and
burnt away.

In the stormy days which followed those feverish
pleasures of the Restoration, England, and London
especially, had more serious matters to think and
write about than the pleasures of the town at Vauxhall. There were Stuart kings to get rid of, bishops
to acquit, papists to be packed off bag and baggage,
a new Protestant king to be brought over from
Holland, and a whole line of Protestant successors
to be secured for the English throne by an Act of
Settlement. It is not strange, therefore, to find little
mention of our garden up the river in the annals of
those days, though we know that it still opened its
gates to the subjects of King William as it had done
to those of Charles and James, with pleasures a little
chastened no doubt, to suit the more serious spirit of
the times. The whole place was for sale, apparently,
in 1694, and any one wishing to know all particulars
could have them by inquiring of " Mrs. Eliz. Plant at
Foxhall, near the Garden," as we learn from the *London
Gazette*, and the sale included " the Great Spring

Garden, commonly called the New Spring Garden at Foxhall, with several acres of land and houses." Whether they were sold we do not know, and whether Mrs. Eliz. Plant was one of the early proprietors to whom pleasure-loving London owed so much, is also a matter of surmise. It is certain that the amenities of the place were still provided for such as chose to enjoy them, and that by the time England began to settle down under Queen Anne the fame of the gardens at Vauxhall, as one of the attractions of the town, had in no way diminished since the delights recorded by Mr. Pepys.

In the last year of the seventeenth century we learn from Mr. Tom Brown, the facetious historian of many of the diversions of those times, that " the ladies have an inclination to take delight in the close walks of Spring Garden, where both sexes meet and mutually serve one another as guides to lose their way, and the windings and turnings in the little wildernesses are so intricate," adds Mr. Brown slyly, " that the most experienced mothers have often lost themselves in looking for their daughters." There is still, we observe, the old tradition of the whispering lover about Vauxhall, the attraction of the dark walks and shady groves, which drew successive generations of youths and maidens to the place until their discreet reticence disappeared a century later in a blaze of vulgar fireworks. Doctor Swift, we find, took Lady Kerry and Miss Pratt to hear the nightingales a little later, and Mr. Thoresby, of the Diary, was " surprised

with so many pleasant walks so near London," in the
Vauxhall of 1714.

It is in such allusions as these that we trace the
London *al fresco* through those early days, days during
which its trees grew, and the habits of its patrons
formed themselves in a manner which made it easy
for the managers of the palmy days which were to
come to fill the groves of one with continuous and
delighted crowds of the other. It happens that the
rather scanty annals of the Vauxhall of the days of
Anne were enriched by an essay on the beauties of the
place and the aspect of its company, which are as convincing as the vivid pages of Mr. Pepys himself. No
less a light of those times than Mr. Addison devoted
a day and a whole *Spectator* to a visit to Vauxhall. It
has been often quoted, but in these days when *Spectators* and *Tatlers* and *Guardians* we suspect are little
read as a whole, we make no apology for recalling the
Spectator's visit to Vauxhall with Sir Roger de Coverley on the evening of May 20, 1712.

We all know, or we ought to know, that famous
description of the journey by water to Vauxhall.
There is the crowd of importunate watermen at the
Temple stairs, from whom the knight picks out one
with a wooden leg as a reward for the loss of the
limb at La Hogue. We see the short-faced Spectator
taking his seat, and Sir Roger trimming the boat with
his coachman, "who, being a sober man, always served
for ballast on these occasions." We see the old man
turning about, as the boat swings out into the stream

in the evening light, to take a survey of the great metropolis, and make "several reflections on the greatness of the British nation; as that one English-man could beat three Frenchmen, that the Thames was the noblest river in Europe, and that London Bridge was a greater piece of work than any of the seven wonders of the world." The badinage of the river is received by the knight in exchange for his kindly good-morrow, and he regrets that he is not in the commission for Middlesex in order to teach "such vagrants that her Majesty's subjects were no more to be abused by water than by land."

"We were now arrived at Spring Garden," continues the Spectator, "which is exquisitely pleasant at this time of the year. When I considered the fragrancy of the walks and bowers, with the choirs of birds that sung upon the trees, and the loose tribe of people that walked under their shades, I could not but look upon the place as a kind of Mahometan paradise." The singing of the birds reminded Sir Roger of the nightingale coppice at Coverley Hall, and he fell a-musing on the widow, the widow who had "certainly the finest hand of any woman in the world," "when a mask who came behind him gave him a gentle tap on the shoulder, and asked him if he would drink a bottle of mead with her. But the knight, being startled at so unexpected a familiarity . . . told her she was a wanton baggage, and bid her go about her business." There is allusion to the modest refreshment of the place in the record

of the glass of Burton ale and slice of hung beef
which the Spectator and the knight took together,
the famous animadversion of Sir Roger to the lady
at the bar about the paucity of nightingales and the
plenty of wanton baggages, and we are certain that
Mr. Addison's picture of the Spring Garden at Vauxhall in the days of Queen Anne will not be improved
by a single touch of our own.

A great silence fell over Vauxhall after the days of
the *Spectator*, a silence which hushed all report of its
doings, and remained unbroken until the first year of
the reign of the second George, when one of those
geniuses who took the amusements of Londoners
into their keeping arose and did for Vauxhall what
Heidegger did for the masquerade, or Francis White
for the clubs, or Astley for the circus. Historians
of London find no record of Vauxhall and its pleasures
for fourteen years, with the single exception of its
mention as one of the sights of the town in the " New
Guide to London" of 1726. But the *al fresco* entertainment in which we are interested was by that time
out of danger, and was providing London, as we know,
with a score of tea gardens in the most pleasant spots
of the town and its suburbs. Mr. Wroth thinks that
the place had somewhat declined in the interval of
silence, that the attractions had become stale and
scanty, and its management lax. So much was hinted
later when a grateful London took to praising Mr.
Jonathan Tyers for his enterprise,—Mr. Tyers, who
took a lease of the place from Mrs. Elizabeth Masters

in 1728, who eventually acquired the freehold of the original gardens and of some additional acres, and who was the real author of the famous Vauxhall Gardens of George the Second and George the Third, the Vauxhall of Fielding and Smollett, of Horace Walpole, of Goldsmith and Dr. Johnson, of the Duchess of Devonshire and the Prince of Wales.

Tyers was in no hurry, as it would seem, to force the attractions of his place upon the town. He obtained his lease in 1728, as we say, and for no less than four years he continued to crouch, as it were, for a final spring in 1732. The place was doubtless open during those years, but one reads nothing of it, and there is little doubt that Jonathan saved the greatest of his efforts for the season of 1732, when he made a bid for the patronage of the great by his famous *Ridotto al fresco* of that year.

The idea itself was almost of the nature of an inspiration, the idea of removing the masquerade, which was providing Heidegger with a fortune at the Haymarket, from the hot rooms of the opera-house to the cool shades of Vauxhall in the balmy surroundings of the evening of an English June. The company did not meet till between the hours of nine and eleven, so all the garishness which sunlight was calculated to shed upon mask and domino was avoided, and the mystery which was a necessary part of those joyous functions was happily preserved. It requires little imagination to recall the famous *Ridotto al fresco* of 1732; the river still without bridges, boat-loads of happy people in fancy dress going up stream, as the evening closed in, in boats preceded by others playing music, the lights of the flotilla and the fancy dresses and the music giving a touch of Venetian gaiety to the lovely but sober reaches of the Thames. There were some hundreds only of the *élite* of London Society admitted to this *fête*, as we are told, and Prince Frederick, Prince of Wales, came down the river in his barge from Kew. The night was fine, and they kept it up till the birds sang and the daylight came at four o'clock the next morning. There was some little excitement when a pickpocket was detected in the act of taking the purse of one of the company with fifty guineas, and comic relief was not wanting when a tipsy waiter reeled in among the fine ladies in an improvised fancy dress.

Such was the opening ceremony of the famous Tyers management of Vauxhall Gardens, which established their vogue and made of them the most famous open air entertainment in Europe during a century. Of the details of that management there is no lack; after 1732 we are on firm ground, and the difficulty is not one of the collection of information but of its sifting and selection. For there is a chorus of praise chiefly, but of comment and criticism also, on the attractions of Vauxhall from the days of Horace Walpole to those of Thackeray and Albert Smith.

There survives a tradition that the first years of Mr. Tyers at Spring Gardens were not unclouded with anxiety. He was meditating, indeed, if we are to believe that tradition, on the easiest way out of the troubles by which he was beset, and had arrived at a consideration of the respective merits of hanging and drowning. While in this mood he happened to meet Mr. Hogarth the painter, who had lodgings near the gardens for the summer. Mr. Tyers imparted his griefs to the painter, and Mr. Hogarth bade him be of good cheer and call at his studio later in the day for a discussion of the business. The conference which followed is said to have led to a suggestion which resulted in the production of the *Ridotto al fresco*, which founded the fortunes of the place and of Mr. Tyers. The legend is difficult to confirm or refute, nor is it a matter of great importance. Mr. Hogarth was undoubtedly associated with the place; he certainly painted one decorative picture for the embellishment of one of Mr. Tyers' saloons himself, and he allowed Francis Hayman to copy another for the same purpose. He also designed those delightful little season tickets in silver or bronze, which are now eagerly sought by collectors of the memorials of past times in London; little tokens delicately wrought in ovals, or of a lozenge shape, with borders in the rococo style, and hinting at the pleasures of the gardens by pretty relievos of nymphs, in classical attire, reclining gracefully in the shade of its groves, or Amphion twanging his harp on the dolphin's back. Mr. Hogarth himself received a life ticket in gold to admit "a coachful," and inscribed with the legend, *in perpetuam beneficii memoriam.* This identical token recently brought the amazing price of £310 by auction at Sotheby's, and its existence may, or may not, be accepted as a confirmation of the Hogarth legend to which we have alluded.

It is not difficult to reconstruct the pleasaunce which Mr. Tyers prepared for his patrons, for many of the scribes of the next half-century recorded its delights, and not a few of the capable artists of those times transferred its beauties to the copper plate. The place was a parallelogram, and its main features were groves of trees which eventually assumed the dignity of forest timber, intersected by gravel walks crossing each other at right angles. It was entered by a gateway through an ordinary-looking house of brick of three storeys, which with a high brick wall enclosed the gardens on the western side bounded by Kennington lane. On the three other sides its borders were the hayfields of the open country. As you entered the place from the gateway through the manager's house you looked up the Grand Walk, planted with a stately avenue of elms, and extending the whole length of the demesne. Parallel to the Grand Walk on the right hand ran the South Walk, an avenue of much the same length and dimensions, which was crossed by three triumphal arches of a rather debased Renaissance design. A third avenue, the Grand Cross Walk, ran across the whole garden at right angles to the two avenues we have named. On the right the Grand Cross Walk gave access to the Dark Walks, the Druids' Walk, or the Lovers' Walk, the secluded alleys of Vauxhall which gave the place much of its fame and not a little of its attractions for some of its patrons. On the left the Grand Cross Walk led to the Wildernesses and Rural Downs, more open shrubbery-like spaces which afforded a view of the country towards the river. The whole place covered about twelve acres, and you may trace its general plan quite perfectly in the excellent bird's-eye view drawn by Mr. Wale in 1751.

It was thus that Mr. Tyers prepared a loafing-place for half a century of the social life of London; he spared neither time nor money nor ingenuity on its attractions, and he had his reward in a long popularity. He placed at the end of his two grand walks represen-tations of the ruins of Palmyra, and colossal statues, which by concealing its boundaries added to the apparent size of the place. He employed sculptors of ability to carve him statues in marble; one of Mr. Handel, whose music was often heard in the gardens, was much admired, and is yet in the possession of Mr. Alfred Lyttleton. Milton in lead sat blind and forlorn in the rural downs, and representations of Apollo gave an air of classic taste to his groves. He dug out caves in his wildernesses, where he buried his musicians, from whose fiddles arose mysterious music in the solitudes known as the Musical Bushes, until, as he announced, he was obliged to abandon that ingenious attraction, " the natural damp of the earth being found prejudicial to the instruments." He built a fine orchestra in what he called his Grove, a space of nearly five acres near the entrance on the right, where bands of the ablest musicians in London played good music in most imposing cocked hats, and tenors and prima donnas trilled and quavered for half a century.

The Grove was the square enclosed by the Grand and South Walks, and by the Cross Walk and the western wall of the gardens, and it was the centre of the buildings of Vauxhall which came to be as famous as its groves and arbours. Round and about the Grove were clustered the temples, the pavilions, the rotundas, the great rooms, the music rooms, the picture rooms, the covered colonnades for wet weather, above all the famous supper boxes built in straight rows or curving sweeps. In those famous supper boxes, where generations of Londoners ate the noted Vauxhall chicken and ham, were the paintings which gave a quaint interest to each, every picture displayed by its own little oil lamp. There were the "Four Times of the Day," copied by permission from Mr. Hogarth's noted compositions of the same title, and the varied productions of Mr. Francis Hayman and other artists; scenes from Shakespeare and from popular comedies; representations of the favourite sports of the people—the Play of See-saw, the Play of Cricket, Leap-Frog, Sliding on the Ice, milkmaids dancing round the Maypole, Phyllis and Corydon, pipe and tabor, sheep and shepherds and shepherdesses and what not. Mr. Hogarth himself painted a picture for one of the larger saloons, of Henry the

Eighth and Anne Boleyn; and in his blunt way, it is said, pointed to a famous scandal of the day by painting Henry with the face of Frederick, Prince of Wales, and Lady Archibald Hamilton as Anne Boleyn. Above all, Mr. Tyers lighted up the darkness of his groves " with above a thousand lamps so disposed that they all took fire together, with such a sudden blaze as was perfectly surprising."

It was that same lighting of the groves which formed one of the chief attractions of Vauxhall and captivated all beholders for half a century. There is a continual rhapsody on the lamps at Vauxhall by generations of writers, and a blaze of artificial light seen through a foreground of overhanging trees at Vauxhall provided a subject for a succession of artists, who produced those delightful vignettes on copper for its programmes and song sheets, where the beauties of the place are best preserved. The illuminations of Vauxhall were undoubtedly arranged with much taste, and the sudden lighting of the lamps, with a simultaneous crash of music from the orchestra, had a considerable effect. Moreover, the illuminations of Vauxhall gained greatly by contrast with the aspect of the town of that day. Long after the general use of gas, London after nightfall was a dull and gloomy place. The streets were generally narrow and ill lighted, and quite without the blaze of light to which we are accustomed from the modern shop window. Even at the theatres, the stage effects, with which this century is familiar, were unknown, and Vauxhall was really the only place

where the citizen could see anything of the beauty
of artificial light intelligently employed. Modern
caterers are fully aware of the value of a judicious
investment in gas and white paint, and there is little
wonder at the success of the efforts of Mr. Tyers and
his successors to produce "a rich blaze of radiance"
by their coloured lamps and chandeliers and illuminated stars and revolving mirrors in an age when the
ordinary surroundings of the Londoner gave them so
much help by their contrast.

Mr. Tyers also lost nothing by any lack of enterprise in his methods of advertising the place. Grub
Street was eloquent about the joys of Vauxhall, the
fashion of its patrons, the beauty of its groves, the
chaste sobriety of its solitudes where, as we learn,
"even bishops have been seen without injuring their
character." "The whole place," says another scribe,
"is a realisation of Elizium." Gazetteers descanted
on the surprising fashion of the company to be met in
its walks, which were "often honoured with some of
the Royal family, who are here entertained with the
sweet song of numbers of nightingales in concert with
the best band of musick in England." Frederick
Prince of Wales really did haunt the garden a good
deal, would command songs which were favourites of
his Royal Highness, and allowed Mr. Tyers to dedicate
a pavilion to him, which was duly surmounted with
the royal plumes. The minor poets, too, often broke
into song about the beauties of Vauxhall, as when one
of those tuneful gentlemen described the impressions

of Farmer Colin from the country, after a visit to
Lambeth :—

> " O Mary! soft in feature,
>   I've been at dear Vauxhall;
> No paradise is sweeter,
>   Not that they Eden call.
>
> Methought when first I entered,
>   Such splendours round me shone;
> Into a world I entered,
>   Where rose another sun.
>
> While music never cloying,
>   As skylarks sweet I hear;
> The sounds I'm still enjoying,
>   They'll always soothe my ear."

You may read reams of verses like these if you have
time and inclination to explore the collections of the
fugitive literature of George the Second and George
the Third.   We probably do no great injustice to Mr.
Tyers in surmising that a great deal of such poetry
drew as much inspiration from his strong box as from
the charms of his gardens.

Tyers was more original, perhaps, in one other of
his methods of advertising.   He was accustomed to
dress up presentable agents of both sexes in the height
of fashion, and to send them to mix with the assemblies of great people who took the air in the park or
in the Mall at St. James's.   These " decoy ducks," as
as they came to be called, met at such places as if by
accident, remarked on the beauty of the weather in
tones audible to bystanders, and supposed that they

would have the pleasure of meeting each other later
at Vauxhall. By these devices, and the general enterprise of his management, the astute manager contrived
to make his gardens the summer playground of
London society for half a century, and a history of
Vauxhall during the Tyers management is a history of
one phase of that society itself.

That was a typical evening at Vauxhall on the
23rd June, 1750, when Lady Caroline Petersham
arranged a party and sent Mr. Horace Walpole a
card. We see in our chapter on the parks how
Lady Caroline beat the Mall for recruits on that
occasion, and enlisted such lights of the society of
that day as the Duke of Kingston, Lord March,
"a pretty Miss Beauclerc and a very foolish Miss
Sparre, little Miss Ashe and Mr. Whitehed." "The
ladies," says Horace, "were as handsome as crimson
could make them, having just finished their last
layer of red." They took the water at Whitehall
Stairs and rowed up the river, with the customary
boat of French horns as a vanguard, Miss Ashe
lending the additional charm of her voice. At
Vauxhall Stairs they picked up Lord Granby, who
had just come from the joys of duck hunting at
Jenny's Whim at Chelsea, and was deplorably drunk,
as Horace unkindly records. This was the heroic
Granby of Minden, whose head was on half the inn
signboards in England for the next half century.
"At last," says Walpole, "we assembled in our
booth, Lady Caroline in front, with the visor of

her hat erect and looking gloriously jolly and handsome. She had fetched my brother Orford from
the next box, where he was enjoying himself with
his *petite partie*, to help us to mince chickens. We
minced seven chickens into a china dish, which Lady
Caroline stewed over a lamp with three pats of butter
and a flagon of water, stirring and rattling and laughing, and we every minute expecting the dish to fly
about our ears." The mixture does not sound
appetising, but they seem to have made a meal of
it. Lady Caroline had brought Betty the fruit girl
from St. James's Street with hampers of strawberries,
who waited on these great people, and was honoured
by being allowed to sup at a little table of her own by
their side. You may follow if you like the conversation of the party of social celebrities in Walpole's
gossiping pages. A Mr. O'Brien, a fortune-hunting
Irishman, had lately arrived from Ireland, too late,
however, to claim the Duchess of Manchester from
Mr. Hussey. "I took up the biggest hautboy in the
dish," says Walpole, "and said to Lady Caroline,
'Madam, Miss Ashe desires you would eat this
O'Brien strawberry;' she replied immediately, 'I
won't, you hussey.'" And who shall say that wit
and repartee were dead in June of 1753? "In
short," says Horace, "the whole air of our party
was sufficient, as you will easily imagine, to take
up the whole attention of the garden; so much so
that from eleven o'clock till half-an-hour after one we
had the whole concourse round our booth. At last

they came into the little gardens of each booth on the side of ours, till Harry Vane took up a bumper and drank their healths, and was proceeding to treat them with still greater freedoms." The party got home, as we learn, at three o'clock in the morning, and the entertainment was in every way typical of a fashionable party at Vauxhall during the prosperous days of Mr. Tyers' management.

Those same viands of Vauxhall chicken and ham had a reputation which was as renowned as the lamps and the groves of the gardens; the chickens for their smallness, the slices of ham for a thinness past belief. There was much humorous comment on the eatables at Vauxhall from the beginning of Mr. Tyers' management to the days of Thackeray, who speaks of "the twinkling boxes in which the happy feasters made believe to eat almost invisible slices of ham." The old citizen of the *Connoisseur* of 1755, Mr. Rose, found the chickens no bigger than a sparrow, and estimated his mouthfuls at groats and threepenny pieces; you may still see him in a delightful little copper-plate engraving which illustrated that periodical, holding up a reproachful forkful of ham at the waiter. It was contended that a famous carver of the gardens obtained and held a lucrative situation by his proved ability to cover the whole twelve acres of the premises with slices from a single joint. It was unsafe, as was asserted, to carry a plateful from one table to another, the slices being subject to abduction by the zephyrs of the groves.

Constant patrons of the gardens also declared that you could read the *Postboy* or the *Chronicle* with perfect ease through the transparent medium of the delicate Vauxhall ham.

During the height of their vogue there was a certain etiquette at the gardens; ladies came in full evening dress, and the men walked bareheaded, with their hats under their arms. A stately promenade of the main walks of the garden was usually a function which began the delights of the evening for the more fashionable of the company. Then followed the concert, invariably composed of sixteen pieces; songs alternating with instrumental performances—the songs of a very sentimental cast—the sonatas and symphonies for the band being often of a higher musical quality. Tyers, however, engaged the finest voices of his day to warble the tender ballads for which the place was famous; and men like Thomas Lowe and Vernon, and lady singers like Mrs. Arne, Miss Stevenson, Miss Wright, Mrs. Baddeley, and Mrs. Weichsell, no doubt supplied the charm which the songs themselves—all about Strephon and Delia and Cupid—seem to lack to-day. There were set spectacles, like watermills and tin cascades, for those who preferred them to music, and great opportunities for ogling on a grand scale for the younger members of Mr. Tyers' patrons. "A young lady, who was at Vauxhall on Thursday night last in company with two gentlemen," says an advertisement in the *London Chronicle* for August 5th, 1758, "could not but observe a young gentleman in blue and gold-laced hat, who, being near her by the orchestra during the performance, especially the last song, gazed upon her with the utmost attention. He earnestly hopes (if unmarried) she will favour him with a line, directed to A. D. at the bar of the Temple Exchange Coffee-house, Temple Bar, to inform him whether fortune, family, and character may not entitle him upon a further knowledge to hope an interest in her heart." Who does not wish a happy ending to the sighs of this modest young gentleman in blue and the gold-laced hat, his oglings of the fair restrained within prudent limits by the presence of the two other gentlemen, but still culminating in a killing effort during the last song, and fully expressed later in the accommodating columns of the *London Chronicle*?

The other famous attraction of Vauxhall was provided by the romantic qualities which generations of young people found in Mr. Tyers' dark walks. Frisky maidens from the city delighted in braving the dangers of those solitudes, and there were not wanting gallant youths who provided the necessary excitement. It was the destiny of most of the famous heroines of fiction, from Amelia to Evelina, to meet with adventures in the recesses of Mr. Tyers' famous solitudes; readers of Fielding will remember how Amelia fared at the hands of Jane and my lord before the arrival of Booth and Captain Trench; and the meeting of Evelina and Sir Clement Willoughby, and the declaration of love which followed, is surely an everlasting model for all ladies who write love scenes between prim maidens and impetuous lovers.

The dark walks of Vauxhall had quite naturally different aspects for different minds. There was an innocent gentleman, for example, who wrote a description of Vauxhall which was very popular and several times reprinted during the last century, who pointed out its beauties for minds of a contemplative cast. "It is very agreeable," he says, "to all whose minds are adapted to contemplation and scenes devoted to solitude, and the votaries that court her shrine, and it must be confessed that there is something in the amiable simplicity of unadorned nature that spreads over the mind a more noble sort of tranquillity, and a greater sensation of pleasure than can be received from the nicer scenes of art.

> 'How simple nature's hand with noble grace,
> Diffuses artless beauties o'er the place.'

This walk in the evening is dark, which renders it more agreeable to those minds who love to enjoy the full scope of imagination, to listen to the orchestra and view the lamps glittering through the trees."

We take this good gentleman to have been one of Mr. Tyers' literary men, because there is much critical matter affecting the reputation of the chaste solitudes which he describes which issued from other pens almost at the same moment. We read of "loose persons of both sexes," who frequented the dark walks, "yelling in sounds fully as terrific as the imagined horrors of Calvacanti's bloodhounds," of ladies driven from their friends and half-frightened to death, and of much reprehensible rowdyism and horseplay. The magistrates indeed interfered in 1763, and compelled Mr. Tyers to fence off the famous Dark Walks and provide watchmen to keep the peace. The bloods, however, would have none of the restrictions, and forcibly removed Mr. Tyers' new fence, and the humours of the Dark Walks undoubtedly continued for another quarter of a century much as they were described by our last quoted authority. Quite late in the century, as we learn from Sir Gilbert Elliot, there was a certain manifestation from the Dark Walks, known as the "Vauxhall squeak," which was a signal for the more reputable members of the company to retire. There is record too of a humorous custom amongst people of a certain social standing which had a great vogue during one or two seasons just before George the Third came to the throne, which throws a not un-interesting light on the manners of society in public places in those days. Parties of well-dressed ladies, we are told, prided themselves on their proficiency in imitating the crowing of cocks at Vauxhall, one, Mrs. Woolaston, being reckoned particularly distinguished in that pleasing mimicry. The gentlemen of the party were accustomed to respond antiphonally with the not inappropriate burden of the braying of asses.

We believe, however, that such incidents, of which,

it is true, there is record during the whole of the
Tyers' management, were exceptional, and that the
main features of the entertainment of Vauxhall for
half a century were distinguished by a decorum which
was uncommon at similar places of amusement about
the town.   It is quite certain that Tyers found patrons
among the chief men of his day in most walks of
life.   We think of the great figures of those times,
each in its particular environment : Johnson and Goldsmith in their modest lodgings off the Strand ; Sir
Joshua at the painting-room in Leicester Fields ;
Garrick at Drury Lane or the Adelphi ; Fox and
Fitzpatrick at Brooks's or the House of Commons ; the
wild Prince of Wales and the Duke of York chafing
under the parental curb at the Queen's House at
St. James's ; any or all of the great ladies of society,
from the " beautiful Molly Lepel " to the Duchess
of Devonshire and Mrs. Crewe, and Lady Elizabeth
Foster, in their great town houses or great country
mansions—but we may think of them all with the
greatest historical propriety at Vauxhall.   Those
gardens at Lambeth were a kind of social exchange,
where Londoners of all ranks could and did meet for half
a century, and partook together of Mr. Tyers' harmless entertainments.   Vauxhall was, in fact, the only
place of its kind in Europe, during a century, which
saw nearly every capital except London devastated at
one time or other by the occupation of hostile armies.
Certain it is that whole generations of Londoners
revelled in its delights, and have left blessings upon its

memory, and Vauxhall was either a very pleasant place, or else the town of George the Third was much more easily amused than the town of to-day. "That excellent place of amusement," said Dr. Johnson, "must ever be an estate to its proprietor, as it is peculiarly adapted to the taste of the English nation, there being a mixture of curious show, gay exhibition, music, vocal and instrumental, not too refined for the general ear, for all which only a shilling is paid, and though last, not least, good eating and drinking for those who choose to purchase that regale." Goldsmith delighted in the place, and his description of the company and the pleasures of Vauxhall in the "Citizen of the World" —of Mrs. Tibbs and the pawnbroker's widow, of the shabby beau and the man in black, and the raptures of the Chinese philosopher—is almost as much a classic of our literature as Mr. Addison's essay of half a century before. The great people went, and it followed, as a matter of course, that lesser people followed to gaze at them. Vauxhall was the place where any one aspiring to the notice of the fashion of the day was obliged to appear at proper intervals: the rising actor, the poet looking out for a patron who was good for twenty guineas for a dedication, the parson wanting preferment. Famous toasts of the town displayed their beauties in its walks; the fascinating Miss Chudleigh, who was a maid of honour and Countess of Bristol and Duchess of Kingston almost at one and the same moment, was very fond of its promenade; and Horace Walpole will tell you how the incomparable Miss Gunnings were so mobbed by a crowd of eager admirers of their beauty that they had incontinently to retreat. The periodical unbending of a proud society in public, which appeared to perfection in Walpole's account of his famous party, was no doubt much appreciated by the ordinary citizen, and Vauxhall was almost the only place where he could enjoy occasional contact with great people in such propitious moods. There is a pleasant flavour about many of the anecdotes of Vauxhall which are recorded in the light literature of the last century. It must have been pretty to hear Lord Sandwich and his party, which included the mellifluous Miss Rae no doubt, tuning up after supper, and starting a glee from their box, to the delight of the bystanders. General Haile, in the next box, moved by his lordship's example, prevailed on a young lady who accompanied him to sing a solo, "which the band obligingly accompanied, to the delight of the audience." The ordinary citizen, we should imagine, usually got his shilling's worth, quite apart from the entertainments provided by Mr. Tyers. A little excitement was occasionally provided by a row between well-known men about town like Parson Bate and the ruffian Fighting Fitzgerald, or when Captain Allen and Mr. Kelly called each other rascal and scoundrel, drew their swords, and provided the pamphleteers with a subject for a month's writing.

In the later days the attractions of Vauxhall were not diminished by the chance of meeting the handsome

young George Prince of Wales, who would break out
of the windows at St. James's and appear suddenly at
midnight in more or less of disguise with Hanger, or
Barrymore, or Lake, or St. Leger, or it may be Mr.
Charles Fox, if he were not engaged in the House of
Commons or at faro at Brooks's.   They were very fond
of the Prince of Wales at Vauxhall, dedicated pavilions
to him, and exhibited his face and figure in transparencies, his Royal Highness leaning against a horse
held by Britannia, Minerva bearing his helmet, Providence fixing his spurs, and Fame blowing a trumpet
and crowning him with laurel.   Then the famous
baritone, Mr. Darley, would come to the front of the
orchestra and sing the praises of the royal youth—

> " Endowed with each virtue the dignified youth,
>   Ere reason enlightened his mind,
>   Burst forth on the world in example and truth
>   The boast and delight of mankind "

—verses which could not have been without humour
to all who knew the history of George Prince of
Wales in 1791.

"The Prince of Wales was at Vauxhall," says the
British Magazine for August of 1782 . . . "but when
the music was over, being discovered by the company,
he was so surrounded, crushed, pursued, and overcome
that he was under the necessity of beating a hasty
retreat.   The ladies followed the prince ; the gentlemen pursued the ladies; the curious ran to see what
was the matter ; the mischievous ran to increase the

tumult, and in two minutes the boxes were deserted; the lame were overthrown, the well-dressed were demolished, and for half-an-hour the whole company were contracted in one narrow channel and borne along with the rapidity of a torrent, to the infinite danger of powdered locks, painted cheeks, and crazy constitutions."

The great period of Vauxhall Gardens lasted, as we believe, until the year 1791, when the ordinary price of admission of one shilling was doubled by a new management, and a series of entertainments were begun which we shall examine shortly later on, and marked the inevitable period of decline. Jonathan Tyers died in 1767, was succeeded by his son of the same name, and the old traditions of his management lasted until the year we have named. That management, we hold, marked the height of the London *al fresco*, the almost forgotten entertainment which filled so large a place among the pleasures of our ancestors, which it has been our pleasant task to investigate and describe. Vauxhall, as we have seen, was fortunate in many of its historians, and there is a drawing by that admirable artist, Mr. Thomas Rowlandson, well known to connoisseurs by the fine engraving, which preserves for us much of the charm of its prime and the portraits of some of its patrons.

The two beautiful women in the centre of the composition are the Duchess of Devonshire and her sister Lady Duncannon, the upright figure on the left with the eyeglass that of Captain Topham, the proprietor and editor of the *World*, an early specimen of the now common "society" paper. Admiral Paisley is the particular hero represented as the veteran with the wooden leg on the duchess's right, and the parson who looks over Lady Duncannon's shoulder is Sir Harry Bate Dudley, the editor of the *Morning Post*, who was more than a match for Fighting Fitzgerald and his bruising footman in the famous Vauxhall Affray. By his side is James Perry, the editor of the *Morning Chronicle*, a great amateur of the claymore, and therefore represented in Highland costume. On the right of the picture are his Royal Highness the Prince of Wales and Perdita Robinson, the latter coyly trifling with her locket, containing Florizel's picture no doubt.

Under the orchestra in the box is Dr. Johnson, with Boswell on his left and Mrs. Thrale on his right, supported by Oliver Goldsmith. Mrs. Weichsell is warbling from the orchestra, and any one interested in the smaller musical matters of the time may recognise among the musicians Barthlemon the leading fiddle, Fisher with his hautboy, and Mr. Hook the conductor, father of the facetious Theodore of the next generation.

Before passing on to the later history of those famous gardens, it may not be inappropriate to take leave of Jonathan Tyers, to whom the pleasure-loving Londoners of his day owed so much. Many years before his death Mr. Tyers had the reward which attends those who are diligent in business, and retired to the banks of the Mole, at a country place called Denbies. Here he contrived to indulge his old love of gardens and groves, but his efforts were all inspired by a strain of chasteness and morality suited to his years, and suggested perhaps by his experience of the vanities of the world at Vauxhall. The Dark Walk at Vauxhall was represented by "the Valley of the Shadow" at Denbies, which seems to have been one of the sights of the county. "Awful and tremendous the view on the descent into this gloomy vale," writes Mr. Hughson, a visitor evidently much impressed by the solemnity of Mr. Tyers' landscape gardening. "There was a large alcove divided into two compartments, in one of which the unbeliever was represented as dying in great agony; near him were the books which had encouraged him in his libertine course, Hobbes, Tindal, &c. In the other was the Christian, represented in a placid and serene state, prepared for the mansions of the blest." The last glimpse of all of old Tyers is in a rather pathetic paragraph which records that a few days before his death, in 1767, he was carried at his own request and placed in a chair in the middle of the old gardens at Vauxhall, so that he might take a dying glance at the place which had engaged the energies of his prime.

Although there were still nearly seventy years of life, and perhaps half that number of prosperity, in store for Vauxhall, its history after 1791 interests us less, as students of the London *al fresco*, than the period we have already examined. The old social features of the gardens are much less in evidence during its later history, the spectacular and the sensational much more. We read in 1792 of grand galas and masquerades, with crowds of haymakers, sweeps, sailors, and punches, and of a company which in no way compared with that of Mr. Tyers' *Ridotto al fresco* of 1732. A few years later were introduced the fireworks, which invariably marked the decline of an open air entertainment in London from the old, simple standards of music and refreshment. The change was, no doubt, inevitable, and fireworks, acrobats, and tight-rope dancers became features of the management so long as the place kept open. The taste of Londoners progressed if it did not improve, and the new views of life and its opportunities, which began to prevail after the Revolution in France, were no longer satisfied with the placid joys which had delighted earlier generations. There are scores of prints and programmes showing the new attractions, and the alterations in the old plan which they entailed. There was a firework platform erected at the eastern end of the grounds, a fire-work tower, and a mast sixty feet high, from which the "ethereal Saqui" descended on the tight-rope in a blaze of blue flame and Chinese fire. The ethereal Saqui is represented as a very material-looking lady of masculine appearance, dressed in a Roman helmet surmounted by enormous plumes, a tunic of classic cut, and white linen trousers tied round the ankles, like

the typical school-girl of the period of Miss Austen.
She descends the tight-rope very cleverly, on one toe
apparently, in the painting by Mr. Hutchison of Bath.
As the present century ran into its teens, there were
changes which may have caused old Jonathan Tyers
to turn in his grave. They cut down many of the
trees in his grove, and two sides of that pleasant enclosure and a great part of the Grand Walk were
covered in by a colonnade with cast-iron pillars. The
place was still in the possession of the Tyers' family,
represented by a Mr. Barrett, who had married the
daughter of Jonathan Tyers the younger, but there
was little other association between the Vauxhall of
the early years of George the Third and those of his
successor, the patron of the place who, in 1822, conferred the privilege of the royal title upon the proprietors of that year, Mr. Bish, Mr. Gye, and Mr.
Hughes. The later Vauxhall is the Vauxhall of
Thackeray and Dickens and Albert Smith and Theodore
Hook, the Vauxhall of the 20,000 additional lamps,
the Vauxhall where Jos Sedley drank too much arrack
punch and called Becky Sharp his " tiddy iddy darling," and where Pendennis danced with Fanny Bolton.
That Vauxhall is still remembered by persons living,
and its latest aspect is best preserved in the drawing
of Mr. Doyle in *Punch*. It was a Vauxhall of dancing-
floors and balloon ascents, of spectacular panoramas of
Arctic regions, of Indian jugglers and Mr. Ducrow's
equestrian entertainments—above all the Vauxhall of
Mr. Simpson, the wondrous master of the ceremonies,

the "gentle Simpson, that kind smiling idiot," whose
personality is preserved in the wonderful etching by
Robert Cruikshank. There must be people living yet
who remember Mr. Simpson, the very incarnation of
humility—Simpson with his knee breeches and shirt
frill, his tasselled cane and his dress hat, his wondrous
attitudes and his surprising Vauxhall addresses, and his
last will and testament, hoping that " the managers
would dispose of his humble body as they deemed fit."
We glance at this later story of Vauxhall, with its gas
lamps and its battle of Waterloo, which the Duke
himself went to see and admired, but which Talfourd
hoped might be ended by the immediate arrival of the
Prussians, as a sort of duty which we owe to the
obsequies of the London *al fresco*. The stout at
Vauxhall grew muddier, the slices of ham, if possible,
thinner, the chickens more skinny, and the company
more raffish as modern England became transformed
by railways and Reform Bills. There was no place in
London for an entertainment which in anyway represented the old pleasant tradition of the *al fresco*.
Even the vulgarity and sensations of the later Vauxhall failed to please at last, and the positively last
appearances which were announced in successive seasons
after the year 1850 became a standing joke of the
town. The " last appearance," however, came in the
end on July 25th, 1859, and the London *al fresco*
was at length laid to rest after a rather discreditable
old age, unless, indeed, it still lingered in the doubtful keeping of the projectors of the Cremorne.

We do not propose to examine that question, but to content ourselves with the pious hope that modern London may one day see a resurrection of a form of pleasure of which it stands, year by year, in greater need.

CHAPTER VIII

THE FAIRS

SOME obscure instinct of the English has chosen the late summer and autumn as the season in which to seek its chief relaxation and enjoyment. It is often suggested that the modern exodus of the population of our great towns to the sea or to the hills of the north, is governed primarily by the fact that Parliament rises in the late summer; indirectly also by the love of sport which prompts our legislators to bid good-bye to the Speaker at the time of the year when sport is easiest to find. The appearance of our great railway stations in August is a plausible argument in favour of this proposition. But a short study of the ways in which our forefathers amused themselves, and the times at which they took their diversion, leads to the conclusion that such a theory is superficial at the best. Field sports, as we understand and practise them, were until quite recent times the amusement of a very small part of the population, who lived constantly in the country, and yet Parliament still rose in the autumn. August and September were the busiest months in an England whose resources were drawn

from agriculture and the care of flocks and herds
rather than from the profits of manufactures and
commerce. And yet it was in those months that
this instinct of the English taught them to lay aside
their cares and get what enjoyment they could from
the means nearest at hand. Before the era of railways
and cheap travelling the great mass of the population
of London never went twenty miles from St. Paul's,
and the sport they enjoyed took the form of the
delights provided by Hockley in the Hole, the
Ducking Ponds, and the Cockpits, as we see in
other chapters. And yet, as the summer passed
away, and the dog-days raised a heat from the
cobblestones which drove the dogs themselves into
the shade of alley and entry, the common people of
London, instead of panting for the water-brooks or
the sea-shore, prepared themselves for the great
carnivals which were prepared for their delight in
one or other of the great fairs of the town.

These annual gatherings followed each other in
quick succession in the hot months of the year in
the not very promising surroundings of Smithfield,
or Southwark, or Westminster. The glory of these
entertainments was at its zenith at the beginning of
the eighteenth century, and we propose to examine
them here as the periodical diversion of great numbers
of the inhabitants of London during the next three-
quarters of a century.

In one or other of the admirable treatises which
have been written on the historical aspect of these

fairs, you may discover that their origin was religious, their development commercial, and their apotheosis an unrestrained indulgence in pleasure or license, as you may choose to regard their diversions. St. Bartholomew Fair, for example, the crown and glory of the whole set, originated in the pious jugglery of Rayer, the abbot of the priory of that saint, who obtained a charter from Henry the First, which enabled him to fleece the pilgrims during the three days' festival of his patron at Smithfield. This holy man, who began life as jester to the king, died in great sanctity in 1143, "leaving a flock of thirteen monks, who did very well on the oblations of rich Londoners." The gathering of pilgrims soon gained a commercial aspect by the establishment of a cloth fair, where other oblations of the pilgrims went to the enrichment of the city merchants, whose good broadcloth protected the pilgrims' bodies while the monks continued to look after their souls. We may read how the city contrived to get a large share in the management of the festival through the efforts of these cloth merchants, and gradually extended the fair beyond the limits of the priory; and how Henry the Eighth took over that religious institution, and reformed it in his thorough-going fashion into the hospital "for the continual relief and help of a hundred sore and diseased," which we still cherish as Bartholomew's Hospital; and how all the privileges of the fair came in time to be divided between the Corporation of London and a patentee of the Crown, Lord Rich.

We shall find that by the time of Queen Elizabeth, the cloth merchants of London having found markets elsewhere, the original three days' fair had expanded into a fourteen days' carnival, which had no pretence of any object but pleasure, and provided Ben Jonson with a subject for a play, which is an epitome of some aspects of the life of his time. All these are explanations of the fact that when modern England began, Bartholomew Fair, after many vicissitudes, had become a great popular festival, opened in state by the Lord Mayor, who drank "a cool tankard of wine, nutmeg, and sugar" at Newgate on his way to Cloth Fair to inaugurate the annual diversions. There he read his proclamation which opened the revels, which were looked forward to for months by the simple and hearty populace of those days as the great annual festival of their lives.

As the evening of the 22nd August came round in each year, the citizens who lived in the parts adjacent to Smithfield were reminded of the imminence of this annual merrymaking by the doings of a mob which seems to have sprung into existence soon after the Long Parliament. It was the custom and the pride of a perennial gang of ruffians, who came to be known —nobody knows why—as "Lady Holland's Mob," to inaugurate the eve of the feast by very singular proceedings. These humourists were accustomed to anticipate the Lord Mayor's proclamation of the morrow, by going round the streets occupied by the fair, ringing bells, pushing and hustling foot-passengers, and breaking lamps. Lady Holland's Mob was accepted as "a good old custom," and was little interfered with except when their gaiety degenerated into highway robbery. So much was this the case, that it was reckoned inadvisable to put a light in your window on that particular evening in the neighbourhoods of Smithfield or Clerkenwell; and any one whose curiosity prompted him to look out from his upper chamber, accepted the volley of stones which usually greeted his appearance as a matter of course.

It was after preliminaries such as these that the Lord Mayor, as we say, with his officials and trumpeters, went to the entrance of Cloth Fair, after calling at Newgate for his tankard, to open the show, which was the delight of the true citizen and his wife and children, his apprentices, and the lower orders of the town for the time during which it was open. We may note in passing that Lord Mayor Sir John Shorter came to a sad end in 1688 in performing that same function at Newgate. His lordship let down the lid of his tankard with so violent a snap that his horse started, threw him on his head in the Old Bailey, and instead of going on to the Cloth Fair, he was carried back dead to the Mansion House.

On the 24th of August, then, the people of London flocked in their thousands to taste the annual joys of the fair thus inaugurated with all state by their chief magistrate. For the ordinary citizen there was nothing but amusement in the incidents of the fourteen days' carnival, but for the survivors of the Puritans of the Commonwealth there was little but deadly sin in the same occasion. The puritanical spirit, as we know from present experience, dies hard. At the opening of the eighteenth century there were men alive who had seen King Charles's head roll on the scaffold at Whitehall, and thousands of others whose youth had been formed in the austere school of the men who surrounded Cromwell. We find, accordingly, that there were continual protests from the god-fearing against what they considered the license of the fairs. The cakes and ale of this annual holiday were little in favour with these gentry, and the gin stalls, the gaming-booths, the shops where sausages were eaten in derision of the Jews, above all, the booths of the players, of which the fair was largely composed, were the objects of much of their active hatred.

In the first year of the eighteenth century there was a presentment of the Grand Jury of Middlesex on the subject of Bartholomew Fair, when these good gentlemen attempted to put the clock back to the times of Henry the Seventh at least, by a proposal that all shows and booths should be abolished and the fair restored to its original character of a sale of merchandise, "we esteeming," said the Puritans, using the Grand Jury as a mouthpiece, "the renewing of their former practices at the fair a continuing of one of the chiefest nurseries of vice next to the play-houses."

This double-edged stroke at the fairs and the play-

houses was well timed, for the reason that Bartholomew Fair was on the eve of a very remarkable
development in the direction of dramatic entertainments.   A few years earlier the elder Penkethman, an
actor well known at the patent theatres, had unob-
trusively set up a booth and offered a theatrical entertainment among the tight-rope dancers, jugglers,
puppet shows and monstrosities, of which the fair
was chiefly composed.   Penkethman was followed by
many imitators from the great theatres.   There was
Dogget, for instance, the charitable comedian whom
we still remember in the annual race for the waterman's coat and badge on the Thames, an actor
described by his contemporary Cibber as the most
natural of his day ; Miller, another player well known
at Drury Lane ; Bullock, Simpson, and many others
who set up booths at the fair during the first few years
of the century.   The theatrical movement, in fact,
became so pronounced that as time went on most of
the favourite actors of the day did not disdain to tread
the boards in the temporary booths of the fair.   Colley
Cibber himself, the poet laureate, a man of fashion and
a member of the great club at White's, came later, and
Quin, Macklin, Woodward, Shuter, were among the
lights of the drama who eventually gave a distinguished
vogue to the booths of Bartholomew Fair.   The dramatic entertainments which were in fashion at the
fairs were in the strongest possible contrast to anything we associate with the theatre to-day.   They
consisted almost invariably of some prodigious long-

SOUTHWARK FAIR

DRAWN BY WILLIAM HOGARTH, 1733

winded scheme dealing with such portentous subjects
as "The Loves of the Heathen Gods," "The Creation
of the World," "The Siege of Troy," "Jephthah's
Rash Vow," "Tamerlane the Great," lightened up with
much comic relief, in which an eccentric English
character took a part totally irrelevant to the particular
epic comprised in the plot. These productions came
to be called "drolls," and you may trace in these
drolls the germs of many forms of variety entertainment popular to-day, including, perhaps, that of the
English pantomime. The plots were set out in the
greatest detail in the handbills, which are now the
rarities of great collectors, a form of advertisement
which was greatly relied upon by the managers in a
day when newspapers were few and little read by the
common folk. From these handbills we may gather
that the good British public delighted for generations
in an entertainment which simply rang the changes
on one or other of the plots we have mentioned.
The puppet - shows of Powell and Penkethman
followed the dramatic taste set by the actors, and
"Phaeton's Fall," "The Story of the Chaste Susannah,"
or "The History of Solomon and the Queen of Sheba,"
were presented with all the impressiveness which
accompanies the judicious employment of pasteboard,
glue, and copper wire.

"At Crawley's Booth, over against the Crown
Tavern in Smithfield," we read in 1716, "during
the time of Bartholomew Fair, will be presented a
little opera called 'The Old Creation of the World,'

yet newly revived with the addition of Noah's Flood;
also several fountains playing water during the time of
the play. The last scene does represent Noah and his
family coming out of the Ark with all the beasts two
by two, and all the fowls of the air seen in the
prospect sitting upon trees. Likewise over the Ark
is seen the sun rising in a most glorious manner. A
multitude of angels will be seen in double rank, which
presents a double prospect, one for the scene, the other
for the palace, where will be seen six angels ringing
of bells. Likewise machines descending from above,
with Dives rising out of Hell and Lazarus seen in
Abraham's bosom, besides several figures dancing
Jiggs, Sarabands, and Country Dances to the admiration of the spectators, with the merry conceits of
Squire Punch and Sir John Spendall, completed by
an entertainment of singing and dancing with several
naked swords by a child eight years of age."

Was ever such a medley known, and all to be seen
for sixpence! If you went early you would see Noah
and the angels strutting on the stage outside the
booth. If you made up your mind to sit out the
performance to the end, you would towards the finish
see a man put his head into the tent and inquire in a
loud voice, "Is John Audley here?" This was a
signal for the management that another audience was
already gathered at the door waiting for admission,
and the play which you had gone to see would then
be brought to a close with such decency as the
circumstances allowed.

In another "droll" of the same period, called "The Tempest, or the Distressed Lovers," the audience was enticed by a very circumstantial bill of the play. There are full particulars of "The English hero and the Island Princess, and the comical humours of the enchanted Scotchman, or Jockey and the three witches." We read how the nobleman, after surprising adventures on the "Indian shore," married the princess; how "his faithful Scotchman fell in among witches, when between 'em is abundance of comical diversions. There in the tempest is Neptune and his Triton in his chariot drawn with sea horses and mair maids singing, with variety of entertainment performed by the best masters; the particulars would be too tedious to be inserted here. Vivat Regina."

In another presentment the story of Tamerlane the Great would be varied with the humours of an Italian scaramouch; in another "the History of the Chaste Susannah" would be "exhibited with a pair of new Elders;" or Punch would add variety to the story of the Queen of Sheba by making rude remarks about King Harry and the French, and "lay his leg upon the queen's lap in a very free manner," as we are informed by Mr. Joseph Addison. In a new opera called "The Cruelty of Atreus," says one of the advertisements of the day, "the scene wherein Thyestes eats his own children is to be performed by the famous Mr. Psalmanazar, lately arrived from Formosa, the whole supper being set to kettle drums."

It was productions of this character which engaged

the energies of the managers both of the puppet-shows and the theatrical booths, and which provided parts for actors who were afterwards well known. Bartholomew Fair indeed became so great a nursery of dramatic talent that many actors afterwards famous obtained their first chance at Smithfield. The fair became a sort of theatrical exchange, where managers during their annual visits were often able to find valuable recruits, and where strolling players from the provinces were accustomed to attend in the hope of engagements with the regular companies. Thus Booth found Wilkes, the original Macheath, playing a part in the Siege of Rhodes at Bartholomew's; and Mrs. Horton, a stroller of only one year's standing from Windsor, was so captivating in Cupid and Psyche that she was translated forthwith to Drury Lane, where she achieved a gratifying success.

The theatrical importance of the Fair, indeed, became so well established that the managers of the great theatres found it profitable to close their houses altogether during its continuance and take their companies to Smithfield, where they found they could earn more money from the audiences who flocked to their shows during the whole day than from the single performances of the patent theatres. Then pieces were removed bodily from the Haymarket and played at Bartholomew's by the same actors. Great names came to be identified with the booths as time went on. There was Mr. Henry Fielding, for instance, fresh from Eton and Leyden, but without a guinea in his pocket, who set up a booth, and for ten years provided an entertainment for the people at the fair, in partnership with such actors as Reynolds and Hippesley, Oates and Hall. Fielding produced "The Beggars' Opera" at Smithfield, occasionally trod the boards himself, and received the honour of a visit from the Prince and Princess of Wales in 1732, who were much delighted with his historical drama of "The Fall of Essex." Fielding, indeed, added much to the repute of the fair as a home of the drama by the superior quality of his productions. We learn from an advertisement of his that there was "a commodious passage for the quality and coaches, and care will be taken that there shall be lights and people to conduct them to their places."

There was thus a continual development of the dramatic entertainment at Bartholomew's during the first half of the last century, a progress, however, which was often harassed by persecution from the puritanical bodies. The efforts of these busybodies frequently succeeded in closing the booths, and often left the fair to the gin-stalls, gaming-tables, and jugglers, diversions which were presumably less vicious in their eyes than the dramatic entertainments we have examined. At other times the persecution took the form of an indictment of a particular actor as a rogue and a vagabond. It was always open to the patentees of Drury Lane and Covent Garden to suppress the performance of any player who was unprovided with a licence, and the law was often capriciously invoked upon the information of some interested informer. The officers would then swoop down upon some obscure player and hale him off before the justices, as when, in 1733, they carried off poor Harper, "a very meek man," upon the information of one High-more.   Harper was committed to Bridewell, but appealed to Westminster Hall, and carried the day, among the acclamations of hundreds of his patrons.

At other times the puritanical spirit would move the Corporation of London to prohibit the booths on the very eve of the fair, even after many of them had already been set up.   On such occasions as this, Lady Holland's Mob would be much in evidence. The ordinary attractions of the fair would then be enlivened by a riot of first-class dimensions, which always resulted in assault and battery, and sometimes in sudden death.   Mr. Birch, the City Marshal, for example, was killed in attempting to suppress the booths in 1751.   Such interference, however, came only at intervals; the theatrical element was, as a rule, left undisturbed, and it remained the chief attraction of Bartholomew Fair for fifty years. Great people from the west did not disdain to visit these humble places of entertainment, and it is on record that the brotherhood of the theatre was so strong at the fair as to prevent the booth-keeper taking Mr. Garrick's money when he went there with his bride in 1749.   "No, Mr. Garrick," said the doorkeeper, in refusing the half-crown, "we actors never take money from one another."

The change which at last broke up the supremacy
of the theatrical booth at Bartholomew's was the
curtailment of the revels from fourteen days to three.
There had been many attempts between 1735 and
1750 in the direction of shortening the duration of
the fair; and when in the latter year the curtailment
was effected in perpetuity, the theatrical glory of the
fair was gone. It paid no good actor to take an
engagement for so short a period, or a manager to
move his company and appointments from one of the
theatres of the west. The fair then began to develop
attractions of a more varied character.

Very popular among such attractions was the
menagerie of wild beasts. Until quite modern times
the natural wonder of a homestaying population at
the beasts of the field, and especially the dangerous
beasts of foreign parts, had little opportunity of satisfaction. The dens of the Tower were great attractions
for many generations of Londoners as the one place in
London where such fearsome beasts as live lions could
be seen. We find accordingly, very early in the last
century, that any beast which could be exhibited in a
booth was much appreciated. As early as 1702 the
good people at Smithfield were regaled with the sight
of "a tyger warranted to pluck the feathers from a
fowl." A year or two later much excitement was
occasioned by the appearance at Smithfield of a
menagerie which, from a naïve advertisement, we
gather included such rarities as the "Noble Cashaware
brought from the Island of Java in the East Indies.

. . . He eats iron, steel, and stones, and he hath two spears grows by his side." There was "a leopard from Lebanon," a "possum" from Hispaniola, an eagle from Russia, and a "great mare of the Tartarean breed;" also a "little black hairy monster, bred in the deserts of Arabia—a natural ruff of hair about his face, walks upright, takes a glass of ale in his hand, and does several other things to admiration."

With our knowledge of the Zoo of to-day, it is not difficult to identify most of these surprising creatures; but they were rare enough in 1708 to induce the inquisitive antiquary and man of science Sir Hans Sloane to haunt the booth for a fortnight, and to employ a draughtsman to make studies of such curiosities.

Later were to be seen "two rattlesnakes, one of very large size, and rattles that you may hear him a quarter of a mile almost, and something of music that grows in the tails thereof." There was a "bovine curiosity or double cow," which had "given uncommon satisfaction to the several learned bodies by whom it has hitherto been seen; a surprising young mermaid, taken on the shores of Aguapulca, that the generality of mankind believe there is no such thing." Such doubts, however, could be satisfied by a visit to Smithfield, and the payment of the nominal sum of sixpence. As the dramatic interest of the fair decreased with the persecutions of the players and the reduction of the rites of the festival to a poor three days, those of the menagerie increased.

Snakes manœuvred up silk ropes to the sound of music at the bidding of some wandering Indian who had strayed to London in 1778. There was "the eagle of the sun that takes the loftiest flight of any bird that flies; the panther from Turkey, on which are thousands of spots, and no two of a likeness; pelicans that suckle their young on their hearts' blood from Egypt; the noble vulture cock, having the finest tallons of any bird that seeks his prey; a beautiful large tyger brought from Bengal by Captain Webster, and the right man tyger brought from Angola by Captain Dalbiac in the Portfield East Indiaman."

It was a happy state of society, we think, which could find continued amusement in such sights as these, but as the last century drew to its close the *naiveté* of the audiences diminished, and dramatic effect apparently became necessary even in the menagerie. It was about that time that the spectacle of the keeper's head in the lion's mouth began to thrill audiences who were no longer moved by a plain "he panther" or the "right man tyger from Bengal." It was then, we believe, that the venerable declamation, which has, nevertheless, a semi-modern ring about it, took its origin. "Does he whisk his tail?" said the keeper with his head in the lion's mouth to his understudy outside the cage. "He does, mate." "Then I am a dead man."

We have touched upon two prominent features of the fair of Bartholomew's only; its other delights comprised such a collection of attractions as have scarce been seen together elsewhere, among which, however, you may discover the parents of many of the still popular items of variety entertainments. The tight-rope and slack-wire dancing, which are very hardy annuals at such places as the Pavilion, differ little from such performances at Smithfield in the reigns of Anne and the early Georges. There was "Lady Mary," a very favourite artist on the tight-rope for many years, whose beauty attracted and whose modesty resisted the gilded youth of a generation. Lady Mary it was said, was the daughter of a Florentine noble, who eloped with an English acrobat named Finley and married him, learned his trade, and helped to support him until her career was ended in tragedy, when she fell on the boards in 1703, and died a day or two later. There was Clinch, the famous vaulter, "who, being arrived from Italy, will show the world what vaulting is," as we read from his modest advertisement, and whose performance differed little from some we pay our shillings to see to-day. Such men as Fawkes the conjurer, and Pinchbeck the "machine man," originated that pleasing illusion the flower trick, which has delighted successive generations of sightseers and helped to support other generations of conjurers right down to our own times. It is pleasant to learn that these old showmen died with handsome fortunes acquired by their efforts to amuse the people at Bartholomew Fair and elsewhere. Flockton made £10,000 at the fairs by his puppet-shows, which we remember little changed as marionettes. There were natural curiosities, which do not seem to have survived, like that of the gentleman with stentorian lungs who undertook " to break a glass and shatter window-panes by the loudness of his vociferation," but we may all recognise "the wonderful man who talks in his belly and can fling his voice into any part of the room," in one of the commonest of our entertainments. Peep-shows of the Siege of Gibraltar and the like, gingerbread stalls, and many other humble joys of a similar kind at these old fairs are still alive and are drawing the pence of children in the provinces, if not in London.

With attractions such as these Bartholomew Fair kept London amused for centuries, and provided the chief diversion of the year for a great number of citizens. Nor were its delights alone prepared for the humbler classes of the city, who were its chief supporters, for an occasional visit to Smithfield was recognised as a mild and acceptable excitement by greater people further west, and the ordinary citizen from Holborn or Cheapside had often the advantage of rubbing shoulders with a great personage. It was no uncommon sight at Bartholomew's to see an exquisite like Chesterfield, or a great minister like Sir Robert Walpole, with his star on his breast, tasting the diversions of the fair alone and on foot. Parties of bloods from White's and Almack's were not above exchanging humorous badinage with the fruit-sellers or the prettier of the strollers or acrobats, or even chucking

them under the chin.   In the middle of the century
might be seen so well-known a member of the quality
as Horace Walpole escorting a party of ladies through
the dust of Smithfield.   The magazine writers of the
same period are eloquent upon the visits of royalty
itself.   There would be a flare of torches brighter
than the lamps and candles of the booths, the sound
of measured steps, a pressing of the crowd from the
middle of the alleys, a cry of " Room for his Royal
Highness, room for Prince George," and Frederick
Prince of Wales would walk through the alleys between
the booths preceded by little Mr. Rich, the Master
of the Ceremonies, from Covent Garden Theatre,
surrounded by his beefeaters, and leading the little
Prince George by the hand.

In addition to all other attractions of the fair was
that chance of turbulence, disorder, and horseplay
always dear to a crowd of Englishmen.   Lady
Holland's Mob was an evergreen which flourished
through season after season, and was always ready
at a moment's notice to join issue with the powers
represented by the constables of the corporation.
The periodical suppression of the booths in the early
part of the century was a frequent opportunity for
their exertions, in which, as we have seen, bailiffs
were sometimes killed.   At another time some
aggrieved tradesman who resisted the tolls demanded
by the authorities on his industry of gin or gingerbread selling, would provide the mob with a chance
of asserting themselves and defying the authorities.

Their operations would then add an attraction to the fair which was much appreciated by large numbers of its patrons. When such incidents failed, the mere breaking of a swing-boat was excuse enough for the burning of the entire apparatus, and for an organised expedition throughout the precincts of the carnival in search of similar erections, and a general conflagration followed, in which the benches and tables of the sausage vendors were added to the flames. Altogether, however, there is very little record of loss of life or damage to property in connection with the fair during its vogue of five centuries. A stage broke down occasionally when the piety of Noah or King Solomon, or the wings of the angels or the godhead of Apollo or Jupiter, failed to save them from broken limbs. A juggler or a tight-rope dancer paid with his life for his courage and temerity on occasion. But disaster was rare, and the fact that a congregation of such inflammable material as mustered annually in Smithfield escaped serious fire is a standing wonder to this day.

Bartholomew Fair was hardly closed before preparations were in train on St. Margaret's Hill, near Southwark Town Hall, for another festival of the same character. Southwark Fair was also of very respectable antiquity, for the festival originated in a charter of Edward the Sixth granted in the year 1550, and like most of the London fairs was at its zenith in the opening years of the eighteenth century. It came to an end only after a continuous career of two hundred and thirteen years. As the 7th of September came round in each year, the same gin stalls, gaming-tables, gingerbread stalls, and theatrical booths which had delighted Smithfield were packed up, taken across the river, and displayed in all their attractiveness to new audiences of South Londoners at Southwark.

Thus, although not on the same scale as Bartholo-mew Fair, that of Southwark differed little from it in character. You may trace the same booth proprietors, the same actors, and the same pieces in the handbills of both; Fielding, Miller, Powell, Penkethman, all extended their operations to those fresh audiences across the river. There was one performance, how-ever, that took a greater breadth at Southwark than at Smithfield, that of the acrobat or rope dancer. Such performers were little troubled by municipal authorities in those days, and in the absence of the restrictions of Boards of Works or County Councils, their displays at Southwark were often organised on a generous scale. It must have been quite thrilling to see a man swing across the street from St. George's Church tower to the Mint, as was the custom of Mr. Cadman at Southwark. The incomparable Violantes, too, in their prime never missed the fair, the geniuses who had established their reputation by sliding down a slack rope from the steeple of St. Martin's Church in the Fields right across St. Martin's Lane to the Royal Mews, in the presence of royalty itself. Mr. Cadman, as we learn, came to a sad end in attempting a bold flight across the Severn at Shrewsbury, and a poet of

his day, moved by the tragedy of the occasion, spread
his feelings over poor Cadman's tombstone, as all may
read in Shrewsbury churchyard—

"No, no, a faulty cord being drawn too tight,
  Hurried his soul on high to take her flight,
  Which bid the body here beneath good-night."

The humours of Southwark Fair inspired Mr.
Hogarth in one of his finest efforts, wherein are
reflected so admirably the life of his times, and that
excellent plate of Southwark Fair is as good an illustration as need be of the importance of the festival
among the popular diversions of the middle of the
eighteenth century. The greatly daring acrobat on
the rope stretching from the church tower to the
Mint, which is out of the picture, is the great Mr.
Cadman himself; the artist on the slack rope on the
other side of the picture is a back view of the Vio-
lante. Mr. Figg, the famous "Master of the Noble
Science of Self-defence," displays his honourable
wounds on the right. His booth is round the
corner, and he is riding through the fair with a
very martial aspect to gather clients to witness a
set-to between himself and some other bald-pated
hero of the sword or quarter-staff. On the right of
the pretty girl with the drum and the black page,
who is effectively advertising the show which she
represents, is Tamerlane the Great in full armour
being arrested by a bailiff. The enormous posters of
the background, which almost blot out the church,

and display the attractions of the Fall of Troy, the
Royal Waxworks, and the wonderful performance of
Mr. Banks and his horse, are all quite typical of the
London fair, and Mr. Hogarth's grim humour appears
to perfection in the title of the show which he represents as tumbling into the street on the right, with
its actors and orchestra and monkey on the pole, the
"Fall of Bagdad." Note too the peep-show and the
hag presiding over the gaming-table, and the pleasant
glimpse of open country between the houses.

There is little in the prim locality which to-day
spreads itself north of Piccadilly to Oxford Street and
westward from Bond Street to Park Lane to remind us
of the revels of a distinctly low-class populace. And
yet Chapel Street and Hertford Street were the centre
of a popular carnival, dating from the times of
Edward the First, a carnival which opened on "the
25th day of June, the eve of St. James's," and had a
reputation distinct in many ways from the similar
merrymaking at Smithfield and Southwark. The
name of those revels still survives in that of the
district "Mayfair," though there was nothing in
them of the aristocratic flavour which one associates
with that district to-day. The proceedings in Mayfair were at times even too strong for the stomach
of the Restoration, for we find in 1664 that it was
suppressed "on account of looseness and irregularity."
The Puritans were again active in the reign of Anne.
"Oh the piety of some people about the Queen," says
one of them in the *Observator*, "who can suffer things

of this nature to go undiscovered to her Majesty, and consequently unpunished. Can any rational man imagine that her Majesty would permit so much lewdness as is committed at Mayfair for so many days together, so near her royal palace, if she knew anything of the matter. I do not believe the patent for that fair allows the patentees the liberty of setting up the devil's shops and exposing his merchandise for sale."

What was the precise vanity of Mayfair which so moved this honest gentleman we are unable to discover. We meet again at Mayfair the puppet-shows of Smithfield and Southwark, as, for example, "an excellent droll called Crispin and Crispianus, or a Shoemaker and a Prince, with the best machines, singing and dancing ever yet in the fair." Woodward, the admirable comedian, made his first appearance in a booth "opposite the Three Jolly Butchers," from the humble boards of which establishment he was soon translated to those of the great theatre in Covent Garden. Pennant remembered the locality of Mayfair "covered with booths, temporary theatres, and every enticement to low pleasures;" and the place had undoubtedly a raffish flavour over all its amusements which was peculiar to itself, and unshared by the older institutions further east.

On the other hand, many of the attractions, records of which have survived, are just as vicious or as virtuous as the diversions at other gatherings of the sort. There was an obliging Frenchman who exhibited, with a *sang-froid* born of safety to his own skin, his wife, a thin woman of much beauty, raising an anvil with her hair, and supporting the same implement on her breast, while a company of three blacksmiths forged a horseshoe upon it with the usual heavy hammers.   Another great attraction of Mayfair was the beheading of puppets " in a coalshed attached to Mr. Smith's, the grocer's."   A shutter was fixed horizontally, upon which a puppet laid his head.   After much formality, it was decapitated by another puppet, armed with a portentous axe. Sidney, Raleigh, Charles the First, Russell, and other martyrs of history, bled thus again in effigy through many years at Mayfair.

Other features of the fair, less innocent, at times caused great riots, in which men lost their lives, both on the spot and at Tyburn afterwards.   Undesirable women were excluded from the precincts ; the guards from St. James's took the frail ones' side ; bailiffs and constables were killed, and the general license of the meetings at Mayfair was forced upon the attention of the town by very deplorable proceedings.   There was certainly no moral strictness in society in the year 1720, so we may assume that the presentation of Mayfair by the Grand Jury of Middlesex for several successive years was justified by the facts.   A royal proclamation hushed its revels for ever in that year— a result aided perhaps by considerations connected with the interest of an influential nobleman, Lord Coventry, whose property suffered much by the low character of the company which the fair never failed to attract. The neighbourhood shortly afterwards was covered with the streets and houses which to-day form that compact quarter of the town which as Mayfair keeps the memory of the old popular institution alive.

We have glanced at most of the attractions of the three great London Fairs which provided amusement for the great body of Londoners through many centuries. They are typical only of many others, for the annual fair was a great institution at scores of villages round the town and its suburbs, and indeed throughout the country. Westminster had a fair dating from the year 1257, held in St. Margaret's Churchyard and Tothill Fields, which had a continuous career until the year 1819. Peckham gained a royal charter for a fair by a propitious accident and the good offices of Nell Gwynn, when his Majesty King Charles, highly pleased by a successful stag hunt which ended at that village, granted the charter upon the intercession of that lady. There was a highly organised fair called Tottenham Court Fair, held on or near the site of the Adam and Eve Tavern, which still stands at the corner of the Euston and Hampstead Roads. Tottenham Court was a fair attended by all the better class of theatrical booths from Smithfield and Southwark, and it presented another great attraction in the booth of Jack Broughton, the father of the prize-ring. Enterprising Londoners would go as far as Edmonton, Blackheath, Kingston, Parson's Green, and Wandsworth, and by their presence and their shillings help the success of annual meetings at those places, which are only examples of similar festivals which had a vogue of centuries in villages a little further afield. Many of these, of which that of Greenwich is the best remembered, continued well on into living memory; but they had most of them passed their prime before the opening of the present century.

The palmy days of Bartholomew's, the greatest of all the fairs, began to depart as early as the middle of last century, when the great people of St. James's withdrew their patronage, and St. Giles's and Blooms-bury, bewailing the loss of tone, followed their example. The company grew more raffish, more sophisticated, and consequently harder to please, and we find the eulogies of the early writers exchanged for the patronising descriptions of the papers of the West End, with columns of facetious raillery, and numbers of the dreariest and most feeble jokes printed in italics, in order, perhaps, that their point might not be missed. There were often interesting figures to be seen at Smithfield, even in its later days; the Pata-gonian Giant of the 'nineties was no other than the great Egyptian traveller Belzoni of a later date. But things were getting in a bad way when Belvidera, in " Venice Preserved," came out of her booth and knocked down the King's Trumpeter for having de-manded his fees. The further history of Bartholo-mew's, as of all other fairs, is one of decline. In 1825 its shows were banished to Islington, and for a further twenty-five years the festival struggled on with such poor attractions as merry-go-rounds, swing-boats, and gingerbread stalls. In 1850 Lord Mayor Musgrave, going to read his proclamation at Cloth Fair, found his occupation gone, even the gingerbread sellers had seceded from participation in the maimed festival, and the revelry which had prevailed at Smithfield during centuries was at last hushed for ever.

It was at one or other of these old gatherings, as we say, that ordinary commonplace London found its chief diversion during the summers of many centuries. Upon a review of the whole subject it is possible to admire the simplicity which could find amusement in their rather limited attractions for so long, and to envy the state of mind of a public which could be so easily pleased. There was, as we have seen, little variety, and the same attractions amused the same audiences year after year at the great fairs of the town, and at the smaller gatherings of the suburban villages. Humble personages reappeared season after season with such regularity as to establish themselves as public institutions. There was Tiddy Doll, for instance, the merry-andrew who joked for a guinea a day at Bartholomew Fair and Southwark, and sold gingerbread for the rest of the year in Covent Garden. During that long period of preparation Tiddy Doll maintained a demeanour as solemn as that of a bishop, without the cracking of a single joke or the concession of a single smile which might diminish his stock for the short days of those joyous festivals. That there was humour of a sort at these meetings in plenty, we make no doubt. There was Mr. Lane, for example, "first performer to the King, who played off his snip, snap, rap and thunder tricks so that the grown babies stared like worried cats," and the other obliging gentleman who undertook " to drive about forty twelvepenny nails into any gentleman's breech, place him in a loadstone chair, and withdraw them without the least pain." Humour, too, could not be quite dead at a meeting where you could get the ballad of "The Delicate History of the Ferret and the Coney" for a penny. The title alone was surely worth the money.

There are pleasant glimpses too of some prettier aspects of the fairs to be gleaned in their old records, as when Mrs. Pritchard charmed her hearers with her dainty singing of "Sweet, if you love me, smiling turn"; there is music in the line yet, and one is glad to know that her charm in the song at Bartholomew's resulted in a prosperous career at the theatres of the west. You may find much pleasant allusion to these and other aspects of the fairs in such admirable histories of their pleasures as Mr. Morley's "Memoirs of Bartholomew Fair," and Mr. Frost's "Old Showmen." And we feel that with much that was trivial and vulgar, coarse and riotous from our modern standpoint, there must have been much in these old entertainments to justify the hearty pleasures they excited. In any case they are not lacking in human interest as the relaxations of generations of our forefathers who have now been many years asleep.

CHAPTER IX

THE PRIZE-RING

"YESTERDAY," says the *Protestant Mercury* for January 12th, 1681, "a match of boxing was performed before his Grace the Duke of Albemarle between the duke's footman and a butcher. The latter won the prize, as he hath done many before, being accounted, though but a little man, the best at that exercise in England."

The historians of pugilism, who are many and laborious, are agreed that the *Mercury's* quaint report of his grace's diversion is the earliest record of a public boxing match in England. That early encounter presents many of the essential features of others which followed it in later times and went to make up the glory of the prize-ring. Here was a noble patron looking on at two men, with no quarrel between them, engaged in punching each other's heads for the sake of a monetary consideration. Later, as we shall see, the prize-ring claimed all kinds of virtues for its principles and professors. It was "the noble science of self-defence," "the nurse of the true British spirit," and many other fine things beside, if we are to believe its votaries and supporters. The

71

prize-ring was in reality a spectacular entertainment which provided amusement for many generations of loafers who found the money to keep it going, and occupation for a relatively small number of courageous men who lived by that strange industry of head-punching. It differed in degree only, and not in kind, from those ancient gladiatorial combats about which Lord Byron wrote so touchingly in a famous passage, his lordship being at that moment a distinguished supporter of the " fancy," as the cult was then affectionately styled by its votaries. It is in this aspect of an amusement for Londoners that we wish to consider the subject of pugilism, and by no means as an athletic exercise. The athleticism was confined to the men who fought, who numbered altogether about 1500 in 150 years. The athletic part played by the vast proportion of the " fancy " was displayed in getting to the ring and back again, or in evading the police. The prize-ring, nevertheless, had a surprising vogue as a show among men of all classes for a great number of years. We ask the reader to accompany us through its rather dubious records, and to determine, perhaps, the place it is entitled to claim among the diversions of past generations of Londoners.

We saw in another chapter how Londoners of all classes, the lower perhaps in a majority, flocked to Hockley in the Hole, to Figg's theatre in the Oxford Road, or to his booth in Southwark Fair, and to other establishments of the same kind, to

taste the joys of the prize-fight as presented by Figg
and his satellites, then an affair of swords mainly, like
the students' duel of Germany to-day ; of swords used
to produce shallow cuts in the limbs or face, and
without thrust or serious attack on a vital. It would
appear that the ancient cult of the fist was at a discount during that ascendency of the sword. Such
references to pugilism as exist apply mainly to the
semi-comic encounters between women which we have
noticed ; but there was silently establishing itself among
the sporting characters of those days a taste for the
encounter with the naked fist, which lacked but a
leader and the patronage of the great to develop into
a great national institution, destined to become the
plaything of certain classes for a century and a half.

We must look, as we say, for the birth of that
great organisation of the London prize-ring to those
lowly establishments of which Mr. Figg's theatre was
the most reputable. Mr. Figg's business card, designed
for him by Mr. Hogarth, describes that gladiator as
'Master of ye noble science of defence, on ye right
hand in Oxford Road, near Adam and Eve Court,
teaches gentlemen ye use of ye small sword, backsword, and quarterstaff at home and abroad." There
is nothing said here as to Figg's skill in pugilism, and
we believe that most of the exhibitions in boxing
which took place at Figg's were subsidiary to the
affairs with the sword, or stick, or quarterstaff, and
were produced as additional but minor attractions to
those exhibitions. Figg, indeed, is often spoken of as

the first pugilistic champion, though there is no record
of any pitched battle in which he took part. His
establishments, nevertheless, both in the Oxford Road
and at Southwark Fair, were the nurseries for many of
the earliest exponents of pugilism. "At Figg's Great
Til'd Booth on the Bowling Green, Southwark, during
the time of the Fair," to quote one of his handbills,
among the attractions set forth were "the manly
arts of foil play, backsword, cudgelling, and boxing.
Buckhorse and several other pugilists will show the
art of boxing, to conclude with a grand parade by the
valiant Figg, who will exhibit his knowledge in various
combats with the foil, backsword, cudgel, and fist."
Besides Mr. Figg's establishment, there were others
conducted on quite similar lines, though with less
success, at Smithfield, Moorfields, and St. George's
Fields. A Mr. Andrew Johnson, who was said to be
an uncle of the great Doctor, presided at Smithfield;
a man nicknamed "old Vinegar" at Moorfields; and
a gentleman named Remington, called Long Charles
by his clients, was the patron of another establishment
known as the Ring. It was in such establishments as
these, and in the temporary booths at all the great
fairs, that the London prize-ring took its origin.

Historians of pugilism, which has still its fascination
for many sportsmen, judging by the volumes which
have been written upon it, have spent much labour in
discovering and recording the names and the exploits
of its earliest heroes. They are all indebted to the
invaluable Captain Godfrey, who told us so much of

interest about the swordsmen. It is to him alone, indeed, that the disciples of the great Figg are indebted for their rescue from oblivion. There is a "character" of each of these worthies in the Captain's quarto, the men who originated the tradition of spectacular pugilism, and who carried it forward until John Broughton, a few years later, gave it shape and regulations, and attracted patronage which established its vogue and secured its place among the amusements of the town.

The prize-ring, in its career of a century and a half, produced many famous professors whom we shall have to leave without mention; but the Captain's gallery of portraits all claim enumeration, because his remarks upon each throw much light upon the nature of the science they practised in its origin, and enable us to compare its early beginnings with the later developments which filled so large a place in the sporting life of half a century ago.

One of the earliest of Mr. Figg's scholars seems to have been Tom Pipes, " Pipes " who, says the Captain, " was the neatest boxer I remember; he put in his blows about the face, which he fought at most, with surprising time and judgment." Pipes' great opponent was George Gretting, " who was the most artful boxer, much stronger made than Pipes. Gretting had the neatest way of going to the stomach, which is what they call the mark, of any man I knew; but Gretting had not the bottom of the other." "Bottom," as we learn from the Captain, was " wind, spirit, or heart, or wherever you can fix the true residence of courage."

Figg's other disciples were Bob Whitaker and Ned Peartree.   The Captain's remarks on these gladiators and the fights with which their names are connected, are very instructive as to these early encounters and as to the motives which set the men fighting.   In the year 1733, it seems, a gigantic Venetian came to England in the suite of an English nobleman who had been the grand tour.   This man had a reputation as a great boxer, and the patrons of the sport were at once determined to find a man to match him.   Captain Godfrey happened to be at Slaughter's Coffee-house when the match was made, and gives us many interesting particulars.   "A gentleman of advanced station" sent for Figg to procure a proper man to oppose the Venetian.   Upon arrival Mr. Figg was admonished to be careful in his choosing, as the Gondolier was famous for breaking the jawbone.   "I do not know, master, but that he may break one of his countrymen's jawbones with his fist," replied Figg in his "rough manner," "but I'll bring him a man and he shall not be able to break his jawbone with a sledge-hammer."

The match was arranged to take place at Figg's amphitheatre, and we have the great advantage of the Captain's report of this early battle as an eye-witness.

"The battle was fought at Figg's amphitheatre before a splendid company, the politest house of that kind I ever saw. . . . The Gondolier pitched himself forward with his right leg and his arm full extended, and as Whitaker approached gave him a blow on the side of the head which knocked him quite off the stage, which was remarkable for its height. Whitaker's misfortune in his fall was then the grandeur of the company, on which account they suffered no common people in, that usually sit on the ground and line the stage round. It was then all clear, and Whitaker had nothing to stop him but the bottom. There was a general foreign huzza on the side of the Venetian pronouncing our countryman's downfall; but Whitaker took no more time than was required to get up again when he . . . with a little stoop, ran boldly in beyond the heavy mallet, and with one English peg in the stomach, quite a new thing to the foreigners, brought him on his breech. The blow carried too much of the English rudeness for him to bear, and finding himself so unmannerly used, he scorned to have any more doings with his slovenly fist."

Mr. Figg here stepped on the stage, we learn, to make the most of the fashionable company and of the enthusiasm which the victory of Whitaker called forth. Gentlemen might suppose that he had picked the best man in London to meet the Gondolier. Not at all. " He engaged to produce to them that day se'nnight a man who should beat Whitaker in ten minutes by fair fighting. This brought very near as great and fine a company as the week before," records the Captain, who was again present. " The man was Nathaniel Peartree, who, knowing the other's bottom

and his deadly mode of flinging, took a most judicious
method to beat him. . . . He knew Whitaker's hardi-
ness, and doubting of his being able to give him beating
enough, cunningly determined to fight at his eyes.
His judgment carried in his arm so well that in about
six minutes both of Whitaker's eyes were shut up,
when, groping about awhile for his man and finding
him not, he wisely gave out with these odd words,
'Damme, I am not beat,' but what signifies my fighting when I cannot see my man.'"

We have in the accounts of these two old encounters all the typical features of the organised
prize-fight of later times.   No quarrel between the
men, an array of patrons looking on, and two pugilists
punching each other into a jelly for the sake of the
stakes, swollen by a certain proportion of the very
considerable sum obtained by the gate money.   These
are all points to be borne in mind as we proceed.
There has been much rubbish talked and written
about the virtues of pugilism, its encouragement of
fairplay, its fostering of the British spirit, its assumed
credit of suppressing the use of the knife among
Englishmen, and much more.   But it is quite certain
that the motives which brought Mr. Figg on to the
stage to announce the second encounter between
Whitaker and Peartree were the same which kept the
successors of those heroes face to face for the next
century.   Prize-fighting, in short, was in its origin
and development a spectacular entertainment, conducted on a sound commercial basis, and so it con-

tinued until public opinion, recognising the fact, suppressed its vices and its virtues together well within living memory.

Among Mr. Figg's gladiators was a youthful pugilist of much promise named George Taylor, and when death claimed the champion in 1734, George the Barber, as he was known to his admirers, found means to take over the amphitheatre in the Oxford Road. We have a "character" of George from our invaluable Captain, and we look upon him as a link between his predecessor Figg, who was mainly a swordsman, and John Broughton, his successor, whose fame rests entirely on his eminence as a bruiser. Taylor did the honours of the amphitheatre with much success, opened another establishment four years later, the Great Booth, Tottenham Court, and was noted for his proficiency in the science of the sword, his exposition of the mysteries of the hanging guard being reckoned particularly fine. But he interests us here chiefly as the organiser and improver of the pugilistic side of his show. He surrounded himself with a crowd of boxers, and was himself proficient in the art. Captain Godfrey describes Taylor as "a strong, able pugilist, with a remarkable judgment in the cross buttock fall." If George had been "unquestionable in his bottom," which was unfortunately not the case, the Captain opined that he would have been a match for any man. The boxers, nevertheless, gathered round him and challenged each other to combat at his booth

in the approved style of the old swordsmen.   Says
one of these quaint old announcements in the *Daily
Advertiser* of May 4th, 1742 :—

"At George Taylor's Booth, Tottenham Court Road.   There
will be a trial of manhood here to-morrow between the following
champions, viz. :—

Whereas I, John Francis, commonly known by the name of
the Jumping Soldier, who have always had the reputation of a
good fellow, and have fought several bruisers in the street, &c.,
nor am I ashamed to mount the stage when my manhood is
called in question by an Irish braggadocio whom I fought some
years ago in a bye-battle for twelve minutes, and though I had
not the success due to my courage and ability in the art of
boxing, I now invite him to fight me for two guineas at the time
and place above mentioned, where I doubt not I shall give him
the truth of a good beating.   JOHN FRANCIS."

The Irishman's answer :—

"I, Patrick Henley, known to every one for the truth of a good
fellow, who never refused anyone on or off the stage, and fight as
often for the diversion of gentlemen as for money, do accept the
challenge of this Jumping Jack, and shall, if he don't take care,
give him one of my bothering blows which will convince him of
his ignorance in the art of boxing.

PATRICK HENLEY."

It was such men as these, as we say, who found
employment at Taylor's Booth in Tottenham Court
Road, and drew their share of the gate money, the
gate money which, as we learn from Mr. Miles'
excellent "Pugilistica," often amounted to £150.
Of this Taylor took one-third, and the remaining
two-thirds were parted between the combatants, the
sum so allocated being again divided into three parts,

of which the winner took two and the loser one. The whole arrangement strikes one as fair and business-like, but it is well to recognise that finance was the basis of the prize-ring from the first, and that it was no abstract admiration for "the noble science of self-defence," or the "British spirit," which set and kept that remarkable organisation agoing.

At Taylor's booth then were to be found the small band of men who a few years later found a leader in the incomparable John Broughton, and supported that eminent pugilist when he successfully organised their profession into a recognised institution of the town, in providing it with a set of rules and regulations which held the field unaltered for a century. Here were Pipes and Gretting and Whitaker already mentioned, Prince Boswell, Stevenson the Coachman, Will Willis, Tom Smallwood, Buckhorse, Jack James, Field the Sailor, and last and greatest of all, John Broughton himself.

Captain Godfrey helps us to the understanding of the sporting personalities of some of this group; we like quoting the Captain, because he evidently believes in himself and his subject, and his language is direct, and refreshing in its simplicity by the side of the greater portion of the literature of the ring, much of which, indeed, is but an inflated maltreatment of the Captain's own honest story. James was "a most charming boxer and delicate in his blows," Smallwood and George Stevenson the Coachman "were the best bottomed men of the modern boxers." The Captain saw Stevenson fight Broughton for forty minutes "in one of the fair booths at Tottenham Court, railed at the end towards the pit." "Smallwood wanted but weight to stand against any man." Boswell the Prince was the son of a gipsy king, with a particular blow "with his left hand at the jaw which came almost as hard as a little horse kicks, but he wanted the courage to qualify him for a compleat boxer." . . . "Fye upon his dastard heart that mars it all," exclaims our author; the Captain could not away with "his wormdread soul," his "nurse wanting courage," his terrible lack of the "true British bottom."

For Jack Broughton, however, was reserved the height of Godfrey's eloquence as well as the honour of the foundation of the London prize-ring. "Advance, brave Broughton," he says, "thee I pronounce Captain of the Boxers . . . strength equal to what is human, skill and judgment equal to what can be acquired, undebauched wind and a bottom spirit never to pronounce the word enough." No "fly flap blows such as the pastry-cooks use to beat those insects from their tarts and cheesecakes" were Broughton's. "No, Broughton steps bold and firmly in, and his firm body seconding his arm, pours the pile-driving force upon his man."

This paragon among prize-fighters, who really was, as we believe, a good fellow, has been found worthy of a place among the immortals of the great national biography. We learn there that he was born in 1705; began life as a waterman's apprentice, and found his true vocation quite early in life by thrashing a fellow-waterman. He then went to George Taylor's booth, beat that hero, and so claimed the championship, and set up an opposition establishment of his own in Hanway Street. Here he had a successful career of unbroken victory, during which he organised pugilism as a profession, and retired, after his only defeat, on a modest fortune to Lambeth. John Broughton died at the age of eighty-four, in 1789, and left some £7000 behind him, and lies buried in Lambeth churchyard under a tombstone with a Latin inscription on it.

Such in brief is the life history of the founder of the prize-ring, but for us its closer details have interest. We have said that he gave laws to his profession; he also drew to the ring the valuable patronage of the highly placed, including that glory of the Hanoverians, the young Duke of Cumberland. Some say, indeed, that Broughton was his highness's coachman, but we do not take upon ourselves to correct the orthodox life of the hero as set out in the biographical dictionary in that particular. It is claimed for him by some of his admirers that he was the inventor of all stopping and guarding blows, and that before his day pugilism was a mere unscientific display of hard hitting. He was certainly one of its chief pillars, and his organisation of its practice set it upon a basis as a diversion of the people which it had lacked before his time, and which it retained subsequently for a century.

It is not uninstructive to turn again for a moment to the candid Godfrey and consider the objects which the professors of the noble science of self-defence had in their minds as they faced each other in the ring. We have examined the nature of the mainspring which set the whole machine of the prize-ring in motion, and Godfrey leaves us in no doubt as to the character of the science itself and the objects of its practitioners. The Captain has a cold-blooded list of the deadliest strokes it is possible to inflict upon your adversary, with sound anatomical reasons for each. If you listen to this appalling expert you may learn " the blow under the ear to be as dangerous as any, because in this part there are two blood-vessels both considerably large," and from his further physiological researches, in which we need not follow him, the Captain deduces great virtues for the well-planted blow under the ear. You may so punch a man on that magic spot, indeed, that " his blood is forced up to his brain and back upon his heart," and with luck you will see it gushing from his eyes, ears, and mouth. If fortune is more than ordinarily kind, you will soon see follow a " cardiaca or suffocation." There is much virtue also in a blow between the eyebrows, because the eyelids "swell almost instantaneously, which violent contumescence soon obstructs the sight. " A man thus indecently treated," continues the Captain, "and artfully hoodwinked, is beat about at his adversary's discretion." Of course he was. We saw poor Mr. Whitaker say " Damme " in those em-

barrassing circumstances, and we shall still see Broughton the peerless lose his championship and his patrons'
money in bearing witness to the virtues of the blow between the eyes. Blows on the stomach were also highly
recommended by the Captain, "because the diaphragm
and lungs share in the injury." The object of the
pugilist, indeed, was to disable and, if needs be, kill
his adversary as soon as possible, and it was a solemn
farce played by five or six generations of parasites, who
looked on in safety, betted on it, wrote about it, and
made money out of its atrocities, which represented
the prize-ring as a mere school for the art of self-
defence and the embodiment of all the manly virtues.
Self-defence could be taught and practised with gloves,
as it is to-day, without all those degrading exhibitions
of broken limbs and jaws and blinded eyes, punctuated
every few years by the bleeding corpse carried out of
the ring to the nearest tavern.

Returning to the eminent Mr. Broughton, he went,
as we have said, to Mr. Taylor's establishment, the
"Great Booth" in Tottenham Court Road, where he
quickly established himself as the star of the company.
He beat nearly all the eminent hands we have mentioned—Pipes, Gretting, Stevenson, James, Taylor
himself, and no doubt others whose names have not
survived. Broughton was the life of Taylor's establishment until the year 1742. It was his eminence in
the same profession, no doubt, which led to the difference with Taylor, to the separation and newspaper
controversy with that pugilist which followed, and to

Broughton's building the brand new Amphitheatre in Hanway Street, "the back of the late Mr. Figg's," and his final establishment at the head of the profession.

The important event of the opening of the new Amphitheatre was thus announced in the *Daily Advertiser* :—

"AT BROUGHTON'S NEW AMPHITHEATRE,
OXFORD STREET,
The back of the late Mr. Figg's,
On Tuesday next, the 13th instant,
Will be exhibited

THE TRUE ART OF BOXING

By the eight following men, viz. :—

ABRAHAM EVANS,	—— ROGER,
—— SWEEP,	—— ALLEN,
—— BELAS,	ROBERT SPIKES, and
—— GLOVER,	HARRY GRAY the clogmaker.

The above eight men to be brought on the stage and to be matched according to the approbation of the gentlemen who shall be pleased to honour them with their company.

N.B.—There will be a BATTLE ROYAL between the

NOTED BUCKHORSE

And SEVEN or EIGHT more, after which there will be several BYE BATTLES by others.
Gentlemen are therefore requested to come by times.
The doors will be open at nine ; the champions mount at eleven ; and no person is to pay more than A SHILLING."

Mr. Taylor at once replied to this advertisement of his rival by one of his own :—

" To the patrons and encouragers of the manly art of boxing.

" Whereas Mr. Broughton, well knowing that I was to fight Mr. Field on Tuesday next, the 13th of March 1743, in order to injure me has maliciously advertised to open his amphitheatre on that day, and where several battles are then to be fought. To prevent the public from being deceived I feel it my duty to inform them that the principal part of the persons mentioned were never made acquainted with such circumstances, and have no intention of so doing. Mr. Broughton wishes it to appear that he never imposed upon any of the pugilists who had been concerned with him in any transactions whatever; but his imposition shall soon be made manifest to the world. And to show Mr. Broughton that I have no animosity against him as a pugilist or any jealousy concerning his amphitheatre, I am willing to fight him as soon as he may think proper wherever it may please him, not regarding, as he loudly sets forth, the strength of his arm.

"GEORGE TAYLOR."

We are afraid that Mr. Taylor's jealousy was more real than he pretended. There followed between the pair much exchange of hard sayings in the public papers. Taylor accused Broughton of taking the " lion's share " of the gate money; Broughton satis-fied his patrons that he had taken only the orthodox third. Broughton, indeed, was as successful against Mr. Taylor with his pen as he was with his fist. Taylor like a wise man gave in, joined the opposition establishment in Hanway Street, and the incomparable Broughton, thus overcoming all opposition, gathered the talent of his profession about him at the Amphi-theatre, and took his place at its head.

That eminent position had advantages which Brough-ton was quick to seize upon in order to produce that

set of regulations for the conduct of the prize-fight
upon which his fame chiefly rests.   These rules,
which held the field until 1838 without verbal alteration, are to be found in all histories of the prize-ring ;
they are too long to quote here in full, but their substance is of interest.   The rules very curiously omit
the size of the stage, but are quite clear in other
particulars.   They established the all-important principles of the "round" or "set-to," defined as "a
set-to after a fall or being parted at the rails"; the
institution of a time limit between the rounds; the
appointment of umpires and referee, and the humane
regulation "that no person is to hit his adversary
when he is down, or seize him by the ham, the
breeches, or any part below the waist; a man on his
knees to be reckoned down."   They also confirmed
the usage of the division of the gate money between
victor and vanquished, and if one admits the ex-
pediency of prize-fighting at all, he will probably
admit also the efficacy and even the beneficence of
Mr. Broughton's famous regulations.

Broughton, endowed as he was with the muscles of
the prize-fighter, which made him the best pugilist of
his day, and with the ability which enabled him to
conduct the commercial side of his profession with
success, was also very fortunate in the patronage he
received.   There are many stories of his connection
with the Duke of Cumberland.   His royal highness, it
was said, took him on the Continent ; showed him the
famous guardsmen of Frederick the Great, and asked

him how he would regard a set-to with one of those redoubtable giants. "I should have no objection, your highness, to fight the whole regiment if you would allow me a breakfast between each battle," was the legendary reply. It is said that the duke's illustrious brother, Frederick Prince of Wales, gave much encouragement to the clever bruiser and to his undertaking at the Amphitheatre. Broughton undoubtedly stepped into the place of the great Figg, who had been accepted as a pet by the great people of his day, and sung as such by Mr. Pope and Mr. Bramston in some racy couplets. He opened another establishment in the Haymarket as an academy for imparting the principles of his interesting science to the noble youth of his times. Above all, he invented the boxing-gloves, or "mufflers," as he called them, and so made the initiation to the mysteries as easy as possible to his patrons. Mr. Broughton's advertisement of this subsidiary venture, which appeared in the *Advertiser* of February 1747, seems worth quoting :—

"Mr. Broughton proposes with proper assistance to open an academy at his house in the Haymarket for the instruction of those who are willing to be initiated in the mystery of boxing, where the whole theory and practice of that truly British art, with all the various blows, stops, cross buttocks, &c., incidental to combatants will be fully taught and explained; and that persons of quality and distinction may not be debarred from entering into a course of these lectures, they will be given with the utmost tenderness and regard to the delicacy of the frame and constitution of the pupil, for which reason mufflers will be provided that will effectually secure them from the inconveniency of black eyes, broken jaws, and bloody noses."

There is no doubt whatever that the " proper assistance " was duly forthcoming, and that Mr. Broughton's
academy was prominent among the amusements of the
youth of the London of George the Second until the
final catastrophe overtook its proprietor.

It was mainly the confidence born of fatness and
prosperity which led to Mr. Broughton's downfall;
the proverbial danger to those who put their trust in
princes also appeared in the disaster. The Duke of
Cumberland continued his caressing of the pugilist,
and had unlimited faith in his invulnerability.
Broughton went to a race meeting, met with one
Slack, a Norwich butcher, a pugilist of some note,
but who had been well beaten by Taylor, who had,
as we have seen, yielded the championship to the
unconquered Broughton. Broughton in his pride
threatened a horsewhipping to Slack as a settlement
of the slight difference which had arisen between
them on the racecourse. That gladiator replied with
a challenge to a battle for £200 a side; the gate
money, estimated at £600 clear, was added to the
stake, and the challenge being duly accepted by the
champion, the meeting was arranged for the 10th of
April 1750. The fixture excited great interest in
the sporting circles of that day, but the champion
thought lightly of his risk, and "refused to take
training preparation, although he had not fought
for a long time." His only fear was that Slack
would fail to appear, and he announced to his patrons
on the eve of the combat that he had arranged to

present his opponent with ten pounds in order to make sure of his appearance.

No one of Broughton's following had any doubt of the issue, and the result of the first few minutes of the fighting only increased their confidence. The betting rose to ten to one on the champion, and his royal highness the duke gave the odds in thousands at that figure. Suddenly Mr. Slack made a surprising jump which nobody had anticipated—Mr. Broughton least of all—and dealt that hero a prodigious blow between the eyes, the very stroke, indeed, recommended so highly by Captain Godfrey. Mr. Broughton appeared stupefied, and seemed to be "feeling" for his man. His royal highness, apprehensive for his appalling odds of ten to one in thousands, called out with some lack of delicacy, "What are you about, Broughton? You can't fight; you're beat." Broughton replied, "I can't see my man, your highness; I'm blind, not beat. Let me see my man, and he shall not gain the day." Mr. Slack pursued his advantage, and pommelled the blinded man into submission "under fourteen minutes;" the duke lost his ten thousand pounds, swore he was sold, and turned his back on his pet of former years, and the whole incident is thoroughly typical of the amenities of the prizering, the nurse of the "British spirit" and the breeder of the true "British bottom."

It is curious to notice that as soon as the great man had discarded the pugilist, the authorities stepped in and closed Mr. Broughton's amphitheatre. We have

not discovered the reasons given for that step, no
doubt the perennial charge which was brought up
against pugilists during a century or more—the
charge of a breach of the peace—was sufficient for
the magistrate. In any case, Broughton lost the
championship, and retired from the ring. One
would like to believe the report that the duke
pensioned him off and gave him a place among the
yeomen of the guard. But that report does not
find a place in his biography which we have quoted,
and does not agree with some well-known anecdotes
of his later years.

It was in such surroundings, and by the aid of such
agencies as we have recalled, that the great institution
of the London prize-ring took its origin. Broughton's
rules gave the cult of pugilism a definite shape, and
provided its professors with a ready-made code, which
made the arrangement of their encounters the easier
by saving an infinity of preliminary wrangling. But
the interests of the whole fraternity suffered terribly
from the consequences of Mr. Broughton's mishap
with Slack, and from the delicate position in which that
misfortune left his relations with the Duke of Cumberland. We saw the constables coming in and shutting
up his establishment; the withdrawal of the royal
countenance from its head had, we are afraid, a chil-
ling effect upon the whole profession. One reads
very little about the pugilists or the British spirit
or the true British bottom in the few years which
followed Mr. Broughton's disaster. The duke's sore-

ness about the loss of his £10,000 was no doubt quite sufficient to put the taste for boxing out of fashion among the youth of White's, who, to be sure, about this time were usually engaged in exploring the mysteries of hazard and faro. Boxing, in fact, languished; the reporters were silent in the columns of the *Advertiser* and the *Gentleman's Magazine*; and the great champion, Mr. Slack himself, found it advisable to take a trip in the provinces. We read of him at Bristol, at Acton Wells, in his own county of Norfolk, and elsewhere, fighting rustics, colliers, and Frenchmen, but always emerging victorious. The tradition of the prize-ring, indeed, fled to the country for a while, rested there to recuperate, and came back to London, refreshed and reinvigorated, some years later. If you are curious to explore the dreary records of these old provincial fights, one just like the other, you may read of encounters for small stakes taking place all over the country between those artless provincials with interesting and mechanical names—Bill the Nailer, Smiler the Bricklayer, Joe the Tinman, and the rest. The "fancy" in town remained under a cloud the while, and when, some seven years later, pugilism began to return, it was in a timid and tentative manner, and by way of the more sequestered villages near London—Hounslow or Putney or Islington.

It is not without interest to note that it was the patronage of the Duke of Cumberland which again revived the vogue of pugilism in London.

Slack had carried all before him in the provinces, and, for a space of ten years, after he had overthrown Broughton in his own establishment in the Haymarket, had been accepted as champion without challenge. But in 1760 the Duke of York, finding a likely-looking bruiser in one Bill Stevens, the Duke of Cumberland, his brother, was quite ready to make a match, and, not unnaturally, placed his confidence in the champion whom he had seen knock over Mr. Broughton and his own £10,000 at one blow. The princes made a match of it accordingly; a stage was set up in the Tennis Court, James's Street, Haymarket—a building which exists in an altered shape to this day—and the nominees of the royal sportsmen faced each other on the 17th June 1760. "Slack entered the field with all the confidence of a veteran," says Mr. Miles, quoting some older authority, we presume, "and was acknowledged to have the advantage in the first part of the battle; but the Nailer, with an arm like iron, received the ponderous blows of his antagonist with ease, while with his right arm he so punished the champion's nob that he knocked off the title, picked it up, and wore it." The Duke of Cumberland was thus a second time a loser by Slack, and it is not surprising to learn that his royal highness retired disgusted from the ring. It is a fact, too, which is indisputable, that the ring in London again languished for want of the royal support.

The modern apologists of the prize-ring who saw

so much virtue in its principles and practitioners, and deplored its exit within living memory almost with tears, are very ready to attribute the decline of the "fancy" to the enormities of raffishness and swindling which undoubtedly attended its later years. They are apt to contrast its last unhappy state with the virtue and innocence of its youth and prime, but with very little justification, as it would seem. Mr. Miles, for instance, who in "Pugilistica" lifts up a very eloquent voice in lamentation of the departed glory of the ring, supplies in his own pages very curious information about some of the earlier contests. In 1759 a fight between a boxer of a noted family, Joe James by name, and "Tom Falkner the Cricketer," was obviously sold by the former, "the indignation of the spectators being very highly expressed by their hissing him off the ground." A couple of years later another fight, arranged between Bill Stevens and George Meggs at the Tennis Court by such a pillar of the profession as the ex-champion Slack, was openly and shamelessly given away by Stevens, who owned to having received the stake of twenty guineas, and fifty guineas as well, from Slack, to lose the fight—Slack, of course, finding his account in the heavy backing of Meggs, whom he had trained. No one who knows much of the sporting per- sonalities of the last century will be surprised to hear that Colonel O'Kelly bought Mr. Darts for the sum of £100 when he fought Mr. Corcoran at Epsom in 1771. Of a fight between Sellers and Duggan in

1780 we read "the battle lasted one minute and a half, when victory was declared in favour of Duggan; the amateurs were swindled to a large amount," and they included the promising young Prince of Wales and Mr. George Hanger.

The mention of those names is a reminder that the bruisers received much countenance from his royal highness and the young men who shared the pleasures of his youth, Mr. Hanger, Lord Barrymore, Col. Lake, St. Leger, and the rest. There was little patronage of the prize-ring and its doings to be expected from George the Third, and the countenance of his sons, including the distinguished patronage of the heir-apparent, came as a godsend to the "fancy," which was getting into bad odour. Although there was no longer any recognised amphitheatre in the town like the establishments of Taylor and Broughton, fights took place regularly at various points in the outskirts of London, Stepney Fields, Bloomsbury, Marylebone Fields, and at Islington and Blackheath. But the personnel of the fighters and of the bulk of their patrons had sadly deteriorated since the palmy days of Broughton and the duke. The ring was constantly recruited by roughs, drovers and bargemen, and was in great danger of losing what little respectability it had ever possessed. The interest which the royal youths began to take in its doings naturally brought a crowd of patrons of an assured social position. Fitzpatrick, the Duke of Hamilton, Windham, Sir Thomas Apreece, well-known men like Brady the eminent brewer, the Whig brewer

HUMPHRYS AND MENDOZA

and good fellow Harvey Christian Combe, and scores of other less well-known men of substance and respectability, all supported the prince in his patronage of the ring. By great good fortune too, for its own interests, the profession at this time began to attract practitioners who were in all respects more reputable than their predecessors. There was the Jew Mendoza who replaced the crude brutalities of the earlier professors with a scientific system of boxing which was unknown before his day; Humphrys, whose manners and bearing earned him the title of the Gentleman; and Jackson, whose good-nature and good-humour, generosity and fine presence, seem almost to have entitled him to that distinction. As the century drew towards its close, it became the fashion to take an interest in the ring and its doings amongst men who had hitherto looked upon its vulgarities with contempt. White's and Brooks's did not disdain to put on the mufflers at Harry Angelo's in St. James's Street. The palmy days of the ring indeed were approaching when it became the fashion for a man of position to keep a tame prize-fighter of his own, the Duke of Hamilton and Lord Barrymore being two well-known patrons who enjoyed that luxury. It was the custom of the latter nobleman to introduce his gladiator to his guests after dinner at Wargrave, where they were allowed to judge the strength of his arm by the whizz of his fist an inch off their noses. By the time the 'nineties came in too, if you got into a street row or were hustled at Vauxhall, it was thought just as well to be able to take your part with your fists, swords by that time being rarely worn.

The accounts of the battles of this period and of their circumstances do not show any marked difference from those of the earlier days, nor do they explain the fascination which the ring undoubtedly exercised upon men of birth and good breeding. We have noticed typical battles of the other times, however, and it may be of interest to consider for a moment the sort of thing to which votaries of prize-fighting exposed themselves even in its best days. Here, for example, is one incident of the fight between Gentleman Humphrys and Mendoza, which was arranged to take place at Mr. Thornton's park, at Stilton in Hunts., in the year 1782 :—

"In the twenty-second round Mendoza having struck at Humphrys, the latter dropped. The articles of agreement particularly specified that whichever combatant fell without a blow should lose the battle, consequently a general cry of 'Foul, foul' took place, and it was decided by Mendoza's friends that he had won the battle. Humphrys, Johnson, and the spectators interested in that side of the question contended it was fair, asserting that Humphrys had stopped the blow before he fell. The partizans on the opposite side as vehemently insisted on the contrary, and the whole was a scene of uproar and confusion. Sir Thomas Apreece as the umpire of Mendoza declared it foul, but Alderman Combe refused an opinion. During the affray Captain Brown, Mendoza's second, in a moment of irritation, called Johnson a liar and a blackguard, which was answered by the approach of Johnson in a stern and menacing manner. This led to the expectation of a bye-battle between the seconds. Humphrys came several times to his adversary calling on him to fight out the battle. After much wrangling, Mendoza was taunted into continuing, when Gentleman Humphrys violated the agreement unmistakably by going down to avoid a blow, and the stakes were awarded to the Jew."

This was no obscure encounter between two disreputable coalheavers or drovers, but a great fixture between the ornamental heads of the profession in the presence of the most select of its patrons.

Enthusiasts of the " fancy" point to this period, when Mendoza and Humphrys with their contemporary Jackson were its particular stars, as that in which the whole system attained its meridian. Men of assured position flocked to these encounters, and the ring began to count a large proportion of the male fashion of the day among its supporters. When Mr. Jackson, for example, fought his memorable battle with Mendoza at Hornchurch in 1795, and held that Semitic hero by the hair of his head as he pommelled him, a great number of the peerage made the journey to see that exciting spectacle. A little later when Mendoza met Lee at Grinstead Green there were present many famous men from the White's and Brooks's of that day, Lord Albermarle and General Keppel, Sir W. W. Wynne, Sir John Shelley, Mr. Thornhill, and Sir E. Nagle. There began to arise, too, among the bloods of those days a mild taste for physical exercise, not athletic by any means as yet, but still a step forward from the eternal lounging in card-rooms which had held the field as the main diversion of the young man about town for nearly a century. Mr. Charles Fox and his friends at Brooks's had made a fashion of an affected negligence in dress, and the gradual disappearance of the laced ruffle, powdered wig, and embroidered waistcoat from the figures of the generous youth of the town and clubs made the change easier. The sporting young men of the period began to take an interest in driving and even in hunting, and to dress more like their stud grooms. Boxing as an exercise came to share in this gratifying movement, and it was reckoned the correct thing to put on the gloves with a professor at proper intervals.

The chief of these fashionable instructors was John Jackson, at his famous rooms No. 13 Bond Street, the friend and " corporeal pastor " of Byron, the "emperor of pugilism " and the model of all prize-fighters. Every one grew enthusiastic about Jackson, his manly beauty, his generosity, the astonishing fashion of his clients; "to attempt a list of which," says one scribe, "would be to copy one-third of the peerage." It is certain that some of the asperities of other periods of the ring were toned down by Jackson and his contemporaries. Mendoza was the first who made tours and gave sparring exhibitions, which did much to bring the use of the gloves into fashion. Jackson only fought three battles in his life, and established his great reputation upon those few professional engagements. His fortune was made by the *bona fide* teaching of boxing in his saloons in Bond Street, where Byron capered round with his lame foot and fondly believed he had the makings of a pugilist in him. His lordship talks of a " pugilistic club," and was

very delighted to dine with Mr. Thomas Cribb, another
of the champions of the early years of the century.
By 1814 boxing with gloves had come so much into
fashion under these distinguished auspices of patron
and professor, that the allied sovereigns were regaled
with an exhibition, and Mr. Jackson was dragged out
of his retirement to make sport for those potentates
and for old Blucher and Platoff and the others at Lord
Lowther's in Pall Mall, and at Mr. Angelo's fencing
rooms in St. James's Street. Later still, when his
Majesty King George the Fourth came to the throne,
that monarch, apprehensive, perhaps, of the way in which
his subjects would regard his relations with his queen,
testified to the esteem in which he held the profession
which had owed so much to his patronage by employing its chief professors as a sort of bodyguard at
the ceremony of the coronation. A band of those
gladiators, headed by Mr. Jackson and resplendent in
the scarlet and gold livery of the royal pages, were told
off to keep the ring, so to speak, on that exciting day.
His Majesty presented a single gold medal to the
body to commemorate the occasion, and the prize-
fighters decided to raffle the royal token, which was
won by Mr. Cribb.

Boxing, indeed, was in the air, and was much culti-
vated by the crowds of idle men of fashion who were
set free and provided with leisure by the great peace
which followed Waterloo. Besides Jackson's rooms,
the Fives Court in St. Martin's Street, Leicester Fields,
was another great place of resort for the amateurs.

Here was set up a stage, and here all the noted professors of the art gave exhibitions of sparring with gloves to crowded and delighted audiences at three shillings a head. There are famous prints of the Fives Court with the whole "fancy" of the period displayed at their favourite diversion. It was, indeed, a very famous lounge of the Regency and George the Fourth, and its exhibitions were very innocent, and if the prize-ring had confined itself to such contests, real exhibitions of the "noble art of self-defence," it would never have encountered an enemy in the world.

The club which Lord Byron mentioned in his diary as "increasing daily" was undoubtedly the Pugilistic Society, and was another evidence of the great popularity of the prize-ring and of pugilism in London during the first quarter of the present century. The Pugilistic Society was an organisation which aimed at supplying for the prize-ring the authority which the Jockey Club has given to the turf or the Marylebone Club to cricket. The inimitable Pierce Egan, to whom we are indebted for its early particulars, gave it a greater ambition. According to Mr. Egan its "great object is to keep alive the principles of courage and hardihood which have distinguished the British character, and to check the progress of that effeminacy which wealth is too apt to produce." Anyway, it held its first meeting at the Thatched House on the 22nd May 1814. Sir Harry Smith was in the chair, and Lord Yarmouth made a speech on the occasion. There were stirring events abroad in 1814, which, as we know, had a more or less fortunate conclusion for this country, and his lordship was pleased to see in the cult of pugilism a very good reason for the happy military posture in which we then found ourselves. The members of the society imposed upon themselves the duty of hunting out of the ring all degenerate professors who sold battles to the betting men; they gave purses of from ten to fifty guineas in order to encourage a continuance of battles in out-of-the-way parts of the country; they had stakes and ropes of their own, with P.C. marked on them; and they wore "a uniform dress of blue coats and yellow kerseymere waistcoats, with P.C. engraved on their buttons."

This institution displayed the fashionable side of pugilism; another which was probably more interesting was Daffy's Club, held at Mr. Tom Belcher's at the Castle Tavern, Holborn. At Daffy's Club the "fancy" gathered once a week, and the most noble patrons of the ring did not disdain to appear on occasion and take their glass of spirits and water with the professors of the art. You may read all about Daffy's in that extraordinary work, "The London Spy," by Bernard Blackmantle, otherwise Mr. Westmacott, the book which now produces such figures at Sotheby's by virtue of the delightful aquatints and wood-engravings by Mr. Robert Cruikshank which illustrate its pages. There is a very carefully drawn plate of Daffy's among those, and its portraits have more real eloquence than the dreary prose of its facetious author. "Jemmy

Soares," we learn, " was the president of the club,
Lucky Bob made a 'nation good vice," there are the
"immortal typo, the all-accomplished Pierce Egan,"
Tom Spring with his cock bag, Watts with the Duck
Lane Dossman, Brother Adey, the heroes Scroggins
and Turner, and many more, all looking out of
Mr. Cruikshank's able aquatint.

That same extraordinary phraseology reminds us
that Mr. Westmacott formed his style upon that of
the "immortal typo," Mr. Pierce Egan, in whom the
ring found its high priest and its oracle, and in whose
prose English style surely sank to depths which it has
never reached before or since.   It may be said of Mr.
Pierce Egan that he touched nothing which he did not
disfigure.   He took the plain tales of all the reporters
of pugilism from the earliest days, the honest and
enthusiastic sentences of Captain Godfrey, the quaint
paragraphs of the news-sheets of the middle of the
century, the sober pages of the *Gentleman's Magazine*
and the *Annual Register*, the works of the writers on
pugilism of his own contemporaries, like the anonymous author of " Pancratia," and he converted them
all into that astonishing concoction which he called
"Boxiana," and the idea of which he purloined from
poor Mr. Smeeton.   The English language, as we contend, has never been distorted as it was in the hands
of "the immortal typo," Mr. Pierce Egan, with his
cant expressions in italics, his jokes in capitals so that
you may not miss them, his fawning upon those in
high places, his drearily facetious banter of those who

were not.   Mr. Miles in " Pugilistica " has followed
Pierce over the same ground, and you may there read
how he has played as much havoc with the matter of
those early historians as he has with their manner, expanding a few words into a circumstantial paragraph,
and exchanging their simple statements of fact for his
own inaccurate imaginings.   And yet Pierce Egan had
a prodigious success.   His " Life in London," which
to-day seems the dreariest of his performances, took
London by storm, and fascinated every youth of the
day who was pining for the delights of the town.
Thackeray himself tells us of the fascination which
that wondrous tale of Tom and Jerry, Logic and Cor-
inthian Kate, had for his generous but youthful mind ;
of the disillusionment also which came, thank goodness, upon a later reading.   But Egan, as we say, was
the very figurehead of the " fancy " at any time between
Waterloo and the accession of her present Majesty,
and they both seem worthy of each other, the theme of
the historian and the historian of the theme.

As we have quoted descriptions of the early encounters, we select extracts of two accounts of the
times we are considering as illustrative of the change
which Mr. Egan brought into the literature of the
prize-ring.   The first describes some rounds in the
contest between Mr. Gully and Mr. Gregson, fought
at Sir John Sebright's park, in Hertfordshire, in the
year 1808—a very typical battle of the great period,
which drew thousands of patrons of the ring as
spectators :—

"Round 1. The combatants both sparred about a minute, the utmost silence prevailed in every part of the ring, and every one had his eye fixed steadily on the contending champions. Here Gully displayed one of the most signal specimens of the art of boxing that perhaps ever was witnessed, by putting in two most dextrous hits through his opponent's guard in the mouth and throat at the same moment. Gregson fell like a log and was instantly covered with blood. The greatest commotion was now excited, and peal succeeded peal of applause. The odds were six to four on Gully.

Round 3. Gregson successfully planted a hit in Gully's breast and rallied, but Gully had the advantage of putting in most blows although Gregson threw him. Gregson's head had now begun to swell, and he continued to bleed freely. Odds two to one on Gully.

Round 6. At the close of the round Gregson put in a tremendous blow on the side of his adversary's head, and both fell out of the ring.

Rounds 7 and 8. Gully rallied, put in six successive hits on Gregson's head, and at length knocked him off his legs. . . . Gregson's left eye was now almost closed, his nose broken, the blood flowed copiously, and his head was most hideously disfigured.

Round 9. Gregson evinced distress, and Gully hit him again severely on the face. Gregson fell on his knees.

Round 12. Gregson struck Gully on the breast, who immediately knocked him off his legs by a flush hit in the mouth.

Round 17. In this round Gregson became intemperate and ran in upon his adversary, who continued hitting him and avoiding him in a most surprising manner. Gregson twice turned his back upon his opponent and made towards the ropes, but Gully followed him, changed his front, fibbed him, and kept him from falling until he had hit him into an almost senseless state, and then dropped him gently between his arms.

Round 27. Gregson was brought down by a heavy blow under the ear, and the twenty-eighth round decided the contest, Gregson being too much exhausted to be brought to the mark in time. The battle lasted one hour and a quarter."

This is a plain tale of the reporter's, and obviously true, and we may discover how much of the noble science of self-defence there was displayed in Mr. Gully's exposition of its pleasing intricacies. Now let us listen to a much shorter epic by Mr. Pierce Egan :—

" 1. The men came to the scratch with good-humour painted on their mugs.

2. Vipond came up bleeding from the left ogle, not quite so confident, but nothing loth, and wishing to pay with interest the favour received. But, alas! he was not the first man disappointed in good intentions, for he was met in so tremendous a manner by Pat's right hand on the temple, that he was sent to the ground as if kicked by a horse.

3. Paddy brought him to his recollection by a blow on the victualling office, following it up with another on the box of knowledge.

4. Vipond's ivory box was visited by Pat's left mawley. . . . Unfortunately for Matthew there was a magnetic attraction between Paddy's left and the Lancashire man's frontispiece which kept the claret continually streaming."

The fight was an unimportant one between Langan and Vipond, and we quote it only as an illustration of Mr. Egan's style, but this was the sort of stuff which delighted the sportsmen of those days, inspired half the writers of *Bell's Life* for the next twenty years, and secured for Mr. Egan's *chef d'œuvre* "Boxiana" a place in "every gentleman's library."

That same Mr. Gully, who in the sober report of the first quoted of our authorities "most hideously disfigured" Mr. Gregson, was the other great figure of the most reputable period of the ring, that of

Humphrys, Mendoza, and Jackson. He remains to
this day the shining example of what virtues may be
engendered in its bracing atmosphere, a veritable industrious apprentice of the " fancy." He fought only
three battles in his life, but diligent in the business
which engaged his later years, he lived to stand before
princes. " After a few years passed in the occupation
of a tavern-keeper," we read, " he was so fortunate in
turf speculations, and so well served by sound judgment in racing matters, that he retired and became
the purchaser of Ware Park, Hertfordshire. Here he
associated with the first circles in the county." Mr.
Gully's social and sporting successes were indeed only
a step to further greatness, to the ownership of
collieries in Yorkshire, and to the representation in
the first Reformed Parliament of the borough of
Pontefract, an event which provided Mr. James Smith
with some poetic inspiration :—

> " You ask me the cause that made Pontefract sully
> Her fame by returning to Parliament Gully.
> The etymological cause I suppose is
> His breaking the bridges of so many noses."

One hears little but good about Mr. Gully, and
some of his contemporaries were much impressed by
the splendours of his hospitality. Says one of his
biographers who had sat at his table, " the turbot
came by express from Billingsgate, and the haunch
from his own park ; Moet purveyed the champagne,
Marjoribanks the port, and Griffiths the Lafitte. We

had no skulking host, be assured, but the most entertaining and liberal one alive."

We believe that the fashionable craze among the amateurs in London for the practice of boxing was not of very long duration, and that it was soon eclipsed by the real interest of pugilism for its true votaries, that of seeing two courageous men knock each other out of time with the naked fist. The Fives Court in St. Martin's Lane and the Tennis Court in the Haymarket were still great institutions it is true, but they were attended by amateurs in the capacity of spectators only and not as partakers in the fierce joys of the "set-to." These institutions provided exhibitions where new aspirants for pugilistic honours displayed their abilities with the "mufflers," and where the graduates of the prize-ring took their benefits, a function where the stage was occupied by a succession of the most eminent professors of the art punching each other in pairs, and where the beneficiary himself made his bow and speech of thanks to his patrons, who signified their approval of his past by an eleemosynary shower of half-crowns which fell upon the stage. Disputes as to the terms of forthcoming contests were arranged with much eloquence on the stage of the Fives Court by trainers and seconds, who piloted aspirants (for a consideration) through the dangers, financial and otherwise, which they had themselves passed. The Fives Court indeed came to be the centre of the professional interest of the ring, until in more modern times the editor and staff of *Bell's*

Life, the forerunner of our own sedate *Field*, practically took the organisation of the London prize-ring into their own keeping.

The more fashionable members of the " fancy " were accustomed to gather at Limmer's Hotel; Limmer's still standing, but translated from the Limmer's of those days; Limmer's where the traditions of the eighteenth-century coffee-house lingered latest, the Limmer's celebrated in song :—

> " My name is John Collins, head waiter at Limmer's,
> Corner of Conduit Street, Hanover Square;
> My chief occupation is filling of brimmers
> For spicy young gentlemen frequenting there."

Here the great powers of the ring, the patrons who found the stakes which sent the pugilists off to their trainers, and alone made possible the classic encounters of those days, forgathered, and manipulated the figures at the Fives Court. "Full many a well-known pugilist, with Michael Angelo nose and square-cut jaw, has stood cap in hand at the door of that historical coffee-room, within which Lord Queensberry, then Lord Drumlanrig, and Captain W. Peel, and the late Lord Strathmore were taking their meals. In one window stand Colonel Ouseley Higgins, Captain Little, and Major Hope Johnston. A servant of the major's with an unmistakable fighting face enters with a note for his master. It is from Lord Longford and Sir St. Vincent Cotton, asking him to allow his valet to be trained by Johnny Walker for a proximate prize-fight." So writes a very interesting contributor to a magazine speaking of a day a little later than that we are recalling. But we may place the patrons of the ring from Waterloo to Inkerman with the greatest propriety at Limmer's, a period which would include such lights of the "fancy" as Parson Ambrose, Colonel Berkeley, Sir Edward Kent, the Myttons, Captain Barclay, Lord Pomfret, Squire Osbaldestone, Lord Longford, Lord Winchilsea, and Lord George Bentinck.

To complete our survey of the organisation of the London prize-ring during the first half of the present century, we must add to the institutions we have already described a whole group of what were known as "sporting houses" scattered all over the town. The sporting houses were public-houses kept by re-tired prize-fighters, trainers, seconds, or other in-dividuals who had been connected with the prize-ring in their earlier days. A chief part of the business of the proprietor of a sporting house was to "give the office," that is, to furnish to the properly qualified member of the "fancy" the latest intelligence as to the movements of the principals in a forthcoming fight and of the police who were dogging them. Prize-fights were no longer possible near the town, except, as it were, by accident. But the location of a forthcoming battle, the exact hour, the best means of reaching the place of the encounter, the state of the odds on the combatants, and other information of a like interest might always be had at the nearest sport-ing house by any *bona fide* member of the fraternity.

The Three Tuns off Seven Dials was the typical sporting house of the central district of the town, where there was a constant procession of male fashion from St. James's to consult the old oracle Alec Keene, and every quarter of the town had a similar place of resort well known to all local patrons of the ring, and of which lists were regularly published in the sporting periodicals. With the improved organisation of the police, London had become the headquarters only of operations which were conducted on lines of secrecy in sequestered parts of the home counties, and imitated on a smaller scale in the provinces by organisations of a similar character in the great towns like Birmingham and Manchester.

It is worthy of observation that the whole noble science of self-defence had been in strife with the legal authorities ever since the constables went to shut up Mr. Broughton's Amphitheatre after the Duke of Cumberland lost his £10,000 in 1760, and that the whole organisation of the ring had grown up in defiance of the law. That strife continued, indeed, to the end of the chapter, when the police stepped in and prevented the finish of that greatest of all encounters, the heroic struggle between Heenan and Sayers at Woking just forty years ago. But the war had gone, on the whole, in favour of the authorities, and had produced a state of things which limited the enjoyment of the "fancy" in London itself mainly to the organisation of campaigns in districts where the police were less well organised or more complacent. The newspapers are full of long descriptive accounts of the periodical expeditions made by the "fancy" into the provinces on these occasions. As soon as "the office" had been given to the initiated at the sporting houses of Holborn, Soho, Houndsditch or Chelsea, and the date and place of meeting determined beyond any reasonable doubt, the "fancy," chiefly on horseback, started off on a pilgrimage to the favoured spot. Three days were often spent on the journey when the tactics of the enemy had driven the suffering profession very far afield, to the Sussex or Hampshire downs for instance, Salisbury Plain or the fens of Cambridgeshire. There are most humorous accounts of these old expeditions to be dug out of the quarries of the old sporting papers in the newspaper room at the Museum ; tales of advance and retreat, of strategical manœuvring over two or three counties, of dreadful losses at the hands of brigands in the shape of innkeepers and postmasters. A very typical campaign of this description was that which preceded the classic battle between Mr. Gully and Mr. Gregson, the faithful reporter of which we have already quoted.

The contest had been arranged to take place at a rural spot about two miles from Woburn. The Marquess of Buckingham, however, who was evidently a degenerate outsider, objected as *custos rotulorum* of the county to the engagement taking place within his jurisdiction, and issued an edict against it. The "fancy," nevertheless, flocked to Woburn and the adjacent villages during the two days preceding the date of the fixture, until all that pleasant vicinage hummed like a hive. The Marquess got out his bench of magistrates, his *posse comitatus*, his constables, and his Dunstable volunteers, "with drums beating, flags, cartouche boxes double provided, bayonets fixed, and all in military array, until the peasants thought the French had landed," as the reporter of the *Morning Chronicle* faithfully records. At Woburn, on the second evening, thirty shillings a head was the price claimed and realised for a night's shakedown in a kitchen by the thrifty inhabitants, who thoughtfully removed the boots of their guests as security for the payment. "There were fifteen gentlemen," we read, "laid on the floor of one room, and hundreds reposed in their carriages." On the morning of the third day a ring was thrown up on Ashley Common, and between six and seven A.M. "many of the amateurs came dashing direct from London." Bill Richmond was at the "Magpie" to direct the favoured ones to the proper spot; the multitude soon got "the office" and "followed the bang up leaders" to the common. Mr. Mendoza there rode up to the assembled "fancy" and solemnly assured them that the Marquess and his magistrates would prevent the fight at that spot. The expectant multitude followed that eminent man, who was training Gregson, to his own inn, "where they found the hero seated in Lord Barrymore's barouche with the horses turned towards Woburn, and escorted by about a hundred and fifty noblemen and gentlemen on horseback and an immense retinue of gigs, tandems,

and curricles of every species of vehicle." It appears
that several other places had been selected for the exhibition, in the event of any unfortunate interference,
such as the Marquess's, taking place. The first of
these was Sir John Sebright's park in Hertfordshire,
seventeen miles from Ashley, and the reporter assures
us, with some generosity of imagination, no doubt,
that the whole seventeen miles were covered with one
solid mass of passengers. "Broken-down carriages
obstructed the road, knocked-up horses fell and could
not be got any further, and many hundreds of gentlemen were happy in being jolted in brick-carts for a
shilling a mile." They most of them reached Sir
John Sebright's demesne by two o'clock, however,
where the ring was formed; "the exterior circle was
nearly an acre, surrounded by a triple ring of horse-
men and a double row of pedestrians, who, notwithstanding the wetness of the ground, lay down with
great pleasure, and the forty-foot ring was soon completed." The incidents of these wanderings and of the
contest we have already described are, as we say, quite
typical of a hundred prize-fights organised from London during the pre-railway era of modern England.

There was a slight change of tactics in later times,
rendered necessary by railways, telegrams, and the improved organisation of the police, but the strategy
remained the same. The base lay in London between
Limmer's, the Pugilistic Association, and the Fives
Court, with outposts in the sporting houses of the
suburbs, and the campaign was directed along the

strategical lines of railway where local considerations determined the exact sites of its battlefields. Sometimes this was only decided on the train itself; the railway companies were monstrously polite to the "fancy" in those days; the special train would run on past a waiting band of constables into the next county until a sequestered field was reached, disgorge its combatants, ring-makers, and horde of riff-raff, run on to the next station and return for the whole caravan after the issue had been decided. Another favourite plan was to hire a steamer or two at some down-river jetty, take the train there, embark on the waiting flotilla, and pitch a ring on some presentable spot near the water's edge, in one of the desolate marshes of the estuary, on Canvey Island, or on the embankment of the river itself below Long Reach. There were dolorous complaints against Jews from Houndsditch who, having got "the office," chartered other steamers, filled them at half-prices, and diluted the chaste circles of the real "fancy" with the vulgarity of the East End. By the time that her Majesty came to the throne a successful meeting, which was not unduly harassed by the police, would assemble as many as thirty or forty thousand people, anticipating, indeed, the vast crowds which gather to watch a match of the Football League to-day. The two fixtures had other points of similarity, in that the referee often went in danger of his life.

The actual incidents of the fighting itself differed little through all these years from the incidents of the earlier contests. There is a strange similarity between the accounts of one combat and another in the columns of the *Sporting Magazine* and of *Bell's Life in London*. The style of the reporters alone changed with the years, and variations upon the chaste model of Mr. Pierce Egan enriched the language with a delightful play of phrase and synonym. The odds were stated in quaint terms. It was "Chelsea Hospital to a sentry-box" on the Deaf 'Un, or the "Glass-case of '51 to a cucumber-frame" that the Tipton Slasher beat Tom Paddock. The faces of the heroes were "frontispieces" or "dial-plates"; their mouths "potato-traps" or "gin-traps," or "kissers," or "ivory-boxes"; their heads "nuts," "nobs," or "knowledge-boxes"; their blood "currant juice" or "claret"; their eyes "ogles" or "optics"; their stomachs "bread-baskets" or "victualling offices"; their noses "conks," "snouts," or "smellers." It is only when we read the epics written in such language as this that we realise what we have lost in the prize-ring.

The style of the recording angels of the "fancy" thus changed, as we say, but the subject-matter which inspired them remained much as it had been in the days of Broughton and Slack. Training became better understood, indeed, and the encounters as a consequence were much prolonged, both by reason of an improved defence and of the stamina which was acquired by the abstemiousness of the improved training. Bendigo and Caunt fought ninety-three rounds in September of 1845, and would have fought

more but for the bludgeoning of one of the combatants by the mob; Sayers fought Pineson to a finish
through one hundred and nine rounds, lasting three
hours and eight minutes, in January of 1856; fights
of fifty and sixty rounds were the rule. Punishment
was undoubtedly more severe for men trained to
endure such ordeals as these, and deaths in the ring
were not uncommon. Turner killed Curtis at
Moulsey Hirst in 1816; in 1833 Byrne at St.
Albans was carried off dead after ninety-three rounds
in three hours and sixteen minutes with Deaf Burke.
But all these contests, as we say, differed only in
degree from those reported by Captain Godfrey, and
it is in the reports of exactly similar encounters,
varied only by the style of the reporters through a
century and a half, that the history of the prize-ring
is recorded.

That curious institution, whose history we have
attempted to summarise, had, as we have seen, a surprising vogue, and that among men who were accomplished in many ways and eminent in many walks of
life. Enthusiasts claim Mr. Charles James Fox as
a supporter of the ring; they are certainly entitled
to Mr. Windham, who supported the institution
in Parliament, as he did those of bull and bear
baiting, because, as he believed, it fostered the
"British spirit." A man of a different stamp, the
Lord Althorp of the Reform Bill, whose personal
character inspired the trust both among his own ad-
herents and among his opponents, which alone made

the passage of that great measure possible, made a very curious confession of faith to Speaker Denison. Lord Althorp was a boxer himself, and he declared "that he had carefully considered whether it was not a duty which he owed to the public to attend every prize-fight which took place so as to encourage the noble science to the extent of his power." And yet he himself described how he had seen "Mendoza knocked down for the first five or six rounds by Humphrys, and seeming almost beaten until the Jews had got their money on, when a hint being given he began in earnest and soon turned the table," a proceeding which was surely on a moral equality with pulling a horse in a race, which his lordship would certainly have deprecated. Breezy politicians like Melbourne and Palmerston were, of course, staunch upholders of the ring; Palmerston especially, who intimated in the House of Commons that although the lawyers did not agree with him, he could not see how it was that the peace was broken by two pugilists who had no quarrel or animosity between them.

It all seems very strange now, the place prize-fighting filled in the lives of many people still alive, and the entire lack of any regret for its disappearance at the present time. Listen to Professor Wilson, who devoted one of his famous papers in the *Noctes* to the subject. Crusty Christopher was in one of his most confident and oracular moods. "The English are the most courageous people in the world, and they have chosen of their own accord to settle such differences as cannot be settled otherwise, to be settled with the fist. I regard pugilism as one of the chief causes and effects of the 'British spirit.' I laid emphasis, James, on the words 'British spirit,' and I lay emphasis on the words 'fairplay.' But there are fools, and I suspect knaves eke are they, who while they have not the audacity to libel the whole people nor choose to have their own filthy lick-spittle blown back in their own faces from

'The bold peasantry, the country's pride,'

assembled at rural feast and festival all over Merrie England, squirt their venom like toads from holes at the London Ring, and seem to think that the legislature will listen to the croak of incarcerated reptiles."

The real issues were, of course, avoided in this choice rhetoric. The fairplay upon which Mr. Wilson laid such emphasis became impossible when the betting, which was the mainspring of the whole organisation of the prize-ring, was allowed to inspire such outrages as were the common incidents of its meetings. The fight between Caunt and Bendigo was, as we have seen, stopped by ruffians who had money to lose by the defeat of one of the combatants. The referee at Doncaster in 1831 had to withdraw Brown in his fight with Sampson after he had been kicked in the eye by one of the "fancy" and beaten on the head with a stake until his life was endangered. The Fairplay

Club itself was an organisation of bruisers which had
its headquarters in the editorial sanctum of *Bell's Life*,
the object of which was to keep a ring for the combatants by the attendance of its members armed with
metal-mounted hunting-stocks. Fairplay could not
have been so common among the "fancy" when such
an organisation as the Fairplay Club was necessary.

As to the British spirit, the British people might
still settle their real disputes with the fist, when the
occasion arose, without the assistance of the prize-ring;
such happy arrangements were surely independent
of the professional prize-fight, where two men with
no quarrel between them broke each other's jaws and
beat each other blind and insensible, only to provide a
spectacle and an occasion for gambling for a set of
rowdies, who were careful to preserve their own skins
from the same danger. We are happy to think that
the British spirit has survived such nurses and such
circumstances as these, and that interest in the prize-
fight has been exchanged for a more healthy interest
in more healthy forms of athletics. It is certainly a
matter for rejoicing that the only trace of the old
passion for the "milling match" to be recognised
to-day appears in those gatherings at the sporting clubs
of the West End, where degenerate youths contend in
light gloves for the opportunity of the knock-out
blow.

CHAPTER X

THE PARKS

WHEN in the year 1536 King Henry the Eighth persuaded, by means perfectly understood at the time,
"the Right Reverend Father in God, William Boston,
and the Convent of Westminster," to make over to
him "the scyte, soyle, circuyte and procyncte of the
Manor of Hyde" in exchange for the priory of
Hurley in Berks, he established a tradition of pleasure which has clung to the manor of Hyde ever
since. The motives which induced his Majesty thus
to pack off the abbot and monks to the provinces
appear plainly enough in the royal proclamation issued
in the same month with the Act of Parliament which
completed the transfer, "with their whole assent, consent and agreement," as is quaintly recited in the
statute. "As the King's most Royal Majesty," says
the proclamation, "is desirous to have the games of
hare, partridge, pheasant and heron preserved in and
about the honour of his palace of Westminster for his
own disport and pastime, no person, on the pain of
imprisonment of their bodies and further punishment
at his Majesty's will and pleasure, is to presume to
hunt or hawk from the Palace of Westminster to St.

Giles' in the Fields, and from thence to Islington, to our Lady of the Oak, to Highgate, to Hornsey Park, and to Hampstead Heath."

Such a proclamation serves to remind us what a very modern nation modern England is. The successive lifetimes of only four or five old men would form a chain which might connect our own with a time when Henry coursed hares, and flushed pheasants and herons for Anne Boleyn's tiercels in a royal chase which began on the banks of the Thames and included the present Hyde, St. James's, Green and Regent's Parks, together with the square miles of unlovely bricks and mortar which to-day cover the western and northern suburbs of London. In his present surroundings it is a pleasant occupation for the jaded citizen to think, now and then, of a wild pleasaunce stretching over that wide area, a country of woods and thickets and forest glades, springs and marshy pools, peopled by wild creatures only, and its silence little disturbed except when the "King's most Royal Majesty," with Anne on her palfrey and her train of ladies, rode through its valleys and uplands, with London, little bigger than a modern county town, lying purple in the distance in the hollow by the river between the Tower and the Savoy. Above all, the Londoner of to-day may thank his stars that so much of that open space has been rescued from those same bricks and mortar, and reserved, as it has been, for the "disport and pastime" of the lieges of Henry's successors.

For sport, or pleasure, or merrymaking for one class or another of Londoners have controlled the destiny of the parks, and of Hyde Park especially, ever since that memorable year when Henry laid out his happy hunting-ground. The young Edward the Sixth was there accustomed to give great hunting parties to the foreign ambassadors. The traditions of pleasure which we find clinging to the parks in no way suffered at the hands of Queen Elizabeth, who erected great stands both in Hyde and Marylebone Parks (the last of which we to-day know as Regent's Park) for the better viewing of the chase by herself and her guests. The love of sport which so often took King James the First to the parks, with Jowler and Jewel and the rest of the favourite pack, was not the least agreeable quality of that monarch's character in the eyes of his English subjects. Charles the First certainly had in mind the capabilities of Hyde Park as a pleasure-ground rather than its utility, when he revoked a permission given to an enterprising gentleman of Chelsea to convey the water of its springs to the inhabitants of Westminster, upon the representation of his keepers that such a proceeding would interfere with his Majesty's deer. It may be counted also to Charles for righteousness that, without any pressure at all, he admitted his subjects to share the pleasures of the royal demesne, and by generously throwing open its gates to the public dedicated Hyde Park to the enjoyment of the people "for ever."

It little affects our proposition of the continued

tradition of pleasure in Hyde Park, that in the troubled days which followed, the Parliament converted it into a huge entrenched camp, with bastions and earthworks on the site of the present Hamilton Place and of the Marble Arch; or that a few years later a resolution of the House of Commons decreed "that Hyde Park be sold for ready money," and that the Park, its timber and its deer, were disposed of in three lots for about £18,000. It only followed that the speculators who bought the ground calculated upon the existing popularity of the place as a playground, and imposed a price for admission. Londoners still drove their coaches and rode their nags in Hyde Park in the spring, grumbled sadly, but paid their shillings and sixpences nevertheless, and flocked there as usual to flirt and ogle in its drives, or to watch the horse matches and chariot races, the foot races and the games of hurling, which had a surprising vogue from the very year the gates were opened to the public. There was little real interruption of the gaiety of which Hyde Park was the chosen retreat, and the traditions of the Restoration were in no way violated when the enterprising purchasers of the royal property found their titles treated as null and void by the courts of law.

That same epoch of the Restoration marks the first great period of Hyde Park as a public pleasureground. All classes had been quick to appreciate the value of a breezy open place, where fashion, jaded in the stuffy rooms and playhouses of the London of that day, could forgather in its chariots or on its horses, exchange its repartees, and gaze over an open country right on to the hills of Surrey and Kent on the one hand, and to the northern heights of London on the other. To the attractions of foot races and horse matches which drew crowds of the people to the Park, came to be added that of a rendezvous of fashion, which never fails to draw the great world and the aspiring body which hangs ever on its skirts, to any place which a freak or fad of its leaders may indicate as worthy of its notice. Here was a spot near the town where birds sang and wild flowers grew — a spot in those days much less suburban than Richmond and Hampton to-day. And so we find people of condition flocking to Hyde Park from the first. Even in the dark days of the Puritan ascendency there is record of Cromwell himself in the Park, where he came near to grief in attempting the driving of a coach and six; used the whip too much, as one might expect of him, was flung on the coach pole, and from there to the ground, with his foot in the tackling, " and was carried a good while in that posture, during which time a pistol went off in his pocket." The whole incident pleased the faithful vastly, and was the occasion of some bad verse from the royalist scribes.

The world of fashion of the Restoration being a body of small proportions compared with that of to-day, a much smaller space served for its exercises. Any man or woman entering Hyde Park, either by

the Oxford Road or from Piccadilly, made for a
spot which lay about midway. between the entrances
from those avenues.   A few hundred yards due north
of the Royal Humane Society's present building, probably at the very spot where to-day converge the six
or seven footpaths crossing the Park in that neighbourhood, was fenced in a circular space of some three
hundred yards in diameter.   Round the circumference
of this space ran a carriage road, the whole being
enclosed in a rough fence of stakes and rails.   The
fence and the means of watering this rather primitive
promenade, which was used by the best blood of
England, often excited the derision of the intelligent
foreigner ; the road was extremely dusty as a rule,
and the water-cart was merely a large cask on wheels
with the bung withdrawn.

The great function of the promenade in " the Ring,"
as the enclosure was called, took place in the small
area we have described, and it consisted merely of a
traversing of this circular road in one direction on
horseback or in a coach, at the time when another
row of horses and coaches traversed it in the other.
There were thus two concentric rings of beauty and
fashion continually passing each other.   No stopping
was allowed unless King Charles himself pulled up,
which, to be sure, he often did when the proper lady
appeared in the other circle.   It was the mode to
exchange witticisms with the acquaintances you saw
for a moment in passing from your coach window or
your saddle, and it requires little imagination to recall

the nature of much of that badinage during the palmy days of the Restoration.

It is very easy to trace the increasing fashion of the Ring in Hyde Park in the records of those days. Its pleasures were the theme of the Grub Street poetasters; and it went hard but that a Restoration playwright dragged in a scene placed in the Ring into half the comedies he wrote. The news-sheets would not describe a review of troops without opposing the eyes of Myra or Sacharissa in the Ring to the deadly weapons of the Guards. Anonymous Puritans flooded the town with what they called "satyrs" on the place, and the customs which flourished there; they held up to eternal perdition the chin chucking of orange girls by the beaux, the delivery of *billets doux* between lovers by the same convenient means, the appalling thickness of the paint on the ladies' faces. The diarists, with Pepys and Evelyn at their head, are eloquent on the subject of the Ring. Pepys was there constantly, or wishing himself there, when a fine day elsewhere reminded him of the amenities of the place. He tells us that "the Dukes of York and Gloucester do haunt the place much," which was quite a good reason for the aspiring Samuel to affect the same locality. You may, if you like, imagine with the greatest propriety most of the originals of those simpering beauties of Lely taking a turn in the Ring—Castlemaine, Stewart, Hamilton, Chesterfield, and the rest. Pepys will give you particulars of Castlemaine "lying impudently on her back in the coach asleep with her mouth open," or driving in yellow satin "with a pinner on," and ogling the king, in another coach in the other circle, dreadfully; or riding on a white palfrey with a crimson velvet saddle and a gold bridle, and pulling up for a chat with his Majesty for a whole hour with all London looking on and waiting to go on with their promenade. You may see in the annals of that day how her ladyship, or another like her, would drive into the Ring with a handsome young actor from the playhouse in the very dress he had worn on the stage in the early afternoon performances of those days, or begin an intrigue with a fashionable author by leaning from her coach and abusing him roundly, as when the Castlemaine gave great hopes to the handsome Wycherley by the greeting, "Sir, you're a rascal; you're a villain." De Grammont will tell you of the dreadful struggle between the Castlemaine and the Stewart for the first ride in the Ring in the king's new coach from Paris, with the glass windows—the coach which had been built for his Majesty by the Duc de Guise for two thousand guineas.

Turning again to Mr. Pepys' pleasant gossip we may trace the origin of the lady's riding-habit, which first appeared in the Ring on the fair persons of the "Amazones," as he calls them; "ladies with coats and doublets and deep skirts," says Samuel, "just for all the world like mine, and their doublets buttoned up their breasts, with periwigs and with hats, so that only for a long petticoat dragging under their men's coats nobody would take them for women in any point whatever." All the splendour of that irregular court and the fashion and beauty of those days were indeed focussed upon that circle of three hundred yards diameter in the Park; the deer were banished to the north-west corner, and as all thoughts of the utility of the pastures came gradually to be superseded by considerations of pleasure, Hyde Park was made over as a playground to Londoners of all classes who had time and inclination to take their pleasure there.

The promenade in the Ring strikes the busy man of to-day as a very ponderous function. By the time England had settled down under Anne and the first George a fashionable turnout in the Park had become a serious undertaking. The private coach of that day was a sprawling structure as large as a modern hearse, its ugly body hung on straps between widely separated legs, and its team no less than six grey Flanders mares. Its panels bore the quarterings of the coats-of-arms of its owners on a generous scale, and its coachmen and footmen were in liveries of a splendour which survives only to-day in those of the Mansion House. It was only the magnate of an assured position who could turn out in proper style in the Ring; the aspiring man of fashion of modest income, if he were wise, confined his equipage to the more modest proportions of a well-groomed hack, and made up for the modesty of his stable by the fineness of his wardrobe and the gallantry of his bearing.

There is a classic example of a disaster which happened to a gentleman who was less well advised. Beau Fielding, following the example of a Welsh family of the same name, thought fit to claim descent from the great family of the Hapsburgs. He appeared in the Ring, accordingly, in a chariot of surpassing splendour, with the arms of that family finely emblazoned on its panels. The Lord Denbigh of that day, who was really entitled to the same arms, was moved to indignation at the presumption of the Beau. His lordship engaged a house painter with a can of yellow paint, waited for Fielding in the Ring, set the artisan to daub the offending panel completely over, and left the Beau to retreat amidst the derision of the assembled fashion of the town.

There has never been a lack of a sense of humour in Londoners, and the absurdity of the equipage required by fashion for a drive of a few hundred yards in the Park, no doubt inspired the parody of that equipage which appeared quite suddenly in the Ring in the season of 1724. At the close of the preceding century, the ordinary hackney coach had been forbidden entrance to the Ring. The occasion of the ordinance had been the appearance of a coachful of young men and women in masks, who had horrified the exquisites of the fashionable promenade by the appalling freedom with which they greeted every passing equipage. In 1724, however, some well-born young men about town hired a large but dilapidated hackney coach, harnessed the prescribed number of six broken-down horses, placed themselves inside, mounted scavengers on the box as footmen and chimney-sweepers as postillions, and drove through the gates ere the astonished keepers could recover themselves. They were in the Ring before they could be stopped, and duly performed the function of the promenade in their strange equipage. This was completed by half-a-dozen shoeblacks hanging on the footboard behind, wearing bags with brushes and blacking on their shoulders, and crowned with their three-legged stools by way of hats.

During the public feeling of unrest which preceded the Jacobite rising of 1715, General Cadogan marched the Life Guards and Horse Grenadiers, the Duke of Argyll's regiment of foot, and three battalions of Foot-guards, with field pieces and ammunition waggons, from the Tower into the Park, encamped them under canvas on the south side, just within the wall along Knightsbridge and Kensington Gore, and London was regaled with the first of those military displays which later became one of the chief attractions of Hyde Park. There were great doings on the 1st of August, the anniversary of the king's accession. The Guards were paraded in their new uniforms to the admiration of the people, and the day concluded with fireworks and illuminations. There followed reviews by the king, the Prince of Wales, and the Duke of Marl-borough at intervals during two months, and as the weather broke up in October, the troops went into winter quarters by exchanging their canvas tents for wooden huts, and wooden stables were provided for the horses. When the Prince of Wales' birthday came round in November there were prodigious rejoicings. The officers commanding gave great presents to the troops. We read of the Duke of Montague providing five hundred pounds of pudding, two hogsheads of wine, two of ale, and an ox to be roasted whole at the head of the first troop standard. We can imagine the joy of the open-mouthed Londoner at such proceedings, at the terrific huzzas as they drank his royal highness's health in illuminated circles at night, at the volleys of cannon and small arms which followed each toast. The Ring was deserted, and one immediate result of the presence of the soldiers was the unwonted safety of the Park for passengers, the footpads being quite disconcerted.

In 1722, again, no less than 7000 men, with a field-train, took up their position in Hyde Park. The display of 1715 had given the people a taste for the military, and the camp was the great attraction of the season. The whole town flocked to the Park, and the popularity of the meeting was so great that a full-blown fair arose on the skirts of the camp, with dancing saloons, puppet-shows, and billiard-tables and dice for the people of quality. Bartholomew Fair, in fact, was anticipated at Whitsuntide, the tea gardens of the town were denuded of their customers, and the proprietors bewailed the competition of the camp in the public prints of the day. Those prints are eloquent upon the grandeur of the review on the king's birthday, of the king and the Prince of Wales dining in my Lord Cadogan's pavilion, "taken by Prince Eugene from the Grand Vizier at the siege of Vienna." You might see "almost sixty dukes and other peers, besides abundance of other persons of distinction," among them "the Right Honourable Sir Robert Walpole, the famous Prime Minister;" also the Bishop of Durham, finely mounted, and wearing a "long habit of purple with jackboots, his hat cocked and his black wig tied behind him like a military officer."

No wonder that the Ring was deserted, and the ladies, from duchesses to nurserymaids, flocked to the camp. They even adopted military habits, and red cloaks were much in vogue out of compliment to the soldiers. Grub Street grew furious at the luxury of the officers' quarters, at the tea-parties, and the invitations to drink ratafia, at the gravel walks and gardens laid out round the marquees of the higher officers. A screen of plaited branches to keep the sun from the tent of the Prince of Wales reminded the scribes of the ivy trained over the huts of the young Romans, which was followed by such disaster at Pharsalia. The floors of the tent were boarded and carpeted, and the camp beds adorned with green and red curtains. A great pen like that of Mr. Pope was employed in recording the glories of the camp of 1722. "The maidens with all their charms displayed provoke the spirit of the soldiers, tea and coffee supply the place of the Lacedæmonian black broth. The camp seems crowned with perpetual victory, for every sun that rises in the thunder of cannon sets in the music of violins."

To look forward another half century into another reign in order to complete our glance at the military attractions which have from time to time amused Londoners in Hyde Park, there were 10,000 men in tents in 1780 when the Gordon Mob was like to lay London in ruin, and King George the Third was to be seen daily on foot conversing with the officers in the most affable manner. The popular prerogative of enjoyment in the Park was on this occasion a little infringed. The "quality" were admitted freely, but a shabby coat meant exclusion for its owner. The spectacle of 1780 was altogether much less popular than others of an earlier date. The town began to grow jealous of the presence of so many soldiers, after the disturbance which drew them together had been quelled. England had had twenty years' experience of King George's personal rule by that time, and his Majesty even found it necessary to give his people his solemn assurance that he contemplated no infringements of the liberty of the nation. The camp was picturesque enough to engage the attention of Paul Sandby, and his pictures, which duly appeared in the Academy of the following season, have been perpetuated in engravings. The public were at last pacified by the removal of the troops to Finchley Common and Blackheath, where they lay for the rest of the summer.

Hyde Park, as a resort of fashion, gained greatly by the adoption of Kensington Palace as one of the royal residences. William the Third gave London the first experience of a well-lighted road when he placed lamps along the carriage-way leading to Kensington Palace through the Park, and a new name to that road itself, which was called the King's Road. "Route du Roi," some hold, supplies the derivation of the modern "Rotten Row." The gardens of the palace at Kensington, too, were the resort of the highest "quality" from the beginning of the eighteenth century, where full dress only was allowed, with small-sword, knee-breeches, and shoe-buckles, ordinary people being admitted on Saturdays. George the Second conceived the plan of a new road a little more direct to his palace, and the road which now runs just inside the south railing of the Park to Kensington is the result of his Majesty's thoughtfulness in 1733. Queen Caroline, too, had very definite views about the parks, and Hyde Park especially. The opening of the new road seems to have relieved the old King's Road of all the wheeled traffic and to have given it a vogue as an equestrian promenade, a fashion which resulted in the decay of the inconvenient Ring. The queen, with the aid of Sir Robert Walpole and the Privy Purse, began to dream of vast schemes. These seem originally to have included a new royal palace in the Park, but the most tangible result of her Majesty's activity is the present Serpentine. There were numerous pools in the hollow which is now filled by that sheet of water connected by the little West Bourne, which rose near Paddington. The queen's men of business, Mr. Withers and Mr. Jenkinson, threw a dam across that hollow, the dam which is now crossed by the road, and the Serpentine was the result.

We are convinced that Queen Caroline had her own interests chiefly in view when she did this; the Serpentine was made more as a pleasing adjunct to the royal gardens at Kensington than as an embellishment of a public resort. About the time that the work was drawing to a conclusion, paragraphs began to appear in the papers which bear much evidence of courtly inspiration. We read of royal pleasure-boats for the lake, including a " little vessel for the exercise and diversion of his Royal Highness the Duke of Cumberland," and the queen had already added to the royal gardens at Kensington three hundred acres taken from the Park. It then occurred to her Majesty that the disused Ring might be included in her demesne with advantage. "The Ring in Hyde Park being quite disused by the quality and gentry, we hear that the ground will be taken in for enlarging the Kensington Gardens," says a newspaper of 1736. Sir Robert Walpole had given great assistance to Queen Caroline in carrying out her views; they had between them hoodwinked the king into believing that the queen was paying for the whole of the operations in the Park out of her privy purse, when public funds were being freely used for the purpose. But the most valuable advice Walpole ever gave the queen was perhaps that which set a limit to her schemes. The Ring, as we know, was not included in Kensington Gardens, and a more ambitious scheme still was happily nipped in the bud. Caroline thought that St. James's Park would make a very noble garden if added as an appanage to the palace, and asked the old minister what it would cost. "Three Crowns, your Majesty," was the reply.

When to-day we speak of the Park we have usually Hyde Park alone in our minds, but the expression had a different meaning during the Restoration certainly, and probably for many years after that happy period. Henry the Eighth, as we saw, included St. James's in his royal chase, built his palace of St. James's, and made the swampy meadows, then often overflowed by the river, an appanage of the court. But St. James's Park remained a wild boggy tract fit for little but the flushing of herons until the Stuarts were well established, and the first tradition of social pleasure in St. James's was established only when the young princes, the Prince of Wales and Charles, and their companions, set up a tilting-ring and made a playground in the fields. Then the Park gradually became a walk for the courtiers, people of condition were afterwards admitted, and the tenants of the houses on the Westminster side obtained leave of entrance, a privilege afterwards extended to the general public. Later still the popularity and fashion of the place, aided by the fondness of King Charles the Second for its walks and shades, converted St. James's into the park *par excellence* of London.

Londoners, indeed, owe much to Charles the Second. He was the first to seize upon the capabilities of St.

James's as a playground, and had not the slightest objection in the world to sharing its pleasures with his subjects. The "waterworks" which so pleased Mr. Pepys in the making were the king's own device, and resulted in the piece of water then known as the Canal, which has since developed into the Long Water, the prettiest lake in London. Charles planted groves round the little lake known as Rosamond's Pond, which covered a spot very near that upon which the Guards now learn the goose-step, and so started the tradition of whispering lovers for which Rosamond's Pond was known for nearly a century. He filled the Canal with water-fowl, and fed them with his own royal hand at the cost of some £300 a year for corn, and so colonised that corner of London with a feathered population whose lineal descendants have delighted successive generations of cockneys, and to-day dispute with seagulls for the oblations of whole troops of nursemaids and children. Just where the lake widens out and sweeps round towards the Foreign Office, was the king's pet fancy Duck Island. Duck Island was an acre or two of wild land covered with willows, rushes, and water plants, and intersected in all directions by canals fitted with strange appliances for the rearing and trapping of ducks. The governor-ship of Duck Island was one of those strange court appointments which carried pensions, the invention of which amused the humorous fancy of the king. It was on a par with that famous office which solaced poor Martha Jackson for her ill treatment by some of Cromwell's lambs, when the king made her Gentlewoman of the Horse, Countess of Pall Mall, Viscountess of Piccadilly, Baroness of the Mews, and Lady of the Crupper to the Queen.

But Charles laid the foundations of the future fashion of the Park of St. James's only when he drove that splendid road along its northern border from Spring Gardens to Buckingham Palace, planted it with trees, added subsidiary walks with avenues on each side, and founded what we now know and love as the Mall. The king was quite naturally thinking of his own pleasure when he made the Mall. The game of Pall Mall, which seems to have been of Italian origin, came into England in the reign of his grandfather King James, and was first played in London, "in a very decent and regular manner," along the road planted with a row of elms on each side which still perpetuates the name of the game. The dust of the passing coaches in Pall Mall, it seems, annoyed the players of the Restoration, and the king decided to remove the game to St. James's Park. Pall Mall seems to have been a species of croquet, on a heroic and athletic scale. The game required a long straight course, finely kept, down which a wooden ball could be driven with a mallet, and through a bridge of iron at either end. Players scored by the fewness of their strokes, as at golf, and the driving of the ball a long distance in a proper direction was one of the qualifications for success, qualifications possessed by the king and his brother James in an eminent degree.

So the king, as we say, drove that fine course through the Park, boarded it over, spread it with earth mixed with powdered cockle shells, provided its edges with scales marked with distances in figures which you may still see figured in old prints of the period, and appointed a Keeper of the Mall, or " Cockle Strewer to the King." In so doing he provided that famous promenade over which the fashion and beauty of a century displayed itself, when, after a few years, the vogue of the game expired with the advancing years and troubles of the king, its chief supporter.

It is not difficult to trace the growing fashion of the Park of St. James's in the records of those joyous days, a vogue which followed as a natural consequence of the king's fondness for the place. Charles planted acorns from the oak of Boscobel as mementoes of his former dangers, his newly-made lake was a perpetual delight, his ducks were always there to be fed, and a Dutchman records that his Majesty often stripped in the summer heats and swam in its waters. Then the king brought all sorts of strange creatures to his playground—an albino raven was a public character for years ; Mr. Evelyn saw solan geese, pelicans, Balearican cranes (one with a wooden leg with a practicable joint, the work of an ingenious soldier), many sorts of deer, Guinea goats and Arabian sheep. There was a large aviary for pheasants on the ground now occupied by Marlborough House ; the whole Park, indeed, was a menagerie and an unfailing attraction for Londoners at a time when Zoological Gardens were unknown, and a taste for wild creatures could only be gratified by a visit to the mangy collections at the Tower.

Then the Park provided a background for half those pictures of the court which light up the pages of Pepys or Evelyn or De Grammont. It was the direct way from Whitehall to Hyde Park, and Mr. Pepys describes with much detail the return of a royal party from a promenade in the Ring on the queen's birth-day. A strange procession it was with the "great crowd of gallants," Catherine herself looking "mighty pretty" in her white-laced waistcoat and short crimson petticoat; the Castlemaine, neglected on this occasion, alighting by the aid of her own servant and looking "mighty out of humour" as a consequence; "and had a yellow plume in her hat, and yet is very hand-some," says the susceptible Pepys; "but above all Mrs. Stewart, with her hat cocked and a red plume, with her sweet eye, little Roman nose and excellent taille, is now the greatest beauty I ever saw in all my life."

No wonder the people flocked and dodged the king in the walks of the Park until his ministers beseeched him to discourage their attentions, and everybody but Charles himself was afraid of some lurking fanatic with a dagger. But the king, as he told his brother, was certain that they would not kill him to make James king, and continued his walks in the Park, touched for the king's evil, and encouraged the troops of his subjects who followed him about, to their huge delight. The common people thought more of the urbanity of such a monarch than of his deficiencies in political and constitutional matters, of which they understood little, and there was little cause for scandal among the bulk of his subjects when he was seen to hold "a very familiar discourse" for half-an-hour with "the impudent comedian" Mrs. Nelly Gwynn, on her terrace at the top of the Mall with his Majesty standing on the green sward beneath. Evelyn was "heartily sorry for this scene," and Mr. Pepys seeing the king come from the Castlemaine's lodgings across the Park thought it "a poor thing for a prince to do." But the majority of the Londoners who affected the place in that day were certainly unmoved, and held such doings as a distinct attraction to the Park where they were so freely admitted.

For a century and a half after King Charles inaugurated the fashion of St. James's there was scarcely a dull day. The amusements provided in the Park during the Restoration were often of a surprising character. A sporting nobleman, the Earl of Arran, undertook in 1664 to run down on foot a full-grown buck of the king's herd and kill it. He accomplished the feat without hounds of any sort, but with the help of another peer, Lord Castlehaven, who no doubt headed off the devoted buck at convenient moments. A year or two later the court organised a great wrestling match for a thousand pounds between the "western and northern men," and Cornwall and Cumberland were perhaps first brought together in those early days. The king and "a world of lords" looked on, and Mr. Secretary Morris and Lord Gerard were the judges and awarded the stakes. Later again, when Queen Anne was on the throne, all London flocked to see Dr. Garth and the Duke of Grafton run "the short course of two hundred yards," as it would to-day to witness a similar match between Mr. Lecky, say, and the Duke of Devonshire. The Park, indeed, became the constant scene of strange matches. In default of others, sporting squires would arrange a race between servants, as when Mr. Cunningham matched a coffee-house boy against Captain Light's negro servant in a race round the Park. The whole fashion of the Mall would often be arrested in its morning walk by the spectacle of two chairmen wearing nothing but a pair of shoes, and running for dear life and a hundred pounds down the length of the Mall. Fashion would make way for these strange competitors, the gentlemen cheer the leader, and the ladies simper and hide their faces behind their fans, and this so late as 1738.

About the same time, fashion was greatly interested in hopping matches, usually against time and distance, as when a man engaged to hop a hundred yards in fifty hops, and won much money by accomplishing the feat in forty-six. Later again, all society looked on delighted at the spectacle of a fat cook running a lean footman. The respective figures of the pair can be gauged by the weight carried by the footman by way of handicap, which we learn was 110 lbs., and it is

1784, or THE FASHIONS OF THE DAY

not surprising that the poor footman fell and dropped some of his weight, and so left the race to the man of flesh. Fashion was perhaps most easily pleased when it hung breathless on the performance of a little maid of eighteen months old, whose parents and guardians, who should have known better, backed her to walk the three-quarters of a mile of the Mall in a space of thirty minutes, and realised a great stake when she toddled in with seven minutes in hand.

There was in those early days a freedom of deportment among the company which met in the Mall which no doubt had its attractions as well as its inconveniences. It was quite orthodox for a lady of birth and breeding to exchange badinage with a man she had never seen before. Skittish women without any thought of evil exchanged pleasantries with well-dressed strangers, and gave assignations which they never intended to keep. In all these pleasantries they were much aided by the fashion of wearing masks, which was revived from Tudor times at the Restoration, and continued in fashion during the reigns of Anne and George the First at least. One does not take the plays of the Restoration too seriously as a picture exact in detail of the prevailing manners, but they doubtless give a general reflection of the times and the manners with sufficient accuracy, and they are often corroborated by evidence of a more literal character. Sir Solomon, in Cibber's " Double Gallant," steps into the Park with the expectation of finding his wife in a mask flirting with a stranger. A lady in Dilke's "Pretender," too, describes with much spirit the operations of a freakish girl of the day who enjoyed playing with fire. "I am going to my chamber to fetch my mask, hood, and scarf," she says, "and so jaunt it a little. That's to take a hackney coach, scour from playhouse to playhouse till I meet with some young fellow that has power enough to attack me, stock enough to treat me and present me, and folly enough to be laughed at for his pains."

In "St. James's Park, a Comedy as it is acted every day during the hours of twelve and two during this Season," published in 1733, the amenities of the Mall and of its indiscriminate intercourse are perfectly defined. "These times of park walking," says a character in the play, "are times of perfect carnival to the women. She that would not admit the visit of a man without his being introduced by some relation or intimate friend, makes no scruple here to commence acquaintance at first sight, readily answers to any question that shall be asked of her, values herself on being brisk at repartees, and 'to have put him to it,' as they call it, leaves a pleasure upon her face for the whole day. In short, no freedoms that can be taken here are reckoned indecent, all passes for raillery and harmless gallantry."

The letters and diaries, too, are full of allusion to this custom of promiscuous acquaintance in the Park. Steele will show you a spark of his day beginning a flirtation with an unknown damsel, stepping up to her coach with his hat under his arm and his hand

on his heart, with the remark, "Madam, it is dainty
weather." The correspondence of the second Earl
of Chesterfield contains a letter addressed "To one
who walked four whole nights with me in St. James's
Park, and yet I never knew who she was." "Why,"
says his lordship to the lady, "if your face be suitable
to the rest, which I can hardly doubt, do you refuse
to have it seen, and deny the king, the duke, and all
the court, who it is they so much admire?" The
custom led to occasional marriages, which often made
a stir. There was the famous match, for example,
which Sir Francis Delaval made in 1750 with the old
Lady Isabella Paulet, a widow with £90,000 in the
funds and £150,000 in other property. A confederate took the place of a fortune-teller in the city
whom Lady Isabella was accustomed to consult. From
this prophet she heard that she would marry a handsome stranger whom she would meet in the Mall.
Delaval took care to provide the meeting, and the
marriage duly followed in two days. The rogue
had the impudence to speak of his "harvest moon"
instead of his honeymoon, and remarked *a propos* of his
lady's bulky person and plain looks, "Look you, I
bought Lady Delaval by weight, and paid nothing for
fashion." The custom of indiscriminate acquaintance,
indeed, lasted almost as long as the fashion of the
promenade in the Mall itself. Mr. Samuel Richardson
was humbugged for months by Lady Bradshaigh, who
expressed a wish to meet him by letter, induced him
to describe himself with the richest detail ("one hand

generally in his bosom, the other, a cane in it, which he leans upon under the skirts of his coat usually, of a light brown complexion, teeth not yet failing him, smoothish face and ruddy cheek, a grey eye, too often overclouded by mistiness from the head, by chance lively," &c., &c.). One can imagine the old bookseller concocting the picture in front of his looking-glass. Lady Bradshaigh parodied it perfectly in one of herself, and kept the old fool walking "every warm day" for a sixmonth, until he at last realised the lady's archness, and gave up the quest with the remark, "Lud, Lud, what a giddy appearance."

It is not surprising that the fashion of St. James's should have supplied whole generations of pamphleteers with material for much copy. Here was a subject concentrated in a small space close at hand and full of inspiration for the ancestry of the scribes of the modern society paper. You may find pamphlets describing the Mall and its company in almost every year from the times of Anne to those of George the Fourth; and if these gentlemen fail, the story is taken up by one or other of the intelligent foreigners who visited our shores so regularly and left such valuable notes of their impressions. There are two writers of 1707 who favour us with their estimate of the beauty of the ladies frequenting the Mall in that year—an attractive subject no doubt. We may learn from the " British Court " that there were forty-four ladies of distinguished beauty to be met in that fortunate year, "thirty-three being Court Belles and the rest from the east of Temple Bar." The Duchesses of Marlborough, of Ormond, and Bridgewater, the Countess of Sutherland, Mrs. Dench, Lady Mary Wortley Montagu, open the century well. The Duchess of Marlborough, indeed, was much identified with the Park, until Walpole persuaded the queen to withdraw the royal permission to drive her coach and six along the Mall, a privilege much valued by those who enjoyed it, and the loss of which was bitterly resented by the terrible Sarah. The Mall, too, was the scene of some little embarrassment for the duke. His close-curtained carriage was mistaken for that of Prince Eugene, and was heartily cheered by the crowd. The duke put out his head, and modestly deprecated the ovation, was recognised, and greeted with cries of "Stop, thief!" This was on the queen's birthday, and his daughters, to show their contempt of the court, appeared ostentatiously in the Mall in their dressing-gowns, instead of the gorgeous "birthday clothes" which fashion demanded for the occasion.

"The beauty of the Mall in the summer is almost past description," said an enthusiastic author of a Trip through London in 1727. "What can be more glorious than to view the body of the nobility of our three kingdoms in so short a compass, especially when freed from mixed crowds of saucy fops and city gentry. The Ludgate Hill hobble, the Cheapside swing, the City jolt and wriggle in the gait, being easily perceived through all the arts these smarts and perts put upon them." This gentleman saw an impudent *valet de chambre* parading in the Mall in his master's clothes, followed by "six Monmouth Street Jews bidding against each other for the raiment." We see the benches filled with loungers, tempted out of the coffee - houses by the fine weather, whose chatter "raised regiments of horse, foot, and dragoons, and the most formidable armies, without beat of drum, towns taken, sieges raised, and legions vanquished, and the nation not put to the expense of a shilling." The Park, indeed, was a great place for the loafer, then as now. It was an appanage of the court which was free from the tyranny of the king's writ, and any one guilty of a crime less heinous than high treason was safe in its precincts from bailiff or Bow Street officer. This immunity brought together a constant population of unpromising individuals, who sunned themselves on the grass, filled the benches, begged alms or told fortunes, and picked pockets. Their only enemy was the press-gang, which enjoyed privileges denied to the officers of the law, and swooped down at intervals to make hauls of as many as 150 in one day.

The hours of the promenade in the Mall were fixed, of course, by the habits of the people of condition, who gave it its vogue as a meeting-place of fashion. The morning chocolate in the bedroom and the elaborate toilette filled up the early hours of the day for the beau or the belle of Anne and the first two

Georges, and a promenade in the Mall between mid-day and two o'clock was usually their first public ap-pearance.   In the Mall appointments were arranged for the afternoon or evening, and parties made up for the play or for Ranelagh or Vauxhall.   A lady or a man wishing to find a friend for a jaunt turned naturally to St. James's.   Walpole left us an account of the custom when he described how he and Lady Caroline Petersham and Miss Ashe "issued into the Mall to assemble our company, which was all the town if we could get it."   They gathered together " Harry Vane and the Duke of Kingston, Lord March, Mr. Whit-head, a pretty Miss Beauclerc, and a very foolish Miss Sparre," and we accompany them, in another chapter, by water to Vauxhall.   It was the mode to eat fruit and biscuits in the Mall, and the fruit girls, if pretty, were much patronised by the exquisites of both sexes, both as purveyors of fruit and carriers of love-letters. The peerless Mrs. Abington began life as a flower girl in the Mall, where her beauty attracted much notice, and whence she was promoted to Drury Lane, and from there to the office of *arbiter elagantiarum* of the female fashion of London, which paid her large sums for her advice in matters of dress.   Another figure of the Mall was the female hawker who sold " pomatum of all sorts, lip salves, night masks and handkerchiefs for the face and neck, right chemical liquor to change the colour of the hair, trotter's oil and bear's grease to thicken it, fine mouse skin eye-brows that will stick on so as never to come off."   The

whole tradition of the Mall, indeed, is that of flounce
and furbelow. The evening promenade was made in
full dress, after the early dinner of five or six o'clock,
and was ordinarily even more rich in feminine splendour
than the earlier function at midday. An enthusiastic
German traveller, after describing the greatness of the
crowd of the evening, and the pretty effect of the innumerable lamps, records that on the following morning "when the sun shines the ground sparkled with
pins which have been dropped from the ladies' dresses."

The rural character of St. James's Park, which it
long retained, is very well illustrated by an incident
which is recorded of the days of George the Second.
Bluff old Sir Robert Walpole sent all the way to
Houghton for his pack of otter hounds to hunt an
otter which had come across from the river at Westminster, and had grown fat and lazy upon the king's
carp in the Long Water. Pasturage in St. James's and
in Hyde Parks for milch cows long provided opportunities for the pleasant custom of eating syllabubs in
the open air, which prevailed for a century. " A can of
milk, a can of red cow's milk," was one of the cries of
London in the parks for many years. Sometimes the
privilege of grazing cattle in the parks was bestowed
by royalty as a sort of pension. An interesting case
in point was that of the two old ladies named Searle,
who had the distinction of being the aunts of the
peerless Beau Brummell, and dispensed milk and syllabubs at a gatekeeper's lodge in the Green Park which
stood opposite Clarges Street.

The town continued to grow, however, and its growth led to changes which destroyed much of the old rural character of St. James's. Considerations of drains and sanitation led to the removal of Duck Island, and to the filling in, in the year 1770, of Rosamond's Pond. Rosamond's Pond had acquired an evil name as a place where maidens who had begun their love story in the groves which surrounded it, sought refuge from the troubles which followed later in its waters, and its disappearance seems to have caused little regret. But the aquatic interest of St. James's was not diminished by the addition of the open water which replaced the marshes and willows of Duck Island. The wild fowl continued to prosper and increase in number, and their ranks came to include strange personalities like that of Old Jack, the royal swan, who was a public character for half a century. That delightful fowl was bred and reared in the gardens of Buckingham Palace, and was placed upon the Long Water by Queen Charlotte, whose favourite he was. He drowned dogs who molested him by holding their heads under water, pulled small boys who annoyed him into the lake by their small clothes, and persistently resisted the introduction of strange birds as long as his strength remained, but perished under the continued attacks of a flock of Polish geese in the year 1840.

The Mall of St. James's continued to hold its vogue as a meeting-place of fashion until near the end of the century. The reporters of the newspapers of a hundred years, in recording the appearance of any celebrity, usually placed him in the Mall. That was a historical airing in 1753 when Charles Edward, the Young Pretender, taking off his star and ribbon only, and seeking no other disguise, took a turn through the Mall of what he considered his own park, to the full knowledge of George the Second, as Mr. Hume, who had it direct from the Earl Mareschal, records. Lord Holdernesse, with much fencing, asked his Majesty's pleasure in the matter. "My lord, I shall do just nothing at all," replied the stout old king; "when he is tired of England he will go abroad again." Famous Frenchmen, like the Comte de Grasse, Rodney's prisoner from Dominica, escorted by Sir Hyde Parker, would walk in the Mall as a matter of course, much cheered by the people, who recognised their brave enemy. The female loveliness of a beauteous generation of women of condition was to be seen in the Mall between 1770 and the end of the century, the ladies whose personalities inspired the finest labours of Reynolds and Romney and Gainsborough, and whose effigies in mezzotinto are the subjects of the contests of the West End salerooms to-day; Lady Townshend and her sisters the Montgomeries, Lady Derby, Lady Barrymore and Lady Hinchinbrooke, Lady Stanley, Miss Pitt, the Duchess of Gordon, the Duchess of Rutland, Lady Sefton, Lady Harriet Foley, Lady Jersey, Lady Anne Stanhope, Lady Melbourne, Mrs. Crewe, Mrs. Bouverie, and the incomparable Duchess of Devonshire.

An ingenious journalist of the *Morning Post*, with tastes of a mathematical and statistical order, drew up a scale of attractions in which twelve of these ladies were allotted marks for "beauty, figure, elegance, wit, sense, grace, expression, sensibility, and principle." We presume that this gentleman was intimate with them all, for he gives us some very private information on the subject of his inquiries. It is shocking to learn that the Duchess of Gordon, who kept Mr. Pitt's country gentlemen together session after session, had no elegance; that Mrs. Crewe, who fascinated the Whigs, from the prince downwards, had no grace; Lady Melbourne no figure, Lady Jersey no sense and no principle. Nineteen was the highest score under each of the headings of the contest, and the Countess of Barrymore was an easy winner with eighteen and one-third, Lady Anne Stanhope a bad second with twelve, and Lady Jersey at the bottom of the list with five.

The vogue of the Mall expired somewhat suddenly. About 1786 fashion left its shades and avenues to the middle-classes, the city ladies, and the country cousins, and moved off unaccountably to the Green Park. The Green Park, since Charles the Second enclosed it about 1660, had been little more than a hunting-ground for footpads and a duelling-ground for drunken or quarrelsome combatants. The king had made a harbour for deer at the western end, and some ice-houses of his Majesty built near its centre might be seen until the beginning of the present century. But though Queen Caroline made the walk which runs along the backs of the houses in Arlington Street in 1730, and was often seen there with her children in the spring, it attracted little fashion or attention as a meeting-place for people of condition until about 1780. Then it suddenly became the habit of the well-bred to make their evening promenade up the Queen's walk and round the reservoir which filled the north-eastern corner of the Green Park, the hollow of which may still be seen filled with white mist on a damp evening. Here for a few seasons fashionable London displayed itself in its evening dress after dinner, and incidentally and accidentally gave a great value to the houses on the west side of Arlington Street. Great sums were then paid to the Crown for the privilege of building those balconies, bow-windows and terraces which diversify the Park front of Arlington Street to-day. We read of Mr. Rigby paying £4000 for a bow-window, and Warren Hastings and others in a like proportion for a like concession. The view across the Green Park at that time was very impressive. There was no building in Pimlico or Belgravia; the Thames could be seen from these windows; Lambeth was a marsh with pastures, ponds, willows and cattle, recalling a Dutch landscape, and behind all rose the hills of Sydenham, covered with wood unspoiled by building and un-clouded by smoke.

Out-door fashion thus moved up from St. James's through the Green Park to find its final resting-place in Hyde Park and Kensington Gardens, but it became sadly shorn of its earlier glories as the last century

drew to its close. The continually-growing lateness
of the dinner-hour robbed fashion-on-foot of much of
its fine plumage and of the attractions of feminine
beauty in evening dress. The promenade in the parks
gradually declined and was last represented, perhaps,
by that extraordinary mode of the last years of the
eighteenth century, when ladies of all ages displayed
their charms in scanty dresses of light material in the
classic taste, dresses with waists under the armpits, and
of a delicacy of texture which suggested more than
concealed the figures of their wearers, and provided
rich material for the caricaturists of the times. This
poor survival of the earlier glories of the promenade
was at last absorbed by the taste for the riding and
driving of horses and chariots of the last quarter of
the century, and expired amidst the lamentations of the
old school who remembered the palmy days of the Mall.

That curious revival of a love of equipage, and its
display in Hyde Park after the lapse of nearly a century, was preceded by a change of fashion in dress
among the men, a change which allowed the gentleman to dress himself in the habit of his coachman and
drive his own chariot in the Park. The Whigs who
surrounded Charles Fox at Brooks's during the Ameri-
can War gave the fashion a great impetus. Any time
after 1780 it was quite usual to meet men of an
assured position, like Fox himself, Lord Derby, or the
Duke of Norfolk, dressed with a studied negligence
in a costume suitable for following hounds or riding
post. Then came men like Sir John Lade, "in an

elegant suit of buff," who took to driving as a diversion or sport. The new amusement was patronised in feebler fashion by the Prince of Wales, who would drive through the Park with St. Leger or Lake in a carriage and pair, "with blue harness edged with red, the horses' manes decorated with scarlet ribbons and the Prince's plumes on their crests, the carriage lined with rose-coloured velvet, with cushions of rose-coloured satin and festoons of rich gold braid." The second Lord Rodney was another of these early Jehus, and the first to drive nag-tailed horses in his carriage. Mr. Charles Finch, the brother of the Earl of Aylesford, was another, perhaps the first, to turn out with a four-in-hand, "disguised in a livery coat, it being an unusual thing for a gentleman." Mr. Thomas Onslow, afterwards Lord Cranley, the "Little T.O." of the caricaturists, was another. Driving in the parks became the fashion, and there, as the present century opened, might be seen those strange vehicles from which all modern carriages have been evolved. The phaeton of that day was a spider-like arrangement with four sprawling wheels, four horses, and holding but two persons. There was the curricle, an invention of more sanity, but still requiring three horses and carrying only two persons. The gig was the father of the tilburies, whisks, and all other two-wheeled vehicles, many of which still survive. The horses, as we learn, were of a heavy breed, "Cleveland blacks and long-tailed bays," approaching in type those used for light drays and omnibuses to-day.

With materials such as these the youth of both sexes of the Regency and George the Fourth superseded the old promenades of the Mall, and revived the tradition of equestrianism and equipage of Hyde Park which survives in our own day, and has produced such organisations as the Four-in-Hand Club. The young men, we read, in their noble ardour to emulate the professional, had their teeth filed so that they might be able to expectorate in the manner approved by the stage-coachmen; the women startled the ordinary inhabitant of the streets by the recklessness of their driving. There was Lady Archer, for example, who was the terror of the West End from the pace at which she drove; Lady Stewart with her famous four greys, and a "Mrs. Garden from Portland Street" who, as early as 1783, won a considerable bet by driving her phaeton and bays from Grosvenor Gate through the Park to Kensington in five and a half minutes.

We believe we have given in outline the features of the life in the parks of London which have made of them places of recreation and enjoyment from Tudor times until our own; the details may be filled in from a wealth of accurate material collected in such admirable works as that of Mr. Jacob Larwood, the "Story of the London Parks." If space and the scheme of our undertaking had permitted we might have peopled the walks and drives of them all with many notable figures of modern social England, and traced some diversions which have become part of the lives of numbers of Englishmen in their origin or early developments in the same pleasant surroundings. Skating, for example, was perhaps first seen in England by Mr. Pepys and his contemporaries on the ice of the canal in St. James's; and a century later fashionable London flocked to admire the agility of Lord Carlisle and Mr. Benjamin West, the painter, on the Serpentine, when my Lord March came up in a carriage wrapped in three bearskins, with his hands in a muff, and his carriage warmed with a portable stove, and watched a company of his friends walking through a minuet on the ice. There was much primitive cricket too in Hyde Park in the reign of George the Second, when the citizen could watch Frederick Prince of Wales and a dozen of men of birth and great station at the humble exercises of the game in its earlier and undeveloped periods. Improvised prize-rings were another attraction of the second half of the eighteenth century, when Ben Green of Carnaby Market would fight "Chitty" Myers of the Adelphi on a Sunday morning, and provide so popular an entertainment that thirty sportsmen who were watching the fun on one limb of an elm came to the ground by the breaking of the branch, and half of them were conveyed to Chelsea Hospital. Finally, although no one ever perhaps fought a duel for pleasure, the chance of seeing an encounter was a distinct addition to the joys of Hyde Park for certain minds, and from the days of Hamilton and Mohun to those of Fox and Adair, the mere rumour of such an encounter would bring such crowds as would often prevent the meeting taking place at all.

We all know the part which the parks fill in the
lives of Londoners to-day, or if we sometimes forget
it, it may be easily realised by imagining for a moment Hyde Park and St. James's, the Green Park and
Regent's Park, to say nothing of Battersea Park, Victoria
Park, and Finsbury Park, and others farther afield, cut
up and devoted to streets of smug villas or workmen's
dwellings. The pleasures which we have recalled have
been exchanged for others which are shared by thousands of humbler people, and the parks themselves
have surely changed for the better in every respect but
that of a quaint rusticity since Sir Robert Walpole
hunted the otter in St. James's. There are even
compensations for the Londoner in that same connection of the *rus in urbe*; the intelligent manipulation
of shrub and flower border, with their masses of lovely
colour, which greets one in most of our great parks is
surely a model for all operations of the sort; and there
are certainly worse places in which to study the amusing idiocyncrasies of many wild creatures, ringdoves
say, or water-hens or seagulls, than the little garden
at the foot of the Serpentine, or the Long Water in
St. James's Park.

CHAPTER XI

THE CLUBS AND COFFEE-HOUSES

THE great modern institution of organised leisure which has its headquarters at the almost innumerable club-houses of London, and is so important a part of the social life of to-day, has reached its present vast proportions only in quite recent times. If you look back over the last fifty years you will find club-life and its habitations in London shrinking indeed in bulk and in numbers, but still of considerable dimension. Go back another fifty years to the opening days of the nineteenth century, and you will find record of a bare dozen clubs only in London. Then take as your stand-point the year 1750, and you will find one club certainly, and perhaps two. Finally, recede to the last years of William the Third, and you will discover that the club, as we know it, was as yet in its embryo stage, that is to say, it was a mere assembly of congenial spirits meeting at the coffee or chocolate houses, institutions just then coming into great vogue. It is for this last reason that we include coffee-houses in our inquiry, and seek in the records of their life the origin of the modern club. For the purposes of that inquiry we define the London club

as a body of men meeting continuously in a house or
rooms of its own. With such limitation and definition
of our subject, it is quite possible to trace the whole
vast system of club-life in England to its origin in a
meeting of gentlemen of condition in the last years of
the seventeenth century at White's Chocolate-house in
St. James's Street, a house occupying a site not far
from the present building at the top of the street
where White's Club still opens its doors and lights
its candles.

It follows therefore that we may, without undue
confusion of cause and effect, ascribe the origin of
club-life in England, an organisation which has transformed the habits of many Londoners and acquired
for the solace of its devotees the choicest sites of the
town, to the introduction into this country of " the
bitter black drink called coffee," as Mr. Pepys described that stimulant. Club-life would doubtless
have found other channels of development in the
absence of the facilities which the coffee-houses provided. But as things are, there is no doubt that the
gatherings of men of all conditions of life to drink
coffee at these places supplied the opportunity for
which social London was waiting. We point, therefore, at this moment with the greatest confidence to a
humble establishment which was opened for the sale
of coffee in St. Michael's Alley, Cornhill, in the
year 1652, as the parent of institutions of such
superfine male fashion as White's, the Turf, or the
Marlborough Clubs of our own day.

Antiquarians have decided after much painful inquiry that the first coffee-house opened in England was at Oxford, "at the Angel, in the parish of St. Peter in the East," where one Jacobs, a Jew, made a venture in the sale of the new drink in the year 1650; "and there it was by some who delighted in novelty drank." It was not, however, until two years later that the habit of drinking coffee in public reached London, at the house in Cornhill which we have already mentioned. The origin of the London establishment was, as it would seem, quite independent of the establishment in Oxford. Mr. Edwards, a Turkey merchant, who was accustomed to travel in the East, acquired the Oriental habit on his travels, and brought home with him to London from Ragusa one Pasqua Rosee, a youth who acted as his servant and was accustomed to prepare Mr. Edwards' coffee for him of a morning. "But the novelty thereof," says Mr. Oldys the antiquarian, " drawing too much company to him he allowed the said servant with another of his son-in-law to set up the first coffee-house in London at St. Michael's Alley in Cornhill. The sign was Pasqua Rosee's own head." And to that auspicious event we owe, as we say, the origin and the subsequent development of the social club in England.

The general acceptation of this new habit of coffee drinking seems at first to have hung fire. In any case, it was not until four years later that there is record of any other establishment of the same kind in

London. In 1656 one Mr. Farr, who then kept at No. 15 Fleet Street the house we still know as the Rainbow, offered the new drink for sale. There was some opposition to the new custom, it is clear, for there is record of Mr. Farr being "presented by the inquest of St. Dunstan's in the West for making and selling a drink called coffee, whereby in making the same he annoyeth his neighbours by evil smells." But the opposition here and elsewhere was unavailing, and by the beginning of the eighteenth century the coffee-houses in the town were so increased in numbers that they were reckoned at 3000 by Mr. Hatton in his "New View of London," and the coffee-house had already taken its place as one of the most remarkable among the social developments of modern England.

For by the time that Queen Anne came to the throne all London had arranged itself into groups of patrons for one or other of the different coffee-houses, and representative bodies of all ranks and conditions of Londoners had each a rendezvous in the house which best suited its taste. City merchants went to Garraway's in Change Alley, Cornhill, a house which combined business with pleasure, and had an auction-room on the first floor. Garraway's was a house of call for the great people coming to the city on business from Lincoln's Inn or Covent Garden, for the buyers and sellers of stock, and for "the foreign Banquiers," as Mr. Defoe has recorded. Much of the gambling in connection with the South Sea Bubble of 1720 was conducted at Garraway's. Jonathan's, also in Change Alley, was another famous house of business devoted to stock-jobbers. Lloyd's, the great organisation of the shipping interest which still flourishes in its rooms at the Royal Exchange, is the development of a coffee-house of the same name; and the Jerusalem Coffee-house on Cornhill was an institution of the same type which has not survived. The doctors had their meeting-house at Batson's at the Royal Exchange, where physicians used to meet the apothecaries and prescribe for patients they were never to see. The clergy, from bishops downwards, went to Child's in St. Paul's Churchyard or the Chapter Coffee-house in Paternoster Row. Leaving the city and proceeding westward, Nando's, the house at Temple Bar which has just been rescued from destruction by the County Council; Dick's, a few doors further west; Serle's in Portugal Street; the Grecian in Devereux Court, Strand; and Squire's in Fulwoods Rents, Holborn, were all houses near the various Inns of Court and much haunted by lawyers.

Going west again, the neighbourhood of Covent Garden supplied, at different periods, a group of coffee-houses which were as a Mecca or holy place for all whose tastes or interests lay in the direction of letters. At Wills's, at the corner of Bow and Russell Streets, the great Dryden held his court, with a chair of his own near the fire in the winter and another on the balcony in summer. Here the great man laid down the law upon all questions of taste in literature and the drama, very good-naturedly, as we believe, but still with authority—

> " As who should say, I am Sir Oracle,
> And when I ope my lips let no dog bark."

Dean Lockier as a boy of seventeen walked into Wills's to hear the wits of that famous house, and happened upon the great man discoursing of his own work, as was his habit. " If anything of mine is good," says Mr. Dryden complacently, " 'tis Macflecno, and I value myself the more upon it, because it is the first piece of ridicule written in heroics." " Macflecno is a very fine poem," says the boy rather nervously, " but I do not imagine it to be the first that was ever writ that way." " How long have you been a dealer in poetry," replies Mr. Dryden after a gasp of astonishment, "and what is that you imagine to have been writ so before." " Boileau's ' Lutrin ' and Tassoni's ' Secchia Rapita,' " answers the boy, naming two works from which, as he says, he knew the poet " had borrowed some strokes." " 'Tis true," said Dryden, " I had forgot them." Such was a typical incident at Wills's, an incident which is as pretty an illustration of life at that famous house under Dryden's kindly rule as need be ; the trembling approach of the disciple ambitious for a word from the great man, or a pinch from his box, and the not unkindly reception of the modest admirer by the presiding genius of the place.

Dean Swift used to think poorly of Wills's ; " the worst conversation I ever heard in my life was at

Wills's," he said, but the doctor, as we know, was often difficult to please. He, with Mr. Addison, Mr. Steele, and some other noted men of letters, helped to make the fame of Button's on the other side of Russell Street, where the literary tradition of the coffee-houses took shelter after the death of Dryden and the decline of Wills's. It was at Button's that Mr. Steele set up his famous Lion's Head Letter-Box, where the scribes of that period are supposed to have dropped in those pleasant communications to the *Guardian*, the famous relic still happily preserved at the Duke of Bedford's mansion at Woburn.

The Bedford was the other literary coffee-house of Covent Garden, the Bedford " in the north-west corner of the Piazza," the house of Foote, Fielding, Churchill, Hogarth, Dr. Arne, Goldsmith ; the Bedford " crowded with men of parts, almost every one you meet is a polite scholar and a wit," as the *Connoisseur* of 1754 enthusiastically records. Prodigious sallies of wit " echoed from box to box at the Bedford," as we are told, and there was a special place where a man with an indecent joke to fire off might discharge it out of earshot of the lady at the bar.

Such houses as these were all of a professional character, and supported each by its own body of professional men. The life which developed within their doors, therefore, hardly falls within the limits of a work dealing with the pleasures of past generations of Londoners. We must look elsewhere for the particular establishments which became the birthplaces

and nurseries of the social club.   Proceeding still
westward we soon come upon a group of coffee-houses
which were entirely supported by lounging men of
fashion, the "pretty fellows" of Anne and the
Georges, and by the adventurers and sycophants who
had fortunes to push in such fine company.   The most
fashionable of these houses were clustered in or near
the parish of St. James's, taking their tone, as was
natural, from the neighbourhood of the court.   Many
of these had a political cast, but all were meeting-
places of men of birth and condition.

The St. James's coffee-house was the last house but
one at the bottom of St. James's Street, on the western
side, and its frequenters were devoted to the Whig
interest from the days of Addison to those of Edmund
Burke.   It was at the St. James's, was it not, that Mr.
Steele dated all his letters to the *Tatler* on foreign and
domestic news ; and where Mr. Garrick, half a century
later, produced his mock epitaph upon Dr. Goldsmith,
which provoked the much more effective "Retaliation."
The officers of the Guards on duty at the Palace were
often of the company at the St. James's.   At the Cocoa
Tree, on the south side of Pall Mall, gathered the
high Tories and those discontented gentlemen who
looked askance at the Hanoverian king at St. James's,
and drank furtive healths to the Pretender at St.
Germains by passing the claret glass over the water
bottle as they pledged "the king over the water."
" The little gentleman in velvet " was another favourite
toast at the Cocoa Tree, in pleasant allusion to the

mole whose earthworks were supposed to have caused the accident which resulted in the death of William the Third. The Cocoa Tree kept its doors open in Pall Mall till about the year 1727; later it removed to what is now 64 St. James's Street, where meets the club of the same name into which the coffee-house developed. Ozinda's was another coffee-house of the high Tory complexion at the lower end of St. James's Street. The Smyrna in Pall Mall was a noted house where a man might hear the latest political rumour at court or the freshest news by ship-letter. White's Chocolate-house in St. James's Street, on the site of the present Boodle's Club, was a meeting-place for the most fashionable exquisites of the town and the court, and for the followers who lived upon them. In the early meetings of that fine company at White's Chocolate-house at the end of the seventeenth century, we find, as we repeat, the origin of the social club in London.

It was in these places of public resort, of which we have mentioned typical houses only, that modern social London may be said to have been evolved. Merchants used the coffee-house as office and exchange, lawyers and other professional men as a place to seek clients, the clergy to get patronage and preferment, the fashionable lounger to gossip and kill time. They were all nominally open to anybody who could pay the modest fee of a penny or twopence, which was always left on the counter upon quitting the room, and there was a fine show of democracy in the rules which were hung up in most of them; but it was a pretence only. Strangers of a class different from the ordinary company were more or less frowned upon by the regular frequenters. At Wills's, for example, it was not usual for a man to make regular use of the place without an introduction from one of its patrons. Smoking was practised at most of the coffee-houses in Covent Garden and east of Temple Bar; but a man calling for a pipe at those about St. James's would have been shown the door. On the other hand, any adventurer who could possess himself of a suit of clothes cut in the prevailing fashion, could appear at the best of them; and it was jocularly remarked that the judge at White's Chocolate-house often rubbed shoulders with the highwayman he afterwards condemned to be hanged at Tyburn.

There are a score of contemporary writers whom we may accompany to the coffee-houses of their day, while the life at them was a new thing, and considered worthy of being depicted. The facetious Mr. Ned Ward, of the "London Spy," will describe for us the men of fashion at Old Man's in Scotland Yard: "A gaudy crowd of Tom Essences were walking backwards and forwards with their hats in their hands, not daring to put them to their intended use, lest it should put the foretops of their wigs into some disorder. The clashing of their snush box lids in opening and shutting made more noise than their tongues. Bows and congees of the newest

mode were here exchanged 'twixt friend and friend
with wonderful exactness. They made a humming
like so many hornets in a country chimney, not with
their talking, but with their whispering over their new
minuets and bories, with their hands in their pockets,
if only free from their snush box." Ned was used
to rougher company, but his naïve satire does not fail
to present a recognisable picture of the decorum of
the fashionable coffee-house of the West End.

A writer of a different type, Mr. Mackay, the
author of the "Journey through England," published
in 1714, will give us some few particulars of life at
the same houses of St. James's. "About twelve
o'clock," says he, "the *beau monde* assemble in several
coffee and chocolate houses, the best of which are
White's Chocolate - house, the Cocoa Tree, the
Smyrna, and the British coffee-houses, and all these
so near one another, that in less than an hour you
see the company of them all. You are entertained
at piquet or basset at White's, or you may talk
politics at the Smyrna or St. James's." Tea, coffee,
and chocolate, and wine were purveyed at these houses,
with light viands like biscuit and sandwiches ; set
meals were supplied only at the taverns—houses of
a different type in which, as to-day, the sale of liquor
was the chief object. "But the general way here,"
says Mr. Mackay, "is to make a party at the coffee-
house to go to dine at the tavern, except you are
invited to dine at the table of some great man."

But the best account of life at the coffee-house is

preserved in the *Spectators*, the *Tatlers*, and *Guardians*
—papers which were put forth at the moment when
the coffee-house was at the height of its vogue, and
were written not seldom at the table of one of them,
and in the midst of the very company they described.
We turn, therefore, to those old papers, and follow
their authors into the different coffee-houses of the
town, and in their company we shall have little
difficulty in watching the companies of most of them
assembling, and in seeing the modern social club
taking shape.

The coffee-house of Addison's day was open at six
in the morning, and from his own pleasant banter we
may gather a fairly clear idea of the life within its
doors during the next eighteen hours. In that lively
Spectator, No. 49, are presented to us the humours
of one of the houses near the Inns of Court—
Nando's, perhaps, or the Grecian. Tom Beaver, the
haberdasher, is one of the first arrivals, the coffee-
house oracle, "who has a levee of more undissembled
friends and admirers than most of the ministers or
generals of Great Britain. Every man about him
has perhaps a newspaper in his hand, but none can
pretend to guess what step will be taken in any one
Court of Europe till Mr. Beaver has thrown down
his pipe and declared what measures the allies must
enter into upon the new posture of affairs."

To Mr. Beaver succeeded the students of the
Temple, "some ready dressed for Westminster Hall,
others in night-gowns—one would think these vir-

tuosos take a gay cap, slippers, a scarf, and party-
coloured gown," says Addison, "to be ensigns of
dignity.   The gentleman in the strawberry sash, who
presides so much over the rest, has, it seems, subscribed to every opera this last winter, and is supposed to receive favours from one of the actresses."
It was not until such triflers as these had cleared
away that the real company of the houses used to
assemble—men like Addison and Steele themselves,
"men who have business and good sense in their
faces, and come to the coffee-house either to trans-
act affairs or enjoy conversation . . . those who
relish calm and ordinary life."   Mr. Addison's happy
phrase is not a bad description of an ideal club
to-day.

It is not difficult, as we say, to people the coffee-
houses from those pleasant pages.   There is the knot
of young fellows hanging about the pretty waitress at
the bar, much to the scandal of the older customers,
who have more difficulty than these generous youths
in getting their orders executed.   We see the etiquette
of claiming acquaintance with a chance stranger at the
coffee-house over a pipe of tobacco.   "I observed,"
says the *Spectator*, "three persons in close conference
over a pipe of tobacco, upon which, having filled one
for my own use, I lighted it at the little wax candle
that stood before them, and after having thrown in
two or three whiffs amongst them, sat down and made
one of the company.   I need not tell my reader that
lighting a man's pipe at the same candle is looked

upon among brother smokers as an overture to conversation and friendship."

If we may take seriously Mr. Richard Steele's
speculation in No. 521 of the same periodical, it was
a recognised diversion of the town "to tell a lie at
Charing Cross in the morning at eight of the clock
and then follow it through all parts of the town until
eight at night." Mr. Addison displays the whole
process for us to perfection in *Spectator* No. 403.
The particular fable he supposes to be under discussion in 1712 is the death of the King of France.
"At the St. James's," he says, "I heard the whole
Spanish monarchy disposed of, and all the line of
Bourbon provided for in less than a quarter of an
hour." At Giles's, "a board of French gentlemen
who had espoused the Whig interest, very positively
affirmed that the king had departed this life about a
week since, and therefore proceeded without any
further delay to the release of their friends in the
galleys." At Jenny Man's was "an alert young
fellow that cocked his hat upon a friend of his who
entered just at the same time with myself, and accosted
him after the following manner : 'Well, Jack, so the
old prig is dead at last. Sharp's the word, now or
never, boy, up to the walls of Paris.'" At Wills's
"the discourse was gone off from the death of the
king to that of Monsieur Boileau, Racine, Corneille,
and several other poets, who would have obliged the
world with very noble elegies upon the death of so
great a prince." At a coffee-house in Fish Street the

chief politician, after taking a pipe of tobacco, opined
" that if the King of France is certainly dead we shall
have plenty of mackerel this season, and proceeded to
show how the death of that great man would affect
our pilchards." At another, "a non-juror and a lace
man were warmly in dispute as to whether the late
king was like Augustus Cæsar or Nero." At another
still, " the haberdasher, who was the oracle of the
coffee-house, called several witnesses that he had declared his opinion, above a week before, that the
French king was certainly dead, and that considering
the late advices we had received from France, it was
impossible that it could be otherwise. As he was
laying these together, and dictating to his hearers with
great authority, there came in a gentleman from Garraway's with advice that the king was in good health
and was gone out a hunting the very morning the
post came away, upon which the haberdasher stole off
the hat that hung upon a wooden peg by him, and
retired to his shop with great confusion."

The pleasant leisurely life of those days in the
coffee-house, the life out of which the club grew, is
very delicately suggested, we think, in those old
Spectators and *Guardians*, and the types of men who
frequented them very happily presented for us. In a
dozen of those papers we meet figures of admirable
humour. There is the loud-voiced young gentleman
with a long purse, who was ever ready to support his
opinion with a wager, to the discomfiture of his less
affluent opponents, who had " five guineas upon

questions in geography, two that the Isle of Wight is a peninsula, and three guineas to one that the earth is round," and who laid twenty pieces with the gentleman "who dealt mightily in antique scandal" as to the precise relations between Cæsar and Cato's sister. Then there is the musical youth given to whistling airs from the opera "in the open coffee-house," and who showed his sympathy generally with the lyric arts, who "danced up to the glass in the middle of the room, and practised the minuet steps to his own humming, and with one hand extended as leading a lady in it, danced both French and country dances, and admonished his supposed partner by smiles and nods to hold up her head and fall back, and who began his exercises only after clearing his throat for a full half-hour."

The social intercourse of the coffee-houses, which is displayed so admirably by these old essayists, was, as we believe, the expression of a feeling of security among all classes of Englishmen after the troubled days of the seventeenth century. It was the expression of a sense of rest and leisure, of possibilities of work and enjoyment, which were felt by plain men only after the convulsions raised in the country by the evils of the Stuart rule had ceased. Men now for the first time for a hundred years saw opportunities both for business and relaxation which had been impossible during the period of civil and religious tumult, of rebellion and revolution, which was only terminated by the Act of Settlement and by the acceptance of the

Hanoverian dynasty. A period of social prosperity and expansion was then beginning which developed later under the wise rule of the sagacious Walpole, and made possible amenities of social life which had been unknown in England since the days of Elizabeth.

Apart and distinct from the intercourse of the coffee-houses, in which, as we shall show, the social club took its origin, were those little gatherings which men of parts and substance began to form, gatherings which assumed the names of clubs, and repeated in the times of Anne and George the First the famous symposia of the Mermaid in those of Elizabeth and James. We do not regard these little meetings at taverns as clubs in the true sense of the word, as we understand it to-day. But a work dealing with the amusements of the last century must on no account omit mention of those famous societies in which were to be found the great men of many generations during their hours of leisure and relaxation, such renowned gatherings as the Kit Kat Club, the Dilettante Society, and the Literary Club of Johnson and Burke.

The Kit Kat Club we take to be the very expression itself of the security and beneficence of the new order of things under the wise Whig rule ; the Kit Kat with its nine members all of the Whig interest, that goodly company of great nobles and men of wit and learning, with its toasting-glasses inscribed with the names of the famous beauties of the day, its generous patronage of arts and letters, its stately pilgrimages in its stars and ribbons to the house of Christopher Kat, the mutton-

pieman in Shire Lane by Temple Bar.   There is no
better memorial to-day of that brilliant social life of
the early years of the last century just then beginning
than that stately set of engravings in mezzotinto after
the famous portraits by Sir Godfrey which are still to
be seen at Bayfordbury.

The uneasy spirits of the other side in politics had
also their social meetings, like those under the influence of Dean Swift, the Saturday, the " Brothers,"
and the " Scriblerus " Clubs, of which there is such
frequent mention in the Journal to Stella.   The
" Saturday " was a small society, composed originally
of four members only—Swift, Lord Rivers, the Lord
Keeper, and Lord Bolingbroke.   Afterwards " other
rabble," as the Dean described it, intruded, the Duke
of Ormond, Lord Anglesey, Lord Dartmouth and the
rest.   The " Brothers " was the outcome of another
social scheme of the Dean, meeting on Thursdays at
taverns and coffee-houses ; " the end of our club," as
the Dean recorded, " is to advance conversation and
friendship, and to reward learning without interest or
recommendation.   We take none in but men of wit
and men of interest, and if we go on as we began no
other club in this town will be worth talking of."
The society grew to nineteen members, " nine lords and
ten commoners," and there is interesting evidence as
to the way in which Swift used his masterful personality
to prevent undesirable additions.   " The Duke of
Beaufort had the confidence to propose his brother-in-
law the Earl of Danby to be a member, but I opposed

it so warmly that it was waived. Danby is not twenty, and we will have no more boys."

The members of this select society met at the Thatched House Tavern in St. James's Street, at Ozinda's Coffee-house, or at the Star and Garter in Pall Mall, and often grumbled terribly at the cost of their dinners. It would seem that each member entertained his fellows in turn, being president for the day only. A symposium at the Thatched House, as we learn, cost the Dean seven guineas; the Duke of Ormond's "treat" cost £20 for a dinner of four dishes without dessert and not counting wine. They occasionally had a dinner cooked in Queen Anne's own kitchen at St. James's and sent over to Ozinda's close by, and at times they took an airing in the country, as when fifteen of them dined together "under a canopy in an arbour at Parson's Green," and the Dean never saw anything "so fine and romantick."

Good fellowship and conversation were the objects of the "Brothers," but there was usually a spice of politics to season their meetings, and benevolent actions were not forgotten. Thus the Dean would often wheedle twenty guineas from one of his great friends for some poor author of the right Tory complexion, and the printer's devil was accustomed to attend the meetings with a proof of the Dean's last new squib against the Whigs.

The convivial feelings of which we take note in those days was nowhere stronger than among the men of taste and knowledge who formed the great learned societies. There was a notable club, which was recruited exclusively from among the members of the Royal Society, which met on Thursdays at various taverns, and called itself the Club of Royal Philosophers, and later, the Royal Society Club. This club seems to have been founded somewhere about 1731, and its early surroundings are very typical of a dining society of the eighteenth century. Sir Joseph Ayloffe, one of its first members, has recorded how Dr. Halley, the famous astronomer, used to come to London from the observatory at Greenwich to Child's Coffee-house, to meet his friends for conversation. That conversation often detained them until after their dinner hour, and on such occasions they arranged to go to "a house in Dean's Court, between an ale-house and a tavern, where was a great draft of porter, but not drank in the house." Mr. Reynell was the landlord, and one of the company was accustomed to go round to Knight's in Newgate Street and buy fish, "having first informed himself how many meant to stay and dine." Five or six were the usual numbers, and the dinner, which was limited to fish and pudding, was cooked by Reynell and cost half a crown.

So originated the Royal Society Club, which followed Mr. Reynell to the King's Arms and the Mitre, developed into a society of forty learned members dining at Pontack's, the famous city restaurant, at the Crown and Anchor, the Freemason's Tavern in Great Queen Street, and in our own day at the Thatched House Tavern in St. James's Street. Those primitive early dinners are very eloquent as to the difference of the wants in such matters between those days and our own; there were some other curious points of interest about this club of philosophers. They were accustomed to make honorary members of such "noblemen and gentlemen as sent them venison and game," and they announced their perfect readiness to pay the carriage and fee the keeper. "Resolved, *nem. con.*," says a rule of 3rd May 1750, "that any nobleman or gentleman complimenting this company with venison, not less than a haunch, shall during the continuance of such annuity be deemed an honorary member, and admitted as often as he comes without paying the fee which those members do who are elected by ballot." The present of a turtle carried the same privileges. Says an entry of 5th August 1751, "The society being this day entertained with halfe a bucke by the most noble the Marquess of Rockingham, it was agreed *nem. con.* to drink his health in claret."

The other learned club of those days which still holds its meetings is the Dilettante Society, formed in 1734 with the double object of social intercourse and the encouragement of the arts. According to Mr. Horace Walpole, in gaining whose approbation the society was unfortunate enough to fail, "the nominal qualification is having been to Italy, and the real one being drunk." Walpole was for some reason or other severely censorious of the Dilettantes. Listen to him nearly half a century later when the society produced

its "Ionian Antiquities." "Those who are industrious
and correct and wish to forget nothing should go to
Greece, where there is nothing left to be seen but that
ugly pigeon house the Temple of the Winds, that
flycage Demosthenes' Lantern, and one or two frag-
ments of a portico or a piece of a column crushed in
a mud wall, and with such a morsel and with many
quotations a true classic antiquary can compose a
whole folio and call it 'Ionian Antiquities.'" Walpole's patronage of the classic taste from the serene
height and chaste severity of Strawberry Hill, with its
sham Gothic and cockle-shell grottos, is not undivert-
ing. But a club which included names like Reynolds,
Fitzwilliam, Charles Fox, Garrick, Colman and Windham was, we think, independent of the opinion in
matters of taste of the Honourable Horace Walpole.
Horry's portrait would hardly have improved those
two famous groups of its members by Sir Joshua
which we know so well from the engravings, with the
portraits of Leeds and Greville, Crowle, Hamilton,
Stanhope and the rest.

The Dilettante Society had a curious rule of fining
their members upon accessions of wealth "by inheri-
tance, legacy, marriage or preferment," and there is
some humour in a list of these fines. Five guineas
were paid by Lord Grosvenor on his marriage with
Miss Leveson Gower. The Duke of Bedford's appointment as First Lord of the Admiralty was held to
be worth eleven guineas to the society. The Duke of
Kingston paid two guineas on his acquisition of a

colonelcy of horse; Lord Sandwich on going out as ambassador to Aix-la-Chapelle paid twenty guineas, and twopence three farthings on becoming Recorder of Huntingdon. The society was certainly lucky in getting nine and a half guineas from Mr. Charles James Fox on his appointment as Civil Lord of the Admiralty under Lord North.

The efforts of the Dilettante Society in the cause of the fine arts were continued until quite recent times; it is claimed for them that they were mainly concerned in obtaining a charter for the Royal Academy, and they were certainly very helpful in securing the Siris bronzes for the British Museum in 1820. Their convivial meetings still survive in their dinners on the first Sunday of every month from February to July.

There are two accounts of the origin of the "Sublime Society of Beefsteaks," but they both point to a room in the original theatre in Covent Garden as its first meeting-place, and both are convincing as to the ease with which the social instincts of Londoners of the last century were excited. One account makes the Earl of Peterborough go into the property-room of Mr. Rich the manager and share his modest hospitality of a steak cooked on the fire of the workroom. The other traces the origin of the society to the reception in his painting-room at the same theatre of " persons of distinction " by Mr. Lambert the scene painter. In both cases the charms of conversation led to a single visitor tasting the artist's steak, helped down with London porter and port from a neighbouring tavern, and to the subsequent formation of a club of twenty members meeting weekly at the same place for the same purpose.

The weekly leisure of a great many notable men was spent at those meetings; William Hogarth, Francis Hayman, Churchill, Mr. Wilkes and Lord Sandwich, Mr. Garrick, Mr. Chase Price and the Prince of Wales. They stretched the limit of their club to twenty-five to include His Royal Highness in the year 1785. A little later came the social Duke of Norfolk, Charles Morris the laureate of the society, John Kemble and the Duke of Sussex. Later still such men as Brougham and Lord Eldon. The tradition of the society was nothing more than the joviality arising from these meetings to eat beefsteak and drink port wine, the only viands allowed by its rules. The chairman of the evening was always the butt of the rest of the company, and it was a rule that the member last elected should perform the office of butler and fetch the wine from the cellar. Lord Brougham was observed performing that useful service with great gravity, as was also the Duke of Leinster.

The club had the misfortune to be burned out of its habitation on two occasions: at Covent Garden in 1808, and at the Opera House in 1830. Of all its effects nothing remains but the gridiron upon which the first steak was cooked in 1735. It is pleasant, however, to remember that the Sublime Society of Beefsteaks still holds its meetings in rooms of its own in the Lyceum Theatre.

The most notable, perhaps, of all these famous gatherings which were the solace of the leisure of men of distinction throughout the eighteenth century, was that renowned society which gathered about Dr. Johnson at the Turk's Head in Gerard Street, Soho. A chance word let fall by Sir Joshua Reynolds gave the Doctor an opportunity for the exercise of those social qualities he so delighted to display, and the result came in those famous meetings of the "Club," christened later the Literary Club, in which the intellectual interest of those times seems to centre. It is too late in the day to attempt any description of those famous gatherings, which have employed the pens of the social historians from the days of Boswell to those of our own. But we mention the Literary Club here as the highest development of the periodical gatherings of men of distinction to dine at taverns which are so typical of the social life of London of that century. The incidents and the circumstances of that famous society are the landmarks of the literary history of modern England. What better presented the certainty of brilliant conversation to be expected in the dining-room at Soho than the admission of the Doctor that he took opposite sides against Burke quite independently of the merits of any particular question, and purely for the sake of the argument? The exclusiveness of that choice society which blackballed bishops and Lord Chancellors, and kept its own friends waiting for years for admission to its charmed circle because they expressed too much confidence of joining, is admirably preserved in another of the Johnsonian anecdotes. "I think I'll be of you," said Mr. Garrick. "He'll be of us," said the Doctor, on hearing of David's remark from Reynolds; "how does he know we will permit him; the proudest duke in England has no right to hold such language." And so Mr. Garrick had to chafe outside the charmed circle for years, until his fault was expiated and an increase in the numbers of the club made his entry the easier.

That same increase was the occasion of one of the Doctor's most characteristic sayings, in which his pride of intellect is very happily presented. "It would give," opined Goldsmith, "an agreeable variety to our meetings, for there can be nothing new amongst us; we have travelled over each other's minds." "Sir," said the Doctor, "you have not travelled over my mind, I promise you."

"The room is before us," wrote Macaulay of that famous society, "and the table on which stand the omelet for Nugent and the lemons for Johnson; there are assembled those heads which live for ever in the canvas of Reynolds. There are the spectacles of Burke and the tall thin form of Langton, the courtly sneer of Beauclerc, and the beaming smile of Garrick, Gibbon tapping his snuff-box, and Sir Joshua with his trumpet in his ear. In the foreground is that strange figure which is as familiar to us as the figures amongst which we have been brought up, the gigantic body, the huge massy face seamed with the scars of disease, the brown coat and the black-worsted stockings, the grey wig with the scorched foretop, the dirty hands, the nails bitten and pared to the quick. We see the eyes and the nose moving with convulsive twitches, we see the huge form rolling, we hear it puffing, and then comes the 'Why, sir,' and the 'What, sir,' and the 'No, sir,' and 'You don't see your way through the question, sir.'"

The small convivial societies of men, of which we have mentioned the famous ones only, have for the most part disappeared without leaving much trace of their influence on the social London of later times. In order to trace the history of the modern club we again turn to the meetings of the coffee-houses which we have described, and particularly to those fashionable and more or less exclusive societies which met at such establishments as White's Chocolate-house in St. James's Street.

It was, doubtless, the very popularity of the coffee-house which first suggested to the regular patrons of the more fashionable of such assemblies the desirability of some place of refuge from the chance visitor of a different condition; the Ned Wards, for example, who called for pipes in houses like Old Man's, devoted only to the cult of the "snush-box." There is no doubt about the inconveniences to the more reputable of the frequenters of the modish coffee-houses which attended the mixed company at the best of them, for the literature of the early years of the eighteenth century is full of allusions to it. We have mentioned the supposed meeting of the judge and the highwayman at

White's, which is no doubt apocryphal.   But there is historical evidence of the visit of that eminent knight of the road, Mr. James Maclean, to Wills's.   Farquhar, too, in " The Beaux's Stratagem," places two of his ruffians at Wills's and White's.   Hogarth, in plate vi. of " The Rake's Progress," which is intended to suggest a meeting at White's Chocolate-house, shows a highwayman, with a pistol protruding from his pocket, waiting by the fire for the winner at the hazard-table to leave the house.   Dr. Swift described White's as " the common rendezvous of infamous sharpers and noble cullies."   It is, therefore, quite natural to find the first idea of a private club meeting daily in its own rooms originating amongst a set of fashionable men of means and leisure, such as that which gave White's its vogue, in order to avoid such doubtful company ; and we may look to the existing White's Club in St. James's Street with the greatest confidence as the parent of all other institutions of the same kind.

The original White's Chocolate-house was the venture of a man named Francis White, who, in the year 1693, opened the place at a house on the site of the present Boodle's Club, No. 28, on the east side of St. James's Street, then a new part of the town.   The undertaking was undoubtedly a bid for the support of the fashionable people, whose residences began to spread westwards towards the court after the great fire of 1666.   It was, in fact, an attempt to adapt the conveniences of the coffee-house to the wants of a

class of patrons who had left the earlier houses of the
same kind to the merchants and lawyers of the city
and the Inns of Court. Francis White's speculation
was quite successful from the first, for four years after
opening his house at the present No. 28, he moved
to larger premises on the other side of the street.
His new house stood on the site of what is now the
northern half of Arthur's Club, and there are portions
of it which still remain and are included in the present
club building. It is of those second premises of old
Francis White that we must think as the famous
White's Chocolate - house, which so soon attracted
the attention of the town by the fashion of its patrons
and their generous views in the matter of gaming.
It was at White's that Dick Steele dated all his letters
to the *Tatler* on the fashionable topics of the day;
"all accounts of gallantry, pleasure, and entertainment," he says, "shall be under the article of White's
Chocolate - house," and in the first number of that
admirable paper he announced that the ordinary
charges of a visit to White's were sixpence as against
the customary penny of the average coffee-house. The
news - sheets, too, of those early days contain many
advertisements which point to White's as a place of
'vantage for modest dealings with people of great
station. Mr. Heidegger issued his tickets for the
masquerade from White's as the best of all places
for approaching the most eminent of his clients, and
if a beau left his sword in a chair, or a lady was
bewailing the loss of her lapdog, it was at White's

that each should be returned in order to secure the promised reward.

It was at this favourite haunt, then, that the men of quality using it determined to have rooms of their own, and in giving effect to that decision they founded the first social club in London. The date of that interesting occasion is unfortunately uncertain. The first records of the existing club date from 1736 only, the year when White's Club, by that time an institution of great importance, reoccupied its old quarters, which had been rebuilt after a disastrous fire in 1733. In that fire all the original records of the club disappeared; a fire, by the way, which had the distinction of being attended at four o'clock in the morning by his Majesty George the Second and his Royal Highness Frederick Prince of Wales.

We know, however, from other sources of information that old Francis White had died in 1711, and had left a modest fortune to his widow Elizabeth; that that lady continued a successful management of the Chocolate-house until somewhere between 1725 and 1729, and that in 1733, when the fire occurred, White's was under the management of John Arthur, who had been head servant to Francis White and his wife. The existing books of the club show that when the new house opened its doors in 1736, after a temporary sojourn at Gaunt's Coffee-house on the site of Mr. Bignell's present racing club at the lower end of the street, on the same side, "the club at White's" had been for years a notable institution of the town.

We take it that club life in London to-day differs little in essentials from the conditions that ruled that venerable institution in St. James's Street in the year 1736. The club, in its origin, was aristocratic, a lounging-place for the leisure of a lazy society, and although the borders of club life have since been widened by the social changes which have given leisure and affluence to other classes, the social club still remains a place where a man lays the cares of his work aside and diverts himself. A thousand tastes or interests to-day group men into clubs, where they find those tastes or interests flattered and supported by the companionship of men of the same way of thinking; sport, politics, social position. But most of those incentives to particular association are forgotten within the walls of a modern club, and it remains a quiet refuge from the distractions of business and from contact with the jostling of ordinary people; its attractions, in fact, are precisely those which led to the foundation of the first of the social clubs at White's Chocolate-house a couple of centuries ago.

There was one phase of the pleasantly easy life at White's which attracted the attention of the town from the first, and gave the club a reputation which clung to it for nearly a century. That was the prodigious rage for play, which we examine in detail elsewhere, and was seen at its high watermark at the fashionable meeting-place in St. James's Street. The whole literature of the century is full of allusions to the gaming at White's; all echoes of real events which

DUCK-HUNTING

DRAWN BY S. ALKEN

from time to time astonished the town. The third
Duke of Bedford lost an immense sum to a notorious
gamester, Sir Theodore Jansen, whose dealings at the
gaming-table were not above suspicion, and the incident was at once enshrined in one of the Satires by
Mr. Pope—

" As when a Duke to Jansen punts at White's."

The Earl of Orford told Swift that at the time of his
ministry "he never passed White's Chocolate-house
without bestowing a curse on that famous academy
as the bane of half the English aristocracy." White's
and its gaming are mentioned several times in the
" Dunciad," and Mr. Pope himself added a footnote
to the effect that it was "a noted gaming-house."

But the gaming at White's was only one phase of
the life which passed within its doors, as is quite clear
from the early records of the club as it was constituted
in 1736, records which include a list of its members.
Gaming was the natural amusement of a group of idle
young men of means who were without a taste for
field sports, athletic games, and the thousand ways of
amusement which engage the energies of the youth
of more modern times. As White's was the favourite
meeting-place of the young men of birth and leisure,
it followed as a matter of course that the club took
the lead in gaming as it did in the other follies of the
time. But a short examination of the published list
of its members is sufficient to prove that White's had
other claims to distinction. It was the club of many

of the great names of those days, the club of the great noble, of the courtier and the statesman, though not of the politician. Politics were laid aside at White's during the two centuries of its existence, except during the few years of the hottest of the rivalry between Mr. Pitt the younger and Mr. Charles James Fox, and the Tory tradition of White's which is so often quoted is really quite unwarranted by facts.

Among the men who met at the White's of the time of George the Second were Sir Robert Walpole on the one side, and William Pulteney on the other, a conjunction of names which would at once relieve White's from any reproach of party politics in those early days. Later came William Pitt and Henry Fox; and a generation later, when the rivalries of the sons of those two eminent men gave White's a party colour as the favourite club of the young Pitt, it is interesting to remember that Charles Fox was also a member of White's, and was frequently seen at the club. White's, indeed, has retained throughout its career the character it assumed from the first as the club of the well-born man of leisure, and that character is admirably supported by the list of its early members. Here were represented most of the great families of that day, Russells, Churchills, Pelhams, Stanhopes, Herveys, and Cavendishes. The witty Chesterfield was a noted member, and was accustomed to prepare his choicest *mots* to fire off "among the lads of quality at White's" until the rise of a later humourist, George Selwyn, who unfeelingly called his lordship Joe Miller, and hinting at the careful preparation of his impromptus and repartees, drove him from the club. Members of White's filled most of the good offices and sinecures about the court and in the administrations of those days, and supplied most of the senior officers in the two services. Social distinction, in fact, was the chief qualification for membership of the first of the social clubs, and its pretensions as an appanage of the aristocracy were never better described than by Horace Walpole, who declared that when an heir was born to a great house, the butler went first to White's to enter his name in the candidates' book, and then on to the registry office to record the birth.

The whole tradition of club life in London is supported by this famous club for half a century at least; in fact, we are inclined to the belief that notwithstanding the claim of the Cocoa Tree to existence as a club, apart from the coffee-house, about the year 1747, White's was the only club, as we understand the word, in London until after George the Third came to the throne, when Almack's and Boodle's added two others to the number. In any case, we are quite safe in relying upon the history of White's as the source of all information worth counting upon regular club life, until the doings of the young men at Almack's startled the town during the few years following 1764.

The most striking feature, then, of the club life of the first half of the eighteenth century was its exclusiveness. Here was the only club in the town, which in 1736 had a total of eighty odd members on its list, watching every candidate for admission with suspicion, and filling up its vacancies in the most leisurely fashion possible. For the first eight or ten years recorded in the existing books of White's Club, the elections averaged a little over half-a-dozen yearly, and club life in London was consequently represented in the days of George the Second by a company of gentlemen well under a hundred in number. The doors of this august assembly opened at rare intervals, and then only to men of great distinction, oftener than not the distinction gained on the field of battle. Among those few rare elections of the early days one notices such names as the Earl of Stair, with his record of fighting from the Boyne to Ramillies, and of his extraordinary diplomacy in Paris, where he astonished the French Court by the success with which he gained information and foiled the plots of the Pretender. Others of Marlborough's lieutenants were thought worthy of admittance to White's, Lord Ligonier and Lord Tyrawley; there were other famous soldiers like the Marquess of Granby, and sailors like Anson, who was elected in 1744 on his return from the famous voyage. The Duke of Grafton owed his election no doubt to his great station rather than to his eminence as a statesman, though he announced his intention of being " first minister, by G—d "; the Earl of Burlington of the first list of White's was the amateur architect and friend of Pope, and one of the few notable commoners of these scanty elections was Mr. Edward Gibbon, the father of the historian.

Such slow processes of election inspired by such fastidious choosing of their company, however, by no means satisfied the aspirations of intending clubmen of those times, and the state of things at White's led in 1743 to a curious proceeding on the part of such gentlemen as were dissatisfied with the ordinary accommodation of the coffee-house. These gentlemen established a second club, meeting at the same house in rooms of its own, and adopting the style and title of "The Young Club at White's," the original institution being thenceforward known as the "Old Club." The elders seem to have looked upon the junior concern with a mild and benevolent eye, and although, as we say, quite separate, with rules and a cook of its own, the Young Club at White's was ultimately accepted by those potentates as a place of purgatory or probation, where the young man might, by the blessing of Providence, become purged from all contamination of intercourse with ordinary people, and worthy of communion with their own charmed circle.

Occasionally a candidate for the Old Club passed quickly from the Young Club, but he was invariably a man of parts and possessed of great influence; young Mr. Charles Fox, for instance, was elected to both clubs at White's in the same year, owing no doubt to the efforts of his father, Lord Holland, who was a noted member of the Old Club. His friend George Selwyn, on the other hand, waited eight years in the junior concern, and another typical clubman of the same set, Lord March, was consistently rejected year after year, and only joined the old society when the two clubs were merged in the year 1781. Most of the young men, indeed, who gave White's its fame as the meeting-place of the generous youth of the period, Horace Walpole, Dick Edgcumbe, Gilly Williams, Lord Coventry, Carlisle, and the rest passed their leisure in the rooms of the Young Club only. We may think therefore of the Young Club as the scene of the later glories of the dice-box; of the Old Club as the austere resort of the more sober members, that long line of stately figures which has given White's so great a distinction among clubs, a line which includes every Prime Minister of Great Britain from Sir Robert Walpole to Sir Robert Peel.

It was the younger men, of whom those we have named are the better known, who gave White's its character for gaiety and dissipation, and obscured for some time the more venerable character of its greater but quieter members. In thinking of White's of the last century one remembers George Selwyn oftener than Chatham, or Horace Walpole than his father the minister, and it is to the records of the doings of such choice spirits that one turns for information upon the typical club life of those days. Horace Walpole, especially, is helpful, Horace with his fine eye for the humorous and his admirable habit of putting all that he saw and much that he imagined on paper. Horry enjoyed himself thoroughly at White's, but with moderation, and when the fun became fast and furious he would walk across the street and round the corner into his house at Arlington Street and write those remarkable letters which reflect the life of his times so admirably and in which doings at White's found frequent mention. There is much illuminative matter of the same sort also in that choice collection of letters from the young men about town at the club, letters which came to George Selwyn by every post whenever he and his friends were separated, half of them indeed written from the club-room itself.

Horry Walpole had gone home one evening in 1752 to Arlington Street, and was undressing when he heard a cry of "Stop thief," ran down into the street and assisted the watch in capturing a burglar in a neighbouring area. He had left George Selwyn at his cards at the club, and knowing that gentleman's taste for criminals, sent round a message, when the coffee-house "drawer" "stalked up into the club-room, stopped short, and with a hollow, trembling voice said, 'Mr. Selwyn, Mr. Walpole's compliments to you, and he has got a housebreaker for you.'" The news is irresistible, the whole club empties itself into Arlington Street and surrounds the burglar, who is walked off to the watch-house. Another evening at the club is realised without much exercise of the imagination from a letter by Mr. Richard Rigby written to George Selwyn in 1745. He was waiting, he said, "to hear the rattle of the coaches from the House of Commons in order to dine at White's." He went there "and sat till three in the morning," when " finding nobody to sit with any longer but Boone, who was not able," he went to the Ridotto. "The next morning I heard there had been extreme deep play, and that Harry Furnese went drunk from White's at six o'clock, having won the dear memorable sum of one thousand guineas. He won the chief part off Doneraile and Bob Bertie." Such, we may suppose, was a typical evening at White's in 1745; supper say at ten o'clock, play all night, one man unable to sit in his chair at three o'clock in the morning, and a break up at six, with the winner going away drunk with a thousand guineas.

Walpole will tell us of a dinner of the club, "a folly of seven young men," as he calls it, which displays an extravagance which was rarer then than it is now. A Mr. St. Leger, "the hero of all fashion," as Walpole calls him, was the Amphitryon, and the arrangements included tarts made of "duke cherries from hot-houses," and the drinking of only one glass from each bottle of champagne. The bill of fare got into print, it appears, and, as Walpole says, "produced the apprehension of another earthquake."

That same earthquake of 1750, which much shocked the nerves of the town, seems to have left White's unmoved. Mr. Rigby and Mr. Leveson, on their way to the club from dining with the Duke of Bedford, thought it an appropriate occasion to assume the functions of the watchmen, who in those days proclaimed the hour of the night and the nature of the weather to the sleeping citizens. They knocked at the doors of half Bloomsbury, and cried in the voice of the watch, "Past four o'clock, and a dreadful earthquake." At the club itself the serious nature of the visitation seems to have been unrecognised. "A parson came into White's in the morning," says Walpole, "and heard bets laid whether it was an earthquake, or the blowing up of powder-mills. I protest," said he, "they are such an impious set of people that if the last trumpet were to sound, they would bet puppet-show against judgment."

That mention of betting at White's reminds one of the extraordinary mania for wagering, in vogue about the middle of the last century among men of leisure, which was so conspicuous at White's, and is recorded at full in the published betting-book. There is a venerable story, quoted by Walpole, that a man dropped dead at the door of the house, was carried in, and the members immediately made bets as to whether he was dead or not; "and when they were going to bleed him, the wagerers for his death inter-fered, and said it would affect the fairness of the bet." This, as Walpole says, was only "a good story made on White's," but there are others no less remarkable recorded. There was Mr. Blake, for example, "one of the youth at White's, who," as Walpole tells us, "betted £1500 that a man could live twelve hours under water, hired a desperate fellow, sunk him in a ship by way of experiment, and both ship and man have not appeared since." Mr. Blake, as it would seem, proposed to renew the experiment.

The betting-book of the club contains no wager quite so outrageous as this, but there are many of an extraordinary character. Births, marriages, and deaths among the small society of that day were very favourite events upon which to risk large sums of money. One member of White's, Lord Montfort, alone registered sixty wagers on subjects of this description in the few pages of the early portion of the book which have survived, bets amounting in all to nearly six thousand pounds. Lord Montfort was reckoned the shrewdest man of his day, but his bets were less productive than was generally supposed, and the loss of his entire fortune at gaming of one sort or another drove him to suicide. On the 4th of November 1754, there was entered on the club betting-book the following wager: "Lord Montfort wagers Sir John Bland one hundred guineas that Mr. Nash outlives Mr. Cibber." The bet refers, of course, to the aged poet laureate Colley Cibber, and to the equally venerable Beau Nash, for so many years a prominent figure at Bath. Below this entry is the very significant note in another handwriting (quite possibly Horace Walpole's, who noticed the wager): "Both Lord Montfort and Sir John Bland put an end to their own lives before the bet was decided."

It was the last day of the same year that Lord Montfort spent his last evening at the club, supped there, and played whist until one in the morning. The following day he made his will, and shot himself almost in the presence of the lawyer and witnesses. Sir John Bland, the seventh baronet of Kippax, who had lost every penny of his fortune at hazard at White's—thirty-two thousand pounds at one sitting, it was said—had shot himself in the previous September on the road from Calais to Paris. These events, as Walpole tells us, drew much attention to the excesses of gaming at the club, and if we are to take him literally, the people came to gaze at the building with awe and wonder. "The citizens put on their double channelled pumps," he writes, "and trudge to St. James's Street in expectation of seeing judgments executed on White's, angels with flaming swords and devils flying away with dice-boxes like the prints in Sadler's 'Hermits.'"

It was quite natural that incidents of the life at White's such as these should be the first to attract attention, and to find a place in the letters of the period to the exclusion of the details of the more regular life of the club which continued at the same time. The levities and tragedies of that life were a godsend to those gossiping scribes, and provided them with the materials for their most effective paragraphs. The letters of men like Walpole, Gilly Williams, and the other correspondents of George Selwyn, were full of the trivialities of the club-room at White's; of the Dukes of Grafton and Devonshire almost coming to blows over the bother caused by that famous *mésalliance* which convulsed the town when Harry Fox ran away with the Duke of Richmond's daughter—" the former defending it, the latter a-tearing it to pieces;" of Lord Cobham forced to apologise to Lord Bristol in the full meeting of the club for having insulted his lordship by spitting in his hat at Lady Cobham's own assembly; of Lord Rockingham blushing when helped to sturgeon at the club, because his sister had run away with a man of low birth of the same name; of Lord Carlisle losing £10,000 at a cast of hazard; of the dreadful financial shortcomings of young Mr. Fox. Such chronicles as these reflect only one phase of the life at White's; the other is recorded in the history of the country. Every member of Mr. Pitt's great administration—that Government which buffeted the French all over the world, and raised the renown of England to a height it has seldom reached—is to be found in the list of members of White's; the great Pitt himself, the Grenvilles, Henry Fox, Newcastle, Bedford, and the rest. Club life in London, which was still represented solely by White's, must have had other attractions for men like these than the trifles we have mentioned which Walpole recorded so faithfully. And for the men, also, who carried out Pitt's schemes in all parts of the world, one would think, Rodney, Boscawen, Saunders, the Keppels, and Clive; and the men who fought later in America under less able direction from home—Burgoyne, Cornwallis, Howe, and Clinton.

Before George the Third came to the throne both clubs at White's had increased their numbers, and had

added these and many other names of distinction to
their lists.   Old White's had unbent to the extent of
fixing a maximum of 120 members; the Young Club
admitted as many as 230, so that the clubs together
numbered 350 gentlemen of condition, who comprised
the whole club life of London in 1755.   This increase
necessitated an increased accommodation, and in that
year Robert Arthur, who had succeeded his father
John as "Master of the House," moved with both
clubs to the present club building, then known as
"the Great House in St. James's Street."   It was on
the occasion of that removal, as we believe, that the
transformation of coffee-house into club became complete, and White's Chocolate-house was extinguished.
It is probable that the present Arthur's Club, established early this century, takes its name from a coffee-
house continued at the old premises under the style of
"Arthur's," and so perpetuates the name of a family
who had been in charge of the premises since the days
of old Francis White until the removal across the way
in 1755.

When the brand new young King George the Third
mounted the throne in 1760, the example of that
young monarch's well-ordered life at St. James's, and
his strict views of morality, had a great influence upon
club life in London.   It led almost immediately to a
complete change in the tone of life at White's, indirectly to the foundation of another famous club,
and eventually to the introduction of politics into
club life.   White's Club, without ever having been a

political organisation, had been a club of courtiers from the first, and was naturally affected by the views taken in social matters at St. James's. Old George the Second was never so happy as when winning or losing high stakes at hazard or faro with his subjects at court, and his relations with ladies like the Walmoden and Lady Suffolk are well known. But the glories of high play at court paled before the doings at the Young Club at White's, and the most celebrated of the ladies of a defined position, Kitty Fisher for instance, were supported by a regular subscription from the youth of the same institution. But when the young king assumed the sceptre one of his first acts was to banish the play tables from court with the Walmoden and the other appanages of his grandfather's establishment, and he marked his sense of the excesses which had made White's so famous by cashiering Robert Arthur, the Master of the House, who had held the office of clerk to the royal cellars under the old king. White's, as we say, was very ready to change its attitude in sympathy with this change in high places. One reads no more of the orgies of the dice-box at the clubs, but Walpole and Williams report continuously of the whispering and intrigues of politicians who were looking to gain or lose places upon the changes which must follow the efforts which the king and Lord Bute were making to trip up Mr. Pitt and the Whigs. Instead of the tale of the midnight sitting and the low jest, we have the remarks of those pleasant writers upon the portent of the Lord Cham-

berlain coming down to the club-room to stick up a
notice as to the exact order in which the Irish peers
should walk in the procession at the king's marriage
with Queen Charlotte. White's, in fact, became a
place of meeting for serious men of affairs, the old
gaiety and revel were sadly curtailed under the new
dispensation, and the careless youth of the period
began to look out for a place more to their liking.

The only institution of the kind which existed in
London and was available for those choice spirits was
the present Boodle's Club, which, as the Scavoir Vivre,
had opened its doors at the present building in St.
James's Street in the year 1762. But the Boodle's of
that year was hardly likely to attract the young men
who had been bored with the dulness of White's.
Boodle's took a tone at first of what in the slang of
to-day is called "preciousness." It gave annual prizes
for the best production in each of the fine arts, its
balls and masquerades were reckoned fine, and it
subscribed purses to famous tragedians and to the
tuneful ladies of the Italian Opera. It is quite
improbable that the present Cocoa Tree Club can be
counted among the regular clubs of London of the
year 1762. The coffee-house of the same name had,
of course, been a meeting-place for Jacobites since the
days of Anne, and later the house had acquired a
name as the rendezvous of some of the noblest of the
plungers at hazard. But the Cocoa Tree company
was a small party of irreconcilables whose existence
was barely acknowledged during the long ascendency

of the Whigs, and was only just beginning to enjoy the importance as a social club which it attained shortly afterwards, when the fortunes of the Tory party brightened under the patronage of the king. As we have said, neither Boodle's nor the Cocoa Tree were institutions likely to attract the superfine youth who failed to amuse themselves at White's.

In 1764, accordingly, we find that twenty-seven young men of the day, all of them well under twenty-five years of age, and most of them hailing from White's, went to one M'Call, trading under the name of Almack as the proprietor of a coffee-house in Pall Mall on the site of the present Marlborough Club on the north side of the street. They enlisted Mr. Almack's services as master of the house, and founded a new club of their own, the famous Almack's, which we now know so well as Brooks's.

This new club became later, as the result of causes which we shall examine, the very head and front of the great Whig party, which eventually ranged itself against the policy of the king. But the origin of Almack's was, as we say, a revolt of the gay youth of 1764 against the ordered decorum of White's, and an effort to discover another place of meeting where the old rites of hazard and faro could be continued unmaimed. Almack's assumed from the outset the greatest pretensions to fashion ; the young Dukes of Roxburghe, Richmond, Grafton, and Portland were among its original members, and its early elections included most of the famous young men about town of those days, Mr. Crewe, Sir Charles Bunbury, Richard Fitzpatrick and his brother Lord Ossory, both the young Foxes, their cousin Lord Ilchester, who was a plunger of the noblest, and the young Lord Carlisle, who seems to have been a typical pigeon of the play tables. A little later came Selwyn and Horry Walpole, Gilly Williams and March, all now ranking somewhat as fogies of an older generation; later still young Mr. Sheridan and the Whigs like Burke, Erskine, and Lord Holland, and the intellectuals like Gibbon, Reynolds, and Garrick; last, not least, his Royal Highness George Prince of Wales and the Duke of York.

Almost from the first life at Almack's or Brooks's, as it was called after the second of its proprietors, was really the life of White's of the first half of the century writ large. The original rules of the club, which are given in Cunningham's " London Past and Present," provided that " every person playing at the new quinze table do keep fifty guineas before him," and that " every person playing at the twenty-guinea table do keep twenty guineas before him." Those rules serve, we believe, as an index of the objects of the founders, as does also the significant enactment that " no gaming be allowed in the eating-room except tossing for reckonings." It was necessary, apparently, to keep one room at least free from the excitement of play. In any case play revived at Brooks's in a splendour which quite surpassed all the early glories at White's, and was perhaps only equalled by the doings at Crockford's during the first half of the present century. "Deep play is removed to Almack's," wrote Rigby to Selwyn in 1765, when the club was barely a year old, "where you will certainly follow it;" and for twenty-five years after that date, a period in which a bare half-dozen of knowing ones had acquired fortunes and the rest of the gamesters of the club had dissipated their substance among usurious Jews in their efforts to keep their places at the faro tables, the gaming at Brooks's was the wonder of the age.

We have examined this phase of life at Brooks's in our chapter on the play tables, and need not pursue it here, except so far as to trace its influence on the fortunes of the club. That influence was indeed a very potent one, and was brought to bear upon the fortune of Brooks's through the personality of one remarkable man, who very early in its history became the most prominent figure at the club. Mr. Charles James Fox was, as we see elsewhere, one of the noblest of the plungers at the play tables, and his eminence in that walk of life and in politics were attained almost at the same moment. Mr. Fox's first notable efforts in public life had taken the form of rather light-hearted revolts against his leader, Lord North, whom he had opposed on such measures as Royal Marriage Bills, and in so doing had deeply offended the king. His Majesty had written to Lord North that he considered "that young man had cast off every principle of honesty," and the royal scruples were increased fourfold by the reports which reached him of the

excesses of wine and hazard at Brooks's, in which Mr.
Fox was the most eminent figure.   Worst of all, the
Prince of Wales, who was eager from the day he
reached manhood to embrace every opportunity of
making himself disagreeable to his Majesty, was
pleased to honour Mr. Fox with his particular friendship and countenance, and to announce his intention
of joining his friend's favourite club.   From that
time forward Brooks's was taboo at court, and party
politics were introduced into club life for the first time.

This political aspect of club life was greatly in-
tensified as time went on.   In the first place, Fox's
astounding abilities, and the wonderful charm of his
nature, outweighed his numerous vices and failings,
not only with his boon companions, but with the
austerer spirits of the Whig party, men like Burke,
Rockingham, Richmond, and the rest, who all gathered
about their favourite at Brooks's.   During all those
distressing family quarrels, too, at St. James's, the
Prince of Wales went to the club for counsel and advice.   Fox, Burke, and Sheridan deliberated over his
concerns, wrote his letters to the king and queen, and
generally took his affairs into their keeping, Brooks's
thus becoming the headquarters of the regular Opposition.   The final seal of politics was placed upon the
club in 1780, when young Mr. Pitt first appeared in
public life.

Mr. Pitt, as we know, was at first hailed as a recruit
by the Whigs; Burke, indeed, declared him to be
Chatham come to life again, and Mr. Fox proposed

his name as a candidate for Brooks's, a fact alone sufficient to insure his election. But Mr. Pitt's sagacious ambition very early warned him that as long as George the Third was a power in the politics of the country, any ministry which contained Charles Fox was doomed. Mr. Pitt, therefore, very naturally elected to play for his own hand, renounced all idea of alliance with Fox and his party, and, as we know, succeeded in keeping the Whigs in opposition for nearly twenty years. Fox and his friends remained at Brooks's, Pitt withdrew to White's, and as long as those two great personalities remained in public life, the stormy politics of their times raged about the two clubs, and were directed from each.

We have no space here to follow the details of those contests which are part of the history of the times; how when the king's first fit of madness struck him, the two clubs almost contended for the custody of his person—Brooks's as representing the would-be regent, the Prince of Wales, Pitt at White's successfully supporting the claims of the queen. All the sordid details of those unseemly quarrels are identified with one club or the other; the Tories at White's read the hopeful bulletins of Willis, the mad-doctor, who reported his confidence in his Majesty's recovery; the more outspoken of the Whigs at Brooks's gloated over the pessimistic reports of their own party physician, Dr. Warren. It was said that the royal sons, George and Frederick, sat by at the card-table without protest, whilst gamesters said, " I play the lunatic," meaning

the king of the suit.   In any case, Brooks's was convulsed with the politics of the next twenty years; it
was agitated even beyond its wont when Mr. Orlando
Bridgman came into the club-room and told Mr. Fox
that the Prince of Wales had recently married Mrs.
Fitzherbert, although that graceless royalty had that
very day put up the innocent Mr. Fox in the House
of Commons to deny that the match had taken place.
All the vagaries of that royal scapegrace, his debts, his
amours, his marriage, were the care of Brooks's Club
until even their devotion could stomach his deceit and
want of truth no longer.   We may think of Brooks's,
therefore, until the end of the eighteenth century, as
the home of a small and dispirited political party; its
social life poisoned by the dissensions which politics
had introduced; even the rage for play which had
founded the club thirty years before burned out among
a body of exhausted spendthrifts.   White's, on the
other hand, was, as from the first, the haunt of a band
of courtiers, a band of courtiers converted into a great
political party by the great part played in politics by
the king for the first time during four reigns.   This
tension of high politics in the club life of London, as
represented by these two famous societies, was really
only relieved by the death of the two great opponents
in the same year, 1806.   Brooks's has retained its
political colour as the home of the Whig party ever
since.   White's almost immediately assumed its old
character of a neutral meeting-ground for men of
birth and condition.

Club life in London during the first ten years of the present century was still chiefly represented by the two clubs with whose origin and history we have been so far concerned. The Cocoa Tree continued a small association of gentlemen which has left little mark upon the social life of the town; Boodle's was gradually acquiring the reputation of a club of country squires devoted to fox-hunting, where all disputes connected with that sport, such as the boundaries of the counties hunted by particular packs, were eventually brought for settlement. There had been, it is true, a small club known as Goosetree's, dedicated to the practice of hazard and faro, which occupied Almack's old house in Pall Mall, now the Marlborough Club, after Brooks's went to the present club building in St. James's Street in 1778. But Goosetree's seems to have had a very short life, and the same may be said of two other unimportant clubs, Miles's and Evans's, of which there is bare mention in the letters of the times. In 1807 a gaming club, at which was played a game of cards called Macao for very high stakes, was opened by Watier, the Prince of Wales's *chef*, at the corner of Bolton Street and Piccadilly, and called after his name. Watier's owed its origin to the Prince of Wales himself, as a place where the members of both White's and Brooks's, who grumbled sadly at the cookery of their own clubs, might get an eatable dinner. It was seized upon by the gamblers, who were now frowned upon at both White's and Brooks's, and came to a premature end in 1819, by which date, as Mr. Raikes of the "Diary" records, the members were, almost without exception, ruined. The officers of the Guards, wearying of their accommodation at the St. James's Coffee-house which had been long their meeting-place, opened the present Guards' Club in 1813, and the present Arthur's Club was founded about the same year in the building on the site of the house occupied by Francis White and his successors, the Arthurs, as we have already said. But to all intents and purposes the club life of London was still centred in the two old establishments in St. James's Street, White's and Brooks's.

Life at both of these clubs underwent a great change during the opening years of the century; the softening of the rivalry between Mr. Pitt and Mr. Fox which preceded the year of their death; the disappearance of both from the stage in 1806; above all, the declining influence of George the Third in political matters, removed most of the distractions from both clubs. The dangerous attraction of faro, which had prevailed up till about 1790 at Brooks's, was now exchanged for the less dangerous fascination of whist for high stakes. At White's, faro had been forbidden by the rules, and the high play of the early period of hazard had never been revived. The unrestrained gaming, which was still a passion with the average man of leisure and property, was indulged in elsewhere, at any of the numerous gaming-houses of the West End, but it was discouraged at the older clubs. The attractions of both play and politics were thus removed from both

White's and Brooks's, and were exchanged for that extraordinary cult of male fashion which had its head-quarters at White's and was practised at both clubs, until the opening years of the reign of her present Majesty, by the relatively small body of men known then and since as the Dandies.

The reign of the Dandies was in reality a social tyranny exercised by a few score men over the great body of their social equals. Here was no question of a proud society resisting the advances of a rank of life below it; the whole movement was the assumption by a small coterie of men of fashion of a social supe-riority above their fellows, and the supporting of their pretensions by an arrogance which had been unknown in polite society before their day. The inspiration was supplied by that pattern of fine gentlemen the Prince Regent, at a time of life when the charm of his youth had disappeared, and it was imparted to such among the younger men in St. James's Street as were found worthy by the incomparable Mr. Brummell.

Mr. Brummell was a man whose origin was dis-tinctly middle-class. His father was factor, or agent, or personal secretary to Lord North, and he had aunts living in the persons of two excellent old ladies named Searle, who by the favour of the old king occupied one of the lodges in St. James's Park, kept cows, and sold syllabubs. It was in their dairy, indeed, that Mr. Brummell first met his patron the prince. That meeting led to the presentation by the prince of a commission in the army which Brummell held for three years only. He sold out in 1798, and was in that year elected to White's. Between that year and the year 1816, when he fled to Calais leaving half the tradesmen of the West End in lamentation, his life work was accomplished. He had placed himself at the head of the male society of his day at White's and had founded the cult of the Dandies.

That extraordinary body has excited great admiration both in its own day and since, but it was really little more than the cult of a coat and a neckcloth at best. "Peel is no gentleman," said his Majesty King George the Fourth; "he parts his coat tails before sitting down." It excluded every really eminent man of the period from its ranks, and its most admirable members were men who were witty and pleasant to their fellows, rude to all others, and a curse to their tradesmen.

One hesitates to believe a tenth of the stories told about Beau Brummell, the very high priest of the shrine—which was the bow-window at White's thrown out over the steps of the old entrance in 1812—of his insolence to the prince, and his brutal rudeness to women, because he undoubtedly went through life with a whole skin at a time when such conduct was apt to produce personal chastisement. But there is little doubt that a general portrait of the man is conveyed in those oft-quoted anecdotes; his request to the prince, "George, ring the bell;" his stress on the word "mistress" in ordering Mrs. Fitzherbert's carriage in the same august presence; his query to Lady Jersey, who was dancing with his royal highness, "Who's your fat friend." He would take a cutlet from his plate at luncheon in a strange house, and throw it to a pet dog, with the remark, "See if you can get your teeth through it, I'll be damned if I can." When asked about his parents he replied, "The poor old creatures both cut their throats years ago eating peas with a knife." He ordered a servant to empty his snuff-box into the fire because a bishop took a pinch unasked at the prince's table. And yet upon the man of whom these stories are told the male fashion of an entire generation was content to model itself, and his influence died only within living memory.

The men who followed Mr. Brummell, and upon whom his mantle descended, were better fellows, but they made club life at White's and Brooks's well-nigh unendurable to any but their own set. At White's they appropriated special seats, used special slang of their own, and frowned upon the ordinary members who were daring enough to dispute such places with them. As Mr. Alfred Montgomery said, he would as soon have thought of taking his seat in the throne in the House of Lords as of taking a place in the bow-window of White's. Their savage blackballing decimated the club during a period of twenty years, and at last rendered necessary an alteration of rules which placed the ballot in the hands of a committee in order to save the club from extinction.

The astonishing pretensions of the Dandies, which made White's and Brooks's impossible for the average man of leisure during the first thirty years of this century, led inevitably to the establishment of other social clubs which might be free from their tyranny. There were many men of assured position who resented the attitude of the superfine band at the two older clubs, and who had little reverence for the memory of Mr. Brummell. "D—n the fellows," said Colonel Sebright of the Guards, as he saw two of them in the bow-window at White's, "they are upstarts, and fit only for the society of tailors." When Waterloo brought peace and a period of rest to the country after a quarter of a century of national anxiety, there came an expansion of social life in London very similar to that we noticed a century earlier when the country settled down after the wars of Marlborough. The antics of the Dandies at the ballots at White's and Brooks's were at once a refusal of those choice spirits to widen their own charmed circle in sympathy with the spirit of the times, and a reason for numbers of eligible men of breeding and condition to form themselves into other societies.

As early as 1808, travelled men of leisure, men of letters, bishops and judges, formed the Alfred Club in Albemarle Street, which was merged in the present Oriental Club in 1855. A similar society was the Travellers', founded in 1814. The Travellers' owes its origin to the initiative of Lord Castlereagh, who projected the club as a meeting-place for gentlemen who had travelled "five hundred miles from London in a straight line," and as a place of entertainment for distinguished foreign visitors. In 1815 military and naval men established themselves at the United Service Club, and in so doing added one more to the two service clubs in being at that time, the Guards' and the Royal Naval Club. The year 1824 saw no fewer than four new clubs established in London, all of which are flourishing to-day. Sir John Malcolm founded the Oriental for travellers and residents from the East; men of science and letters like Sir Humphry Davy, Scott, Moore, and Croker conceived and carried out the idea of the stately Athenæum; old Oxford and Cambridge men formed the University Club; men of substance from the city first foregathered at the Union. In 1828 Lord Nugent was instrumental in gathering together "a society of gentlemen connected by a common bond of literary or personal acquaintance," a society which we still know as the Wyndham. Three years later "the patrons of the drama and its professors" established a society of their own at the Garrick Club, in King Street, Covent Garden.

It is from the years immediately preceding the passing of the Reform Bill of 1832 that we date the first of the great political clubs. The Tories who surrounded the Duke of Wellington and Sir Robert Peel in those days of strenuous politics, "found White's too neutral in tone," as we learn from Mr. Raikes, and established in 1831, in the Carlton, an institution of the right Tory colour. Brooks's, as we saw, became a home of the Whig party only by accident. It never lost the Whig flavour which it acquired in the days of Charles Fox, and the great Reform Bill itself may be said to have been incubated in its rooms. But the Brooks's of 1832 included so many reactionaries in its list that the forward spirits of the Liberals felt the necessity of a meeting-place of their own, and so founded the Reform Club as a counterblast to the Tory Carlton.

Since that year, which was the real beginning of the period we call the nineteenth century, the era of railways, of easy communication, of cheap corn, and of industrial prosperity, club life in London and elsewhere has shared to the full in the wonderful developments of the times. Its present importance in the social life of to-day is evident to all who know the town, and need not be enlarged upon here. The imagination, indeed, reels at the thought of London without its clubs. It is true that the sojourning of men at clubs is popularly supposed to be a domestic grievance of a character as unjustifiable as it is acute. But this is a question which, like every other, has two sides, and its true bearings may perhaps best be grasped by endeavouring to realise some unthinkable convulsion which should in a moment restore the clubmen of London to the bosoms of their families.

CHAPTER XII

OF SUNDRY DIVERSIONS

IF any one familiar with the social annals of the two
centuries which preceded the reign of her present
Majesty were asked to characterise the entertainments
which delighted Londoners of all classes throughout
that term, he might reply without much hesitation
that they were as much distinguished for their naïveté
as for their brutality. There were never, in modern
times, audiences more easily moved to laughter or so
delighted with the spectacle of bloodshed and suffering
as gatherings of Londoners during the two hundred
years which ended with the reign of William the Fourth.
People of condition in the reigns of Anne and the
Georges flocked to the Strand or to Covent Garden
to see waxworks at Mrs. Salmon's, or puppet-shows
at Mr. Powell's, or to watch Mrs. Saraband's dogs
and monkeys going through the operations of a siege
with toy cannons and scaling-ladders. A hundred
years later they were just as delighted with mounte-
banks like Katerfelto and quack doctors like Graham
with his mud-baths and his Celestial bed.

Side by side with these innocent simplicities
flourished the brutalities which we have examined in

our inquiries into the humours of Hockley, the
cockpit and the prize-ring, the last two at least of
which famous institutions depended upon the support of well-to-do people for their prosperity and
development.   So too with the great mass of the
people, separated in those days much more sharply
from the classes than to-day.   They delighted, as we
have seen, in the primitive joys of Bartholomew's
Fair or the tea gardens, and were always ready to see
much fun in the spectacle of a man grinning through
a horse-collar.   From such innocent diversion they
would turn with joy to the horrors of the duck hunt
or the cockshy; and a good place of 'vantage from
which to see old Lovat's head roll on the scaffold at
the Tower, or Jack Rann swing into the air at Tyburn
Tree, was held worth while spending the previous day
to secure.

Both these aspects of the amusements of the town
of our ancestors are strange to modern ideas.   Whatever else may be said of the modern entertainments
which appeal to the tastes and the purses of the
London of to-day, it will not be contended that they
lack humanity or err on the side of simplicity in
execution or design.   The virtues of contrast are not
inconsiderable, and it may therefore be convenient
here to recall to a London sated with the spectacular
glories of the Lyceum or the Haymarket the simple
histrionic entertainments which were good enough for
some of their ancestors.   It may also not be uninstructive, with the spectacle of 60,000 people watching

a League football match at the Crystal Palace in the mind's eye, to recall for a moment the much simpler entertainments of Spa Fields which drew together the crowds of the middle of the eighteenth century. Finally, we do not fully realise what we owe to a better state of public opinion in the matter of our treatment of animals, until we have investigated some of the minor sports which kept lower-class London amused until an Act of Parliament in 1835 established a standard of humanity which the public has happily accepted and improved. Such an inquiry will, as we believe, include some items of interest, and will enable us to conclude our work with the consideration of some minor diversions which fall outside the more or less artificial limits of the separate subjects which the scheme of our task has so far suggested as convenient.

The naïveté of the audiences of the early part of the last century, and the ease with which they were amused, appear very plainly, we think, in the success which rewarded some very simple and curious entertainments of a spectacular character, which, by reason of that success, became serious competitors of the legitimate drama at Drury Lane. We have already glanced at the puppet-shows of the great fairs; but these exhibitions were by no means confined to the audiences of those popular meetings. Great people flocked to Mr. Powell's establishment under the Piazza in Covent Garden in numbers which seriously reduced the takings of the patent houses, and ham-pered the progress of the exotic opera, then lately introduced into England.

It is pleasant to think of well-bred audiences delighted with the productions of Mr. Powell; plays of marionettes beginning with the Garden of Eden, dealing with most of the great names from the Deluge onward, and varied with a *divertissement* of Punch and Judy dancing in Noah's ark, Punch subsequently seating himself on the Queen of Sheba's lap, fighting the Duke of Lorraine, and selling the King of Spain a bargain. It was, as we say, such diversions as these that amused the quality of Anne and George the First, and emptied the patent theatres; puppet-plays founded upon such themes as Dick Whittington, Dr. Faustus, Mother Goose, "together with the pleasant and comical humours of Valentine, Nicolini, and the tuneful warbling pig of Italian race," as one of Mr. Powell's handbills recites. Penkethman and Mrs. Saraband, Crawley and Flockman were all managers who kept alight the sacred fire of the puppet-show until near the end of the century, greatly to their own advantage, and the marionettes of our own time are thus only a revival.

Mrs. Salmon's waxworks, too, exhibited at a house in Fleet Street near Temple Bar, had a success which foreshadowed the later glories of Baker Street. The show included a figure of Mother Shipton near the door, which gave a facetious kick to the visitor on leaving. One envies an age when Mrs. Midnight's Oratory in the Haymarket kept the town amused for years with its "noted ox with six legs and two bellies, its male and female acrobats," its "fire-eater smoking out of red hot tobacco pipes, champing lighted brimstone and swallowing his infernal mess of broth." Then, a good deal later, the ingenious Frenchman M. Bisset astonished the town and cleared £1000 in a few weeks with his Cats' Opera and troupe of other animals; monkeys taking wine together, riding on horses, and dancing minuets with dogs. One of M. Bisset's hares walked on its hind legs and beat a drum, and, it may be, provided the model for those delightful white rabbits of our nurseries which go through the same performance. M. Bisset also induced his six turkeys to walk through the steps of a country dance, and surely well deserved the fortune which a delighted London presented him in exchange for these diversions.

From Mr. Powell's puppets to the pantomime was but a step, and the audiences which patronised the one delighted in the other, to the despair of the poor actors. Pantomime, like Opera, crept into England at the beginning of the eighteenth century, "comique masques in the high style of Italie" were announced, and a ballet at Drury Lane of the Loves of Mars and Venus, where the whole story was told by gesture (with some omissions, it may be hoped), foreshadowed the real pantomime which soon followed. Rich at the Lincoln's Inn Theatre produced a piece called "Harlequin Executed" in 1717, which is accepted as the first real pantomime by historians of the stage.

Mr. Rich brought out his pantomime to compete with Mr. Cibber at Drury Lane, who was there beating him in his presentation of the legitimate drama, and actors as a body deplored the innovation for half a century. Harlequin springing appropriately enough from a bed of tulips or a rainbow, amused the town rather more than the pompous mannerisms of the players of the pre-Garrick period. Harlequin, indeed, played by good actors like Woodward, was a very favourite character until the days when the incomparable Grimaldi exalted that of the clown at his expense. Even Garrick himself found the pantomime a serious rival, and was wont to reproach his audiences in the prologues and epilogues which he turned so neatly. The wits and essayists used to make very merry over the innocent absurdities of the pantomime which the quality found so much to their taste; Mr. Pope, for example—

> " Thence a new world, to Nature's laws unknown,
>   Breaks out refulgent with a heaven its own,
>   Another Cynthia her new journey runs,
>   And other planets circle other suns ;
>   The forests dance, the rivers upwards rise,
>   Whales sport in woods and dolphins in the skies."

To glance at the other end of the century there was no sensation more popular with the leisured classes than the silly performances of the medical mountebank. It was the well-bred idler and his womenkind who supported Katerfelto and Doctor Graham. To modern ideas there seems little attraction in Katerfelto's programme. He took advantage of an epidemic of influenza to work upon the nerves of audiences with magic lanterns and fearsome images of microbes and animalculæ. His darkened rooms, black cats, and electric machines impressed his visitors hugely, instead of anticipating the fairly obvious fact later established by a magistrate, when his fire balloons set haystacks alight, that he was a rogue and a vagabond.

Dr. Graham, we suppose, was a shade better; he certainly had a very gratifying success, but then the Doctor had the advantage of the help of the peerless Emma, in the flower of her youth and beauty, before she began to sit for Mr. Romney or had captivated ambassadors and admirals. At a house in the Adelphi, and later at Schomberg House in Pall Mall, you might see Emma and the Doctor sitting in separate mud-baths up to their necks, Emma's hair being wondrously dressed in the mode with powder, flowers, and ropes of pearls, and the Doctor's wig a marvel of the perru-quier's skill. Another day you might hear the humbug lecture on perpetual youth and beauty, his theories illustrated by the blooming nursemaid in the flesh as the "Goddess of Health." Then there was the Celestial Bed, which held forth great attractions for those wanting heirs, " the rosy Goddess of Health assist-ing at the celestial matters," as we learn from the Doctor's advertisement, "and that sacred Vital Fire over which she watches." " The descriptive exhibition of the apparatus in the daytime is conducted by the junior officiating priest," an announcement which

comes as a distinct bathos. It may interest the curious
in small matters to know that the "junior officiating
priest" became later Dr. Mitford, the father of
the authoress. With such attractions as these Dr.
Graham contrived to fill his rooms with a mob of
silly people at five shillings a head.

A quite different entertainment, which had a
vogue almost at the same time, and may claim the
paternity of all modern developments of the circus,
was the equestrian entertainment of Mr. Philip
Astley in Lambeth. Astley's Amphitheatre, which
was only finally extinguished in 1862, began in
very modest surroundings. Astley himself had
served under General Eliot, Lord Heathfield, who
gave him a horse, which he christened Gibraltar, and
which with another formed his whole stud. Strutt,
the historian of all sports and pastimes, says:
"Riding upon three horses at once, while they are
at full speed, is, I believe, a modern species of exhibition introduced to public notice about forty
years back by a man named Price, who displayed
his abilities at Dobney's, near Islington. Soon
afterwards a competitor of the name of Sampson
made his appearance, and he again was succeeded
by Astley."

Whether Mr. Strutt is here quite accurate does
not concern us; at a guess, Jacob Bates at Newmarket was antecedent to all these artists enumerated by the antiquarian. Astley may have got a
hint from the others, but he was undoubtedly a

pioneer in his business, and should be canonised as the patron saint of all ringmasters. He set up his first show in a field at Halfpenny Hatch, his only enclosure a rope and stakes, and his revenues whatever oblations he could extract from passers-by. The rope and stakes later gave place to a slight paling, on the very spot where now stands Waterloo Station. Here, in the words of his own handbill, might be seen "the activity on horseback of Mr. Philip Astley, Sergeant-Major in his Majesty's Royal Regiment of Dragoons. Nearly twenty different attitudes will be performed on one, two, and three horses, every evening during the summer at his riding school. Doors to be open at four, and he will mount at five. Seats, one shilling; standing places, sixpence."

A strange figure is this of the energetic, strenuous ex-dragoon, which one comes across so frequently in the records of the last quarter of the century—a figure in every way representative of the successful semi-professional men who then controlled so many of the amusements of the town. A midday stroll in the West End would usually bring one in contact with the dragoon himself mounted on his white horse Gibraltar, distributing his own handbills, and pointing with his sword in the direction of his show across the river in a very gallant manner. A creditable career was that just opening for the ex-soldier with his modest stud of two horses, his faithful wife taking the shillings at the gate, and providing

orchestra with a big drum. Astley's prospectus
offered to " teach the true and perfect seat on horseback. Mr. Astley undertakes to break in the most
vicious horse in the kingdom for the road or field,
to stand fire, drums, &c. No gentleman need despair
of being a complete horseman that follows his directions, having eight years' experience in General Eliot's
regiment."

People of all sorts and conditions flocked to Mr.
Astley's modest entertainment ; the patent holders
grew jealous, and lodged an information against him,
and things began to look black for the struggling
ex-dragoon. Then his Majesty George the Third
himself happened to come over Westminster Bridge
on a restive horse, and Mr. Astley recognising his
opportunity, showed his knowledge and presence of
mind, pleased the king by his address, and obtained
a royal licence, which effectually silenced his rivals.
Luck then came to Philip in a shower. He scraped
together £200 from the earnings of his poor show,
and invested it on mortgage of a piece of waste
ground at Westminster. The mortgagor went abroad
and was never heard of again ; and Astley, foreclosing,
walked into a fine site containing a most accommodating stock of timber ready for building purposes.
About the same time he picked up a diamond ring
worth £70 on Westminster Bridge, and his poor
show of stakes and railings was converted into a
handsome riding-school with a roof over the heads
of the most important of his customers, and he was

able to advertise that he would "perform every evening, wet or dry." The town now began to flock to
the new entertainment, reinforced as it was by young
Master Astley, aged five years, who took the title
part in "Billy Button's Ride to Brentford." "White-
field never drew so much attention as a mountebank
does," wrote Boswell; "were Astley to preach a
sermon standing upon his head on a horse's back,
he would collect a multitude to listen to him."
Even the critical Mr. Horace Walpole went to
Astley's and found much to admire. "I could
find nothing to do at all," he wrote in 1783, "and
so went to Astley's, which, indeed, was beyond my
expectation. Astley can make a horse dance minuets
and hornpipes."

There was no end to Astley's enterprise. He
brought out a new acrobatic entertainment, common
enough now, but excellently novel and effective, no
doubt, with the public of his day—a pyramid of men,
four supporting three on their shoulders, the three
two, and the two a single individual, who formed the
apex. "The Hercules Pyramid," as he called it,
gave its name to streets and taverns as well as to
Astley's own house. Then he felt the want of a
roof for the centre of his premises so as to shut out
the elements altogether. Her Royal Highness the
Princess Dowager of Wales happened to die at the
moment, and Mr. Astley bought the timber used
for the scaffolding at her obsequies for a song.
Later he wanted more, and mixing with the mob

at an election, whose playful custom it was to make bonfires of the hustings on such occasions, he intimated that beer would flow in a liberal stream if the timber, instead of being burnt, were carried to his yard. With material thus acquired he roofed in his arena, and as the idea of horsemanship under a roof was much criticised, he met such carpings by painting his dome to represent the branches of trees, and by christening it the " Royal Grove."

A man of infinite resource was Astley. Captain Cook's death moved London to much curiosity and interest, and Mr. Astley provided " a grand equestrian dramatic Spectacle " founded upon that tragedy. An equestrian spectacle upon the death of the famous navigator is rather suggestive of the horse marines to the modern intelligence, but it was very popular with the London of George the Third, and helped Astley to further great successes. By 1792, indeed, Astley was able to turn over the chief cares of his undertaking to his son, and on the outbreak of the Revolutionary war in the following year he made a great success in his management of the embarkation of the cavalry, and finally he went through the campaign with the Duke of York.

" The Grove " was burned in 1794, and Astley's Amphitheatre of Arts arose on its ashes. At the Peace of Amiens he succeeded, much to every one's surprise, in obtaining compensation from Buonaparte for the occupation of his branch circus in Paris as a barrack by the Republican troops. Astley was one of the English who were imprisoned on the renewal of the war, but he escaped to the frontier disguised as an invalid French officer. He reached England only to find his wife dead and his theatre again destroyed by fire, by which stroke of ill luck he lost a sum of £30,000. It was rebuilt as the Amphitheatre which some of us remember. Philip Astley died in Paris during the occupation of that city by the Allies in 1814, and lies buried in Père la Chaise. It was just seven years after that his son died in the same bed of the same room of the same house, and lies buried in the same grave. They both, like Heidegger, Tyers and others, claim mention here as men whose fortunes were made by devoting their energies to the amusement of the London of their day.

Turning from these and other regulated amusements for which coin of the realm was exchanged, let us glance at some impromptu revelries which drew thousands of the people to open spaces like Spa Fields, just off the present Gray's Inn Road. These fields were a very favourite resort for the lower classes of Londoners, and during fine weather there was usually a ready-made audience at the disposal of any enterprising entertainer. Here much cudgel-playing or single-stick took place, and a man might graduate in that art for the brighter glories of Hockley, or Figg's amphitheatre. "Two women fought for a new shift valued at half a crown in the Spa Fields, New Islington," says a newspaper of 1768; "the battle was won by a woman called Bruising Peg, who beat her antagonist in a terrible manner." In the summer of the same year, as we learn, "an extraordinary battle was fought in the Spa Fields by two women against two taylors for a guinea a head, which was won by the ladies, who beat the taylors in a severe manner."

The grinning match, too, was a favourite diversion at Spa Fields and similar places near the town like St. George's Fields or Brixton Causeway. At St. George's for example, in 1711, a Mr. Shanks contrived to assemble a great company for a grinning match. "The prize was a gold-laced hat, and the competitors were exhilarated by music and dancing." Near the same time a gold ring was danced for and a hat given as a prize for skittles at the Greengate, near Lambeth Wells. The authorities were fully aware of the value of such assemblies of British manhood as these delights drew together for the purposes, to put it mildly, of recruiting. In 1779 they offered an ox roasted whole and unlimited beer to the "friends of their king and country," a delicate way of hinting at the virtues of enlistment. They offered also "two gold-laced hats as prizes for the two best cudgel-players; a gown, a shift, and a pair of shoes and stockings, to be run for by four old women; three pounds of tobacco and a silver-laced hat to be grinned for by three old men, the frightfullest grinner to be the winner!" We are fortunate in being able to supply some details of the meeting which these attractions drew together. These appeared in the *Clerkenwell Chronicle* in August

1779. "At seven o'clock A.M.," says the report in that journal, "the ox being roasted, came a sergeant and a number of deputy sons of the sword. The sergeant made an elegant speech, at which every one gaped in astonishment, because no one could understand it. At half-past two the beef was taken up, slices cut and thrown among the crowd, and many an one catched his hatfull to fill his belly." We read that "the winner of the gown was a loser, as she tore off the skirt in attempting to get it on." It was estimated that forty to fifty thousand people were present. "Beer was drunk out of pots without number and without measure," says the *Chronicle*. "Some men were enlisted, but more were impressed, as the bloodhounds were on the scent, and ran breast high," a remark which explains the hospitality of the government as represented by the sergeant and the deputy sons of the sword.

Other assemblies very typical of the ease with which the people of the Georgian times amused themselves were those joyous gatherings known as the Garrat Elections. Garrat is, or was, a hamlet on the south side of the Wandsworth High Street, and included at one time a small common. Some encroachment on the right of the commoners about 1750 led to an association of those worthy people, who elected a mayor to look after their rights. The time of the election of the first mayor of Garrat happened to coincide with that of a general election, and it was decided by the commoners that the office of their representative should endure and expire with each Parliament. The publicans, with a sagacious appreciation of the possibilities of these gatherings and their effect upon their own interests, subscribed a purse for the necessary expenses, and the Garrat Election became a highly popular parody of the real article. As time went on such men as Mr. Garrick and Mr. Wilkes did not disdain to assist by writing the addresses of the candidates.

The first member for Garrat was "Sir" John Harper. The successful candidate, observe, always assumed the style and title of a knight. Sir John in private life was an eminent dealer in brick-dust, and he sat for two Parliaments. Sir Jeffrey Dunstan succeeded Sir John, and retained his seat during no less than three Parliaments. He was a purveyor of old wigs by profession, a man of sardonic wit, and altogether the most famous of the Garrat members. During the alarms of the French Revolution Mr. Pitt thought Sir Jeffrey's political jokes worthy of prosecution and Sir Jeffrey's person worthy of incarceration. In 1797 Sir Jeffrey was defeated by Sir Harry Dimsdale, and incontinently drank himself to death. Sir Harry was a muffin-seller of repute, but he died before his Parliament expired, and no independent candidate being worthy to succeed him the seat has since remained vacant.

These burlesque elections were attended by prodigious numbers of people, and were the occasion of much riotous horseplay. Sir Richard Phillips estimates an average attendance at a hundred thousand, an estimate it is as difficult to accept as to refute. There was much fun of a primitive type at the Garrat Election, the candidates being dressed always in a caricature of the prevailing mode, which would include the dress of Mr. Horace Walpole's middle years, the Macaroni equipment of Mr. Charles Fox of the seventies, and the knee breeches and top boots of Sir John Lade at the end of the century. Peers of the realm unbent so far as to drive the candidates to the hustings in their lordships' own carriages and six; the houses of the neighbourhood were at a premium during the contests, and Mr. Foote paid nine guineas for a single window in 1761, and has recorded his impressions of the scene in a very dull piece.

It would seem that successive generations of Londoners have failed altogether to appreciate the capacities of their fine river as a playground. Until our own times its value as a highway was recognised to the full, so much so, that even as late as the Regency, it was computed that the number of wherries on the Thames exceeded that of the hackney coaches on the streets by many thousands. Hansom cabs, omnibuses, and underground railways have since reversed the relations of land and water in London in this particular. But the scanty festivities which used to enliven the river from time to time have one by one departed, and at this end of the nineteenth century the Thames, for all purposes of delight or solace to the Londoner, remains as barren and as utilitarian as the invisible but useful Fleet Ditch which still flushes our sewers.

The Thames is no longer even possible for bathing; but it is not uninteresting to recall the fact that from Stuart times until the days of George the Fourth it was no uncommon sight to see a well-known man about town disporting himself in the river between Westminster and London Bridge. "Dudley North," says Roger North in his "Lives" of that family, "used to swim in the Thames so constantly, and above bridge too, that he could live in the water an afternoon with as much ease as others walk on land." Nearly a century later the tenth Earl of Pembroke was so fond of the same diversion that the facetious Lord Chesterfield in pleasant allusion to his habit, addressed a letter "To the Earl of Pembroke, in the Thames, over against Whitehall." Mr. Benjamin Franklin, too, has left record of a swim which he took through London from Lambeth to London Bridge in the reign of George the Third. Perhaps the last of the distinguished men to keep up the tradition of public bathing in London was Lord Byron, who in 1807 anticipated his exploit in the Hellespont by taking the water at Lambeth and swimming down three miles with the tide. It is said that until the days of the great riverside embankments, the West-minster boys were still accustomed to disport themselves in the unattractive waters of the Thames of those days. The last vestiges of bathing in the river seem to have disappeared with the floating swimming bath at Charing Cross some twenty years ago.

The waters of the Thames appear to have conferred a privilege of free speech in former days which was not always enjoyed on land, and this may have tended to keep fashion on its banks. It is certain that the great people who took boat to Vauxhall and often hired a satellite bark provided with a band of French horns, did so as much for a protection from the badinage of the river as for any enjoyment to be derived from the music. It was the pride and joy of the average boatload of apprentices from the city to unite the vulgarity of their whole company in an epithet of suitable brevity, and fire it off upon every passing boatload of their betters they encountered on the voyage. Great minds like Dr. Johnson's were often employed in returning an appropriate reply, as we know from a famous rejoinder of that great man. One finds allusion to these pleasantries of the Thames at intervals throughout two centuries. "The Thames," says Malcolm, "seems to have a charter for rudeness, and the sons of Triton and Neptune have not only a freedom of, but a licence for, any sort of speech, and the privilege by being so ancient has become incontestable. Crowned heads did not in former times go scot free." We gather from some particulars which Malcolm proceeds to quote, that when the state barge of Charles the Second went up the river from Whitehall, Queen Catherine was sometimes reminded by her subjects of the largeness of the king's family and the emptiness of the poor queen's own nursery.

One reads, too, of "a brisk bold lass, provokingly well versed in the water language," hovering round one of those periodical expeditions which took George the Second to Hanover at frequent intervals during his reign, and making the court officials, who were awaiting their royal master below bridge, stare and gasp at the vigour of her communications. A journalist of the day describes this lady's criticism as a series of "plaguy broadsides," and "odd, comical, out-of-the-way expressions," which he forbore to repeat, because he questioned "whether they would not even be deemed treasonable." If, as is probable, the "brisk bold lass" knew of some of the attractions which drew King George to Hanover, and spoke her mind freely on the subject, it was no doubt advisable, as the writer in the *Medley* said, "that the phrases she made use of should not be repeated here."

The Thames of those early days, with its wonderfully picturesque front, which one sees best in the delightful pictures of Scott, seems, as we say, to have been handed over altogether to ribaldry. The *Folly*, the only floating place of entertainment of which there is record, a large hulk moored off Somerset House in the days of the Restoration, and fitted up as a musical summer-house for the entertainment of the quality, sank from a resort of the fashionables "to a receptacle for companies of loose and disorderly people for the purposes of drinking and promiscuous dancing."

Even the easy morals of the times of George the Second could not tolerate the *Folly*, and put an end to its pleasantries. And so we find that the Thames has never taken the fancy of the more reputable classes of Londoners as a playground, and its pleasures have been confined to the not very exciting occasions when the Lord Mayor went up the stream in his gilded barge, to an occasional pageant like the Ranelagh Regatta of 1775, or to the more interesting contest between young watermen initiated by the benevolence of the eminent comedian Mr. Doggett in 1728, and still happily an annual fixture. On the 1st of August of every year since, six young watermen just out of their articles row the course from Old Swan Pier at London Bridge to the Swan at Chelsea, for the orange-coloured coat, the silver badge, and a prize in money, which has been much increased in later times by donations from the City Companies.

The regatta of 1775 has an interest as the first of such functions in this country, and was in itself a notable spectacle. There were certain ingenious arrangements made to secure its success which have never been imitated since. For example, the actual day was left dependent upon the weather, and was announced by the flying of a red flag from Westminster Bridge, and by the continuous ringing of the bells of St. Margaret's from ten till one. The proceedings did not begin until six in the evening. An incredible number of private boats then assembled at Westminster Bridge, each with its four rowers dressed in one of the national colours. The reds assembled in and about the four arches of the Middlesex side of the bridge, the blues in those of the Surrey shore, while the whites occupied the middle of the stream, leaving only the central arch free. Through this arch shot a number of watermen's wherries on a race to London Bridge and back, for which prizes of some value were given. Upon the conclusion of this race the whole flotilla moved up the river to Ranelagh at Chelsea. The Lord Mayor and the City Companies were present in state. There was a prodigious saluting of cannon, fine music, and an execrable supper at Ranelagh Gardens, provided by Mrs. Cornelys at a cost of 700 guineas, "the wine being very scarce," as we learn. But the London of 1775 was on the whole much impressed, and the reporters were eloquent upon the splendours of the festival. "The ballast the city barges were used to take in," writes one of them, " was on this occasion filled with the finest ballast in the world, above one hundred elegant ladies, and it is thought that the procession was seen by at least 200,000 people."

Later in the century, the regatta of 1775 suggested certain races for prizes given for sailing-boats by the proprietors of Vauxhall, and out of those simple meetings grew the whole vast system of yacht racing and regattas which we know to-day as a great feature of modern England. It is not uninteresting to recall such modest beginnings of a great national pastime, but one turns from the scanty records of the Thames with the conviction that London has from the first neglected its possibilities as a place of diversion.

Could the taste of Londoners for horrors, the interest in suffering which appeared in half their sports and amusements, be better displayed than in the records of their delight in the exhibitions of Tyburn and Tower Hill? We believe that no spectacle of the last century, no coronation, no triumphal progress of captured standards to St. Paul's, or treasure to the Mint during the first Mr. Pitt's great war, ever drew such crowds into the streets as when Balmerino and Kilmarnock went to Tower Hill, or Lord Ferrers or Dr. Dodd, Jack Sheppard or John Rann, made the long and doleful journey from Newgate to Tyburn, the threefold gibbet which stood in fields opposite the present Marble Arch, somewhere very near the present Connaught Square. When the criminal was notorious, or distinguished, or pitied, or execrated above the common, his agony was prolonged by crowds in such numbers as lengthened the passage through the streets by hours. The space of time which lay between the stroke of the bell at midnight under the condemned man's cell window in Newgate Gaol and the claiming of his body by his friends, or by the surgeons for dissection, as his luck might determine, was a time of revel and merrymaking for his fellow-citizens.

It was doubtless a pious and worthy motive that inspired Mr. Robert Dowe in 1605 to give £50 "for ringing the greatest bell in the church (St. Sepulchre's) on the day the condemned prisoners are executed, and for other services for ever, for which services the sexton is paid £1, 6s. 8d." In fulfilment of other conditions of the bequest, the beadle of the same church was accustomed to go under the condemned cell at Newgate as twelve o'clock struck on the night preceding the execution with a handbell, lest the prisoners should be asleep, and administer some very good advice, conveyed however in indifferent verse ending,

> "And when St. 'Pulchre's bell to-morrow tolls,
> The Lord above have mercy on your souls ;
> Past twelve o'clock."

Thus were the last hours of these poor wretches punctuated by that well-meaning busybody Mr. Dowe, "citizen and merchant taylor of London." The ceremony included also a pious exhortation, "affectingly good," as Mr. Pennant describes it, as the procession turned out of the Old Bailey and came to St. Sepulchre's Churchyard. The great bell tolled as the beadle droned out, "All good people, pray heartily unto God for these poor sinners who are now going to their death, for whom this great bell doth toll."

If the victim were a highwayman, and as such a favourite of the ladies, the cart would stop at the steps of the church. Jack Sheppard say, or Jack Rann, who robbed "the Reverend Mr. Bell of his watch and eighteenpence in money in Gunnersbury

Lane on the road to Brentford," would be in the cart, with his coffin and the chaplain on either side of him. Jack would be dressed in a pea-green coat, with knee breeches of white Nankin tied with ribbons at the knee, and the cart, as we say, would stop at the church and a girl would come down with a nosegay which Jack would receive and wear dolefully all the way to Tyburn. The parson would pray all the time, but there would be much badinage between Jack and the crowd, as the equipage moved on, slowly by reason of the great crush, under windows crowded as if for a royal procession. Jack, in Dr. Swift's pleasant lines,

"while the rabble was bawling,
Rode stately through Holborn to die at his calling.
He stopped at the George for a bottle of sack
And promised to pay for it when he came back.
His waistcoat and stockings and breeches were white,
His cap had a new cherry ribbon to tie't;
And the maids to the doors and the balconies ran
And cried, 'Lack-a-day, what a proper young man.'"

When the whole sorry procession at last came in sight of the gallows at Tyburn, a triangle of beams with a pillar at each corner which gave accommodation on a generous scale, the fields were seen to be occupied by a great crowd of people numbering many thousands. There would be all the fun of a fair going on in those fields; oranges and gingerbread would be on sale and copies of Jack's last dying speech and confession, and the hangman would be sitting astride one of the beams with a pipe in his mouth. It was one

of the pleasantries of the occasion for gangs of black-
guards to dig holes in the ground, cover them with
grass, and watch people fall into them. There would
be front seats, too, reserved at half a crown, for those
who wished to see Jack's last moments to the best
advantage. We are shown the whole thing perfectly
in Mr. Hogarth's last plate of the "Life and Adventures of Tom Idle." The cart would then drive up
very slowly through the crowd and pass under one of
the beams of the gallows, where the hangman would
fit Jack's neck with a noose. There would follow a
long or short delay, according as Jack was of a hesitat-
ing nature or able to make up his mind bravely to
get it all over. In the former case he would pray at
such prodigious length that the crowd would jeer him
and protest that it was time for him to be turned off.
Sometimes the parson would do most of the praying,
and there might be some diversion, as when the eminent Mr. Jonathan Wild stole a corkscrew from the
divine's pocket and died with it in his hand. Jack
would have a handkerchief in his fingers, and the dropping of that handkerchief was the signal for which
the hangman and the crowd waited. However long-
winded Jack might be, he must drop that fateful linen
at last, and then, unless it fluttered out of the cart, in
which case the hangman held on for a moment to
recover it as a valuable relic, the cart was driven on,
and Jack was left dangling in the air.

The drop provided for these poor victims was of
the shortest, and their death was usually that of suffo-

cation. So well was this understood that their friends
would bribe the hangman to hasten their relief by
hanging to their legs or punching them on the
chest to expel the last breath. These were incidents
of the show. The pious offices of relatives were also
at times exerted in attempts at resuscitation, often, it
is declared, with success, for there was no dislocated
neck to be adjusted. There were, indeed, numerous
moments of interest to finish the great holiday of an
execution. The friends would find themselves obliged
to chaffer with Jack Ketch for the clothes of the deceased, as they were a perquisite of that official. Then
the rope, when the time came for cutting down, sold
at a shilling an inch, no less, for a good ordinary
criminal, and at a much higher rate for one of high
caste like my Lord Ferrers, who suffered from his own
chariot in a cord of silk. The saturnalia were often
ended by a riot over the body. When they turned off
Jack Sheppard in 1724, his friends brought a hearse to
take him back to St. Sepulchre's for decent burial.
The mob believed, or affected the belief, that this was
a mere ruse of the surgeons to get possession of this
noted corpse for dissection. They attacked the cortege
therefore, broke the hearse in pieces, and half killed
the mutes and other functionaries. The body, as we
learn, "was passed from hand to hand from Tyburn
to Long Acre, where it at length found rest at the
Barley Mow public-house." The mob now discovered
that they had been acting all along under the leader-
ship of a bailiff who was in truth the agent of the

surgeons, and that the funeral procession they had so despitefully used was, indeed, a pious function of Mr. Sheppard's sorrowing relatives. At this their fury blazed afresh, the police were powerless and sent for the troops, and Jack at last found burial at St. Martin's-in-the-Fields under escort of his Majesty's Guards.

Such were some of the incidents of a public execution at Tyburn, an occasion for holiday-making and diversion, to be present at which people took great pains and upon which they set great store, and these not necessarily the low and debased. We know that an exquisite like George Selwyn never missed an execution if he could help it, and when they turned off Jack Rann in 1774, Mr. Nollekens, the eminent sculptor, led that interesting gossip, Mr. J. T. Smith, then a child, to the end of John Street to see Jack go by in his pea-green coat. "On our return home," records Mr. Smith, "Mr. Nollekens, stooping close to my ear, assured me that had his father-in-law, Mr. Justice Welsh, been high constable we could have walked all the way to Tyburn by the side of the cart," so great were the privileges of high station in those days.

It was the taste which could find amusement in the execution that we may suppose kept alive some of those minor sports, the cock-shy, the duck hunt, and the rat pit which diverted the Sunday mornings of great numbers of citizens from the days of William the Third to those of George the Fourth. The cock-shy or cock-throwing, to be sure, was only an annual feast celebrated on Shrove Tuesday, like the eating of pancakes. An ingenuous Frenchman, indeed, associated the two ceremonials with each other. "The English," said he, "eat a certain cake on Shrove Tuesday, upon which they immediately run mad and kill their poor cocks." There was some justification, it must be confessed, for this excellent foreigner's conjecture. On that holy day you might see, in all open parts of the town, cocks or hens tied by the leg, their owners offering sticks at twopence a throw at a range of a chain, or twenty-two yards, just, in fact, as one used to throw at cocoa-nuts at a country fair. The cock had a certain length of string in which to manœuvre, and his master had trained him to avoid the knock over, which made him the property of his assailant, as long as possible, and so to earn many twopences. As a variation the birds were often hung across the street in an earthen pot, their head and tails being alone exposed. A successful throw broke the shard and released the bird, which brought whatever value it possessed after such battery to its tormentor. It was reckoned humorous at times to put an owl in the pot disguised as a cock, which, upon the breaking of the shell, flew away. That this sport was a recognised diversion of the town is plain from a paragraph taken from a news-sheet of 1700 by Malcolm: "Last Tuesday a brewer's servant in Southwark took his walk round Tower Hill, Moorfields, and Lincoln's Inn Fields, and knocked down so many cocks that by selling them again he returned home some twenty-eight shillings and eightpence richer than he came out."

The joys of the duck hunt were not confined to a day or a season, but filled a score of tavern gardens which contained the necessary pond throughout the Sundays of the year with the devotees of the fancy. There was a famous establishment on the site of what is now the eligible Hertford Street, Mayfair, called the Dog and Duck.   Another noted establishment with the same title, was that which the building of the Bethlehem Hospital extinguished.   The sign of a spaniel with a duck in his mouth, wrought in stone, may still be seen built in the wall of the garden of that institution.   Jenny's Whim was a noted tavern which occupied the site of the present St. George's Row in the Ebury Bridge Road, famous for its duck-hunting and Dorchester ale.   It was at Jenny's Whim that Lord Granby got so drunk before joining Mr. Horace Walpole's party at Vauxhall, as we saw in another chapter.   There were favourite ducking-ponds at Halfpenny Hatch, Rotherhithe, at Islington Green, at White's Conduit House, and in the East Lane, Islington, where the New River reservoirs were afterwards made, and at many other places too no doubt. The proceedings at all were the same, and leave us in wonder at the attraction of the sport for human creatures.

The ducking-pond was a small affair, and boarded to the height of the knee round its edges to prevent the excited spectators from falling in in their eagerness to follow the incidents of the sport.   These all arose from the movements of a pinioned duck which was put into the water and hunted by a spaniel or spaniels. "It escaped," we are told, "as long as it was able by diving." There were variations upon the simplicity of this sport. "Sometimes the duck is tormented in a different manner," records Malcolm, "without the assistance of dogs, by having an owl tied upon her back and so put into the water, where she frequently dives in order to escape from the burden, and on her return for air the miserable owl, half drowned, shakes itself, and hooting, frightens the duck. She, of course, dives again, and replunges the owl under the water. The frequent repetition of this action soon deprives the poor bird of its sensations, and generally ends in its death, if not in that of the duck also."

The taste for the hideous brutality of duck-hunting came to an end in the early years of the present century. It was from no softening of the characters of its patrons, we are told, that it expired, but only because an expanding town drained its ponds and built over the gardens where they were maintained. The present devotees of pigeon-shooting may trace back the beginnings of their sport to the institution of the ducking-pond. It was the sportsmen who found their Sunday mornings deranged by the disappearance of the ducking-pond who invented the pigeon match, a diversion which some consider not unworthy of its origin.

Of the amusements of our ancestors in London which we have examined in our inquiry, how many

have survived to our own times? Practically one, and
one only, the theatre, which to-day perhaps fills a
greater place than ever amongst the diversions of the
town. We hold it impossible to make any valuable
comparison between living actors and those of a
former age, but it may be contended for the theatre
that it has shown a continual development as an
organisation of pleasure since the days of Killigrew and Davenant. The other pleasures of the
London of the past have, almost without exception,
been discarded, or absorbed and translated. The
Parks, of course, remain, but they are no longer the
playground of fashion which London made of them in
the days of the Ring or the Mall. The tea gardens
and Vauxhall were features of the London of other
days, which all who have studied their old delights
must regret; in other respects, the amusements of
the town of Queen Victoria are surely a change for
the better upon those of all her predecessors. We
may congratulate ourselves upon the change in taste
and manners which has rendered the excesses of the
play tables impossible in these days. No one regrets
the disappearance of Hockley in the Hole, or the
closing of cockpits and prize-rings. Whatever faint
survivals of the masquerade may still linger at Covent
Garden are a certain improvement upon the diversions
which went on at the Haymarket or at Soho Square.
The great fairs, we believe, were, on the whole, innocent occasions of enjoyment, but their attractions are
    be seen in a developed form to-day at the music

halls, and that continuously and without an enervating revel of weeks in the hottest time of the year. Speaking generally, Londoners of all ranks have exchanged most of their former joys for diversions in which bodily exercise takes a chief part; the man who formerly lost his fortune at hazard or faro at White's or Brooks's now spends it in healthy forms of sport which take him over the country, and, indeed, over the globe for its gratification. Men of a lower station play cricket and football or ride bicycles when they are young, and look on at others doing the same when age overtakes them. And London and England have surely gained by the change.

INDEX

R

THE END

DATE DUE

9/2			
OCT 8 1970			
NOV 2 2 1971			
NO 27 '72			
NO 30 '72			
APR 2 3 1974			
OC 24 '85			
GAYLORD			PRINTED IN U.S.A.